STAR FIGURES
Plane and Three-Dimensional
with
Physical Applications

Paul Klingsporn

Copyright © 2022 Paul Klingsporn.

All rights reserved. No part of this book may be reproduced, stored, or transmitted by any means—whether auditory, graphic, mechanical, or electronic—without written permission of both publisher and author, except in the case of brief excerpts used in critical articles and reviews. Unauthorized reproduction of any part of this work is illegal and is punishable by law.

Library of Congress Control Number: 2017908252
ISBN: 979-8-88640-508-8 (sc)
ISBN: 979-8-88640-509-5 (hc)
ISBN: 979-8-88640-510-1 (e)

Because of the dynamic nature of the Internet, any web addresses or links contained in this book may have changed since publication and may no longer be valid. The views expressed in this work are solely those of the author and do not necessarily reflect the views of the publisher, and the publisher hereby disclaims any responsibility for them.

One Galleria Blvd., Suite 1900, Metairie, LA 70001
1-888-421-2397

CONTENTS

Chapter 1. Introduction 1

Chapter 2. The Mathematical Five-Point Star 6

    2-1   Geometry of star
    2-2   Connection of the star with the Golden Ratio

Chapter 3. The Golden Ratio ϕ 15

    3-1   Origins of the number ϕ
    3-2   The number ϕ in relation to other celebrated numbers in mathematics

Chapter 4. Three-Dimensional Five-Point Mathematical Stars 26

    4-1   Construction with altitude h at center of plane star of radius R
    4-2   Angles in triangular facet of three-dimensional star and their dependence on h and R. Connection to ϕ
    4-3   Ratio of h to R resulting in isosceles triangular facets, and relationships to ϕ and golden angle
    4-4   Unique conditions on ridge, valley, and triangular facet angles that exist when $h/R = \frac{1}{2}$
    4-5   Angular inclination of triangular facets and unique values when $h/R = \frac{1}{2}$
    4-6   An alternate method for calculating ϕ

Chapter 5. Foldability of a Plane Star into a Three-Dimensional Star 59

    5-1   Description of physical conditions to be met for foldability
    5-2   Mathematical conditions for foldability
    5-3   Examples

Chapter 6. Special Triangles Revealed by Geometry of Five-Point Star 69

    6-1   An unusual indentity in the star geometry
    6-2   Triangles containing any two angles in ratio 1:2
    6-3   Triangles with two angles in ratio 1:3
    6-4   Another class of triangles

Chapter 7. Three-Dimensional Stars with Circumscribed Geometric Figures: Comparison of Areas and Volumes 85

    7-1   Surface area and volume of the star having altitude h, radius R

7-2 Comparison of star area and volume to that of circumscribed figures, for star with $h = R$
7-3 Star area and volume versus ratio of altitude to radius
7-4 Three-dimensional stars circumscribed by spheroids
7-5 Further comparison of star volume and area with that of common geometric figures

Chapter 8. Three-Dimensional Stars Containing Inscribed Spheres 118

8-1 Inscribed spheres tangent to ridge and valley lines in star surface
8-2 Star altitudes for ridge and valley tangencies to a particular inscribed spherical surface
8-3 Two right circular cones related uniquely to the tangencies of inscribed sphere in 8-2

Chapter 9. Five-Point Stars with Variable Tip Angles 132

9-1 Star geometry with variable tip angle
9-2 Three-dimensional star of altitude h formed on base star with tip angle φ. Surface area.
9-3 Volume of three-dimensional stars on base star of tip angle φ
9-4 Foldability of three-dimensional star on base with tip angle φ
9-5 Limiting relationships associated with foldability
9-6 Angles in triangular facet of solid star on base star with tip angle φ
9-7 Examples of folded stars

Chapter 10. N-Point Stars 161

10-1 Geometry and surface area of N-point stars
10-2 Three-dimensional star of altitude h on N-point base star. Surface area and volume
10-3 Angle between ridge and valley in triangular facet of solid star
10-4 Foldability of [N, 2] star
10-5 Foldability of N-point star on base star with tip angle ψ
10-6 Angle α_N in N-point star with tip angle ψ

Chapter 11. Stars of the Type [N, J] 196

11-1 The [N, J] symbology
11-2 Angles and sides in a [N, J] star
11-3 Surface area of [N, J] star
11-4 Three-dimensional star of altitude h on base star [N, J]: volume
11-5 Foldability

Chapter 12. Moment of Inertia of Solid Stars 212

12-1	Solid star with flat, parallel faces	
12-2	Comparison of solid star moment of inertia with that of common geometric figures	
12-3	Solid star with flat, parallel faces but variable tip angle, φ	
12-4	Solid stars with N tips, angle φ at each tip, and altitude h at center	

Chapter 13. Passage of Light Through a Solid Star with Flat, Parallel Faces 246

- 13-1 Index of refraction
- 13-2 Light incident perpendicular on an edge face
- 13-3 Splitting of a parallel light beam into seven individual beams
- 13-4 The solid star as an optical device
- 13-5 Symmetric passage of light in the star, with two reflections in each tip
- 13-6 Symmetric passage of light in the star, with four reflections in each tip

Chapter 14. Passage of Light Alternately Through Tips of a Solid Star and Space Between 286

- 14-1 Refractive index for symmetric passage. Time of travel
- 14-2 Symmetric passage of light alternately through tips and space between, variable tip angle
- 14-3 Symmetric light passage through N-point solid star with variable tip angle. Time of travel
- 14-4 Conditions for passage of white light through tips of a solid star and space between

Chapter 15. Stars Derived from Symmetric Passage of Light in Solid [5, 2] Stars 315

- 15-1 Maximum number of reflections in each tip of [5, 2] star for symmetric light path
- 15-2 Radii of stars formed from extensions of symmetric light path lines
- 15-3 Symmetric light path length for two reflections in each tip
- 15-4 Stars formed by symmetric light paths with four reflections in each tip of star
- 15-5 Light path length with four reflections in each tip of star

Chapter 16. Non-Symmetric Five-Point Stars: Their Origins and Properties 337

- 16-1 Skewed stars formed from non-symmetric light paths
- 16-2 Skewed stars formed on the basis of irregular pentagons
- 16-3 A class of skewed stars formed with five non-uniformly spaced points on a circle
- 16-4 Unusual angle relations in arbitrary non-symmetric five-point stars

	16-5	Skewed stars from non-symmetric light paths with four reflections in each tip of solid [5, 2] star

Chapter 17. Swinging Solid Stars 380

	17-1	Oscillatory motion of solid stars with flat, parallel faces
	17-2	Oscillations of solid stars with variable tip angle
	17-3	Period of oscillation versus distance between axis and solid star center

Chapter 18. Diffraction of Light by a Star Aperture 406

	18-1	Introduction
	18-2	Diffraction based on the wave theory of light
	18-3	Fraunhofer diffraction from a five-point star [5, 2] aperture
	18-4	Diffracted light intensity distributions along the x_0 and y_0 axes

CHAPTER 1
INTRODUCTION

From the earliest of recorded time, the "star" has occupied a special place not only as a mathematical geometric figure, but also as a symbol used in ascribing features to people and their actions. It is often said that "He is a star," or "She is a star," or that he or she has "achieved stardom" at an early age. Indeed, five-pointed geometric star figures, each with a name in it, occupy a sidewalk in Beverly Hills, California, known as the "Hollywood Walk of Fame." So prominent is the star figure in our everyday lives that it appears in many company names and logos. Financial stocks and hotels are rated in promotional literature as "five-star," etc. Even newspapers invoke the use of "star," as for example, *The Kansas City Star* and the *Fort Worth Star-Telegram*. Large Macy's department stores use a large red star as an outdoor emblem at their entrances, and many have sections of interior red carpeting adorned with various sizes of gold stars randomly placed on the carpet.

Throughout Christendom the star has occupied a central role in Christianity because of the gospel accounts that speak about the star as a guiding light leading the Magi to the Christ child. The star is a decorative part of nearly all scenes depicting Christmas. In all of these accounts, the five-pointed geometric star figure is used, but in Judaism the six-pointed star figure is symbolized as the "Star of David."

How and when did the simple geometric star figure come to play such an important role in our thinking that we in turn ascribe to the star all the positive and somewhat mystic aspects in our lives? Evidence of the star as a mathematical figure can be traced to the early Egyptians and Greeks. It is interesting to recount some of this history.[1] Certainly the early Egyptians had a very practical command of geometric figures and developed an excellent skill in exact measurements, for they built the pyramids in the distant past well before the time of Abraham. Their progress in the techniques for exact measurement was phenomenal. They could construct right angles because they knew that triangles with sides of lengths three, four, and five units made a triangle with one 90° angle; i.e., a right

---

[1] Eves, Howard, An Introduction to the History of Mathematics, 3rd ed., New York: Holt, Rinehart and Winston, Inc., 1969, p.27, p.49.

triangle. There is evidence that the Chinese knew this also. But the Egyptians also knew how to construct angles of a square, a pentagon, a hexagon, and a heptagon. It is difficult to divide a circle into five equal parts and more difficult still to divide it into seven equal parts, yet ancient Egyptian designs of temples and pyramids bear evidence that they knew how to construct these angles and associated figures. Although the Egyptians had a mastery of practical geometry for these figures, it is not clear whether they knew the underlying theoretical aspects of their empirical methods. A papyrus contained in the Rhind collection at the British Museum has remarkable writings of the Egyptian priest Ahmes, who lived before 1700 BC. These writings provide details of Egyptian knowledge of geometry and arithmetic. In spite of their extensive practical knowledge of figures, a theoretical basis and interpretation of the figures would have to wait until later for the Greeks.

Thales, who lived from 640 to 550 BC, was a rich Greek merchant from Miletus. He was quite successful and he traveled to many countries as a result of his work as a merchant. A keen observer, he learned much from others in his travels. After early retirement from merchant activity, Thales pursued what he had learned in earlier travels. In particular, because of his bent toward mathematics and philosophy, he followed up on knowledge he had obtained from Egyptian priests and he became popular because, according to legend, he predicted a solar eclipse in 585 BC. It is told that while Thales was walking after dark, gazing at stars, he fell into a ditch and a lady attending him inquired how it was that he could know what takes place in the heavens if he could not see what was happening at his feet. Indeed, he must have been awestruck by stars of the heavens as it is easy to be also today merely by gazing upward on a clear night and contemplating all the mystic unknowns represented by those very distant flickers of light. Thales was able to place the practical observations he learned from the Egyptians on a firm theoretical framework because the following and other propositions are credited to him: the angles at the base of an isosceles triangle are equal, a circle is bisected by any diameter, the angle in a semicircle is a right angle, and sides about equal angles in similar triangles are proportional. He placed a multitude of Egyptian measurement details on a firm general-truth foundation. Throughout his life Thales remembered his debt to the Egyptian priests for all the mensuration determinations he built upon to generalize into a theoretical basis. At an advanced age Thales advised his pupil, Pythagoras, to travel to Egypt and visit the priests. Pythagoras did just that and based on his experience, he became an even more renowned teacher.[2] Pythagoras, who lived from 584 to 495 BC, is perhaps best known for the "Pythagorean Theorem," which states that the square of the hypotenuse of a right triangle is equal to the sum of the squares of the two legs of the right triangle. It is told that Pythagoras was so popular as a teacher that even women, who were forbidden to attend public meetings, broke the law and flocked to hear him along with enthusiastic people of all ranks.

The influence of Pythagoras as a great master became so great that many of his ardent pupils eventually formed a brotherhood or society known as the Order of Pythagoreans, and in time this order exercised great influence across the Grecian world. The members of this order shared common philosophical beliefs, engaged in the same pursuits, and were bound together with an oath not to reveal the secrets and teachings of the school. The common symbol that bound this brotherhood together was the badge of membership in the form of the beautiful five-pointed star, or pentagram, which represented the mathematical symbol or figure that the order had discussed.

The mathematical symbol discussed by the Pythagorean Brotherhood must have been a fitting representation of those heavenly dancing patterns of light known as stars. It must be remembered that in the days of the brotherhood, their starry nights were much more prominent to them than they are for most of our urban population today because they had no interfering lights to compete with the glimmering light from the stars. Being free from what might be called light pollution today, the stars must have appeared more prominent to the ancients than they do for those who view them today in the presence of ground lights in and around towns and cities. The modern-day urbanite can gain an appreciation for this by traveling sufficiently far into the country on a clear night and, in the absence of any nearby town lights, a view upward will reveal the true wonder of these distant sources of light entering the eyes to form retinal images, which we call stars.

Spanning the centuries after the early Greeks, it is not difficult to understand how the rectangular-shaped cloth symbol binding the original American colonies together came to have thirteen five-pointed stars, one representing each colony. Not only was it an honor

---

[2] Newman, James R., The World of Mathematics, Vol.1, New York: Simon and Schuster, 1956, pp. 81-83.

to be bound together, each with a star, but also that cloth with thirteen stars represented the special hopes, dreams, and determination of those colonists in the tasks that lay before them. By way of historical note, the first American colonial flag of record with thirteen five-pointed stars was displayed in 1775 by the armed schooner *Lee*. On June 14, 1777, Congress declared that the official flag should have thirteen stars. In 1795, Congress voted to increase the number of stars to fifteen. Finally, in 1818, legislation was passed providing for the addition of a star to the flag each time a new state was admitted to the union.

Each state in the union has its individual flag. As many as fifteen states have one or more stars on their flags. Arizona, California, Nevada, North Carolina, Texas, and the territory of Puerto Rico each has one five-pointed star on its flag. This is particularly appropriate for Texas because it is known as the "lone star state." The flags of Tennessee and Alabama contain three and eight stars, respectively. Both Michigan's and Rhode Island's flags have thirteen stars, while Ohio's has seventeen, Indiana's has eighteen, and Arkansas' has twenty-eight. The District of Columbia's flag has three stars.

In addition to the United States of America, as many as forty countries have one or more stars on their national flags. The stars are five-pointed figures on the flags of thirty-six of these countries. It is interesting that Australia has a flag with a single five-pointed star surrounded by five seven-pointed stars. Burundi has three six-pointed stars on its flag, Jordan has one seven-pointed star, and the flag of Israel has a single six-pointed star.

During the westward expansion in America in the nineteenth century, badges in the shapes of stars were worn by sheriffs and other lawmen representing the honorable quest for order and justice, a common bond signifying those noble instincts. The star has been ingrained in our culture to represent all that is perfect, honorable, and worth defending.

It is to be noted that a small element of humankind has been known to use the star figure as symbology in acts of satanic ritualistic worship. At first thought, this may seem to belie all those positive aspects of the star discussed earlier. Upon reflection, however, it can be reasoned that the human mind, even when one portion of it is bent down a dark path, still responds in another capacity to the appeal of the star figure itself. So it appears there is something of a universal attraction of the mathematical star figure in human psyche.

No doubt the mathematical star discovered by the Brother of Pythagorean Order is the geometric figure linking those faintly visible shimmering points of light with the captivating feelings of awe for their distant sources of origin. The appeal of the five-pointed star figure in our lives is perhaps greater than that of any other geometric figure, such as the triangle, square, or circle. Certainly the patterns of light from these faraway heavenly bodies registered in the eye more nearly correspond to a mathematical star figure of five or more points than to triangles, squares, or circles. To be sure, the circle holds its own special appeal as a mathematical figure, but that appeal lies in other areas quite unrelated to the mathematical star.

Who has not gazed into the heavens on a clear night and experienced wonderment seeing those jagged bits of star-shaped gleams of light and puzzled over the nature of the surface from which the light came and the celestial bodies it passed near in its travel through intervening space? Our mystic wonder is magnified when we note that astronomers tell us there are approximately two hundred billion (200,000,000,000!) stars in our Milky Way Galaxy, and that there are more than one hundred billion galaxies beyond our Milky Way system. Moreover, the closest and brightest star visible in the Northern Hemisphere is Sirius, which is 8.5 light years distant. The speed of light is approximately 186,280 miles per second, and therefore light travels about 5.87 trillion miles per year, which means that 8.5 light years correspond to a distance of approximately 50 trillion miles from Earth to Sirius. Polaris, the North Star, is forty-seven times more distant than Sirius. Now, we have control to a greater or lesser degree over most things we observe on Earth. That is, we can move objects, heat them, cool them, join them, dissect them, etc. In contrast, when it comes to the stars, we can only gaze upward and allow the light to enter our eyes and arouse feelings of profound amazement and curiosity. Perhaps that is the origin of intrigue for the mathematical star-shaped figures we construct and draw on paper.

CHAPTER 2
THE MATHEMATICAL FIVE-POINT STAR

2-1. Geometry of Star

Before proceeding to analyses of solid three-dimensional star shapes, we begin by establishing some of the familiar relationships connecting line segments and angles in the plane five-pointed star figure. As will be seen, these relationships in the plane star are important to the development of geometric features in the solid three-dimensional shapes to be investigated.

Consider a circle drawn with point O as center as shown in Fig. 2-1, and let the circle be divided into five equal arcs of $72°$ each as represented by the points $P_1, P_2, \ldots P_5$. Let a straight line be drawn connecting the pair of points P_1 and P_3. Likewise, let straight lines be drawn connecting the pairs of points P_2 and P_4, P_3 and P_5, P_4 and P_1, and P_5 and P_2. The resulting system of straight lines in Fig. 2-1 is the famous geometric figure known as the five-pointed mathematical star. It is often represented by the symbol [5,2] and referred to as the pentagram or star polygon. The number 5 in the symbol indicates that there are five equally spaced points on the circle, and the number 2 gives the sequence in which the points are connected by straight lines. That is, in the case of the star in Fig. 2-1, each point on the circle is connected to the second point from it.

To determine the magnitudes of angles and segment lengths within the five-point mathematical star, refer to Fig. 2-2, which is Fig. 2-1 with additional straight lines drawn connecting the center O of the circle to the points $P_1, \ldots P_5$ on the circumference, each of which is merely the radius R of the circle. The point at which the lines P_1P_3 and P_2P_5 intersect is

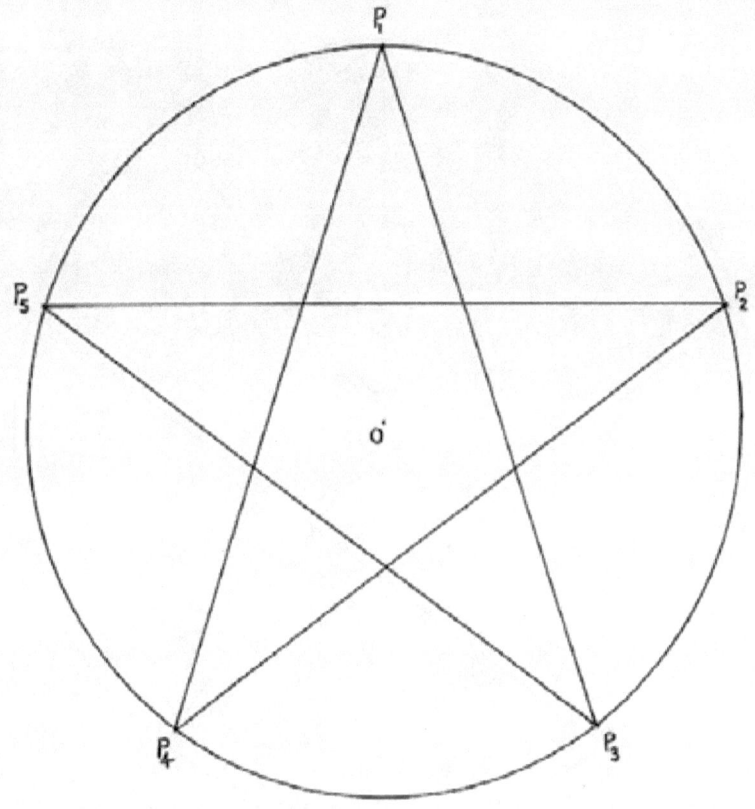

Fig. 2-1. Geometry of the five-point mathematical star [5, 2]. Each adjacent pair of points on the circle subtends an angle of 72° at the center O of the circle.

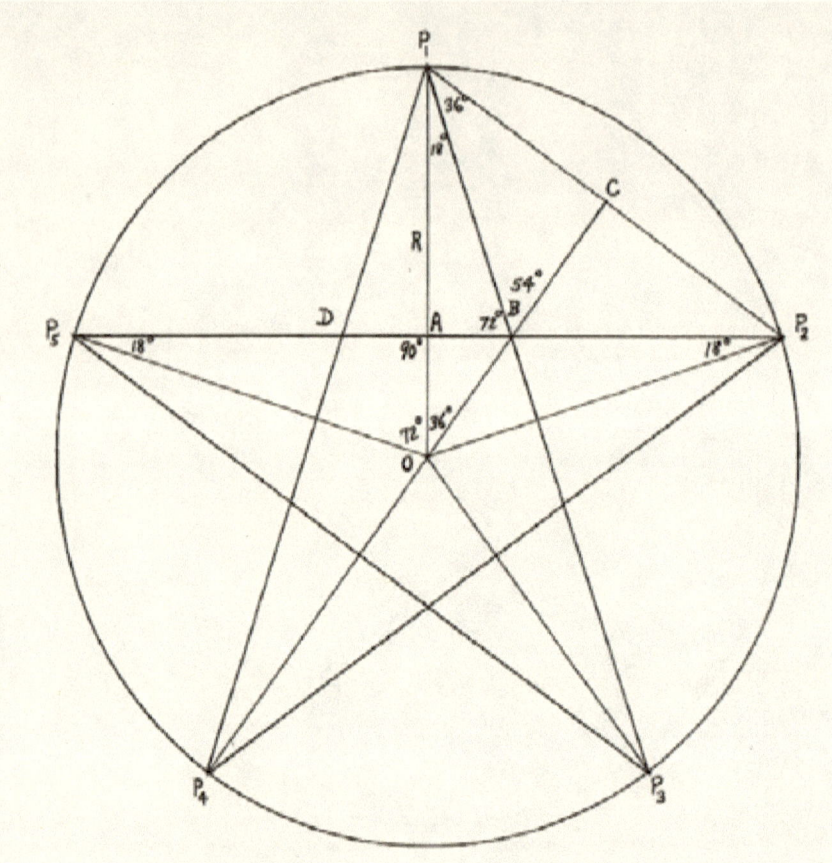

Fig. 2-2. Five-point star with auxiliary lines used in deriving Eqs. (2-1)-(2-8) of text.

designated by B, and the line drawn through the center O of the circle and point B intersects the line P_1P_2 at a point called C.

Now, the triangle P_2OP_5 is isosceles because the sides OP_2 and OP_5 are both equal to the radius R of the circle. Therefore, the apex angle of the isosceles triangle is equal to 144° because it is the sum of the two angles P_1OP_5 and P_1OP_2, each of which is equal to 72°, because the five points $P_1, \ldots P_5$ divide the circle into five equal arcs. As a result, each base angle of the isosceles triangle P_2OP_5 has the value

$$\angle P_2P_5O = \angle P_5P_2O = \frac{1}{2}(180° - 144°) = 18°. \qquad (2\text{-}1)$$

Let A be the point of intersection of the radius OP_1 with the chord P_2P_5. It follows that the segment OA is perpendicular to P_2P_5 because from triangle OP_5A we can write

$$\angle P_5AO = 180° - \angle OP_5A - \angle P_1OP_5$$
$$= 180° - 18° - 72°$$
$$= 90°. \qquad (2\text{-}2)$$

As mentioned above, B is the point of intersection of the chords P_1P_3 and P_2P_5 and therefore in the right triangle P_1AB the angle P_1BA is

$$\angle P_1BA = 180° - 90° - 18°$$
$$= 72°. \qquad (2\text{-}3)$$

In the latter, use was made of the fact that $\angle AP_1B$ is 18°. This is true because $\angle AP_1B$ is a base angle of isosceles triangle OP_1P_3 and, by symmetry, the isosceles triangle OP_1P_3 has the same sides and angles as those shown earlier for isosceles triangle P_2OP_5, leading to Eq. (2-1) for the base angle measure.

The triangles P_4P_1O and P_4P_2O are both isosceles with their equal sides each equal to the circle radius R, and thus their included apex angles at point O are both equal to 144°. It follows that the base lengths P_1P_4 and P_2P_4 are equal. In triangle $P_1P_4P_2$, the radius OP_4 bisects angle $P_1P_4P_2$ because the base angles $\angle P_1P_4O$ and $\angle P_2P_4O$ in isosceles triangles OP_4P_1 and OP_4P_2 are each equal to 18°. Therefore, when the radius P_4O is extended to meet the base P_1P_2 of isosceles triangle $P_1P_4P_2$ in point C, the segment P_4C is perpendicular to the base P_1P_2 in isosceles triangle $P_1P_4P_2$, and it follows that the base angles in the isosceles triangle $P_1P_4P_2$ are each equal to

$$\angle P_4P_1C = \angle P_4P_2C = \frac{1}{2}(180° - 2 \cdot 18°) = 72°. \tag{2-4}$$

Consequently, in the right triangle BCP_1 the angle BP_1C is

$$\angle BP_1C = \angle P_4P_1C - 2 \cdot 18°$$
$$= 72° - 36°$$
$$= 36°. \tag{2-5}$$

Hence the other acute angle in right triangle BP_1C is

$$\angle P_1BC = 180° - 90° - 36°$$
$$= 54°. \tag{2-6}$$

Now, a straight angle contains 180° and therefore from Eqs. (2-3) and (2-6) the two acute angles in right triangle OAB are given by

$$\angle OBA = 180° - \angle P_1BC - \angle P_1BA$$
$$= 180° - 54° - 72°$$
$$= 54°, \tag{2-7}$$

and

$$\angle AOB = 180° - 90° - 54°$$
$$= 36°. \tag{2-8}$$

So, beginning with a circle of radius R in Fig. 2-2 divided into five equal arcs of 72° each, the results of Eqs. (2-1) through (2-8) lead to values of the various angles in the five-point star that are summarized in Fig. 2-3 without some of the auxiliary lines of Fig. 2-2, which are extraneous to the star itself.

2-2. Connection of the star with the golden ratio

It will be seen from Fig. 2-2 that the mathematical five-point star contains, by symmetry, five identical triangles like triangle DP_1B. As shown above, the angles P_1BD and P_1DB are both equal to 72°, so the triangle DP_1B and the others like it are isosceles, with sides $P_1B = DP_1$. Moreover, the apex angle DP_1B is bisected by the radius OP_1, and hence the segment OA is perpendicular to the base DB. It follows that $DA = AB$ and so

$$DB = 2 \cdot AB. \tag{2-9}$$

In right triangle P_1AB, the following trigonometric relation holds

$$\sin 18° = \frac{AB}{P_1 B}, \qquad (2\text{-}10)$$

and therefore from Eqs. (2-9) and (2-10), the ratio of segment P_1B to segment DB in Fig. 2-2 is

$$\frac{P_1 B}{DB} = \frac{AB/\sin 18°}{2 \cdot AB} = 1.618033989 \qquad (2\text{-}11)$$

As it turns out, the latter ratio of the distance P_1B to DB in the five-point star figure is equal to a very intriguing number known as the "golden ratio." This ratio will also appear in further developments related to the three-dimensional star shapes to be presented, and so the following chapter will be devoted to some of the background of this ratio, apart from its connection to the plane star figure.

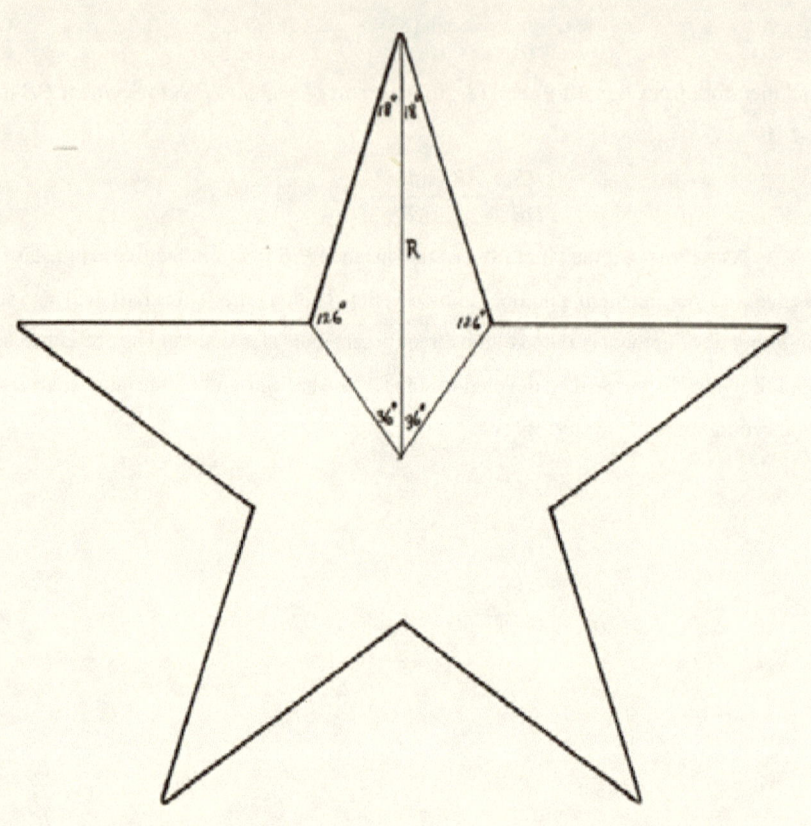

Fig. 2-3. Five-point star [5, 2] of radius R showing the angles in one of the five symmetric regions.

Finally, the lengths of the various segments comprising the five-point star in Fig. 2-2 can be expressed in terms of the radius R of the circle. For example, applying the law of sines to one of the five isosceles triangles, such as triangle P_1P_3O, gives

$$\frac{P_1P_3}{\sin 144°} = \frac{R}{\sin 18°}, \qquad (2\text{-}12)$$

and, correct to six decimal places, this yields

$$P_1P_3 = 1.902113R. \qquad (2\text{-}13)$$

Applying the law of sines to a triangle such as triangle OP_1B leads to the relation

$$\frac{P_1B}{\sin 36°} = \frac{R}{\sin(72°+54°)}, \qquad (2\text{-}14)$$

and, correct to six decimal places, this gives

$$P_1B = 0.726543R. \qquad (2\text{-}15)$$

Using Eqs. (2-11) and (2-15), the length of a side DB of the pentagon formed at the center of the star figure in Fig. 2-1 can be expressed in terms of the radius R, with the result

$$DB = 0.449028R. \qquad (2\text{-}16)$$

The distance OB from the center of the star to the vertex of the pentagon can be found in terms of the radius R by applying the law of sines to the triangle OP_1B to give

$$\frac{OB}{\sin 18°} = \frac{R}{\sin(72°+54°)}, \qquad (2\text{-}17)$$

leading to

$$OB = 0.381966R. \qquad (2\text{-}18)$$

Consider the length of one of the chords, such as P_1P_3 in Fig. 2-1, in relation to the length of one of the tip segments, such as P_1B. From Eqs. (2-12) and (2-14), the ratio of these lengths is

$$\frac{P_1P_3}{P_1B} = \frac{\sin 144°}{\sin 18°}\frac{\sin(72°+54°)}{\sin 36°} \qquad (2\text{-}19)$$

Note that the ratio is independent of the radius R because it cancelled and, further, when the trigonometric factors are evaluated, the result in Eq. (2-19) can be expressed in the form

$$\frac{P_1P_3}{P_1B} = 1 + 1.618033989, \qquad (2\text{-}20)$$

where the second numerical factor on the right is the curious value referred to earlier in relation to the ratio in Eq. (2-11). This value also appears in the relation between the radius R and the distance OB in the star figure because Eq. (2-17) can be put in the form

$$OB = \frac{R}{\sin(72°+54°)/\sin 18°} = \frac{R}{1 + 1.618033989}. \tag{2-21}$$

Because of the appearance of this curious numerical factor, 1.618033989, some attention will be given in Chapter 3 to its origins and other applications.

CHAPTER 3
THE GOLDEN RATIO ϕ

3-1. Origins of the number

Suppose we ask the question, "What positive real number has a reciprocal which is just equal to itself minus one?" To answer this, let u be the number. Then u must satisfy the relation

$$\frac{1}{u} = u - 1. \tag{3-1}$$

which leads to the quadratic equation

$$u^2 - u - 1 = 0. \tag{3-2}$$

The two roots of this quadratic are

$$u = \frac{-(-1) \pm \sqrt{(-1)^2 - 4(-1)}}{2} \tag{3-3}$$

Choosing the positive root gives

$$u_+ = \frac{1+\sqrt{5}}{2}. \tag{3-4}$$

This number, known variously as the "golden ratio," "divine ratio," and "golden section," is usually designated by ϕ and hence from Eq. (3-4), correct to nine places, its value is[1]

$$\phi \equiv u_+ = 1.618033989. \tag{3-5}$$

Therefore, the number ϕ is unique in that it is the only positive real number whose reciprocal is equal to the number itself minus one. Referring to the five-pointed mathematical star figure in Fig. 2-2 and Eqs. (2-11), (2-20), and (2-21), it is seen that the distance ratios are

---

[1] Livio, Mario, <u>The Golden Ratio</u>, New York: Broadway Books, 2002, pp. 75-81.

$$\frac{P_1 B}{DB} = \phi$$

$$\frac{P_1 P_3}{P_1 B} = 1 + \phi \tag{3-6}$$

$$\frac{OB}{R} = \frac{1}{1+\phi}.$$

Another way of arriving at this remarkable number, ϕ, is as follows. Consider the straight line segment of unit length as shown in Fig. 3-1. What is the distance of point P from one end of the segment if it divides the segment such that the difference of the squares of the two segments is equal to the product of the two segments? To meet this condition, z must satisfy the equation

$$z^2 - (1-z)^2 = z(1-z). \tag{3-7}$$

The latter gives rise to the quadratic, $z^2 + z - 1 = 0$, and its positive root, correct to nine decimal places, is

$$z_+ = \frac{-1+\sqrt{5}}{2} = 0.618033989 \equiv \frac{1}{\phi} \tag{3-8}$$

The other segment, $1 - z_+$, has length

$$1 - z_+ = 1 - \left(-\frac{1}{2}\right) - \frac{\sqrt{5}}{2} = \frac{3-\sqrt{5}}{2}, \tag{3-9}$$

but squaring both sides of Eq. (3-8) gives

$$\frac{1}{\phi^2} = \left(\frac{-1}{2} + \frac{\sqrt{5}}{2}\right)^2 = \frac{3-\sqrt{5}}{2} \equiv 1 - z_+ \tag{3-10}$$

and hence from Eqs. (3-9) and (3-10) we get

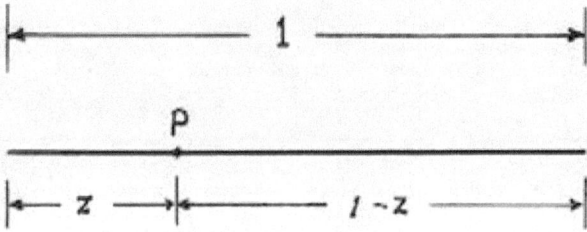

Fig. 3-1. When point P divides the unit segment according to Eq. (3-7), then the two segments are related to the golden ratio ϕ through Eqs. (3-8) and (3-10).

$$\frac{1}{\phi^2} = 0.381966011. \tag{3-11}$$

So, under the conditions set forth for the location of point P in Fig. 3-1, one segment is of length $1/\phi$ while the other segment has length $1/\phi^2$, and we note that $1/\phi + 1/\phi^2 = 1$.

Using the result in Eq. (3-11), it is interesting to note from Eq. (2-18) in Chapter 2 that the relation between the distance OB and the radius R in the star figure of Fig. 2-2 can be expressed in terms of the square of the golden ratio.

$$OB = R / \phi^2 \tag{3-12}$$

Another very interesting way in which the value of the golden ratio ϕ can be obtained is from the well-known pattern of numbers known as the Fibonacci series:

1, 1, 2, 3, 5, 8, 13, 21, 34, 55, 89, 144, 233, 377, ...

Suppose we take the ratio of a number in the Fibonacci sequence to the number just preceding it. For example, 34 ÷ 21 = 1.61905. Note that this is close to the value of the golden ratio ϕ = 1.618033989. Choosing a higher number, 377, in the sequence and dividing it by the preceding number gives 377 ÷ 233 = 1.618026, which is closer still to the value of ϕ. To explore this further, consider Table 3-1 in which the numbers in the Fibonacci sequence are listed on the left, with the running index j = 1, 2, ... denoting the order of ascending Fibonacci numbers, F_j. The quotient of each number in the sequence divided by the preceding number is listed in the column under the heading F_{j+1}/F_j. The last column on the right in Table 3-1 gives a comparison of each quotient with the actual value of the golden ratio ϕ = 1.618033989. In this comparison, the quotient values are subtracted from ϕ. Note that the differences between ϕ and F_{j+1}/F_j alternate in sign because the ratios are alternately larger and smaller than ϕ, but the magnitude of the difference decreases with ascending numbers in the sequence. For example, it is seen from the table that the ratio 377 ÷ 233 differs from ϕ by less than one part in one hundred thousand.

Table 3-1. Relationship of the Golden Ratio ϕ* to the Fibonacci Series.

Index j	Fibonacci Series F_j	$\dfrac{F_{j+1}}{F_j}$	$\phi - \dfrac{F_{j+1}}{F_j}$
1	1		
2	1	1.0	0.618
3	2	2.0	-0.382
4	3	1.5	0.118
5	5	1.666	-4.86×10^{-2}
6	8	1.60	1.80×10^{-2}
7	13	1.625	-6.96×10^{-3}
8	21	1.61538	2.65×10^{-3}
9	34	1.61905	-1.01×10^{-3}
10	55	1.61764	3.87×10^{-4}
11	89	1.618181	-1.48×10^{-4}
12	144	1.617977	5.65×10^{-5}
13	233	1.618055	-2.16×10^{-5}
14	377	1.6180257	8.24×10^{-6}
15	610	1.6180371	-3.15×10^{-6}
16	987	1.6180327	1.20×10^{-6}
17	1,597	1.61803445	-4.59×10^{-7}
18	2,584	1.61803381	1.76×10^{-7}
19	4,181	1.618034056	-6.7×10^{-8}
20	6,765	1.618033963	2.6×10^{-8}
21	10,946	1.618033999	-1.0×10^{-8}
22	17,711	1.618033985	4.0×10^{-9}
23	28,657	1.618033990	-1.0×10^{-9}
24	46,638	1.618033988	1.2×10^{-9}
25	75,025	1.618033989	-6.2×10^{-10}
26	121,393	1.618033989	3.3×10^{-10}
.	.	.	
.	.	.	
.	.	.	

* The value of ϕ used here for comparison is the value $\phi = 1.618033989$, correct to nine decimal places, given in Eq. (3-5).

Going to higher numbers in the series shows that 4,181 ÷ 2,584 differs from ϕ by less than one part in ten million. So, it is seen that the ratio F_{j+1}/F_j converges to the golden ratio ϕ and for relatively small values of j. The value of ϕ used in these comparisons is correct to one part in a billion, and it can be seen from table 3-1 that the ratio $F_{23} \div F_{22} \equiv 28{,}657 \div 17{,}711$ agrees with ϕ to this precision. It is indeed remarkable that the ratio F_{j+1}/F_j converges to ϕ this accurately, using only the 23rd and 22nd numbers in the Fibonacci sequence.

The foregoing provides three quite different ways in which the number ϕ can be obtained. How did this number come to be known as the "golden ratio" or "divine ratio"? Perhaps the most well-known connection of the number ϕ to our senses is its application to the ratio of the length to width of a rectangle that is most pleasing to the human eye. Three rectangles, all of the same length, but with different length-to-width ratios, are shown in Fig. 3-2. The rectangle in the center has its length-to-width ratio equal to ϕ = 1.618034 and by most accounts it is more pleasing to the human eye than the other two rectangles. The rectangle with $l/w = \phi$ is often called the "golden rectangle." Our fascination with the number ϕ and its relation to our senses has prompted many studies over centuries. In particular, a series of psychologists, following the work by Adolf Zeising's *Der Goldene Schnitt* (1884), conducted studies to determine people's preferences of rectangular shapes using thousands of commonly occurring rectangles. Over the rectangular range l/w = 1 (square) to l/w = 2.5, the rectangle with l/w = 1.618 was most often judged to have the most aesthetically appealing shape. Many studies have linked the ratio ϕ to great works of art, such as those of Leonardo da Vinci, Michelangelo, and Raphael, in which it is shown that certain critical portions and sub-portions of the artists' works

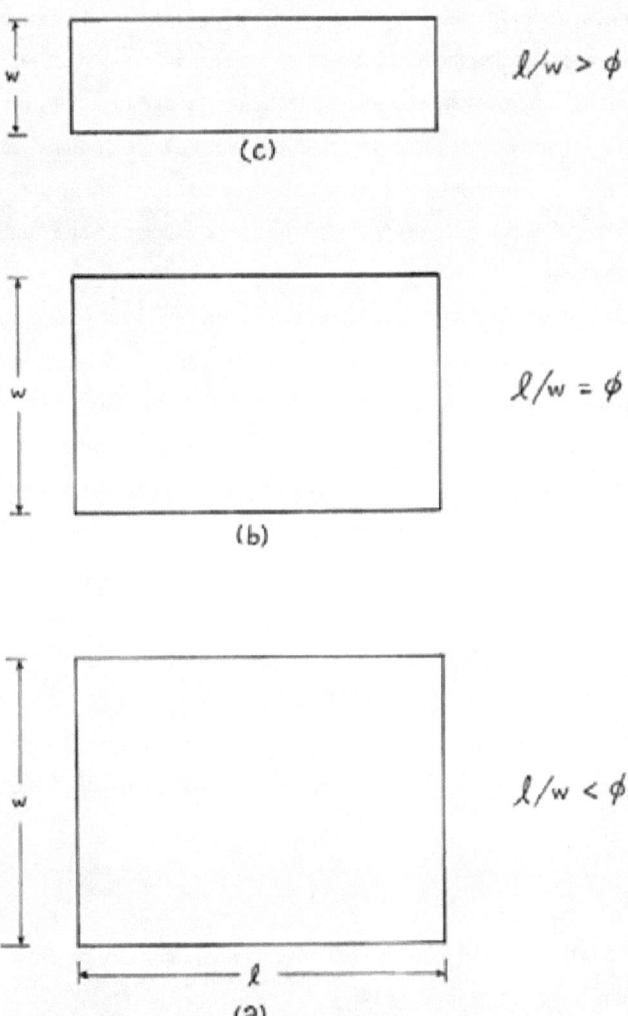

Fig. 3-2. Rectangles of the same length but different widths. Reported studies show that (b) is judged by most observers as the rectangle with relative dimensions most pleasing to the eye.

can be framed in rectangles having the golden ratio ϕ. This has led many to claim that these famous artists either knew of the golden rectangle and consciously incorporated its imaginary boundaries into their art, or if they were not aware of it mathematically, their innate sense of appeal guided them to use relative dimensions close to the ratio ϕ.

In a similar vein, many have studied the relationship of ϕ to architectural structures including the great pyramids, the Parthenon, the Notre-Dame-de-Paris, and Petronas Towers, for examples. There is good reason to believe that the mathematical ratio ϕ was used purposely in these architectures, or at least the aesthetic appeal was a guiding factor in the design dimensions.

In its attributes as a "divine proportion" or "divine ratio," the ratio ϕ can be seen in parts of the human anatomy as for example in the relative dimensions of bones in the hand revealed by x-rays, and in various dimensional aspects of the human face. In regard to human anatomical proportions, a very unusual study reported by Huntley in his book, *The Divine Proportion,* claims that the ratio of women's height to their floor-to-navel distance is very close to the value of $\phi = 1.618$. There is more at a deeper, microscopic level! Harel and colleagues (*Trends in Biological Sciences* II (April 4, 1986)) reported their measurements showed that each cycle of the DNA molecule sine curve had a length-to-width ratio of 1.62, which is nearly identical with the divine proportion $\phi = 1.618$.

It was shown earlier in Eqs. (3-1) through (3-5) that the number ϕ is unique in that it is the only real number that is equal to the reciprocal of itself minus one; i.e., $\phi = 1/(\phi - 1)$. This can also be written as

$$\phi = 1 + \frac{1}{\phi}, \tag{3-13}$$

indicating that ϕ is the only real number equal to unity plus its reciprocal. Now, let a be any positive real number. Then, from Eq. (3-13)

$$a^\phi = a^{\left(1+\frac{1}{\phi}\right)}$$

$$= a a^{\frac{1}{\phi}}, \tag{3-14}$$

or, written in another familiar notation

$$a^\phi = a \sqrt[\phi]{a} \tag{3-15}$$

According to the latter, if a positive real number is raised to the power of the golden ratio, ϕ, the result is simply equal to the real number itself times the $(1/\phi)^{th}$ root of the number. The latter is true only for the power ϕ, because of the particular property that ϕ enjoys in Eq. (3-13). As an additional interesting feature, note that the square of the golden ratio, from Eq. (3-4), can be expressed as

$$\phi^2 = \left(\frac{1+\sqrt{5}}{2}\right)^2$$

$$= \frac{4+2(1+\sqrt{5})}{4} \qquad (3\text{-}16)$$

$$= 1+\phi.$$

Therefore, if a is any positive real number, then

$$a^{\phi^2} = aa^{\phi}. \qquad (3\text{-}17)$$

So, when a real number is raised to the power of the square of the golden ratio, the result is merely the product of the number times the number raised to the power ϕ.

3-2. The number ϕ in relation to other celebrated numbers in mathematics

The number ϕ is fascinating, but there are, of course, other very intriguing numbers in mathematics, perhaps the most famous of which is π, the ratio of the circumference of a circle to its diameter. As close a rival is e, the base of the natural logarithms. Euler, one of the most brilliant mathematicians of all time, is credited with the relation

$$e^{i\theta} = \cos\theta + i\sin\theta. \qquad (3\text{-}18)$$

If we substitute $\theta = 2\pi$ into the latter, then the result is

$$e^{2\pi i} = 1, \qquad (3\text{-}19)$$

which has been called the most astonishing relation in mathematics. To understand why, consider the following. A real number (as opposed to imaginary) is said to be "rational" if it can be expressed as the ratio of two integers, otherwise the number is referred to as "irrational." Now, in number theory it is readily shown that $\sqrt{2}$ and $\sqrt{5}$, for example, are irrational because neither can be expressed as q/p, where p and q are integers. It has been shown that both e and π are irrational and, moreover, both are transcendental numbers, meaning that neither is a root of a polynomial equation with rational coefficients. By comparison, note that $\sqrt{2}$ and $\sqrt{5}$, while irrational, can each be expressed as the root of an algebraic polynomial equation because in the former case $x^2 - 2 = 0$ and in the latter case $x^2 - 5 = 0$ are the equations with solutions $\pm\sqrt{2}$ and $\pm\sqrt{5}$, respectively. Finally, the quantity i in the power to which e is raised in the expression in Eq. (3-18) is referred to as the "imaginary unit," and it was invented so that an equation of the form $x^2 + 1 = 0$, for example, will have a solution where $x = \pm\sqrt{-1}$ is by definition $x = \pm i$. So, the intrigue surrounding Eq. (3-19) is that the transcendental number e = 2.7182818284 ... is raised to a power that is a product of another transcendental number π = 3.1415926536 ... times twice the imaginary unit $\sqrt{-1}$, and the result is simply a real number, namely, unity.

What is the connection between the two transcendental numbers π and e, and the golden ratio, ϕ? So far as this author is aware, there is no formal relation. However, we can make the following very amazing observations. First, using the values of e, π, and ϕ correct to nine decimal places, it is easy to see with a hand calculator that the combination $e\phi/\pi$ is equal to the ratio of two small integers

$$\frac{e\phi}{\pi} = \frac{7}{5}, \qquad (3\text{-}20)$$

to within 1.3 parts per one hundred thousand. Another way to view the latter result is to note that the value ϕ can be calculated from π and e from the simple relation

$$\phi = \frac{7}{5}\frac{\pi}{e}. \qquad (3\text{-}21)$$

Using π and e correct to nine decimal places, the calculated value of ϕ from Eq. (3-21) is ϕ = 1.618018288, which differs from the correct nine-decimal value ϕ = 1.618033989 by only 1.57 x 10^{-5}, or 0.00097 percent!

It is easy to see that an amazingly simple relationship between ϕ and π exists in the form of π/ϕ^2 = 6/5. That is, the ratio of the two small integers 6/5 gives π/ϕ^2 correct to within 1.8 parts per one hundred thousand. Using the relation $\phi^2 = 1 + \phi$ from Eq. (3-16) makes it possible to cast the relation π/ϕ^2 = 6/5 in the simple form $\phi = 5\pi/6 - 1$, from which it can be seen that the golden ratio ϕ can be calculated to within 0.0024 percent. Finally, a simple relation between ϕ and e can be found by combining the latter, $\phi = 5\pi/6 - 1$, with Eq.

24

(3-20) and Eq. (3-16) to yield $\phi = 25e/42$, from which the calculated value of ϕ is correct to within nine parts per million, corresponding to a difference of only 0.00056 percent.

From a purely mathematical point of view, a given number either equals a second number or it does not. In this strict sense, the equality signs in Eqs. (3-20) and (3-21) and in the text of the above paragraph should each be replaced with the "approximately equal" sign, $\cong$. This was not done because emphasis was placed on the limits of precision, comparing one side of Eq. (3-20) to the other side, or comparing calculated values of ϕ to the true value of ϕ. As can be seen, the degrees of precision to which the approximate equalities hold is remarkable.

The numbers π and e are no doubt the most celebrated numbers in all of mathematics. Not only have π and e been dealt with so extensively in analyses of a pure mathematical nature, but also π and e play a prominent role in nearly all of science. So, how does the role of the number ϕ compare to that of π and e? To be sure, ϕ has and continues to enjoy connections to art forms, paintings, architectural designs, patterns in nature, etc., that demonstrate its appeal to the human senses. In this regard, the number ϕ occupies a different and somewhat unique role relative to π and e. Perhaps for this reason it is all the more worthy to note that a simple numerical relationship among ϕ, π, and e has been found, as embodied in the precision of the equality in Eq. (3-20). Regarding the five-point star, one thing is certain, as can be seen from Eq. (2-11) of Chapter 2. The ratio of the line segments P_1B to DB in the five-point mathematical star of Fig. 2-1 is exactly equal to the number ϕ and, as will be seen, the number ϕ will appear in very intriguing ways as three-dimensional star shapes are developed and analyzed in the following chapters.

CHAPTER 4
THREE-DIMENSIONAL FIVE-POINTED MATHEMATICAL STARS

4-1. Construction with altitude h at center of plane star of radius R

A three-dimensional star shape can be formed by imagining the five-point star of Fig. 2-1 to be displaced relative to itself, without rotation, through a distance d in the direction perpendicular to the plane of the star. This gives the three-dimensional star shape of thickness d in Fig. 4-1, with the opposite star-shaped faces lying in parallel planes. Solid star shapes of the type in Fig. 4-1 will be studied in many aspects in later chapters, but a different class of three-dimensional star shapes will serve as the area of focus in this chapter.

Consider again the star figure in Fig. 2-1 and let a segment of length h be erected perpendicular to the plane of the star, through the center at point O. Designate the "top" end of the segment of length h by the letter O', and, using straight lines, connect O' with each of the tips P_1, P_2, ... P_5 of the plane star to give the shape in Fig. 4-2. Because of the symmetry of the five-point plane star figure, and because the segment OO' is perpendicular to the plane at the point of symmetry O, it follows that each line joining O' with a tip of the plane star has length $\sqrt{h^2 + R^2}$. To begin an analysis of the three-dimensional shape relative to the base plane star of radius R, note first that the plane star is comprised of five identical quadrilaterals, each having a diagonal of length R as indicated in Fig. 4-3. Let the line segments OB and P_1B be designated by l_1 and l_2, respectively, as indicated in the figure. The diagonal segment DB, as shown earlier in Chapter 2, is perpendicular to the segment OP_1, i.e., the radius R. Using the angles in the geometry of the star figure, we see from $\triangle OP_1B$ in Fig. 4-3, we can write

$$l_1 \sin 36° = l_2 \sin 18° \qquad (4\text{-}1)$$

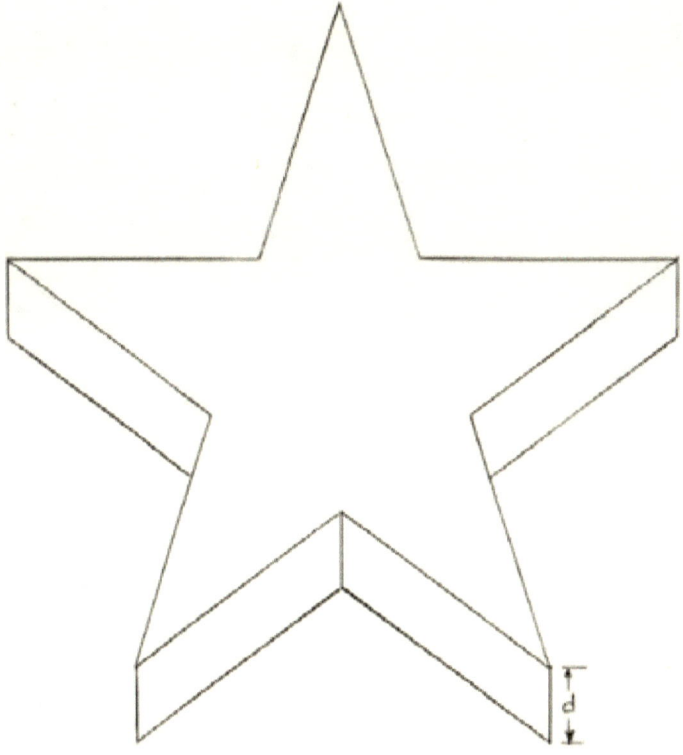

Fig. 4-1. A simple three-dimensional five-point star of thickness d, with opposite parallel plane star faces.

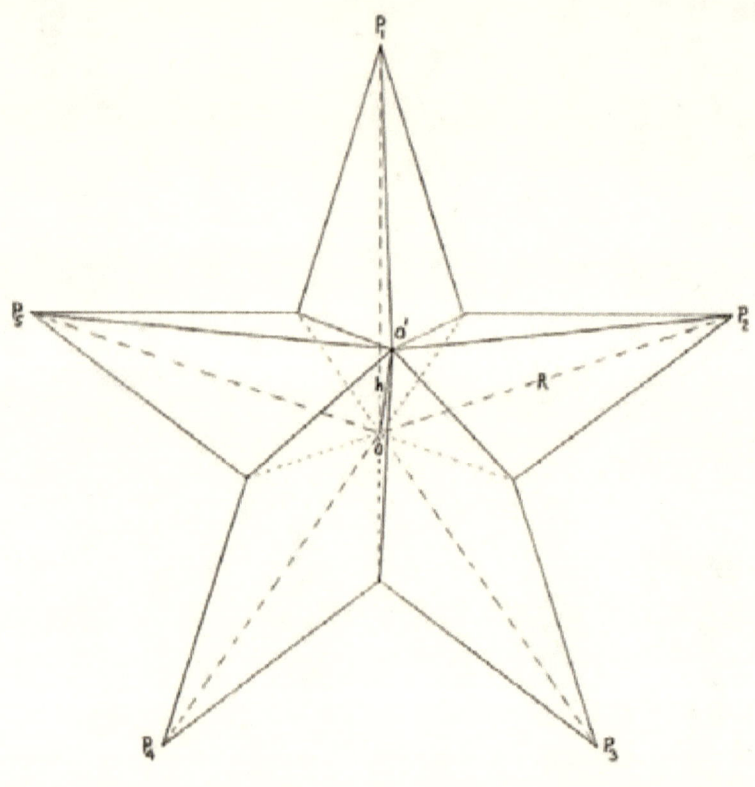

Fig. 4-2. A three-dimensional star of altitude h constructed on a plane five-point star of radius R.

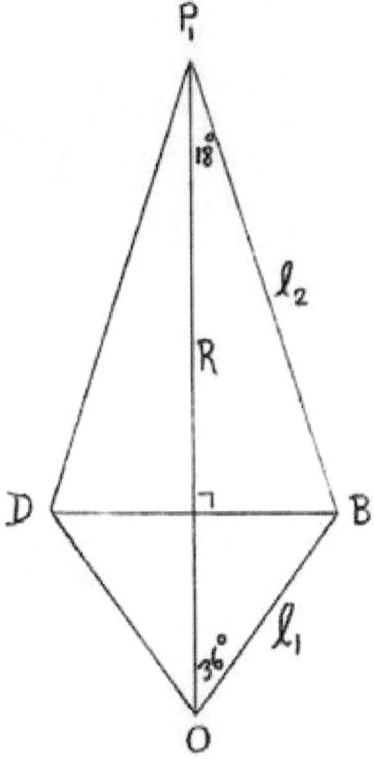

Fig. 4-3. The plane star base in Fig. 4-2 is composed of five identical quadrilaterals like OBP_1D.

$$l_1 \cos 36° + l_2 \cos 18° = R \tag{4-2}$$

Solving Eqs. (4-1) and (4-2) to express l_1 and l_2 in terms of the angles and radius R gives

$$l_1 = R \frac{\sin 18°}{\sin(18° + 36°)} \tag{4-3}$$

$$l_2 = R \frac{\sin 36°}{\sin(18° + 36°)}. \tag{4-4}$$

When the quantities involving the angles are evaluated numerically, the distances l_1 and l_2 can be written as

$$l_1 = a_1 R$$
$$l_2 = a_2 R, \tag{4-5}$$

where, correct to nine decimal places,

$$a_1 = 0.381966011$$
$$a_2 = 0.726542528. \tag{4-6}$$

4-2. Angles in triangular facet of three-dimensional star and their variation with altitude h, radius R, connection to ϕ

In the three-dimensional star shape in Fig. 4-2, each of the five quadrilaterals in the plane star base in Fig. 4-3 has the group of four triangles constructed on the quadrilateral base as indicated in Fig. 4-4. Consider the triangle $O'BP_1$, in Fig. 4-4, which has one side of length l_2 in the base star and one side equal to the length $\sqrt{h^2 + R^2}$, which is the segment drawn from the tip O' of the perpendicular h, to the tip P_1 of the plane star base. Let θ be the angle between the two

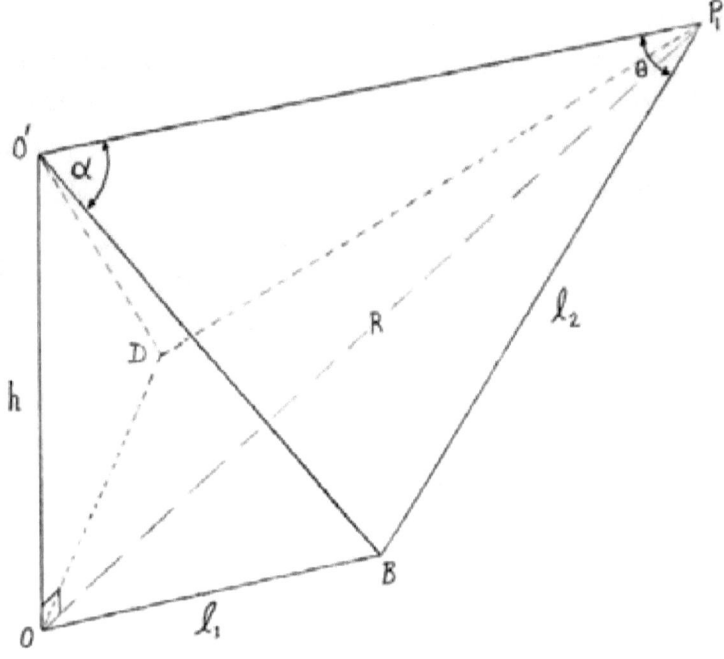

Fig. 4-4. One of five identical pyramidal volume elements comprising the three-dimensional star of altitude h constructed on the base star of radius R shown in Fig. 4-2. A total of ten triangular facets like $O'BP_1$ and $O'DP_1$ make up the surface area having altitude h at O in Fig. 4-2.

sides l_2 and $O'P_1 = \sqrt{h^2 + R^2}$ in triangle $O'BP_1$, and let α be the angle between the side $O'P_1$ and the third side of triangle $O'BP_1$ that connects O' at the tip of h with point B in the plane of the base star. The third angle, $\angle O'BP_1$, in this triangle is simply $\pi - \theta - \alpha$. Note that, as h approaches zero in Fig. 4-4, the lines $O'P_1$ and $O'B$ approach R and l_1, respectively, in the base star and, in fact, when $h = 0$, $O'P_1 \equiv R$ and $O'B \equiv l_1$. Consequently, as h approaches zero, the angle θ approaches 18° and angle α approaches 36° as can be seen from the appropriate angles in the base star.

Intuitively, as the perpendicular distance h increases, one would expect the angles α and θ to increase, and therefore the third angle $\omega \equiv \pi - \alpha - \theta$ would decrease. The actual functions relating the angles α and θ to the altitude h of the three-dimensional figure and the radius R of the base plane star can be determined with reference to Fig. 4-4. Remembering that h is perpendicular to the plane of the base star in which l_1 and l_2 lie, we can use the property of the right triangle $OO'B$ to write

$$(O'B)^2 = h^2 + l_1^2. \tag{4-7}$$

Likewise, because the radius R lies in the plane of the star, the right triangle $OO'P_1$ allows us to write

$$(O'P_1)^2 = h^2 + R^2. \tag{4-8}$$

The law of cosines applied to triangle $O'BP_1$ gives $(O'B)^2 = (O'P_1)^2 + l_2^2 - 2l_2(O'P_1)\cos\theta$, and therefore use of Eqs. (4-7) and (4-8) with the law of cosines leads to the relation

$$h^2 + l_1^2 = h^2 + R^2 + l_2^2 - 2l_2 (h^2 + R^2)^{\frac{1}{2}} \cos\theta, \tag{4-9}$$

which can be solved for the angle θ to give

$$\theta = \arccos\left(\frac{R^2 + l_2^2 - l_1^2}{2l_2\sqrt{h^2 + R^2}}\right). \tag{4-10}$$

The foregoing expression for θ can be expressed in terms of the numerical factors relating l_1, l_2 to R in Eq. (4-5), with the result

$$\theta = \arccos\left(\frac{1 + a_2^2 - a_1^2}{2a_2\sqrt{1+x^2}}\right), \tag{4-11}$$

where x denotes the ratio of the altitude h to the radius R,

$$x = \frac{h}{R}. \tag{4-12}$$

Now, the angle α can be determined by applying the law of sines to triangle $O'P_1B$ in Fig. 4-4 to yield

$$\alpha = \arcsin\left(\frac{l_2 \sin\theta}{\sqrt{l_1^2 + h^2}}\right), \tag{4-13}$$

and again using Eq. (4-5) and the ratio $x = h/R$ allows the latter to be written as

$$\alpha = \arcsin\left(\frac{a_2 \sin\theta}{\sqrt{a_1^2 + x^2}}\right). \tag{4-14}$$

Using the results in Eqs. (4-11) and (4-14), three different three-dimensional star shapes were constructed from paper, each on a base star of radius $R = 3.0$ inches, using different ratios of perpendicular distance h to R. Photographs of the constructions are provided in Fig. 4-5. The ratios used in these constructions were $h/R = 1/3$, $2/3$, and 1.0. These can be regarded as "half shapes" in the sense that they were constructed on one side of the underlying plane of the base star. A full three-dimensional star construction is shown in the photograph in Fig. 4-6. For the latter, the half shape was constructed symmetrically on both sides of the common base-plane star using a ratio $h/R = 1$.

A graph of the angles α and θ, as well as the third angle of triangle $BO'P_1$ in Fig. 4-4, is provided in Fig. 4-7 as a function of the ratio of altitude h to radius R. This was done by first calculating the angle θ versus the ratio $x \equiv h/R$ from Eq. (4-11), using the numerical values for a_1 and a_2 given in Eq. (4-6). Then, for each value of θ, the angle α was calculated from Eq. (4-14) at the corresponding value of x. The third angle in triangle $BO'P_1$ is simply equal to $\pi - \alpha - \theta$.

It is seen in Fig. 4-7 that the angle θ increases as the ratio h/R increases. The increase of θ, while not linear, is nonetheless a continual increase with increasing value of h/R. More will be said about the shape of this curve later. Note that the angle α first increases with increasing values of $x = h/R$, but then the value of α reaches a maximum in the region of $x \cong 0.35$, after which α decreases as x is increased further. Finally, the third angle, $\pi - \theta - \alpha$, in the triangular facet $O'P_1B$ decreases continually as x increases.

The actual value of $x = h/R$ at which the maximum angle α occurs, and the value of α at this value of x, can be determined mathematically from Eq. (4-14). To do this, we first use Eq. (4-11) to express $\sin\theta$ in Eq. (4-14) in terms of x. Thus, remembering that $\sin^2\theta$ +

$\cos^2\theta = 1$, Eqs. (4-11) and (4-14) can be combined to express the angle α as a function of x alone as follows:

Fig. 4-5. Three-dimensional stars of various altitudes constructed on five-point base stars of radius $R = 3$ in. Right: $h/R = 1/3$. Upper left: $h/R = 2/3$. Lower left: $h/R = 1$.

Fig. 4-6. Three-dimensional star constructed on both sides of a five-point base plane star of radius $R = 3$, using $h/R = 1$.

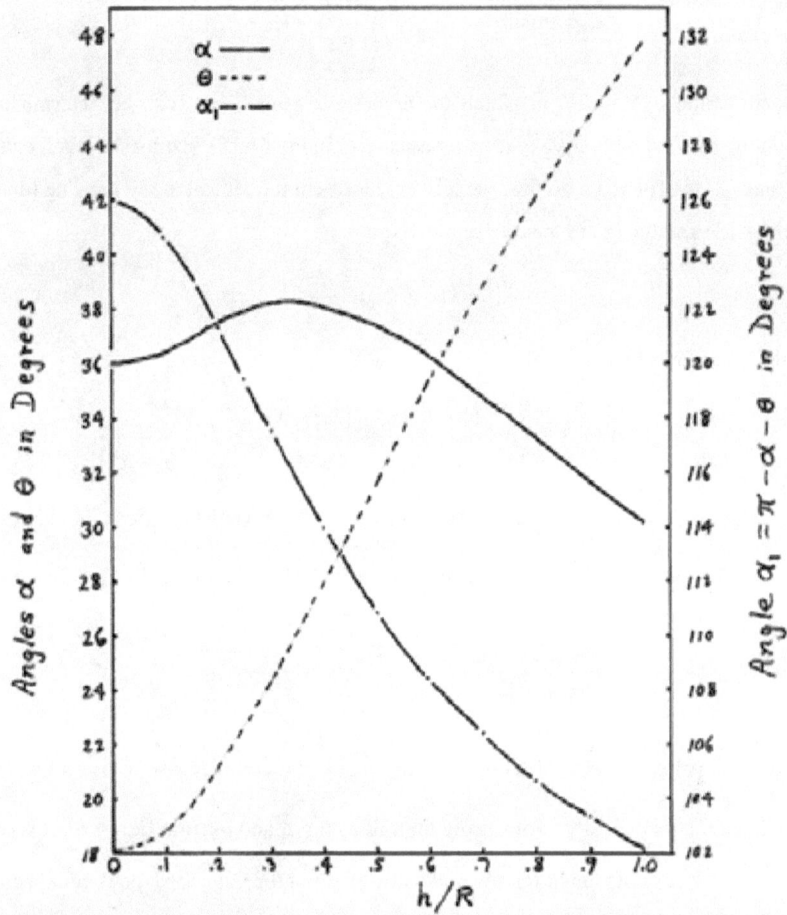

Fig. 4-7. Variation of angles in a triangular facet versus ratio of three-dimensional star altitude h to radius R of base star.

$$\alpha = \arcsin\left[\frac{a_2^2}{a_1^2 + x^2} - \frac{\left(1 + a_2^2 - a_1^2\right)^2}{4\left(1 + x^2\right)\left(a_1^2 + x^2\right)}\right]^{\frac{1}{2}}. \qquad (4\text{-}15)$$

Now, the value of $x = h/R$ at which the angle α is a maximum can be determined by calculating the first derivative of α with respect to x in Eq. (4-15), setting the result equal to zero and solving for x. To do this, we let $V(x)$ represent the radical in the arc sine function in Eq. (4-15) and then note that the first derivative is

$$\frac{d\alpha}{dx} = \left(1 - V^2(x)\right)^{-\frac{1}{2}} \frac{dV(x)}{dx}, \qquad (4\text{-}16)$$

and thus it follows that

$$\frac{d\alpha}{dx} = \left(1 - V^2(x)\right)^{-\frac{1}{2}} \frac{1}{V(x)} \left[\frac{\left(1 + a_2^2 - a_1^2\right)^2 \left(x + a_1^2 x + 2x^3\right)}{4\left(1 + x^2\right)^2 \left(a_1^2 + x^2\right)^2} - \frac{a_2^2 x}{\left(a_1^2 + x^2\right)^2}\right]. \qquad (4\text{-}17)$$

To find the value of x for which the first derivative $d\alpha/dx$ vanishes, the right side of Eq. (4-17) can be set equal to zero and, with the factor $\left(V\sqrt{1-V^2}\right)^{-1}$ divided out, this gives

$$\frac{a_2^2 x}{(a_1^2 + x^2)^2} = \frac{\left(1 + a_2^2 - a_1^2\right)^2 \left(2x^3 + a_1^2 x + x\right)}{4\left(1 + x^2\right)^2 \left(a_1^2 + x^2\right)^2}. \qquad (4\text{-}18)$$

The latter is valid provided $\left(V\sqrt{1-V^2}\right)^{-1}$ does not equal zero because division by zero is not defined mathematically. Now, using the values for a_1 and a_2 from Eq. (4-6), it is found that $\sqrt{1-V^2}$ does not vanish for any real value of x, but the value of V does equal zero for the particular value of $x = 0.55589297$. So, for x not equal to this particular value, Eq. (4-18) can be solved for the value of x that meets the condition for the first derivative of angle α with respect to x to vanish, thereby determining the value of x for which the angle α is a maximum.

Solving for x by combining terms in Eq. (4-18) and simplifying leads to the following equation in x

$$x^4 + 2x^2 (1 - a_{12}^2) + 1 - a_{12}^2 (1 + a_1^2) = 0, \qquad (4\text{-}19)$$

where the quantity a_{12} is defined in terms of a_1 and a_2.

$$a_{12} = \frac{1+a_2^2-a_1^2}{2a_2} \tag{4-20}$$

Eq. (4-19) is a quartic in the variable x, the ratio of altitude h to radius R in Fig. 4-4, and the coefficients and constant term are defined in terms of the quantities a_1 and a_2 relating the sides l_1 and l_2 of the base plane star to the radius R. The cubic term in x is absent, as well as the term containing x to the first power. Therefore, the quartic, containing only the x^4 and x^2 terms in the variable, can be solved by making the substitution $u \equiv x^2$, thereby reducing Eq. (4-19) to the quadratic equation

$$u^2 + 2u(1 - a_{12}^2) + 1 - a_{12}^2(1 + a_1^2) = 0. \tag{4-21}$$

So, we first solve the latter quadratic for u and then find x by taking the square root of u; i.e., $x = \sqrt{u}$. Only positive, real values of x are meaningful in this instance and therefore only a positive value of u is applicable. Substituting the values a_1 and a_2 from Eq. (4-6) into Eqs. (4-20) and (4-21) and using the quadratic formula, the positive root of Eq. (4-21) is found to be

$$u = 0.118033992, \tag{4-22}$$

and hence the root x that satisfies Eq. (4-19), and thereby causes $d\alpha/dx$ in Eq. (4-17) to vanish is

$$x = \sqrt{u}$$
$$= 0.343560754. \tag{4-23}$$

Now, Eq. (4-15) can be evaluated for this value of $x = h/R$ to give the maximum value of the angle α_m. Substituting x from Eq. (4-23) and a_1 and a_2 from Eq. (4-6) into Eq. (4-15) gives

$$\alpha_m = \arcsin(0.618033989)$$
$$= 38.17270765°. \tag{4-24}$$

Comparing Eq. (4-24) with Eq. (3-8), we note the unexpected and very surprising result that the maximum angle α_m is simply the angle whose sine is the reciprocal of the golden ratio, that is,

$$\alpha_m = \arcsin\left(\frac{1}{\phi}\right). \tag{4-25}$$

In summary, with regard to Fig. 4-7, it is to be noted that the three-dimensional star shape in Fig. 4-2, constructed on the five-point mathematical star in the base plane, contains ten identical triangular facets like triangle $BO'P_1$ in Fig. 4-4. A full three-dimensional shape has twenty identical triangles of this type because the star shape in Fig. 4-2 is constructed symmetrically on both sides of the plane star base. The shape of the triangular facet, in terms of its angles, depends only on the ratio of the altitude h to the base radius R, because h and R appear only in the ratio $x = h/R$ in Eqs. (4-11) and (4-14), and the quantities a_1 and a_2 are numerical values independent of h and R. So, whether a three-dimensional star of the type in Fig. 4-2 is constructed on a base star of radius 0.1 inch, or a radius of 10 feet, for example, the angle α in the triangular facet can never exceed the value of 38.1727...° given in Eq. (4-24), and for any ratio of h to R less than or greater than the value 0.34356 ... in Eq. (4-23) the angle α in the facet will be less than 38.1727 ...° Moreover, the trigonometric sine of this maximum value of α is simply equal to the reciprocal of the golden ratio ϕ as seen from Eq. (4-25).

From the shape of the curve of α versus h/R in Fig. 4-7 and the results of Eqs. (4-23) and (4-24), it follows that substitution of a value of h/R less than that in Eq. (4-23) should yield a positive value of slope $d\alpha/dx$ calculated from Eq. (4-17) and a value of angle α less than that in Eq. (4-24), while substitution of a value h/R greater than that in Eq. (4-23) should yield a negative value for $d\alpha/dx$ and, again, a value of α smaller than Eq. (4-24). Indeed, substitution of $x = 0.34$ into Eq. (4-17), for example, yields a slope $d\alpha/dx = 1.23 \times 10^{-3}$, with a value of $\alpha = 38.06°$ calculated from Eq. (4-15) for $x = 0.34$. Then, using $x = 0.35$, for example, as a value slightly larger than that in Eq. (4-23), gives a calculated slope $d\alpha/dx = -2.16 \times 10^{-3}$ and a corresponding angle $\alpha = 37.96°$.

Consider again the angle θ in triangle $BO'P_1$ in Fig. 4-4. From Fig. 4-7, it is seen that θ increases steadily as the ratio of altitude h to radius R increases. However, close examination of Fig. 4-7 shows that the slope of θ versus x, while always positive, appears to increase steadily for values of x up to the range 0.4 to 0.5, but as x increases above this range, the slope of θ versus x no longer increases as fast. Mathematically this means that the curve exhibits what is known as an inflection point in the region $x = 0.4$ to 0.5. The conditions for the existence of an inflection point in the curve of θ versus x are that the second derivative of θ with respect to x be zero and that the sign of the second derivative changes for values of x slightly below and slightly above the inflection point. So, to find the inflection point, we calculate the second derivative of θ with respect to x from Eq. (4-11) and set it equal to zero and solve for x. To do this we first define the function w(x)

$$w(x) = a_{12}(1+x^2)^{-\frac{1}{2}}, \tag{4-26}$$

where $x \equiv h/R$ and the quantity a_{12} is given in Eq. (4-20). Then, θ as a function of x in Eq. (4-11) can be written as

$$\theta = \arccos(w(x)). \tag{4-27}$$

Now, the first derivative of the arc cosine function is

$$\frac{d\theta}{dx} = -\left(1-w^2(x)\right)^{-\frac{1}{2}}\frac{dw(x)}{dx}, \tag{4-28}$$

and therefore from Eqs. (4-26) and (4-27) we have

$$\frac{d\theta}{dx} = \frac{a_{12}x}{(1+x^2)\sqrt{1+x^2-a_{12}^2}}, \tag{4-29}$$

and, after lengthy but straightforward manipulation of terms, the second derivative can be written in the following form.

$$\frac{d}{dx}\left(\frac{d\theta}{dx}\right) = a_{12}\left[\frac{(x^2-1)(a_{12}^2-1)-2x^4}{(1+x^2)^2(1+x^2-a_{12}^2)^{\frac{3}{2}}}\right] \tag{4-30}$$

The necessary condition for an inflection point x_i to exist is that the second derivative vanish. Therefore, setting the result in Eq. (4-30) equal to zero leads to the equation x_i must satisfy.

$$x_i^4 + \frac{1}{2}(1-a_{12}^2)x_i^2 + \frac{1}{2}(a_{12}^2-1) = 0. \tag{4-31}$$

The foregoing quartic equation contains x_i only to the fourth power and second power, and therefore it can be solved easily by substituting $x_i^2 = Z_i$ to reduce it to a quadratic, solvable from the quadratic formula to give Z_i. Then, $x_i = \sqrt{Z_i}$. The quadratic in Z_i becomes

$$Z_i^2 + \frac{1}{2}(1-a_{12}^2)Z_i + \frac{1}{2}(a_{12}^2-1) = 0, \tag{4-32}$$

for which, after evaluating a_{12} from Eqs. (4-6) and (4-20), the positive root is found to be

$$Z_i = 0.195935362, \qquad (4\text{-}33)$$

from which the inflection point x_i is calculated to be.

$$x_i = \sqrt{Z_i}$$
$$= 0.442645865. \qquad (4\text{-}34)$$

Note that the other root of Eq. (4-32) is $Z_i = -0.243681108$, but this root is ruled out because it gives an imaginary result for x_i, which has no meaning for this case.

If the value of x_i in Eq. (4-34) is truly the inflection point, then substitution of a value of x slightly smaller into Eq. (4-30) should yield a value for the second derivative of one sign, while substitution of a value slightly larger should give a second derivative with opposite sign. This is true because, for example, substituting $x = 0.43$ into Eq. (4-30) gives $d/dx(d\theta/dx) = 0.04316$ while $x = 0.45$ gives $d/dx(d\theta/dx) = -0.02368$.

4-3. Ratio of h to R resulting in isosceles triangular facets and relationships to ϕ and golden angle

Referring to Fig. 4-4 shows that as the altitude h increases relative to the base star radius R, all the angles vary in the triangular facet $O'BP_1$ in Fig. 4-3. So, for example, the facet will be isosceles with angles θ and α equal and, estimating from the graph in Fig. 4-7, this should occur for x approximately equal to 0.6. The value can be calculated exactly from Eq. (4-14) by writing it in slightly different form

$$\sin\alpha = \frac{a_2 \sin\theta}{\sqrt{a_1^2 + x^2}} \qquad (4\text{-}35)$$

and then noting that if $\theta = \alpha$, it follows that $\sin\theta = \sin\alpha$ and Eq. (4-35) can be solved for the corresponding values of $x = h/R$ to give $\theta = \alpha$:

$$x = \sqrt{a_2^2 - a_1^2}. \qquad (4\text{-}36)$$

Using the values of the quantities a_1 and a_2 from Eq. (4-6), it is seen from Eq. (4-36) that

$$x \equiv \frac{h}{R} = 0.618033989 \qquad (4\text{-}37)$$

is the ratio of altitude h to radius R that will cause the angles α and θ to be equal, thereby making the facet $BO'P_1$ an isosceles triangle in Fig. 4-4. Note that Eq. (3-8) from Chapter 3 shows that the ratio h/R in Eq. (4-37) can be expressed in terms of the golden ratio:

$$\left(\frac{h}{R}\right)_{\theta=\alpha} = \frac{1}{\phi} \qquad (4\text{-}38)$$

It can be seen from Eqs. (4-11) and (4-14) that the magnitude of the angles for $h/R = 1/\phi$ is

$$\theta = \alpha = 36°. \qquad (4\text{-}39)$$

The third angle in triangle $O'BP_1$ of Fig. 4-4 is $\pi - \theta - \alpha$, which we shall now call α_1, i.e., $\alpha_1 = \pi - \theta - \alpha$. We can now show that the triangular faces of the three-dimensional star can be isosceles only with $\angle\theta = \angle\alpha$. That is, no value of h/R exists for which $\angle\theta = \angle\alpha_1$, and neither for $\angle\alpha = \angle\alpha_1$. To show this we note first that the law of cosines can be applied to triangle $BO'P_1$ in Fig. 4-4 to express angle α_1 in terms of a_1, a_2, and the ratio $x = h/R$. This leads to the following, after some manipulation.

$$\alpha_1 = \arccos\left(\frac{a_1^2 + a_2^2 - 1}{2a_2\sqrt{x^2 + a_1^2}}\right) \qquad (4\text{-}40)$$

If a value h/R exists to make $\theta = \alpha_1$, then $\cos\theta$ must equal $\cos\alpha_1$ and hence from Eqs. (4-11) and (4-40), we can write

$$\frac{1 + a_2^2 - a_1^2}{2a_2\sqrt{1+x^2}} = \frac{a_1^2 + a_2^2 - 1}{2a_2\sqrt{x^2 + a_1^2}} \qquad (4\text{-}41)$$

and solving for x yields

$$x = \left(\frac{\left(a_1^2 + a_2^2 - 1\right)^2 - a_1^2\left(1 + a_2^2 - a_1^2\right)^2}{\left(1 + a_2^2 - a_1^2\right)^2 - \left(a_1^2 + a_2^2 - 1\right)^2}\right)^{\frac{1}{2}}. \qquad (4\text{-}42)$$

Substituting the numerical values of a_1 and a_2 from Eq. (4-6) into the latter results in

$$x = \sqrt{-0.095491503}, \qquad (4\text{-}43)$$

which indicates that θ cannot equal α_1 because the assumption of their equality leads to the square root of a negative number for $x = h/R$; i.e., h/R is imaginary. Now, referring to the discussion following Eq. (3-19) of Chapter 3, we can make use of the imaginary unit i defined by $i \equiv \sqrt{-1}$ and write Eq. (4-43) in the form

$$x = i\sqrt{0.095491503}, \qquad (4\text{-}44)$$

and because of the positive number under the radical sign, Eq. (4-44) gives

$$x = 0.309016994i. \qquad (4\text{-}45)$$

Referring to Eq. (3-8) in Chapter 3, it can be seen that the numerical factor multiplying the imaginary unit $i \equiv \sqrt{-1}$ in Eq. (4-45) can be expressed in terms of the golden ratio, ϕ:

$$x = i\left(\frac{1}{2\phi}\right) \tag{4-46}$$

Therefore, although no real value of the ratio h/R exists to give an isosceles triangular facet with angle θ equal to α_1, their assumed equality implies an imaginary value of h/R that is, nonetheless, expressible in terms of one-half the reciprocal of the golden ratio!

Finally, to show that no value of h/R exists for which the triangular facet is isosceles with the angles α and α_1 in Fig. 4-4 equal, we first apply the law of cosines to the triangle $BO'P_1$ considering the side l_2 opposite angle α, and after manipulation it is seen that α can be expressed in terms of x and a_1 and a_2 as given below.

$$\alpha = \arccos\left(\frac{1 + a_1^2 + 2x^2 - a_2^2}{2\sqrt{1+x^2}\sqrt{a_1^2+x^2}}\right) \tag{4-47}$$

If a value of $x = h/R$ exists for which $\alpha = \alpha_1$, then $\cos\alpha$ must equal $\cos\alpha_1$ and hence from Eqs. (4-40) and (4-47) it is found that

$$x = \sqrt{Z} \tag{4-48}$$

where Z is a solution of the quadratic

$$Z^2 + \left(d_{12} - \frac{1}{4}f_{12}\right)Z + \frac{1}{4}\left(d_{12}^2 - f_{12}\right) = 0 \tag{4-49}$$

and the numerical quantities d_{12} and f_{12} are defined in terms of a_1 and a_2 in Eqs. (4-5) and (4-6).

$$\left. \begin{array}{l} d_{12} = 1 + a_1^2 - a_2^2 \\ f_{12} = \left(\dfrac{a_1^2 + a_2^2 - 1}{a_2}\right)^2 \end{array} \right\} \tag{4-50}$$

Substituting the values of a_1 and a_2 and solving the quadratic in Z shows that both roots are negative, meaning that the corresponding values of x from Eq. (4-48) are imaginary and therefore no value of h/R exists for which the triangular facet $BO'P_1$ in Fig. 4-4 is isosceles with angles $\alpha = \alpha_1$. However, close examination of the magnitudes of the two roots Z_1 and Z_2 of Eq. (4-49) leads to an unexpected observation. The values of x corresponding to the two roots are

$$x_1 = \sqrt{z_1} = \sqrt{-0.472135955}$$
$$x_2 = \sqrt{z_2} = \sqrt{-0.095491503},$$
(4-51)

and using the imaginary unit $i \equiv \sqrt{-1}$ allows these to be written

$$x_1 = \sqrt{0.472135955}\ i$$
$$x_2 = \sqrt{0.095491503}\ i.$$
(4-52)

Upon evaluating the radicals, it is seen that $x_1 = 2ix_{\alpha max}$, where $x_{\alpha max}$ is the value of h/R in Eq. (4-23) for which the angle α is a maximum, and $x_2 = i/2\phi$. So, even though no value of x occurs that will make $\alpha = \alpha_1$, the condition on x that would have to be true if the equality existed leads to imaginary values with numerical factors nonetheless related to the golden ratio in one instance and the actual value of x for a maximum of the α in the other case!

The angle α_1 appears to have an inflection point in the region $x = 0.2$ to $x = 0.3$, as can be observed in Fig. 4-7. To calculate the value, we take the second derivative of α_1 with respect to x from Eq. (4-40), set it equal to zero and solve for x. After considerable algebraic manipulation, this procedure leads to the result

$$x_{\alpha_1\ \text{infl.}} = \sqrt{Z_{\alpha_1}}$$
(4-53)

where Z_{α_1} satisfies the quadratic

$$Z_{\alpha_1}^2 + \frac{1}{2}(a_1^2 - b_{12}^2)Z_{\alpha_1} + \frac{1}{2}(b_{12}^2 - a_1^2)a_1^2 = 0,$$
(4-54)

in which a_1 and a_2 are given by Eq. (4-6) and $b_{12} = (a_1^2 + a_2^2 - 1)/2a_2$. One root of Eq. (4-54) is positive and the other negative. Only the positive root will give a real value for x_{α_1} in Eq. (4-53), and the result is

$$x_{\alpha_1\ \text{infl.}} = 0.2508721.$$
(4-55)

The corresponding angle α_1 at which the inflection occurs is found by substituting from Eq. (4-55) into Eq. (4-40), giving the result

$$\alpha_1 = 119.4257°.$$
(4-56)

The prominent feature of the curve α versus x is the maximum occurring at the value of x in Eq. (4-23), as discussed extensively earlier. However, as can be seen from Fig. 4-7, the curve of α vs. x also exhibits an inflection point at a value of $x = h/R$ approximately one-half the value at which the maximum occurs. Calculation of the second derivative,

$d/dx(d\alpha/dx)$, from Eq. (4-15) leads to a very complicated expression to solve for x to find the inflection point mathematically. Therefore, an interpolative numerical approach was taken that gave the value $x = 0.176465$. A way to check this result is to note that the magnitude of the first derivative, $d\alpha/dx$, should be slightly smaller for a value of x slightly larger than the latter inflection point, and $d\alpha/dx$ should be slightly larger at a value of x slightly smaller than the inflection point. From Eq. (4-47), the first derivative can be put into the form

$$\frac{d\alpha}{dx} = \frac{-x}{\sqrt{(1+x^2)(a_1^2+x^2)-(c_{12}+x^2)^2}} \left[2 - \frac{(c_{12}+x^2)(1+a_1^2+2x^2)}{(1+x^2)(a_1^2+x^2)} \right], \quad (4\text{-}57)$$

where

$$c_{12} = \frac{1}{2}(1+a_1^2-a_2^2).$$

Now, taking $x = 0.180$, a number slightly larger than the interpolated inflection point (0.176465), the value of $d\alpha/dx$ calculated from Eq. (4-57) is $d\alpha/dx = 0.17012$, while substitution of $x = 0.170$ gives $d\alpha/dx = 0.17355$, thus validating that the inflection point lies between $x = 0.170$ and 0.180.

Many of the foregoing results of this chapter are compiled in Table 4-1.

Table 4-1. Summary of angle measures, versus ratio of altitude h to radius R, in triangular facets of the three-dimensional star shape constructed on a five-point base star.

Feature	h/R*	Angles**
θ vs. h/R inflection	0.442646	$\theta = 29.5802°$
		$\alpha_1 = 112.5819°$
		$\alpha = 37.8379°$
α vs. h/R inflection	0.176465	$\alpha = 37.2373°$
		$\theta = 20.5141°$
		$\alpha_1 = 122.2486°$
α_1 vs. h/R inflection	0.250872	$\alpha_1 = 119.4257°$
		$\alpha = 37.8643°$
		$\theta = 22.7100°$

α maximum	0.343561	$\alpha_{max} = 38.1727°$
		$\theta = 25.9137°$
		$\alpha_1 = 115.9136°$
Isosceles	$0.618034 \equiv 1/\phi$	$\alpha = 36°$
		$\theta = 36°$
		$\alpha_1 = 108°$

---

*   Values rounded to six decimal places.
** Rounded to four decimal places.

Consider Fig. 4-8 in which the geometry of Fig. 4-4 is shown for the special case in which triangle $BO'P_1$ is isosceles. As shown earlier in Eq. (4-38), when $h/R = 1/\phi$, the triangular facet $BO'P_1$ is isosceles with $\theta = \alpha = 36°$. Viewing this in another way, the facet is isosceles when $R/h = \phi$. So, triangle $OO'P_1$, which has h and R as two of its sides, is just "half" the golden rectangle with sides $R/h = \phi$. In the golden rectangle, the angle the diagonal makes with the longer side is known as the "golden angle." This angle between the segment $O'P_1$ and the radius R in Fig. 4-8, is

$$\angle OP_1O' = \text{arc tan } (h/R)$$
$$= \text{arc tan } (1/\phi)$$
$$= 31.71747442° \qquad (4\text{-}58)$$

Furthermore, when triangle $OO'P_1$ is golden with $R/h = \phi$, making triangular facet $BO'P_1$ isosceles, then the triangle $OO'B$ in Fig. 4-8 is also golden because, using Eq. (4-5),

$$\frac{h}{l_1} = \frac{h}{a_1 R} = \frac{x}{a_1} = \frac{0.618033989}{0.381966011}$$
$$= 1.618033989 \equiv \phi, \qquad (4\text{-}59)$$

where the value of a_1 was obtained from Eq. (4-6).

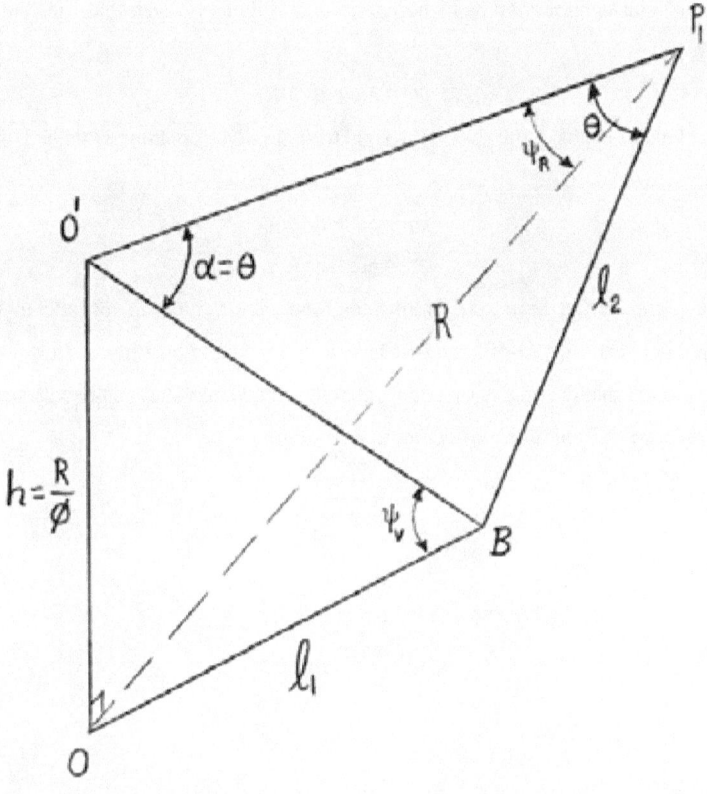

Fig. 4-8. When $h = R/\phi$ in Fig. 4-4, then each of the ten triangular facets of the surface is isosceles with $\alpha = \theta$.

Referring to Fig. 4-8, the right triangle $OO'P_1$ contains the "ridge" of the three-dimensional star construction as its hypotenuse, and it can be seen that each ridge makes the angle

$$\psi_R = \text{arc tan}\,(h/R) \tag{4-60}$$

with the plane of the base star. Now, the right triangle BOO' contains a "valley" that makes an angle

$$\psi_V = \text{arc tan}\,(h/l_1)$$
$$= \text{arc tan}\,(h/a_1 R) \tag{4-61}$$

with the plane of the base star. If the common factor, ratio of altitude to radius, is eliminated between Eqs. (4-60) and (4-61) and the numerical quantity a_1 from Eq. (4-6) is used, it is found that the angles ψ_R and ψ_V that the ridge and valley make with the plane of the base star are related to the golden ratio ϕ through

$$\frac{\tan \psi_v - \tan \psi_R}{\tan \psi_R} = \phi, \tag{4-62}$$

or, equivalently,

$$\sqrt{\frac{\tan \psi_v}{\tan \psi_R}} = \phi. \tag{4-63}$$

4-4. Unique conditions in ridge, valley, and triangular facet angles that exist when $h/R = \frac{1}{2}$.

Next, refer to Fig. 4-9, where it is seen that the triangular facet $BO'P_1$ shares the "valley" of length $\left(h^2 + l_1^2\right)^{\frac{1}{2}}$ in common with the right triangle $OO'B$. Let α_2 be the angle that the valley makes with the altitude h. Then

$$\sin\alpha_2 = \frac{l_1}{\sqrt{h^2 + l_1^2}}. \tag{4-64}$$

Now, α is the angle between the valley and ridge in the triangular facet and, as shown earlier, the angle α can be obtained from Eq. (4-13). Because of what follows, it is interesting to pose the question regarding the value of h/R that would cause the two angles α_2 and α to be equal. If these two angles are to be equal, then their sines must also be equal and therefore after some simplification, we obtain the following from Eqs. (4-13) and (4-64),

$$\sin\theta = \frac{l_1}{l_2}, \tag{4-65}$$

where θ is the angle between sides l_2 and $O'P_1 = (h^2 + R^2)^{\frac{1}{2}}$ in the facet triangle. Eliminating the angle θ between Eqs. (4-65) and (4-10) yields the relation

$$\sqrt{1 - l_1^2 / l_2^2} = \frac{R^2 + l_2^2 - l_1^2}{2l_2\sqrt{h^2 + R^2}}, \tag{4-66}$$

and using the proportionality definitions between l_1, l_2, and R in Eq. (4-5), the latter can be solved for the ratio h/R.

$$\left(\frac{h}{R}\right)_{\alpha=\alpha_2} = \sqrt{\frac{\left(1+a_2^2-a_1^2\right)^2}{4\left(a_2^2-a_1^2\right)}-1} \qquad (4\text{-}67)$$

Substituting the numerical values for a_1 and a_2 into Eq. (4-67) leads to the surprisingly simple ratio of altitude h to radius R for which the angles α and α_2 in Fig. 4-9 are equal.

$$\left(\frac{h}{R}\right)_{\alpha=\alpha_2} = \frac{1}{2} \qquad (4\text{-}68)$$

With $h/R = 1/2$, the magnitude of α can be calculated from Eq. (4-15). However, in this case, because α is equal to α_2, it is simpler to calculate $\alpha_2(=\alpha)$ from the right triangle $OO'B$, noting that $\tan\alpha_2 = l_1/h$. Moreover, using Eqs. (4-5), (4-6), and (3-11), it is easy to see for $h/R = 1/2$ that α_2 is connected to ϕ because

$$\alpha_2 (=\alpha) = \arctan(a_1 R/h)$$
$$= \arctan(2/\phi^2)$$
$$= 37.37736812°. \qquad (4\text{-}69)$$

Now, from Eq. (4-11), the magnitude of the angle θ between the ridge and the segment l_2 of the triangular facet, for $h/R = 1/2$ is

$$\theta = 31.71747442°, \qquad (4\text{-}70)$$

but this is exactly the magnitude of the "golden angle" referred to earlier in Eq. (4-58). Consequently, when $h/R = 1/2$, if we erect a perpendicular from point B to the ridge segment $O'P_1$ and call the point of intersection B', then the resulting triangle $BB'P_1$ in the plane of the triangular facet $BO'P_1$ is merely one-half the golden rectangle. It follows that $B'P_1/BB' = \phi$. In right triangle $BO'B'$, the angle α_3 between the valley segment BO' and the perpendicular BB' is $\pi/2 - \alpha = 52.62263188°$, but this is equal to the angle α_4 between the valley and the segment l_1 in the base star because in triangle $OO'B$, the angle $\alpha_4 = \pi/2 - \alpha_2 = \pi/2 - \alpha$.

So, to summarize the interesting relations that exist when the ratio of altitude h to radius R has the simple value 1/2, note first that the angle α between the ridge and the valley is equal to the angle between the altitude h and the valley, and this is true, of course, for all five pairs of angles $\alpha = \alpha_2$ at the apex of the symmetric three-dimensional construction. Also, for $h/R = 1/2$ the curious result is that the angle θ between each ridge and base star segment l_2, in the plane of the triangular facet, is simply equal to the golden angle, arctan($1/\phi$), and this is true for all ten of the facets (twenty, if we consider a "full" structure symmetric about both sides of the base plane star). In the smaller of the two right triangles that together compose the triangular facet $BO'P_1$ in Fig. 4-9, the angle α_3 opposite angle α is just equal to the angle α_4 between the valley and the segment l_1 in the plane base star, for $h/R = 1/2$, and this is true at all five points B where the valleys meet the base star figure.

4-5. Angular inclination of triangular facets, and unique value when $h/R = \frac{1}{2}$

Each pair of triangular facets in the three-dimensional star shape that shares a point of the star radius tip also shares a common side defining a "ridge." Similarly, each pair of facets having vertices at adjacent tips of the star also share a common side defining a "valley." Each triangular facet defines a plane such as that represented by $BO'P_1$ in Fig. 4-9. So, the planes of two facets with common point on the star tip intersect in a line defining a ridge, and likewise the planes represented by two facets with vertices at adjacent tips of the star intersect in a line defining a valley. Because of symmetry, all ten facets of the shape in Fig. 4-2 are inclined at the

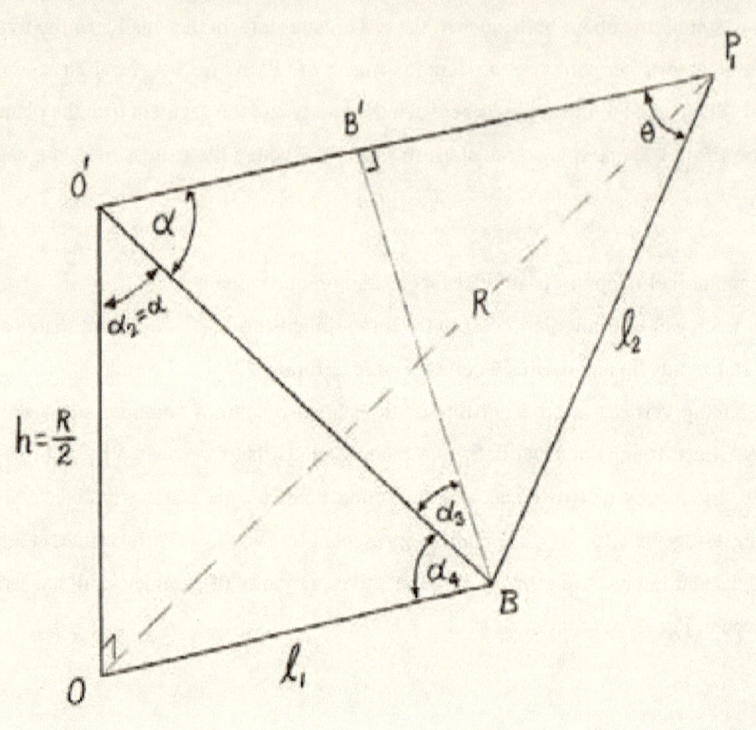

Fig. 4-9. When $h = R/2$, the angle α between a ridge and a valley in a triangular facet is equal to the angle between α_2 between a valley and the altitude in the three-dimensional star of Fig. 4-2. Also, angles α_3 and α_4 are equal.

same angle with respect to the plane of the base star, although, of course, each facet is oriented differently relative to the perpendicular to the base. For given values of altitude h and radius R, the angle of inclination can be found as follows. Referring to Fig. 2-2 of Chapter 2, we note that the segment P_1B of the base star, referred to here as l_2, is collinear with the chord P_1P_3 and as such P_1P_3 lies in the plane of the triangular facet of which l_2 is a side. Furthermore, as shown earlier in relation to Fig. 2-2, the radius R drawn from center O to a tip, such as P_1, is perpendicular to P_2P_5 at point A. Likewise by symmetry radius OP_2 intersects chord P_1P_3 perpendicularly at a point A', and these features of the base plane star are incorporated in Fig. 4-10, which shows Fig. 4-8 with side l_2 extended collinearly to meet OA' perpendicularly as described because OA' is a segment of the radius from O to the tip P_2 adjacent to P_1. Joining O' to A' forms a right triangle perpendicular to the base plane of the star because the altitude h is perpendicular at O. Now, points O' and B, of course, lie in the plane of the triangular facet $BO'P_1$, and the segment $A'B$ is just an extension of the side l_2 of the facet, so the hypotenuse $O'A'$ of right triangle $A'OO'$ also lies in the plane of the facet. Therefore, the angle that the hypotenuse $O'A'$ makes with the base plane star is precisely the angle of inclination of a triangular facet relative to the base, and hence this angle Ω from Fig. 4-10, using Eq. (3-8), can be expressed as

$$\tan \Omega = \frac{OO'}{OA'} = \frac{h}{R \sin 18°} = 2\frac{h}{R}\phi, \qquad (4\text{-}71)$$

where ϕ is the golden ratio. When the ratio of altitude to radius is one-half, then the angle of inclination of each triangular facet is related simply to the golden ratio.

$$\Omega = \text{arc tan } \phi \qquad (4\text{-}72)$$

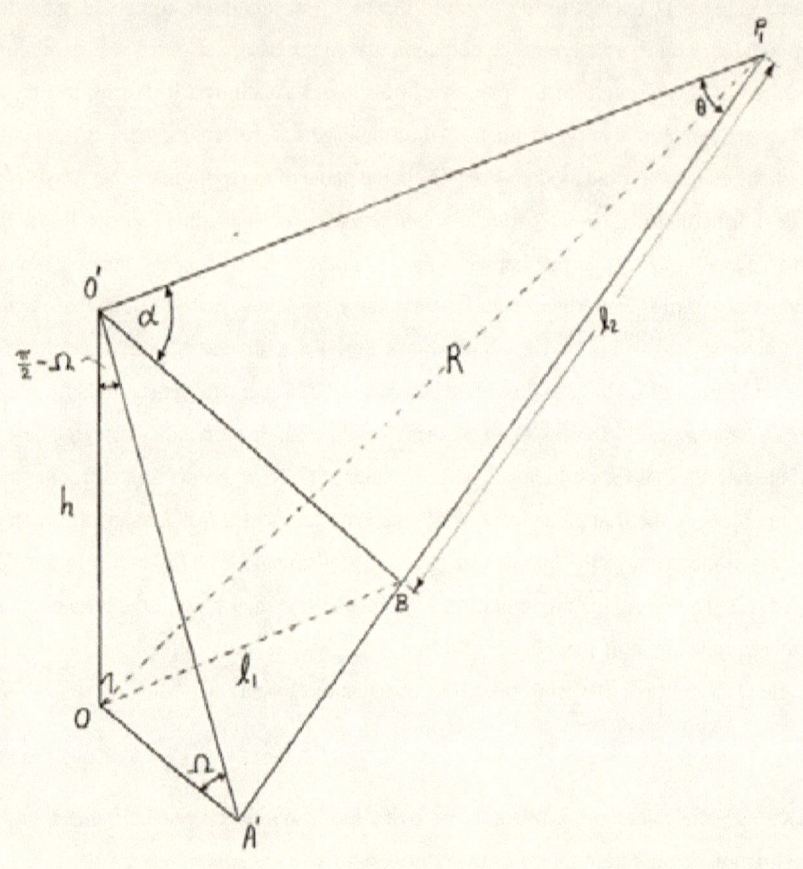

Fig. 4-10. $A'B$ is an extension of side l_2 of the base star, in the plane of the star. The plane of the triangular facet $O'P_1B$ is co-planar with $O'P_1A'$, and angle Ω is the angle between the plane of the triangular facet and the plane of the base star of radius R.

Now, in the right triangle $OO'A'$, the angle between the altitude h and the hypotenuse $O'A'$ is $\pi/2 - \Omega$, but this is the angle that the plane of the facet makes with the perpendicular to the base. Calling $\omega \equiv \pi/2 - \Omega$, we have from triangle $OO'A'$ and Eq. (4-71) the following relation.

$$\tan \omega = \frac{OA'}{O'O} = \frac{1}{2\phi(h/R)} \tag{4-73}$$

For $h/R = 1/2$, the angle ω

$$\omega = 31.71747442°, \tag{4-74}$$

which is the golden angle, and the altitude h is just ϕ times the side OA' meaning that triangle $OO'A'$ is one-half the golden rectangle with $O'A'$ as the diagonal. Remembering that the angle θ in the triangular facet is $31.71747442°$ for $h/R = 1/2$ (see Eq. (4-70)), we can now say that when the altitude is one-half the radius, then not only does the triangular facet contain the golden angle at the base star tip, but also the plane of the facet is inclined at the golden angle relative to the altitude!

4-6. An alternate method for calculating ϕ

Earlier the value of h/R for which the angles α and θ are equal in the triangular facet was obtained by setting $\sin\alpha = \sin\theta$ in Eq. (4-35) and substituting in the numerical values for a_1 and a_2 from Eq. (4-6). Let us, instead, work directly with the definitions of a_1 and a_2 from Eqs. (4-3) through (4-5), after which the right side of Eq. (4-36) becomes

$$\sqrt{a_2^2 - a_1^2} = \sqrt{\frac{\sin^2 36°}{\sin^2 54°} - \frac{\sin^2 18°}{\sin^2 54°}}. \tag{4-75}$$

Using trigonometric identities for the sine of twice an angle and for the sine of three times the angle, the latter can be cast into the following form after some straightforward algebraic and trigonometric manipulation.

$$\sqrt{\frac{\sin^2 36° - \sin^2 18°}{\sin^2 54°}} = \frac{1}{\sqrt{3 - 4\sin^2 18°}}, \tag{4-76}$$

Evaluation of the sine factors on the left side of the latter shows that

$$\frac{1}{\sqrt{3 - 4\sin^2 18°}} = \frac{1}{\phi}, \tag{4-77}$$

which can be written as

$$\phi = \sqrt{3-4\sin^2 18°}. \tag{4-78}$$

Eq. (4-78) provides an interesting alternative to Eqs. (3-5) and (3-8) of Chapter 3 for arriving at the value of the golden ratio ϕ.

CHAPTER 5

FOLDABILITY OF A PLANE STAR INTO A THREE-DIMENSIONAL STAR

5-1. Description of physical conditions to be met for foldability

Based on the analysis in Chapter 4, a three-dimensional star shape can be constructed by choosing a desired altitude h and base star radius R and then constructing ten identical triangular facets per Eqs. (4-10) through (4-14), after which the facets are assembled on the plane base star. An alternate way, which was actually the method used in obtaining the shapes shown in all the photographs in Chapter 4, is to construct five identical pairs of adjacent triangular facets, each pair with common ridge side, and then fold each pair along the common side and assemble the pairs on the plane base star.

Is it possible to construct a star shape on a flat piece of paper such that, when folded alternately along internal lines through its center, will result in a three-dimensional star of the type in Chapter 4, in which the exterior lines of the original star shape lie in the plane and conform exactly to the lines of the base plane star? If this is to be possible, then the angles and dimensions of the star shape must meet certain unique conditions relative to the base plane star. Consider Fig. 5-1 showing a base plane star of radius R and center at O, with points $P_1, P_2, \ldots P_5$ lying on the circle of radius R. One pair of angles, 18° and 36°, is shown and following previous notation in Chapter 4, the sides opposite these angles in triangle OP_1B are designated by l_1 and l_2. For the sake of convenience, the proportionalities a_1 and a_2 between l_1 and l_2, respectively, and R in the five-point mathematical star are repeated in Eqs. (5-1) and (5-2).

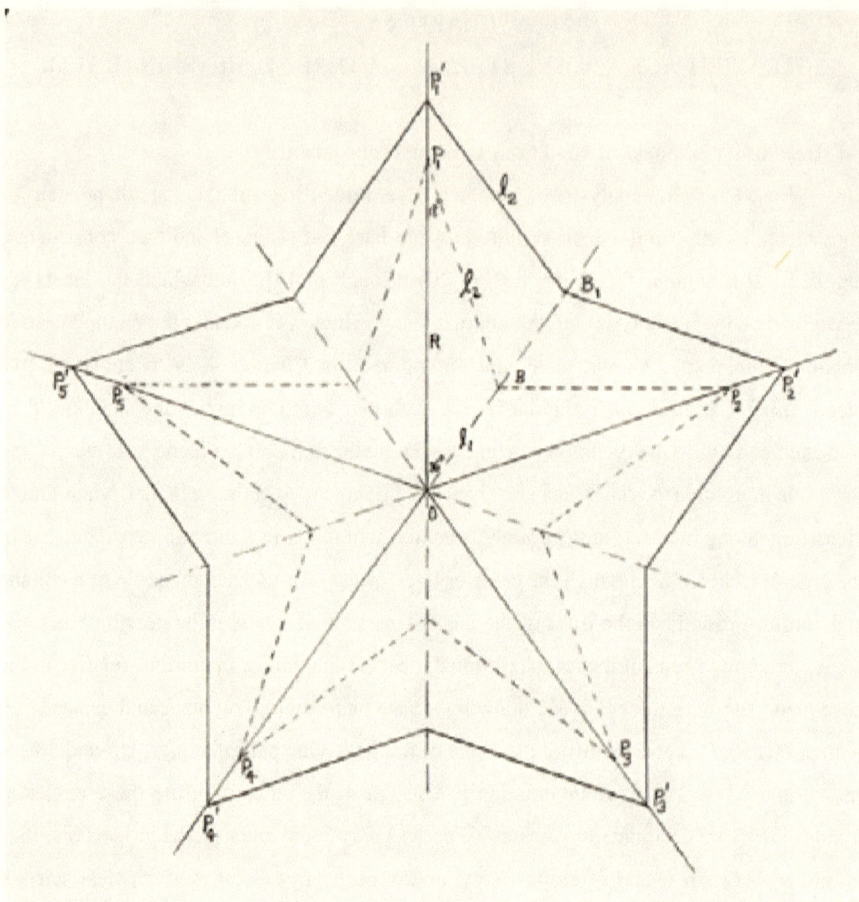

Fig. 5-1. Geometry used in deriving Eqs. (5-3) through (5-11) giving the conditions under which the star of radius OP_1' can be folded convex about OP_1' and concave about OB_1, etc., to make a three-dimensional star of altitude h at O with its plane base periphery coincident with the mathematical five-point star [5, 2] of radius R.

$$a_1 \equiv l_1/R = 0.381966011 \qquad (5\text{-}1)$$
$$a_2 \equiv l_2/R = 0.726542528 \qquad (5\text{-}2)$$

Also shown in the plane of the base star in Fig. 5-1 is a star shape with center at point O and with tips P_1', P_2', ... P_5' lying on a radius OP_1' that is greater than the radius R of the base star. Point B_1 is the point of the outer star figure corresponding to point B of the base star. The outer star shape contains five lines such as OP_1', each of which is co-linear with a radius R of the base star, and five lines OB_1, each of which is co-linear with a segment such as $l_1 = OB$ of the base star. So, the intent is to fold the outer star shape in one sense about each line such as OP_1' and in the opposite sense about each line such as OB_1 so that its center will rise to an altitude h directly above point O and, in turn, each of the tips P_1', P_2', ... P_5' will move inward to coincide with the tips $P_1, P_2, \ldots P_5$ respectively, of the base star while at the same time each point such as B_1 will move inward to coincide with B of the base star. That is, the outer star figure must be partially folded in a convex sense, away from the reader, about each line such as OP_1' while at the same time a partial concave fold, toward the reader, must be made about each line such as OB_1. The lines such as OP_1' will form the five ridges of the resultant three-dimensional structure and lines such as OB_1 will form the valleys of the structure. If each point P_1' is to move inward and mate with point P_1 of the base star and each point B_1 is to move inward and mate with point B of the base, then the segment $P_1'B_1$ of the star shape must be identical in length to $P_1B = l_2$ of the base star, and hence the segment $P_1'B_1$ has been labeled l_2 in Fig. 5-1. The same is true of the other nine segments like $P_1'B_1$.

5-2. Mathematical conditions for foldability

In Fig. 5-2 are shown planes perpendicular to the base that contain the altitude and a ridge, and altitude and a valley. The radius OP_1 which is the radius R of the base star is shown in Fig. 5-2a, along with the co-linear line OP_1' of the star figure to be folded. When the figure is folded in a convex fashion about OP_1', point P_1' will move inward horizontally to point P_1 while the center at O moves upward to altitude h. This means that we must have

$$OP_1' = \sqrt{h^2 + R^2} \qquad (5\text{-}3)$$

because the altitude h is perpendicular to the base plane in which OP_1' initially lies. Similarly, the condition at a valley of the three-dimensional structure is shown in Fig. 5-2b.

The segment $l_1 \equiv OB$ of the base star is shown along with the co-linear segment OB_1 in the star figure to be folded. So, when the figure is folded in a concave fashion about OB_1, the point B_1 moves inward along the direction of l_1, to coincide with point B, while at the same time the opposite end, point O, of OB_1 moves upward a distance h equal to the altitude h of the resultant structure. So, the length of OB_1 in Fig. 5-1 must be

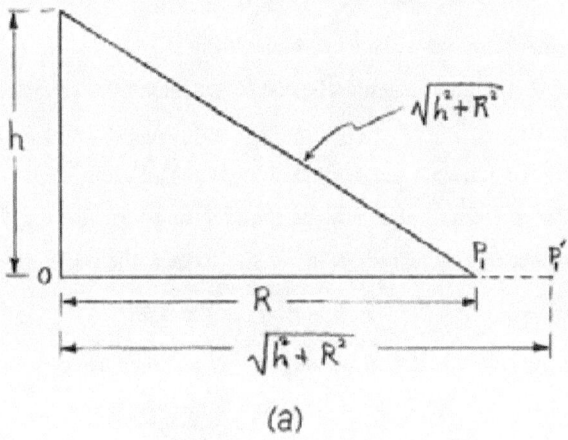

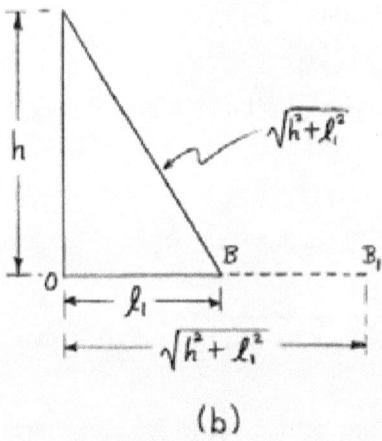

Fig. 5-2. When the star of radius OP_1' in Fig. 5-1 is folded alternately convex and concave to make a three-dimensional star of altitude h, the view in (a) shows a plane containing the altitude and a ridge, and (b) shows a plane containing a valley and the altitude.

$$OB_1 = \sqrt{l_1^2 + h^2},\tag{5-4}$$

because h is perpendicular to the base plane in which OB_1 lies.

The mathematical conditions that must be met so that alternate convex and concave foldings of the star figure $P_1', P_2', \ldots P_5'$ in Fig. 5-1 will result in a three-dimensional structure of altitude h at center, with the peripheral segments all lying in and coinciding with the base plane star of radius R, can now be found. Using Eqs. (5-3) and (5-4) and applying the law of cosines to triangle $OP_1'B_1$ in Fig. 5-1 leads to the following relation.

$$l_2^2 = l_1^2 + R^2 + 2h^2 - 2\sqrt{h^2 + R^2}\sqrt{l_1^2 + h^2}\cos 36°\tag{5-5}$$

Rearranging the latter and squaring to remove the radicals, and then using a trigonometric identity along with Eqs. (5-1) and (5-2) allows the latter to be cast into the following form.

$$\left(\frac{h}{R}\right)^4 \tan^2 36° + \left(\frac{h}{R}\right)^2 \left[(1+a_1^2)\tan^2 36° - (a_2/\cos 36°)^2\right] + \left(\frac{1+a_1^2 - a_2^2}{2\cos 36°}\right)^2 - a_1^2 = 0\tag{5-6}$$

Now, it can be shown that the last two terms in Eq. (5-6) combine to give zero. That is, applying the law of cosines to triangle OP_1B in Fig. 5-1 gives

$$a_2^2 = 1 + a_1^2 - 2a_1 \cos 36°,\tag{5-7}$$

where the relations in Eqs. (5-1) and (5-2) were used. Eq. (5-7) can be rearranged to yield

$$a_1 = \frac{1+a_1^2 - a_2^2}{2\cos 36°},\tag{5-8}$$

and therefore the last two terms in Eq. (5-6) vanish, thereby allowing the solution for the ratio h/R from Eq. (5-6) to be expressed as

$$\frac{h}{R} = \frac{\sqrt{a_2^2 - (1+a_1^2)\sin^2 36°}}{\sin 36°}.\tag{5-9}$$

Substituting the numerical values for a_1 and a_2 from Eqs. (5-1) and (5-2) into the latter gives

$$\frac{h}{R} = 0.618033989,\tag{5-10}$$

and therefore from Eq. (3-8) of Chapter 3 it follows that

$$R = h\phi,\tag{5-11}$$

where ϕ is the golden ratio. This result is truly amazing because not only does it show that a unique ratio of altitude h to radius R exists for which a plane starlike figure can be constructed and alternately folded convex and concave to make a three-dimensional star structure with a mating plane star base, but also the unique relation between h and R is the golden ratio. This is all the more intriguing because not merely is the golden ratio involved mathematically in the solution, but the golden ratio is uniquely and intimately related to the condition under which it is physically possible to fold a plane star figure into the three-dimensional shape while at the same time maintaining the mathematical star in the base plane. That is to say, the plane star folding operations that produce this result can only be achieved if the construction obeys the golden or "divine" ratio.

We note further that the condition for foldability imposed by Eq. (5-10) means that the right triangle formed by the altitude h and radius R in the base is one-half of a golden rectangle. Therefore, the angle that the ridge makes with the plane of the base star is equal to the arctan (h/R) = arctan $(1/\phi)$ = 31.717474°, which is the golden angle. Knowing that we must have $R = \phi h$ for foldability of the star $P_1', P_2', \ldots P_5'$ of Fig. 5-1 into a solid star shape with star base, we can now determine the angle $OP_1'B_1$ at each tip. Using the relation in Eq. (5-4) and applying the law of sines to triangle $OP_1'B_1$ in Fig. 5-1 gives the relation

$$\frac{\sin \angle OP_1'B_1}{\sqrt{l_1^2 + h^2}} = \frac{\sin 36°}{l_2}, \qquad (5\text{-}12)$$

and using Eqs. (5-1) and (5-2) along with $R = \phi h$, where $\phi = 1.618033989$, we get

$$\angle OP_1'B_1 = \arcsin\left(\sin 36° \frac{\sqrt{a_1^2 + (1/\phi)^2}}{a_2}\right), \qquad (5\text{-}13)$$

or

$$\angle OP_1'B_1 = 36°. \qquad (5\text{-}14)$$

Then, the angle $P_1'B_1O$ in the starlike figure $P_1', P_2', \ldots P_5'$ in Fig. 5-1 is

$$\angle P_1'B_1O = \pi - 36° - \angle OP_1'B_1$$

$$= 108°. \qquad (5\text{-}15)$$

Now, the perimeter of the mathematical base star with half angle 18° at each tip in Fig. 5-1 is just 10 l_2. However, as shown above for the foldability condition of the star figure $P_1', P_2', \ldots P_5'$, each segment like $P_1'B_1$ must also be equal to l_2. Therefore, the perimeter of the starlike figure $P_1', P_2', \ldots P_5'$ is 10 l_2, the same as that of the base star.

The area of the star $P_1', P_2', \ldots P_5'$ relative to the area of the base star in Fig. 5-1 is a simple factor, as will now be shown. In the base star, the total area A_b is ten times the area of one of the triangles such as OP_1B:

$$A_b = 5(l_2^2 \cos 18° \sin 18° + l_1^2 \cos 36° \sin 36°) \tag{5-16}$$

Similarly, the area A_f of the foldable star figure is ten times the area of the triangle $OP_1'B_1$, and using Eqs. (5-4) and (5-14) gives

$$A_f = 5(l_2^2 + l_1^2 + h^2) \cos 36° \sin 36°. \tag{5-17}$$

Using the result in Eq. (5-10) relating h to R, and the relations in Eqs. (5-1) and (5-2) connecting l_1 and l_2 to R allows A_b and A_f in Eqs. (5-16) and (5-17) to be evaluated in terms of R, with the resulting ratio expressed simply as

$$\frac{A_f}{A_b} = \sqrt{5} \tag{5-18}$$

5-3. Examples

Using Eqs. (5-10), (5-14) and (5-15) along with Eqs. (5-1) through (5-4), three star figures were constructed on paper, each with a different radius and then each was folded alternately concave and convex about valley and ridge lines, respectively, to produce the three-dimensional star figures shown in the photographs of Fig. 5-3. The radii chosen were 1.0, 2.0, and 3.0 inches for which the altitudes of the resulting three-dimensional star figures were 0.618 in., 1.236 in., and 1.854 in., respectively calculated from Eq. 5-10. As can be seen from the photographs, the bases of the folded three-dimensional stars conform well to the plane on which they sit.

Fig. 5-3a. Three-dimensional stars folded on five-point base plane stars of radii $R = 1$ in., 2 in., and 3 in., each with $h/R = 1/\phi \equiv .618034$.

Fig. 5-3b. Three-dimensional stars folded with $h/R = 1/\phi$ on base star radii $R = 1.5$ in. and 2.5 in.

CHAPTER 6
SPECIAL TRIANGLES REVEALED BY GEOMETRY OF FIVE-POINT STARS

6-1. An unusual identity in the star geometry

Consider again the mathematical five-pointed star shown in Fig. 6-1, with particular attention to one of the ten identical triangles such as OP_1B. It was shown earlier in Eqs. (4-3) and (4-4) of Chapter 4 that the two sides of length l_2 and l_1 are related to the radius R and the angles through the following expressions.

$$l_1 = \frac{R \sin 18°}{\sin 54°} \tag{6-1}$$

$$l_2 = \frac{R \sin 36°}{\sin 54°} \tag{6-2}$$

Now, using the trigonometric identities $\sin 2y = 2\sin y \cos y$ and $\sin 3y = 3\sin y - 4\sin^3 y$, it can be shown from Eqs. (6-1) and (6-2) after some manipulation that the following curious identity is true, regarding the star radius R and the distances l_2 and l_1.

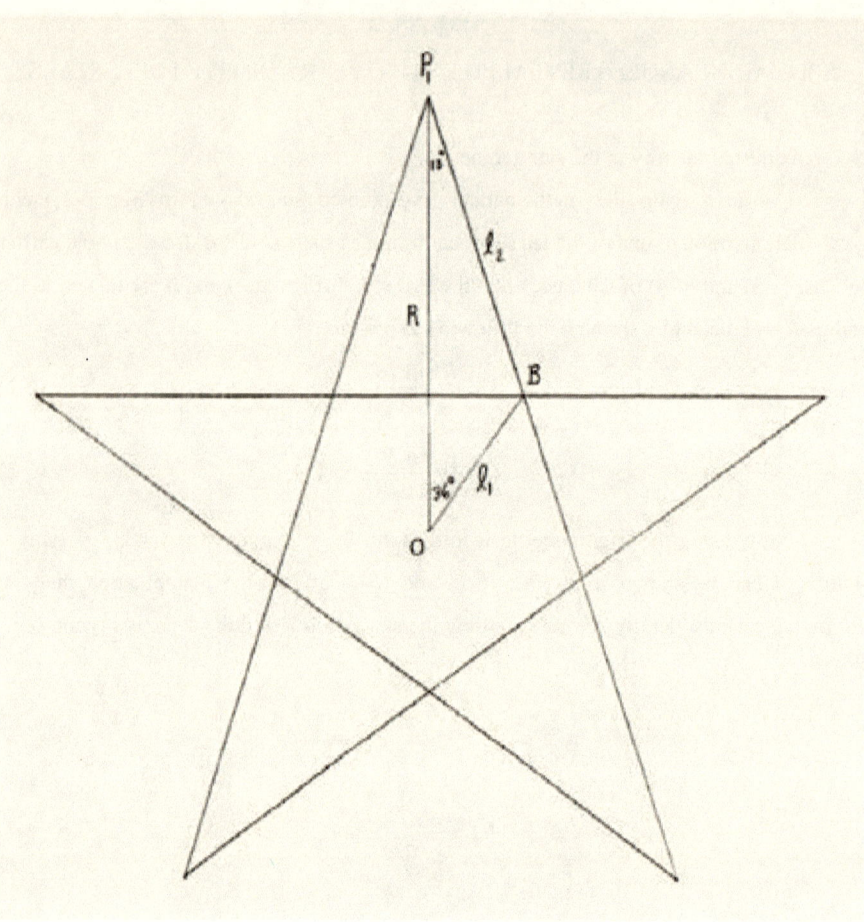

Fig. 6-1. The mathematical five-point star [5, 2], showing angles and sides in one of its ten identical triangles.

$$\frac{l_2^2}{l_1^2 + l_1 R} = 1 \tag{6-3}$$

The latter can be written in the form

$$l_2^2 = l_1^2 + l_1 R \tag{6-4}$$

and this can be interpreted geometrically by referring to Fig. 6-2 in which the triangle OP_1B of Fig 6-1 is shown. The square with side l_2 has area l_2^2 and, according to Eq. (6-4), this area is equal to the area of the square with side l_1 plus the area of the rectangle with one side equal to the star radius R and the other side equal to l_1. This geometric property of triangle OP_1B in the five-point star is reminiscent of the Pythagorean theorem for a right triangle in which the square of the hypotenuse c^2 is equal to the sum of the squares $a^2 + b^2$ of the two legs as depicted in Fig. 6-3.

6-2. Triangles containing any two angles in ratio 1:2

At first thought it may seem that the interesting equality in Eq. (6-4) is a result of the fact that one angle in the triangle OP_1B of the star is 18° and a second angle is 36°. However, it will now be shown that the equality of Eq. (6-4) is true for any triangle containing one angle that is twice one of the other angles. Consider the triangle shown in Fig. 6-4a containing one angle designated by γ and another angle that is twice γ. Let C be the length of the side opposite the angle 2 γ, and let B be the side opposite the angle γ, and let the third side of the triangle be

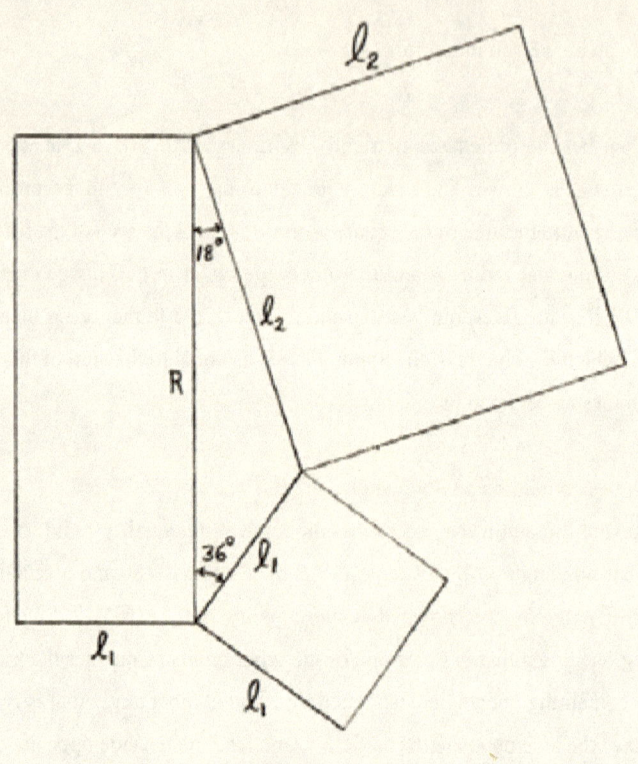

Fig. 6-2. Geometric interpretation of Eq. (6-4).

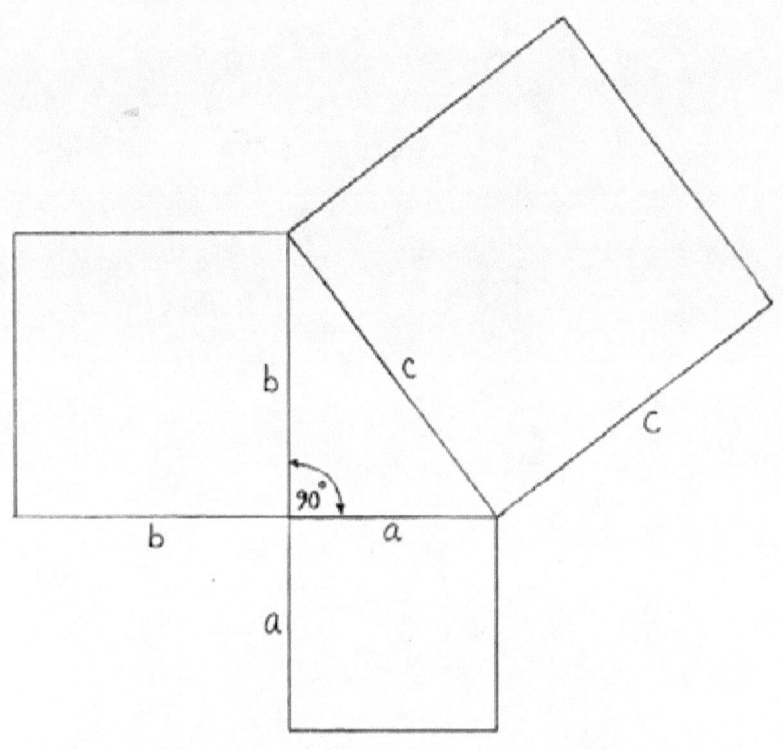

Fig. 6-3. The familiar geometric interpretation of the Pythagorean right-triangle relationship, $c^2 = a^2 + b^2$.

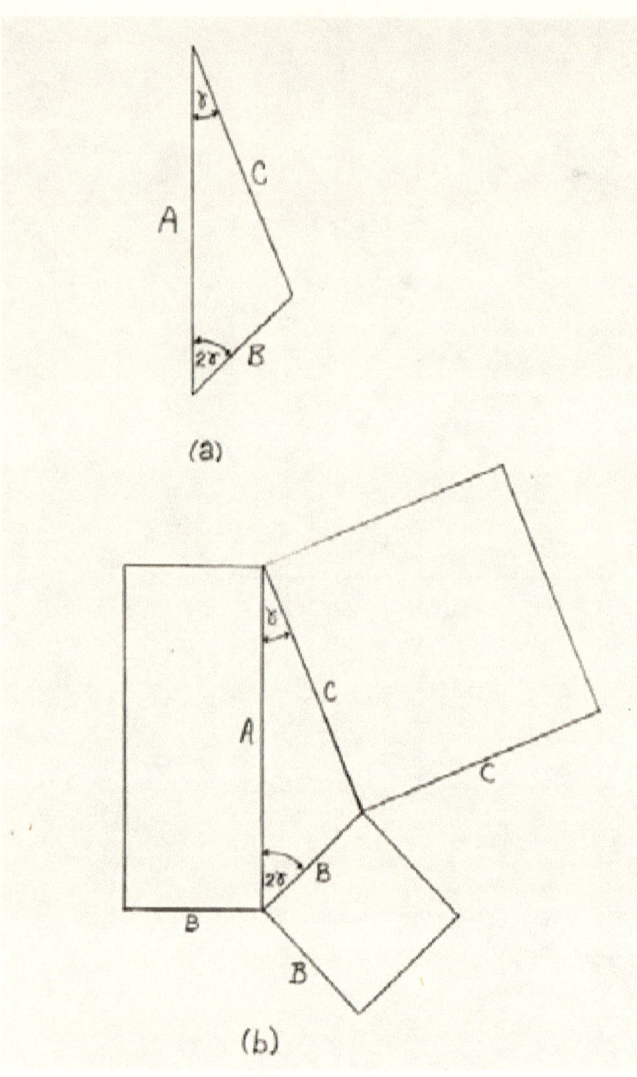

Fig. 6-4. (a) A triangle with sides *A*, *B*, *C*, and one angle equal to twice another. (b) Geometric interpretation of Eq. (6-7) relating sides *A*, *B*, *C* in (a).

designated by A. Applying the law of sines to the triangle in Fig. 6-4a and using the trigonometric identity $\sin 2y = 2\sin y \cos y$ yields

$$\frac{\sin \gamma}{B} = \frac{\sin 2\gamma}{C} = \frac{2\sin \gamma \cos \gamma}{C},$$

or

$$\cos \gamma = \frac{C}{2B}. \qquad (6\text{-}5)$$

Now, taking the projections of sides B and C on side A and making use of the trigonometric identity $\cos 2y = 2\cos^2 y - 1$ leads to the following.

$$A = C \cos \gamma + B(2\cos^2 \gamma - 1) \qquad (6\text{-}6)$$

Substituting from Eq. (6-5) into Eq. (6-6) leads to the following equality, after simplifying and rearranging.

$$C^2 = B^2 + AB \qquad (6\text{-}7)$$

We can interpret the result in Eq. (6-7) geometrically as depicted in Fig. 6-4b and state it in the following theorem:

> In any triangle containing one angle that is twice a second angle, the area of the square constructed on the side opposite the double angle is equal to the sum of the area of the square constructed on the side opposite the single angle plus the area of the rectangle constructed on the third side having its other side equal to the side opposite the single angle.

Comparison of Fig. 6-4b with Fig. 6-3 shows that the result in Eq. (6-7) for the scalene triangle with one angle twice another is analogous to the Pythagorean case of the right triangle.

With a little thought, it is easy to see that Eq. (6-7) applies as well to the special cases of a right triangle, an isosceles triangle, and an isosceles right triangle. This is true, of course, provided each contains one angle that is twice another in the triangle.

6-3. Triangles with two angles in the ratio 1:3

The generalization embodied in Eq. (6-7), which was inspired by the earlier analysis leading to Eq. (6-4) for the triangle OP_1B in the star that contains one angle 18° and another 36°, naturally raises the question regarding what special properties, if any, a triangle may possess when one of its angles is exactly equal to three times another of its angles. In an attempt to answer this question, consider the triangle shown in Fig. 6-5 with sides designated by D, E, and F, in which the angle opposite side E is γ while the angle opposite side F is 3γ. Now, side D can be expressed as the sum of the projections of sides F and E on it, giving

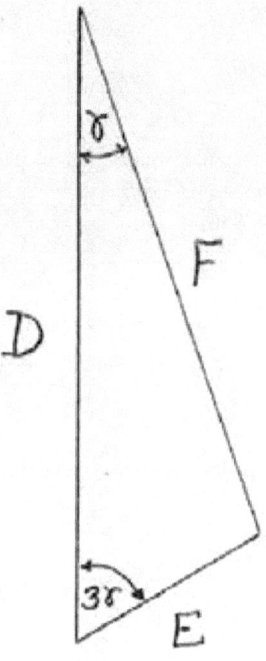

Fig. 6-5. A triangle with sides D, E, and F in which one angle is three times another angle.

$$D = F\cos\gamma + E\cos 3\gamma \qquad (6\text{-}8)$$

and use of the trigonometric identity $\cos 3y = 4\cos^3 y - 3\cos y$ allows the latter to be written as

$$\cos\gamma = \frac{D}{F + E(4\cos^2\gamma - 3)}. \qquad (6\text{-}9)$$

Applying the law of sines to the triangle in Fig. 6-5 results in

$$\frac{\sin\gamma}{E} = \frac{\sin 3\gamma}{F}, \qquad (6\text{-}10)$$

and using the identities $\sin 3y = 3\sin y - 4\sin^3 y$ and $\sin^2 y + \cos^2 y = 1$ allows Eq. (6-10) to be arranged after considerable manipulation into the form

$$\cos^2\gamma = \frac{1}{4}\left(1 + \frac{F}{E}\right). \qquad (6\text{-}11)$$

Combining Eq. (6-11) with Eq. (6-9), after some rearranging, leads to the following.

$$\cos\gamma = \frac{D}{2(F-E)} \qquad (6\text{-}12)$$

An expression involving $\cos\gamma$ can also be obtained by application of the law of cosines to the triangle of Fig. 6-5.

$$E^2 = D^2 + F^2 - 2DF\cos\gamma \qquad (6\text{-}13)$$

Eliminating the factor $\cos\gamma$ between Eq. (6-12) and (6-13) leads eventually to the following relation involving only the sides of the triangle in Fig. 6-5.

$$E^3 + F^3 = D^2 E + E^2 F + F^2 E \qquad (6\text{-}14)$$

The algebraic relationship among the sides of the triangle of Fig. 6-5, given in Eq. (6-14), can be interpreted geometrically per the following statement as a theorem:

In any triangle having two angles in the ratio 1:3, the sum of the cube volumes, each with side opposite the two angles, is equal to the sum of three rectangular parallelepiped volumes: one with square base of side equal to the third side of the triangle and height equal to side opposite the smaller angle; one with square base of side opposite the smaller angle and height equal to side opposite larger angle; and one with square base of side opposite the larger angle with height equal to the side opposite the smaller angle.

The relationship in Eq. (6-14) can be arranged somewhat differently and put into the form

$$(F^2 - E^2)(F - E) = D^2 E, \qquad (6\text{-}15)$$

which lends itself to the following geometric interpretation relative to the triangle in Fig. 6-5:

The volume represented by the difference in areas of squares each with sides opposite the two angles of ratio 1:3, times the difference in lengths of these two sides, is just equal to the volume represented by the square area having sides equal to the third side, times the length of side opposite the smaller angle.

Finally, Eq. (6-14) can be cast into the following form.

$$F^2(F - E) = E^2(F - E) + D^2 E \qquad (6\text{-}16)$$

In this form we can interpret it geometrically as shown in Fig. 6-6 and make the following theorem statement:

In any triangle containing two angles in the ratio 1:3, the square on the side opposite the larger angle times the difference in lengths of the sides opposite the two angles is equal to the sum of the square on the side opposite the smaller angle, times the same difference in these two sides, plus the square on the third side of the triangle times the side opposite the smaller angle.

The latter can be stated equivalently in terms more descriptive of the volumes involved in the geometric interpretation of Eq. (6-16) in Fig. 6-6:

In any triangle with two angles in the ratio 1:3, the volume of a rectangular parallelepiped with square base on the side opposite the larger angle, and altitude equal to the difference in the two sides opposite the angles, is equal to the sum of two rectangular parallelepiped volumes: one with square base on the side opposite the smaller angle and altitude also equal to the difference in the sides opposite the two angles; and one with square base on the third side and altitude equal to the side opposite the smaller angle.

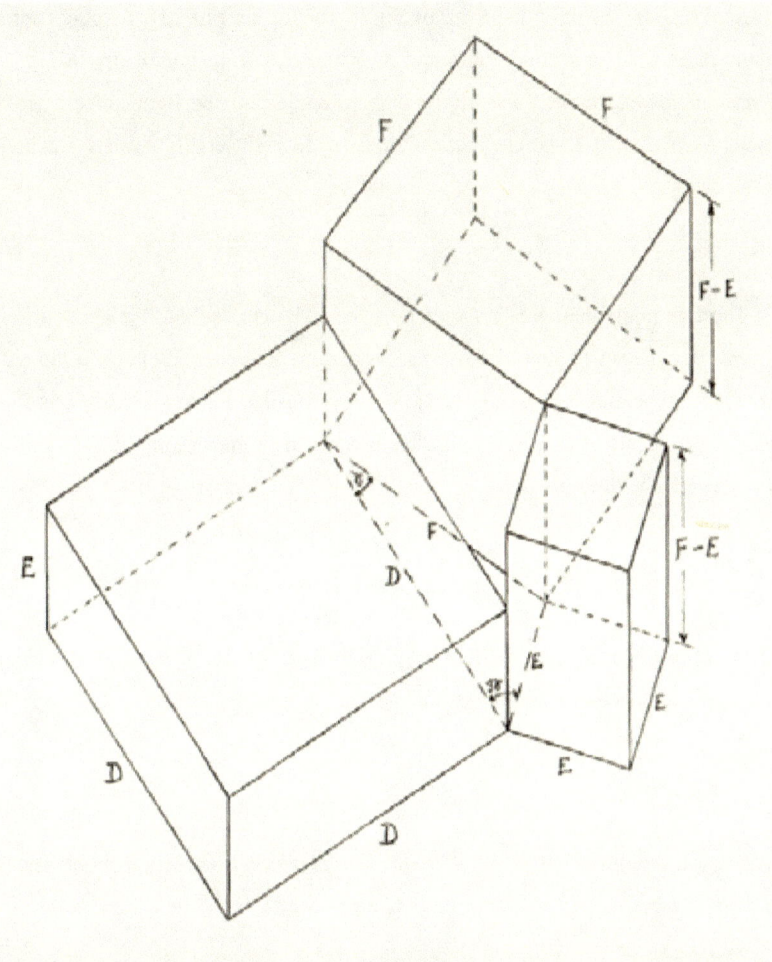

Fig. 6-6. Geometric interpretation of Eq. (6-16) relating to the triangle with sides D, E, and F in which one angle is three times one of the other angles.

So, it can be seen that the form of Eq. (6-16) for the case of a triangle containing one angle three times a second angle and its interpretation geometrically in Fig. 6-6 is somewhat analogous to the case of the right triangle and the Pythagorean geometric interpretation in Fig. 6-3, except that volumes of different configurations are involved instead of areas.

6-4. Another class of triangle

The foregoing analogies between a scalene triangle and the Pythagorean relation for a right triangle can be made somewhat more general, extending beyond the cases in which two of the angles bear a ratio of 1:2 or 1:3. Consider a triangle formed as follows. Let two line segments of lengths A and B be joined at their ends as in Fig. 6-7a so that the angle α between the lines is

$$\alpha = \text{arc cos}\left(\frac{B}{2An}\right), \tag{6-17}$$

where n is a positive real number. In order for the cosine of α to be defined, it is clear that the magnitude of n must satisfy the inequality

$$n > \frac{B}{2A}. \tag{6-18}$$

Although cos α is defined for $n = B/2A$, we would not have a triangle in this case because A and B would be co-linear. Next, let the opposite ends of A and B be joined with a straight line in Fig.

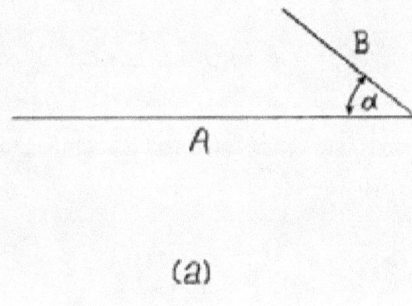

(a)

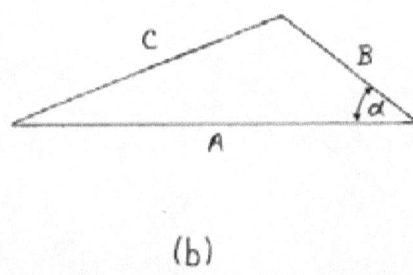

(b)

Fig. 6-7. (a) Two segments A and B are joined at angle α related to their lengths through Eq. (6-17). Then, when a triangle is formed by joining the opposite ends of A and B, as in (b), the length C of the third side is related simply to A and B according to Eq. (6-22).

6-7b and call its length C. Now, side C is opposite the included angle α and therefore we can write

$$C^2 = A^2 + B^2 - 2AB \cos \alpha, \qquad (6\text{-}19)$$

but we are requiring the angle α to depend on A and B according to Eq. (6-17) involving a real number n, so Eq. (6-19) becomes

$$C^2 = A^2 + B^2\left(1 - \frac{1}{n}\right). \qquad (6\text{-}20)$$

Carrying the analogy one step further, we can define a scaled length B', relative to side B, as

$$B' \equiv B\sqrt{1 - \frac{1}{n}}, \qquad (6\text{-}21)$$

and then write Eq. (6-20) in the following form for the scalene triangle.

$$C^2 = A^2 + B'^2 \qquad (6\text{-}22)$$

It can be argued that there are as many scalene triangles obeying the relationship in Eq. (6-22) as there are right triangles obeying the Pythagorean relationship. For example, consider any right triangle for which the legs A and B are known or can be measured. Knowing A and B, a value of n can be chosen meeting the condition in Eq. (6-18) so that the angle α can be calculated from Eq. (6-17). Then, the square of the third side C of the scalene triangle in Fig 6-7b obeys Eq. (6-20), and, of course, Eq. (6-22). Finally, it is to be noted that when n is chosen as an integer, the factor multiplying B^2 in Eq. (6-20) is merely the ratio of two integers.

CHAPTER 7
THREE-DIMENSIONAL STARS WITH CIRCUMSCRIBED GEOMETRIC FIGURES: COMPARISON OF AREAS AND VOLUMES

7-1. Surface area and volume of the star having altitude h, radius R

The surface area of the three-dimensional star shape can be determined by referring again to one of the triangular facets as shown in Fig. 7-1. The area of the triangular facet $O'P_1B$ is one-half the base times the altitude. Taking the base to be the ridge of dimension $(R^2 + h^2)^{1/2}$, the altitude is then $l_2 \sin\theta$, and so the area is

$$A_f = \frac{1}{2}(R^2 + h^2)^{\frac{1}{2}} l_2 \sin\theta, \qquad (7\text{-}1)$$

but the angle θ between the ridge and the side l_2, according to Eq. (4-10) in Chapter 4 is

$$\theta = \arccos\left(\frac{R^2 + l_2^2 - l_1^2}{2 l_2 \sqrt{h^2 + R^2}}\right). \qquad (7\text{-}2)$$

The sides l_1 and l_2 of the facet are related to the star radius R through the proportionalities a_1 and a_2 in Eqs. (4-5) and (4-6) and therefore the area of the facet can be expressed as follows by combining Eqs. (7-1) and (7-2).

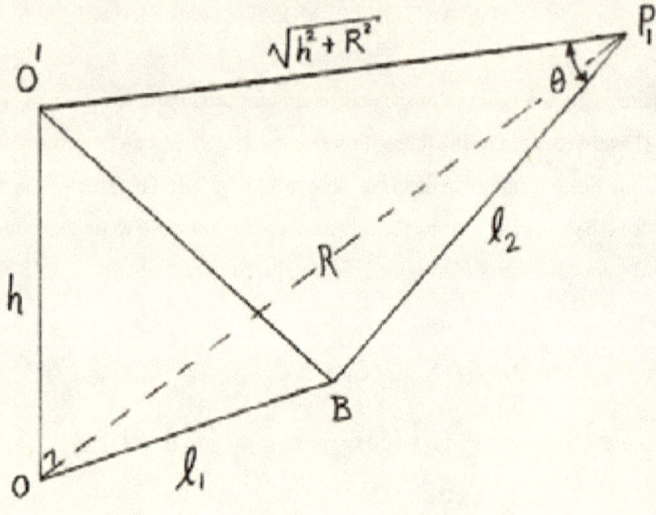

Fig. 7-1. The surface area of a three-dimensional star of altitude h formed on star base plane defined by OP_1B is ten times the area of the triangular facet $O'P_1B$.

$$A_f = \frac{1}{4}R^2\left[4a_2^2\left(1+(h/R)^2\right)-\left(1+a_2^2-a_1^2\right)^2\right]^{\frac{1}{2}} \qquad (7\text{-}3)$$

For a full three-dimensional star shape, symmetric about the base plane, there are four facets each with area A_f at each of the five tips and therefore the total surface area, A_s, is twenty times the value A_f:

$$A_s = 5R^2\left[4a_2^2\left(1+(h/R)^2\right)-\left(1+a_2^2-a_1^2\right)^2\right]^{\frac{1}{2}} \qquad (7\text{-}4)$$

For a given ratio of altitude h to radius R, the total area is proportional to the square of the base radius of the five-point star. At a given value of radius, the increase of area with altitude is slightly greater than linear. A graph of area versus altitude, for unit value of radius, is given in Fig. 7-2, and this was calculated from Eq. (7-4) using the numerical values of a_1 and a_2 in Eq. (4-6).

The volume of the three-dimensional star can be determined by considering one of the elemental tetrahedral prisms such as OO^1P_1B in Fig. 7-1. The base of this structure is triangle OP_1B in the plane of the base star, and the remainder of the prism is formed by the altitude h, a ridge O^1P_1, and a valley O^1B. From solid geometry, the volume is one-third the product of the base triangular area times the altitude:

$$V_p = \frac{1}{3}\left(\frac{1}{2}Rl_2 \sin 18°\right)h \qquad (7\text{-}5)$$

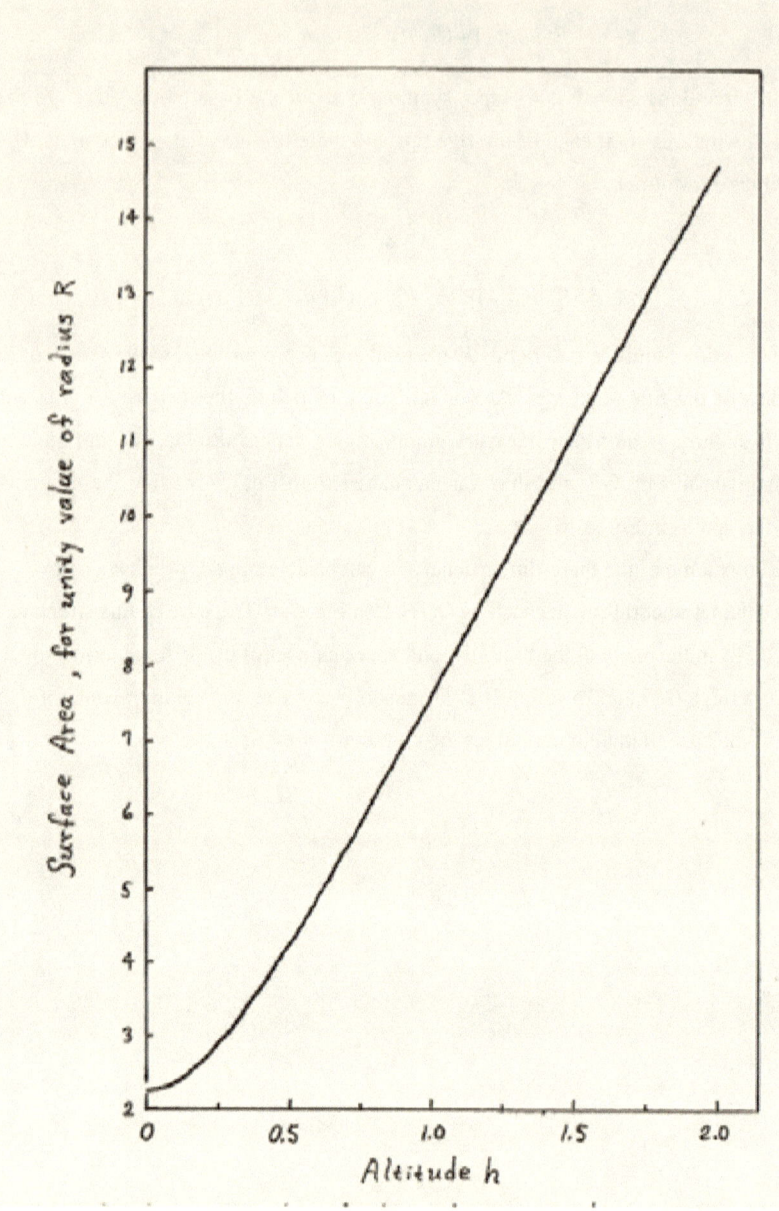

Fig. 7-2. Surface area A_s of three-dimensional star as a function of altitude h, calculated from Eq. (7-4) for unity value of R.

Noting that there are twenty identical elemental volumes of this size contained in the full three-dimensional star symmetric about the base plane, the total volume V_s of the star can be expressed as

$$V_S = \frac{10}{3} a_2 R^2 h \sin 18°. \qquad (7\text{-}6)$$

Using the value of the proportionality a_2, Eq. (7-6) becomes

$$V_S = a_v h R^2, \qquad (7\text{-}7)$$

where the numerical factor $a_v = 0.748379961$. Expressed in terms of the altitude-to-radius ratio, the volume can be written

$$V_S = a_v \left(\frac{h}{R}\right) R^3. \qquad (7\text{-}8)$$

In contrast to the dependence of the star surface area on altitude and radius, the volume is directly proportional to the product of the square of the radius and the first power of the altitude. For a given value of altitude, the volume increases as the square of the radius. According to Eq. (7-8), for a given ratio of altitude to radius, the star volume is proportional to the cube of the radius.

In keeping with the definition of altitude h in earlier chapters, we note that the surface area and volume in Eqs. (7-4) through (7-8) refer to a three-dimensional figure that is symmetric about the base plane star so that h is the perpendicular distance from the apex on one side to the common plane of symmetry. That is, the distance from apex to apex along the perpendicular to the base plane star through its center is $2h$.

7-2. Comparison of star area and volume to that of circumscribed figures, for stars with $h = R$

It is interesting to compare the surface area and volume of a three-dimensional star to areas and volumes of common geometric figures. Consider a three-dimensional star with altitude h equal to radius R. Let a sphere of radius R be circumscribed about the star with center on the center of the base star. It is clear that the star has seven points in common with the spherical surface, five of which are the tips of the base plane star and the other two at each apex. The ratio of star area to that of the sphere is $A_s/4\pi R^2$, while the volume ratio is $3a_v/4\pi$, where a_v has the numerical value given just below Eq. (7-7). Another geometric figure that can be circumscribed about the three-dimensional star with $h = R$ that will share just seven points with it is a right circular cylinder of radius R and length $2R$ with its long axis perpendicular to the base plane star located at the midpoint of the cylindrical axis. The star-to-cylinder area ratio is $A_s/2\pi R(R + 2h)$ and volume ratio is $a_v/2\pi$. Also, a right regular pentagonal prism of height $2R$, with its five vertices at radius R relative to its center, will inscribe the three-dimensional star with seven points in common provided the base plane of the star is perpendicular to the axis and centered on it at the midpoint of the axis. Each apex of the star then lies on the center of the end faces of the pentagonal prism. The surface area ratio is $A_s/10R^2 (2 + \cos 36°) \sin 36°$, and the volume ratio is $a_v/10\sin 36° \cos 36°$. Next, consider a right circular cone with base radius R and altitude R. If two of these cones are joined at their common base, then the star can be inscribed with its plane base lying in the base of the cones. In this case each apex of the star shape coincides with the vertices of the cones and the ridges of the star lie in the conical surfaces. The ratio of areas is $A_s/2\pi R^2 \sqrt{2}$ and the volume ratio is $3a_v/2\pi$. The three-dimensional star with altitude h equal to radius R inscribed in the various geometric shapes are represented in Fig. 7-3.

Finally, let the star shape be inscribed in a rectangular parallelpiped. In this regard, note first that if the star base is inscribed in a square of side $2R$ with its center at the center of the square, then the star can be oriented so that, at most, one of its tips lies on a side of the square. However, if the base star is inscribed in a rectangle of dimensions $2a_2R(1 + \sin 18°)$ by $2a_2R(1 + \sin 18°)\cos 18°$ and oriented as shown in Fig. 7-4, then all five tips of the base plane star lie on sides of the rectangle. If a rectangular parallelpiped with length $2R$ is constructed on this rectangle and the base plane of the star is perpendicular to the length $2R$ at its midpoint and oriented as in Fig. 7-4, then all seven vertices of the three-dimensional star lie on the rectangular faces. The volume of the rectangular parallelpiped is

$$V_r = 8a_2^2 R^3 (1+\sin 18°)^2 \cos 18°, \qquad (7\text{-}9)$$

and its surface area can be expressed as

$$A_r = 8a_2 R^2 (1 + \sin 18°)[1 + (1 + a_2 (1 + \sin 18°)) \cos 18°]. \qquad (7\text{-}10)$$

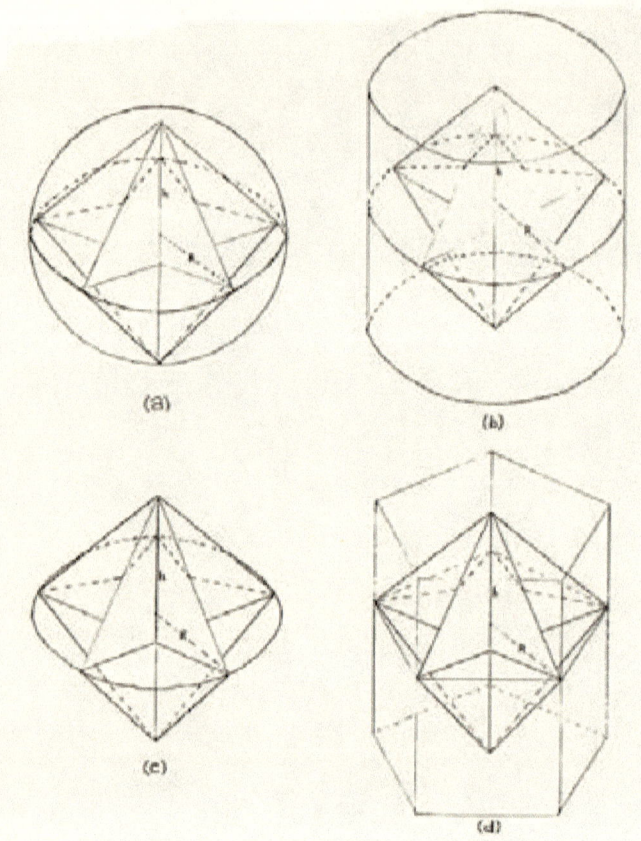

Fig. 7-3. Three-dimensional star with altitude *h* equal radius *R* inscribed in (a) a sphere, (b) a right circular cylinder, (c) two right circular cones, and (d) a pentagonal prism.

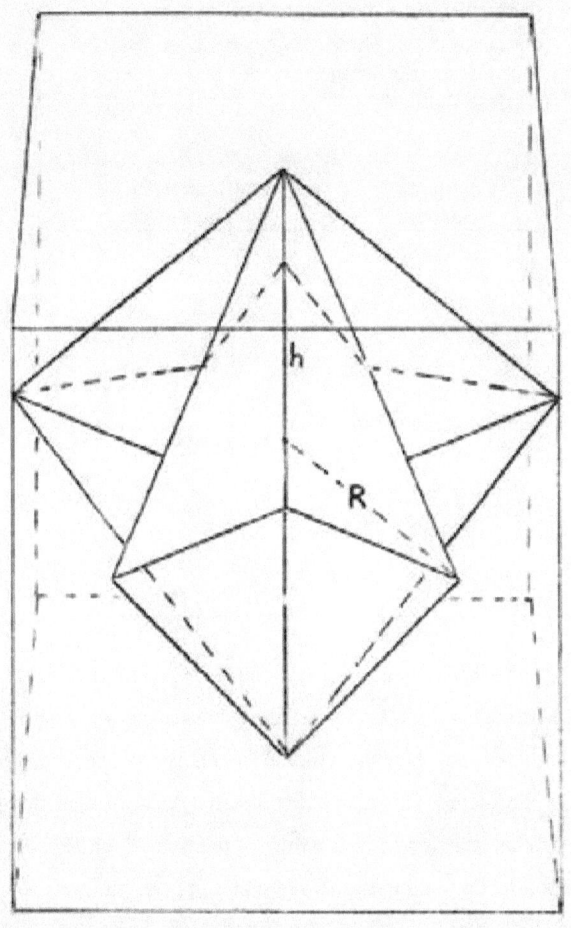

Fig. 7-4. Three-dimensional star with altitude h equal to radius R inscribed in a parallelepiped.

Using all the foregoing relations, the numerical values of area and volume ratios were calculated, and these are given in Table 7-1. The results are listed in the order of increasing fraction of star area and volume relative to the other geometric shapes.

Table 7-1. Comparison* of Three-Dimensional Star Surface Area and Volume to Other Geometric Shapes. For the Star Shape, the Altitude is Equal to the Star Base Radius.

Geometric Shape	Ratio Star Surface Area to Shape Area	Ratio Star Volume to Shape Volume
Rectangular Parallelepiped	0.350007	0.108746
Cylinder	0.403427	0.119108
Regular Pentagonal Prism	0.460567	0.157379
Sphere	0.605140	0.178663
Double Right Circular Cone	0.855797	0.357325

* Numerical values rounded to the nearest sixth decimal place.

It can be seen from the table that the star surface area is a considerably higher fraction of the shape area than the volume is relative to the shape volume, for each geometric shape considered. This is an indication that the ratio of surface area to volume of the three-dimensional star, for a given radius, is relatively high. A comparison of surface area to volume for the three-dimensional star and other common geometric shapes is given in Table 7-2. For the star, the calculations were made using Eqs. (7-4) and (7-8), with altitude h equal to the radius R, and Eqs. (7-9) and (7-10) were used for the rectangular parallelpiped referenced in Table 7-1. For the cylinder and pentagonal prism, the altitudes were taken as $2h = 2R$ for consistency with the data of Table 7-1.

Table 7-2. Ratio of Three-Dimensional Star Surface Area to Volume, and Similar Ratios for Other Common Geometric Shapes for the Case $h = R$.

Geometric Shape	Ratio of Surface Area to Volume
Star	$10.162/R$
Cube*	$6/R$
Sphere	$3/R$
Double Right Circular Cone	$4.243/R$
Rectangular Parallelepiped	$3.157/R$
Regular Pentagonal Prism	$3.472/R$
Cylinder	$3/R$

* Length of side = R.

For ease of comparison with common geometric shapes, all the calculations summarized in Tables 7-1 and 7-2 were for the special case of a three-dimensional star with altitude h equal to the radius R. To be more general, consider first the ratio of the star surface area, Eq. (7-4), to the surface area A_{cyl} of a right circular cylinder of altitude $2h$, which can be expressed as

$$\frac{A_s}{A_{cyl}} = \frac{5R^2 \left[4a_2^2 \left(1 + h^2/R^2\right) - \left(1 + a_2^2 - a_1^2\right)^2 \right]^{\frac{1}{2}}}{2\pi R^2 (1 + 2h/R)}. \tag{7-11}$$

7-3. Star area and volume versus ratio of altitude to radius

How do the foregoing ratios vary with the ratio of altitude h to radius R of the star? If the functional variation exhibits a local minimum or maximum, then the corresponding value of h/R can be found by calculating the first derivative with respect to h/R,

$$\frac{d(A_s/A_{cyl})}{d(h/R)},$$

and setting this equal to zero and solving for the critical value of h/R. Doing this with Eq. (7-11) and solving for h/R gives

$$\left(\frac{h}{R}\right)_{cyl} = 2\left[1 - \frac{\left(1+a_2^2-a_1^2\right)^2}{4a_2^2}\right], \qquad (7\text{-}12)$$

and evaluating it with the numerical values of a_1 and a_2 from Eq. (4-6) of Chapter 4 leads to

$$\left(\frac{h}{R}\right)_{cyl} = 0.190983. \qquad (7\text{-}13)$$

Taking the case of the regular pentagonal prism of altitude $2h$, radius R, its surface area can be expressed in terms of the ratio h/R and then from Eq. (7-4), the ratio of star area to prism area is

$$\frac{A_s}{A_p} = \frac{5R^2\left[4a_2^2(1+h^2/R^2)-\left(1+a_2^2-a_1^2\right)^2\right]^{\frac{1}{2}}}{10R^2 \sin 36°(\cos 36° + 2h/R)}. \qquad (7\text{-}14)$$

To test for a maximum or minimum of the latter, we calculate the derivative of A_s/A_p with respect to h/R, set it equal to zero, and solve for the critical value of h/R. Doing this leads to

$$\left(\frac{h}{R}\right)_p = \left(1 - \frac{\left(1+a_2^2-a_1^2\right)^2}{4a_2^2}\right)\left(\frac{2}{\cos 36°}\right)$$

$$= 0.236068. \qquad (7\text{-}15)$$

Now, the surface area A_r of the right rectangular parallelpiped of altitude $2h$ can be expressed in terms of the ratio h/R as follows:

$$A_r = 8a_2R^2\,(1+\sin 18°)\left[(1+\cos 18°)\left(\frac{h}{R}\right) + a_2(1+\sin 18°)\cos 18°\right] \qquad (7\text{-}16)$$

So, to test for a minimum or maximum in the functional relationship of star area to the area A_r versus h/R, we form the ratio of A_s in Eq. (7-4) to A_r in Eq. (7-16) and calculate the first derivative with respect to h/R, set it equal to zero,

$$\frac{d(A_s / A_r)}{d(h/R)} = 0,$$

and solve for the critical value of h/R. When this is done, the result is

$$\left(\frac{h}{R}\right)_r = \frac{1+\cos 18°}{a_2(1+\sin 18°)\cos 18°}\left(1 - \frac{\left(1+a_2^2 - a_1^2\right)^2}{4a_2^2}\right), \tag{7-17}$$

and evaluating it numerically leads to

$$\left(\frac{h}{R}\right)_r = 0.205979. \tag{7-18}$$

In the case of the double right circular cone, the surface area can be written as

$$A_c = 2\pi R^2 \sqrt{1+(h/R)^2}, \tag{7-19}$$

but when the first derivative of A_s/A_c is calculated and set equal to zero, the derivative vanishes only for the trivial value $h/R = 0$. The same is true for comparison of A_s with the sphere because the first derivative of $A_s/4\pi R^2$ vanishes only for $h/R = 0$.

The functional comparison of areas for the cylinder, pentagonal prism, and rectangular parallelpiped leads to the critical values of h/R given in Eqs. (7-13), (7-15) and 7-18), respectively. For each of these three cases, the ratio of star area to the geometric shape area is a minimum. This is easily seen by calculating the ratio of star area to shape area for a value of h/R, slightly smaller than the critical value and for a value slightly larger, then comparing these values with the area ratio for the critical value. For example, the value of the area ratio A_s/A_p for the pentagonal prism calculated from Eq. (7-14) for the critical value $h/R = 0.236068$ in Eq. (7-15) is $A_s/A_p = 0.37518$, while A_s/A_p calculated for $h/R = 0.22$, for example is $A_s/A_p = 0.37540$ and for $h/R = 0.26$, $A_s/A_p = 0.37560$.

Using Eqs. (7-4), (7-11), (7-14), (7-16), and (7-19) the ratios of star surface area to the surface areas of each of the geometrical shapes listed in Table 7-1 are plotted as a function of the altitude-to-radius ratio in Fig. 7-5. Note that three of the curves exhibit minima in accordance with the results of Eqs. (7-13), (7-15), and (7-18), while the other two do not, as reasoned above.

The ratio of star surface area to volume can be written in the following form, using Eqs. (7-4) and (7-8).

$$\frac{A_s}{V_s} = \frac{10 a_2}{a_v R}\left[1 + \frac{1}{(h/R)^2}\left(1 - \left(\frac{1 + a_2^2 - a_1^2}{2 a_2}\right)^2\right)\right]^{\frac{1}{2}} \qquad (7\text{-}20)$$

Similarly, for a cylinder of radius R and altitude $2h$, its surface area per unit volume can be written

$$\frac{A_{cyl}}{V_{cyl}} = \frac{1}{R}\left(2 + \frac{1}{(h/R)}\right). \qquad (7\text{-}21)$$

In the case of the right regular pentagonal prism referred to above, we can write the ratio of surface area to volume in the form

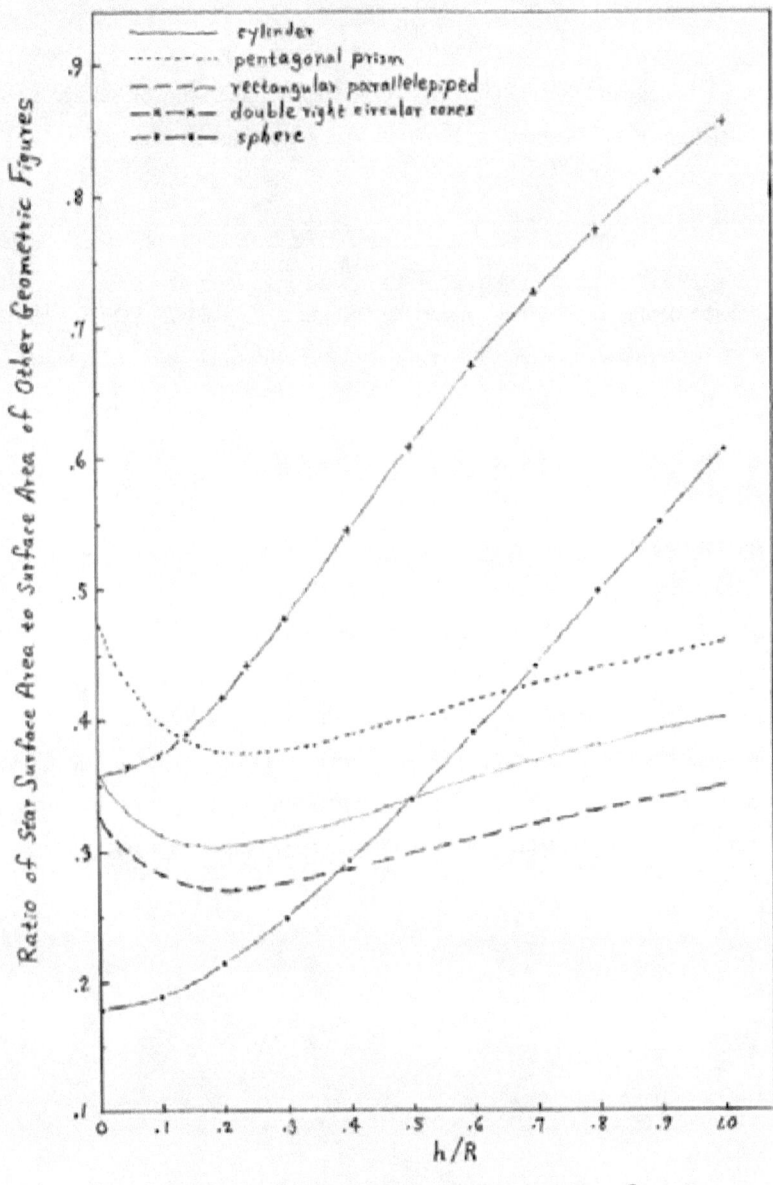

Fig. 7-5. Ratio of three-dimensional star surface area to surface area of other geometric shapes, versus ratio of altitude h to radius R.

$$\frac{A_p}{V_p} = \frac{1}{R}\left(\frac{1}{(h/R)} + \frac{2}{\cos 36°}\right). \tag{7-22}$$

For the right rectangular parallelpiped referenced above, the ratio of surface area to volume, after some simplification, can be put into the following form below.

$$\frac{A_{rect}}{V_{rect}} = \frac{1}{R}\left[\frac{1}{(h/R)} + \frac{1+\cos 18°}{a_2(1+\sin 18°)\cos 18°}\right] \tag{7-23}$$

Finally, for the double right circular cone, the volume is $V_c = 24\pi R^2 h/3$ and therefore, using Eq. (7-19) for its surface area, the area-to-volume ratio can be written as follows.

$$\frac{A_c}{V_c} = \frac{3}{R}\left(1 + \frac{1}{(h/R)^2}\right)^{\frac{1}{2}} \tag{7-24}$$

For the special cases that were considered in Table 7-2, those results agree with the values calculated from Eqs. (7-20) through (7-24), when h is set equal to R.

Eqs. (7-20) through (7-24) were used to calculate the area-to-volume ratios as a function of the ratio of altitude to radius for the three-dimensional star and the other common geometric shapes, and the results are provided in the graph of Fig. 7-6.

In passing, consider again the ratio of surface area to radius for the double right circular cone, as a function of its altitude divided by its radius. As h/R becomes larger, the radical approaches unity and in fact as h/R becomes large without bound, the limiting value is

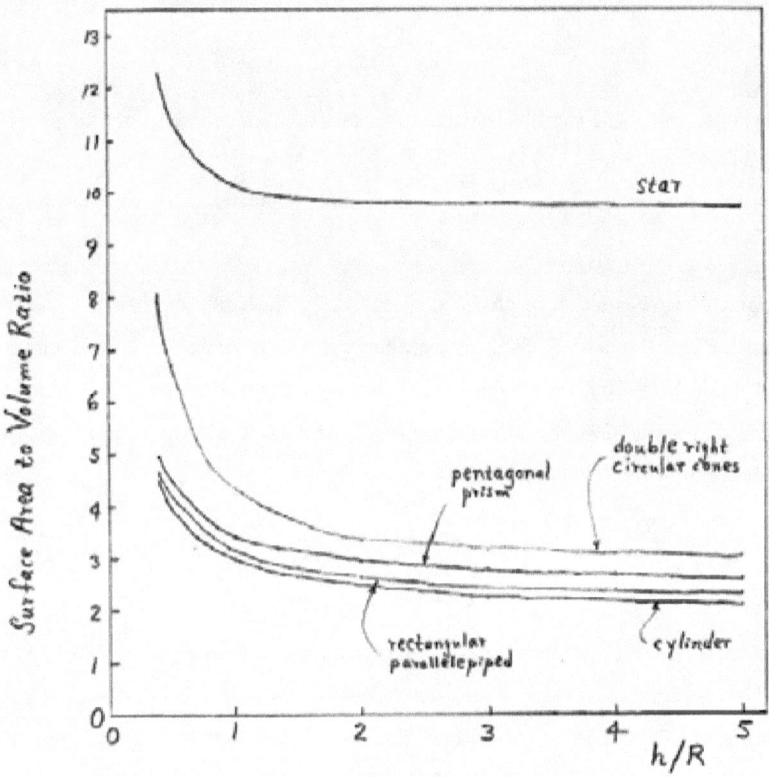

Fig. 7-6. Surface area to volume ratio, in reciprocal radius units, versus ratio of altitude h to radius R for three-dimensional star compared with other geometric figures.

$$\underset{h/R\to\infty}{\text{Limit}}\left(\frac{A_c}{V_c}\right) = \frac{3}{R}. \tag{7-25}$$

Interestingly, this is the same as the ratio of surface area to volume for the sphere.

$$\frac{4\pi R^2}{\frac{4}{3}\pi R^3} = \frac{3}{R} \tag{7-26}$$

A graphical representation is provided in Fig. 7-7. The value of A_c/V_c approaches the limiting value $3/R$ relatively fast because when $h/R = 10$ the value of A_c/V_c is within 0.5% of $3/R$, while $h/R = 20$ gives a value of A_c/V_c within 0.125% of the limit.

From Eq. (7-20), the limiting value of star surface area to volume ratio, as h/R becomes large without bound, is

$$\underset{h/R\to\infty}{\text{Limit}}\left(\frac{A_s}{V_s}\right) = \frac{10 a_2}{a_v R}. \tag{7-27}$$

As h/R increases, the approach to this limit is rapid because, using the values of a_1 and a_2 from Eq. (4-6) of Chapter 4, it is seen that $h/R = 5$ gives a value of A_s/V_s within 0.19% of that in Eq. (7-27), and $h/R = 10$ yields a value of A_s/V_s within 0.048% of the limit. Now, it is quite interesting to compare the limiting value of surface area to volume for the star with the ratio of surface area to volume of the sphere. Using the value of a_2 in Eq. (4-6) and the value of a_v in Eq. (7-8), we find from Eqs. (7-27) and (7-26) that

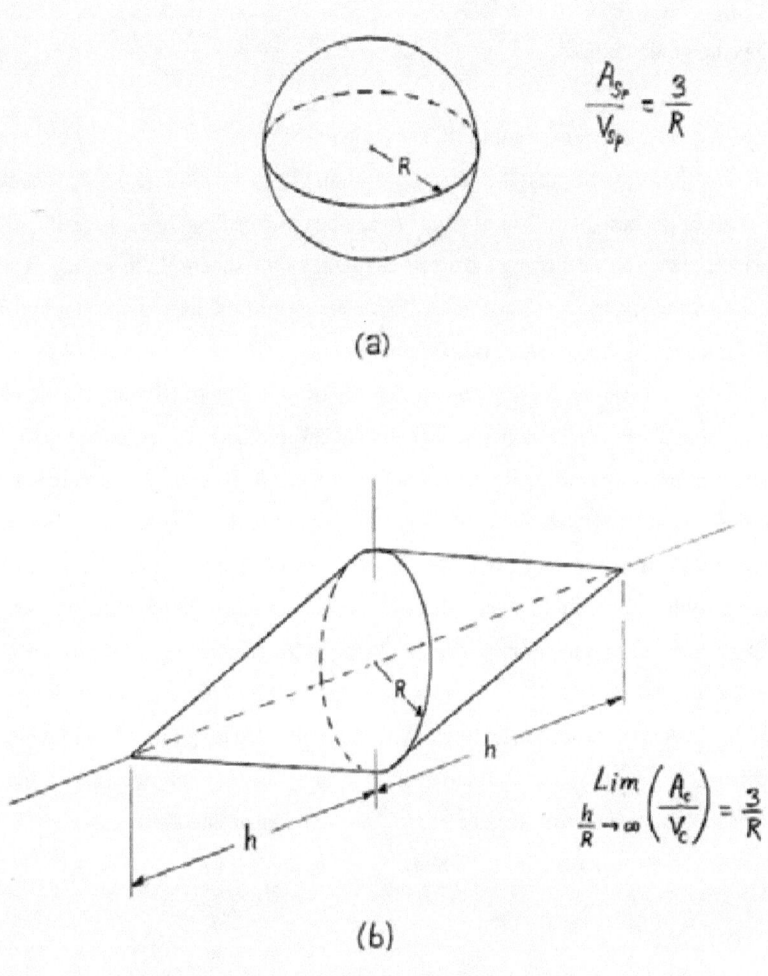

Fig. 7-7. Graphical representation of Eqs. (7-24) - (7-26) for (a) sphere and (b) double right circular cones.

$$\frac{\underset{h/R\to\infty}{\text{Limit}}(A_s/V_s)}{(A/V)_{sphere}} = \frac{10a_2}{3a_v} = 2\phi, \tag{7-28}$$

where ϕ is the golden ratio.

7-4. Three-dimensional stars circumscribed by spheroids

It was shown earlier that the three-dimensional star with altitude $h = R$, symmetric on both sides of the base plane star of radius R, can be inscribed inside a sphere of radius R with the base plane star occupying a diametrical plane of the sphere. In this case, all seven star tips lie on the spherical surface, i.e., all five vertices of the base plane star and both apexes of the star. In the general case, for the altitude $h \neq R$, neither apex will lie on the spherical surface. However, for this general case, there are geometrical shapes in which the three-dimensional star can be inscribed such that all seven of its vertices lie on the surface. Consider an ellipse with semi-major and minor axes R and h respectively, as shown in Fig. 7-8a. If this ellipse is rotated about the semi-minor axis h, the three-dimensional figure generated is known mathematically as an oblate spheroid, represented in Fig. 7-8b. It is clear that the oblate spheroid intersects the x-y plane in a circle of radius R in Fig 7-8b, and that it intersects the Z axis at points $\pm h$. So, if the three-dimensional star with altitude $h < R$ is oriented with its base plane star lying in the x-y plane of Fig. 7-8b, center coinciding with the origin O of the x-y-z coordinates, then all five tips of the base plane star will lie on the oblate spheroid surface in its central circular plane of symmetry, and one apex of the star will lie on the oblate spheroid surface at $z = +h$, the other on the surface at $z = -h$. The volume of the oblate spheroid in Fig. 7-8b is

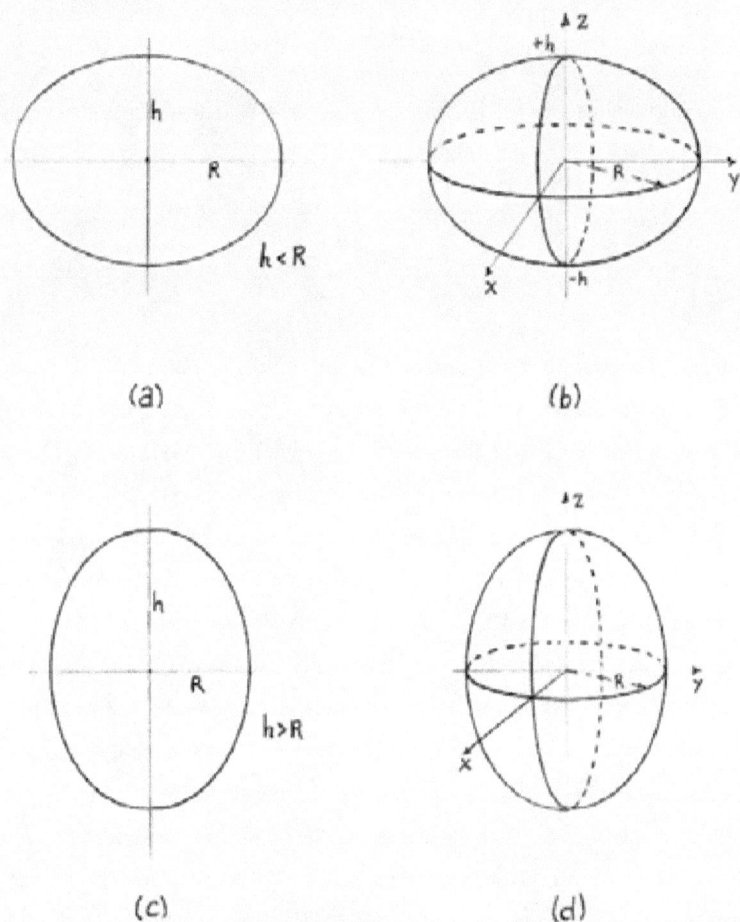

Fig. 7-8. Revolving the ellipse in (a) about its semi-minor axis h gives the oblate spheroid in (b), whereas revolving the ellipse in (c) about its semi-major axis h results in the prolate spheriod in (d).

$$V_{ob} = \frac{4}{3}\pi R^2 h, \qquad (7\text{-}29)$$

and comparing the volume of the star, from Eq. (7-7), to that of the oblate spheroid circumscribed about it gives the following:

$$\frac{V_s}{V_{ob}} = \frac{3a_v}{4\pi}$$

$$= 0.178662555. \qquad (7\text{-}30)$$

We see that both the radius R and altitude h cancel in Eq. (7-30), so that this result is true for all values of h in the interval $0 < h \leq R$. When $h = R$, the oblate spheroid is a sphere of radius R and for this special case, the numerical value in Eq. (7-30) is identical to the value given in Table 7-1, specifically for comparison of the star volume to that of a sphere.

Now, consider the ellipse with semi-major and minor axes h and R, respectively, in Fig. 7-8c and let it be revolved about the major axis h to generate the three-dimensional figure mathematically referred to as a prolate spheroid, represented in Fig. 7-8d. The prolate spheroid surface intersects the x-y plane of Fig. 7-8d in a circle of radius R by virtue of the way in which the surface was generated from the ellipse, and it intersects the z axis at points $\pm h$ where $h > R$, compared to Fig. 7-8b where $h < R$. It is clear that the star for $h > R$ can be inscribed in the prolate spheroid of Fig. 7-7d provided the base plane star lies in the x-y plane, centered at O. Then the star apexes lie on the prolate surface at $\pm h$ on the z axis, while all five-star tips lie on the circle of radius R in the x-y plane of symmetry of the prolate spheroid. For the prolate spheroid with $h > R$, the volume is

$$V_{pr} = \frac{4}{3}\pi h^2 R, \qquad (7\text{-}31)$$

and then from Eq. (7-7) we can express the volume of the star relative to the prolate volume as

$$\frac{V_s}{V_{pr}} = \frac{3a_v}{4\pi(h/R)}. \qquad \text{for } h > R \qquad (7\text{-}32)$$

Using Eq. (7-30) and (7-32) the three-dimensional star volume was calculated relative to the circumscribed spheroid volume, and the results are given in Fig. 7-9.

Finally, consider the surface area of the three-dimensional star relative to that of the oblate spheroid as a function of the altitude h to radius R. For $h \leq R$ for the case of the oblate spheroid, we can arrange the standard handbook formula for the spheroid and write the surface area in terms of the ratio of the semi-minor axis h to the semi-major axis R to give the following.

For the case in which the altitude h is greater than the radius, the handbook formula for the prolate spheroid surface area can be cast in the form below.

$$A_{ob} = \pi R^2 \left[2 + \frac{(h/R)^2}{\sqrt{1-h^2/R^2}} \ln\left(\frac{1+\sqrt{1-h^2/R^2}}{1-\sqrt{1-h^2/R^2}}\right) \right] \qquad (7\text{-}33)$$

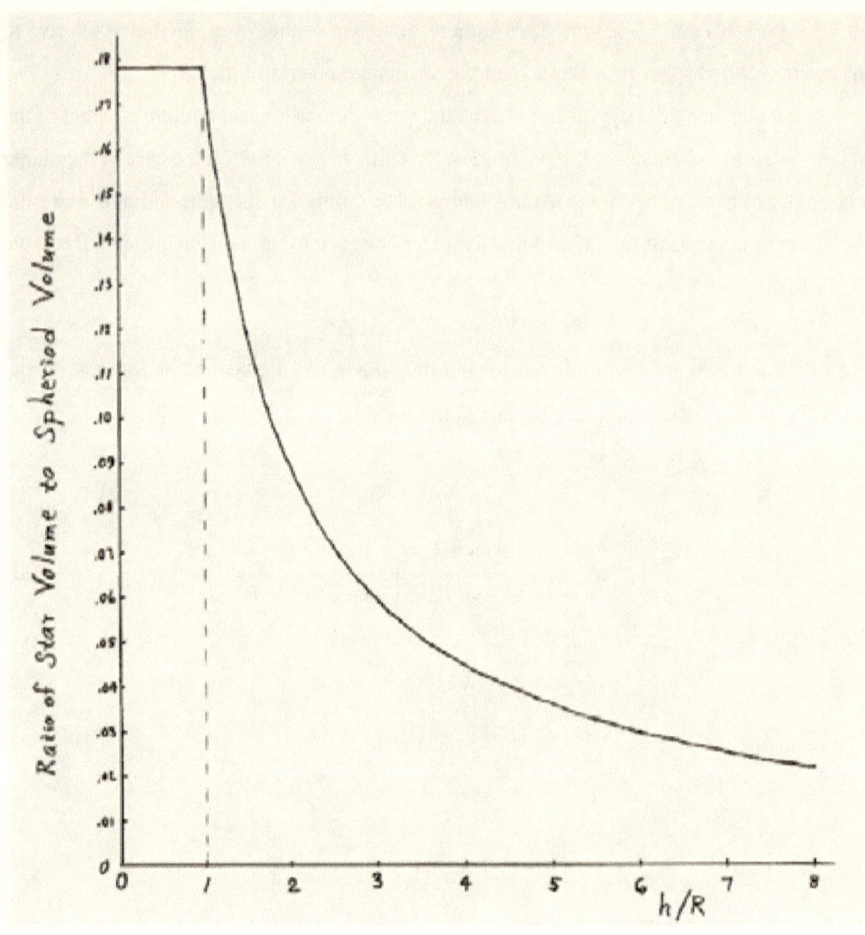

Fig. 7-9. Ratio of star volume to oblate spheriod volume, versus *h/R*, for *h/R* < 1. For *h/R* > 1, the volume ratio is for the prolate spheriod.

$$A_{pr} = 2\pi R^2 \left[1+(R/h)^{-1}(1-R^2/h^2)^{-\frac{1}{2}} \arcsin(1-R^2/h^2)^{\frac{1}{2}}\right] \qquad (7\text{-}34)$$

So, using Eq. (7-4) for the star surface area versus h/R, the ratio of star area to the circumscribed spheroid area for the two regions is

$$\begin{array}{ll} A_s / A_{ob} & h \leq R \\ A_s / A_{pr} & h > R. \end{array} \qquad (7\text{-}35)$$

Eqs. (7-4), (7-33), and (7-34) were used to calculate the area ratios in Eq. (7-35) and the results are presented graphically in Fig. 7-10.

7-5. Further comparison of star volume and area with that of common geometric figures

How does the volume-to-surface area ratio of a symmetric solid star figure with $h = R$ compare to the same ratio for other common geometric figures? There are, of course, a variety of comparative shapes such as those considered earlier (Tables 7-1, 7-2) in the comparisons of the inverse ratios, i.e., surface area to volume. Before further analysis of this, consider first the following hypothetical experiment that is offered as an analogy to the comparison of geometric figures that is to follow.

Suppose we select at random a few pebbles from a beach. These may and very likely will differ in shape, color, size, surface texture, etc. Of the various features or properties of these pebbles that we might use in comparing them, let their mass be the distinguishing factor of

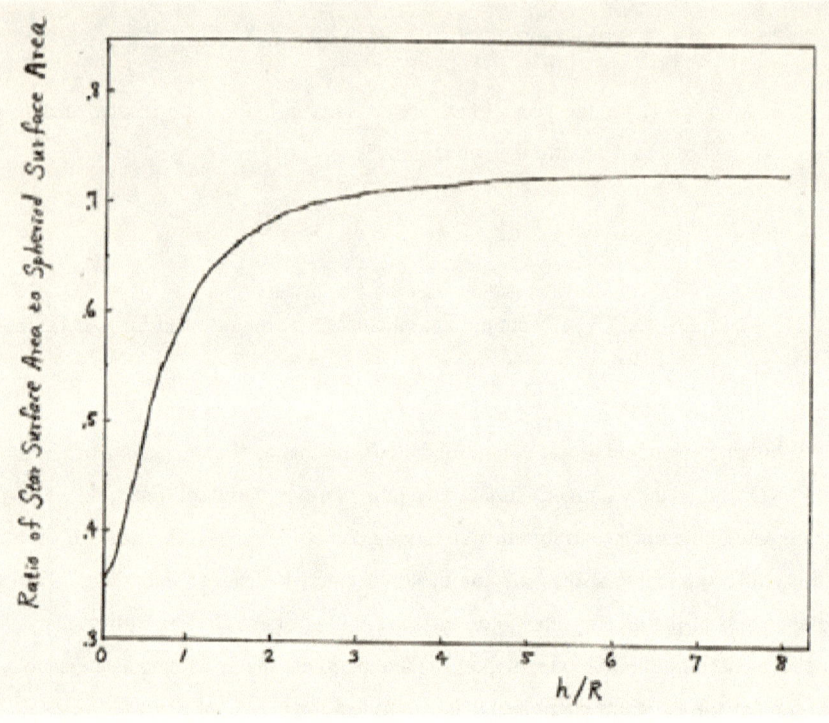

Fig. 7-10. Ratio of star surface area to spheriod surface area versus ratio of star altitude to radius. For $h/R < 1$ the spheriod is oblate, while for $h/R > 1$, the spheriod is prolate.

choice. Actually, in practice, a small weight measurement device could be sufficiently accurate for comparison of mass if one were inclined to pursue the experiment. For now, we imagine that the mass of each of the randomly selected small pebbles has been measured and we list the masses in order of increasing magnitude, giving each pebble a number so that 1, 2, ... N correspond to the order of increasing mass. Now, we inquire as to how uniformly the masses of the pebbles are distributed. That is, m_2-m_1 is the amount by which the mass of pebble No. 2 exceeds that of pebble No. 1; how close is the difference, m_4-m_3, for example, equal to m_2-m_1, and in turn, equal to m_N-m_{N-1}? Again, in the spirit of the hypothetical experiment, suppose that eight pebbles selected at random on the beach have masses according to the order in which they were selected, as listed in column A of Table 7-3. Then, column B gives the number assigned to each pebble in order of increasing value of measured mass.

Table 7-3. Hypothetical Measured Masses of Eight Randomly Selected Pebbles on a Beach.

Column A	Column B
Mass* Per Selection Order	Order of Increasing Mass
2.1	3
5.1	6
1.9	2
2.3	4
0.15	1
6.9	8
3.1	5
6.8	7

* Arbitrary mass units, such as grams, kilograms, etc., as long as all are measured in the same unit.

To assess how nearly uniformly distributed the pebble masses are, we can plot the pebble mass versus assigned pebble number, as shown in the hypothetical graph of Fig. 7-11. Of course, the assigned numbers on the horizontal axis are linearly distributed because each number is one unit greater than the immediately preceding number. Therefore, if the masses of the randomly selected pebbles are exactly uniformly distributed in mass, then the plotted "data" points will lie on a straight line. However, we would not expect the masses to be precisely linearly distributed and so the points would not lie exactly on a straight line, but the degree to which the mass points fall on a straight line is a measure of the degree to which they are linearly distributed. A mathematical technique often referred to as "least squares" or "linear regression" can be used to obtain the equation of the straight line, such as in Fig. 7-11, for which the data points fit most closely, and coupled with this analytic method is a quantity referred to as the "correlation coefficient," which provides a measure of the degree to which the points lie on the straight line. If the points fall exactly on the line, then the correlation is 1.0, or 100%. A correlation of 0.95 or

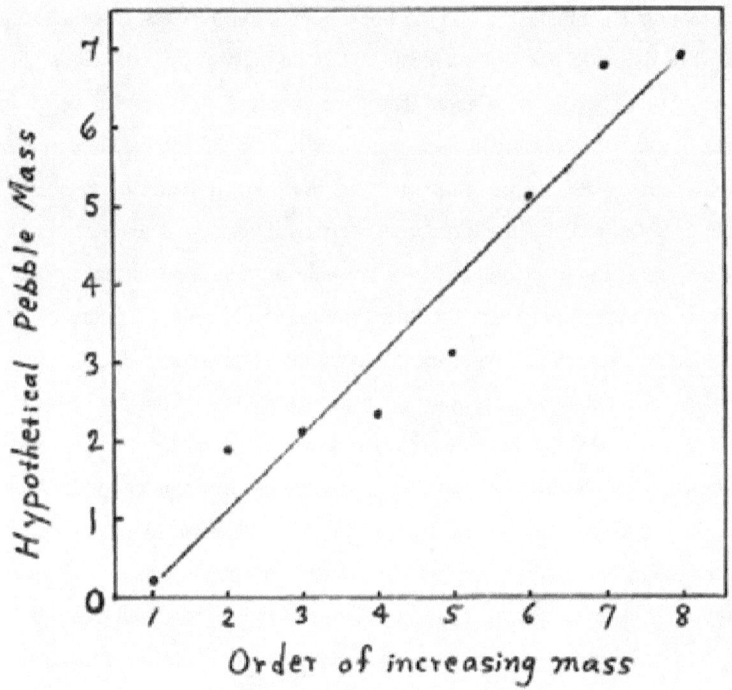

Fig. 7-11. Plot of hypothetical data from Table 7-3. The straight line is actual best-fit linear relationship of the points.

0.90, or even somewhat lower represents a less-than-perfect linear relationship but still indicates that the data points exhibit some linearity. For this hypothetical case of Table 7-3 and corresponding graph in Fig. 7-11 a linear regression analysis gives a straight line represented by slope 0.9708 and intercept − 0.825 on the vertical axis with a correlation coefficient of 0.9669. It is to be noted that if we choose 2, 4, 6 . . . 16, for example, to represent the order of increasing masses, instead of 1, 2, . . . 8, then the slope and intercept of the straight line will change in the analysis, but the correlation coefficient does not change. In what follows, it is the correlation coefficient that is of sole interest.

Now, we return to a comparison of the ratio of volume-to-surface area of a solid star (with $h = R$) to the same ratios for other common solid geometric figures. The sphere, right cylinder, and right circular cone are obvious choices for comparison, but looking over the landscape of solid geometric figures, we must also include the five platonic solids: these are the tetrahedron, hexahedron (cube), octahedron, dodecahedron, and icosahedron. On a historical note, the early Greeks were aware of these five regular solids. Around 350 B.C. Plato attempted to connect the existence of these solid shapes to the basic elements he believed made up the universe, i.e., air, fire, water, and earth. Hence these five regular geometric solids have been referred to as the Platonic solids. It was Euclid who first proved that only five such regular polyhedra are possible, "regular" in the sense that the faces are all identical regular polygons. In the case of the cube, the faces are all squares while the dodechedron contains twelve pentagons as its faces. The remaining Platonic solids contain equilateral triangles as faces, with numbers being four, eight, and twenty, respectively, for the tetrahedron, octahedron, and icosahedron. In comparison, we note that the solid star symmetric about its base plane contains twenty identical triangular facets.

A list of the ratios of volume-to-surface area for all these solids is given in Table 7-4, and the solids are illustrated in Fig. 7-12. From a dimensional standpoint, the ratio of volume (cubic units) to surface area (square units) is a numerical quantity with the dimension of a simple length unit, and this is designated as R in the table. For example, for the sphere, R is simply its radius. For the hexahedron R is the length of a side of a square face and R is the length of a side of a pentagon for the dodecahedron. For the other three, Platonic solids R is the length of a side of an equilateral triangle comprising the surface facets for the particular solid.

Table 7-4. Calculated Ratios of Volume-to-Surface Area for Common Solid Geometric Figures, Compared with the Three-Dimensional Star Having $h \equiv R$.

Geometric Solid	Volume to Surface Area Ratio*	Order of Increasing Ratio V/A
Sphere	1/3	8
Cylinder	1/4	6
Right Circular Cone	0.2357	5
Tetrahedron	0.06804	1
Hexahedron	1/6	4
Octahedron	0.13608	3
Dodecahedron	0.37117	9
Icosahedron	0.2519	7
Star	0.0984	2

* Units of R.

A plot of volume-to-surface area, V/A, versus order of increasing ratio from Table 7-4 is given in Fig. 7-13. Based on a linear regression analysis, the straight line in the figure has a slope 0.0372 with intercept 0.02634R, and the correlation coefficient is relatively high with the value 0.9879.

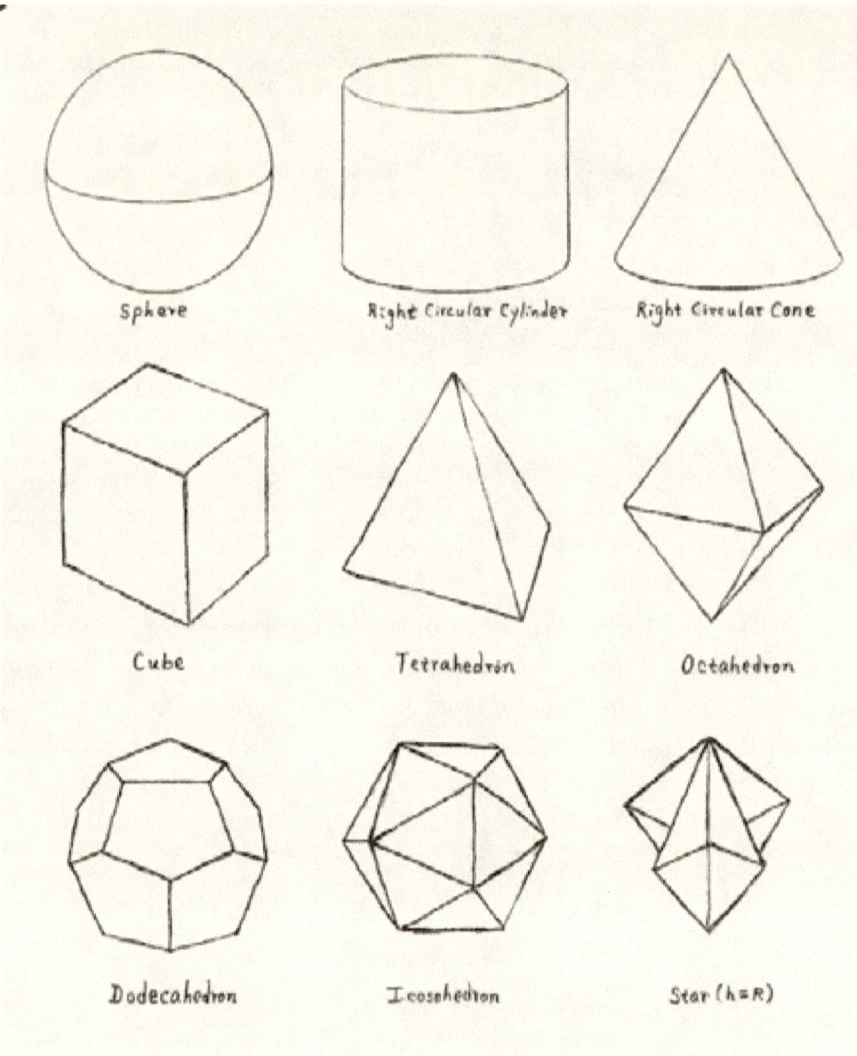

Fig. 7-12. Graphic representations of the solid geometric bodies in Table 7-4, for comparison with the solid star of altitude h equal to its radius.

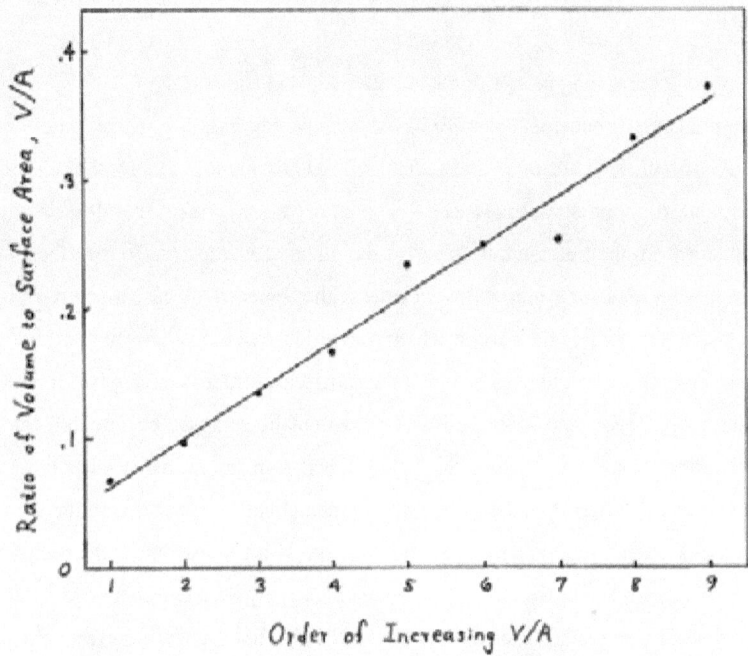

Fig. 7-13. A plot of the data from Table 7-4. The straight line is the result of the best-fit linear regression analysis to the data points, for which the correlation coefficient is 0.9759.

CHAPTER 8

THREE-DIMENSIONAL STAR CONTAINING INSCRIBED SPHERES

8-1. Inscribed spheres tangent to ridge and valley lines in star surface

In the three-dimensional star we have been considering, five "ridge" lines connect the altitude with the five tips of the base plane star, and the same is true for the other side of the base plane of symmetry. Likewise, five "valley" lines connect the altitude with the points inward from the tips, on both sides of the plane of symmetry. To inscribe a sphere inside the three-dimensional star, with its center at the center of the base plane star, we will consider two cases. First is the case in which a spherical surface is tangent to all ten of the ridge lines, and secondly, the case in which the spherical surface is tangent to all ten valley lines. Intuitively, these conditions most likely cannot be satisfied by one and the same inscribed spherical surface because the valley lines from the altitudes meet the base at points closer to the center than the ridge line. Mathematically we can determine the radius of the spherical surface that is tangent to the ridge lines and compare it to the radius of the spherical surface tangent to the valley lines. Each plane perpendicular to the base plane that contains a radius also contains the altitude and two ridge lines. One of these five planes is shown in Fig. 8-1a. This plane, obviously, contains the center O of the base plane star and therefore an inscribed sphere with center at O intersects this plane in a circle. Let the radius of the inscribed circle be r and therefore the radius drawn from O is perpendicular to the ridge line at the point of tangency. Now, by definition of the "ridge" line, it intersects the perpendicular to the base line through O at altitude h from O. Let β be the angle between the radius R and the ridge line. Then, in the right triangle containing the star radius R as hypotenuse we can write

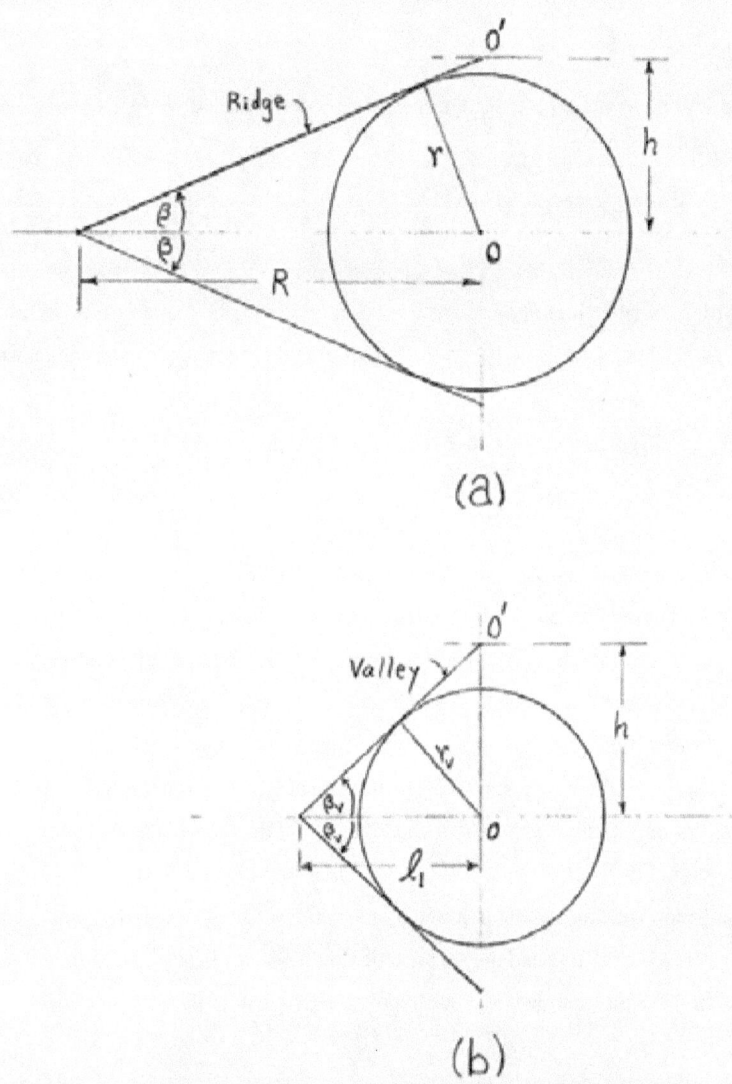

Fig. 8-1. (a) A sphere of radius r is tangent to all ten ridge lines in the three-dimensional star of altitude h, and (b) a sphere of radius r_v is tangent to all ten valley lines.

$$\sin\beta = \frac{r}{R}. \tag{8-1}$$

In the right triangle containing the ridge as hypotenuse and altitude h opposite angle β, the following is true.

$$\tan\beta = \frac{h}{R} \tag{8-2}$$

Using the trigonometric identity $1 + \cot^2 y = \csc^2 y$ allows the angle β to be eliminated between Eqs. (8-1) and (8-2) and then the radius r of the inscribed sphere tangent to all ridge lines can be expressed as

$$r = \frac{h}{\sqrt{1+(h/R)^2}}. \tag{8-3}$$

Each valley line connects the altitude to a point in the base plane, and therefore there are five planes perpendicular to the base that contain the altitude and two valley lines. One such plane is shown in Fig. 8-1b. For consistency of notation with earlier analysis, note that the valley line intersects the base plane at distance $l_1 \equiv a_1 R$ from the point O at the foot of the altitude and, of course, the valley line intersects the perpendicular at altitude h above the center O of the base plane star. The numerical quantity a_1 is given in Eq. (4-6) of Chapter 4. Now, an inscribed sphere with center at O will intersect the plane of Fig. 8-1b in the circle with radius r_v, equal to the spherical radius, and the radius drawn from O to the point of tangency with the valley is perpendicular to the valley line. Let β_v represent the angle between the valley line and the segment of length l_1 in the base plane as shown in Fig. 8-1b. Then, in the right triangle with l_1 as hypotenuse, we can write

$$\sin\beta_v = \frac{r_v}{l_1}, \tag{8-4}$$

and referring to the right triangle with altitude h opposite angle β_v, we have

$$\tan\beta_v = \frac{h}{l_1}. \tag{8-5}$$

Eliminating the angle β_v between Eqs. (8-4) and (8-5) allows the radius of the inscribed sphere tangent to all ten valley lines to be written

$$r_v = \frac{hl_1}{\sqrt{h^2 + l_1^2}}, \tag{8-6}$$

and, alternately, using the proportionality between l_1 and radius R in terms of the numerical quantity a_1, the latter becomes

$$r_v = \frac{h}{\sqrt{1 + \left(\dfrac{h}{a_1 R}\right)^2}}. \tag{8-7}$$

Now, the magnitude of a_1 is less than unity and therefore the denominator in Eq. (8-7) is greater than the denominator in Eq. (8-3), meaning that the radius r of the inscribed sphere tangent to the ridge lines is greater than the radius r_v of the inscribed spherical surface tangent to the valley lines. So, for a given star of altitude h and radius R, if a sphere of radius r given in Eq. (8-3) is inscribed, then the spherical surface will intersect each valley at two points, as can be seen in Fig. 8-2. These two points of intersection can be found as follows. Let an x-y coordinate system with origin located at O in Fig. 8-2 be oriented with x-axis along l_1 and y-axis along the altitude h. The equation of the circle of intersection of the sphere of radius r with the plane of the figure is

$$x^2 + y^2 = r^2, \tag{8-8}$$

and the equation representing the valley line in this system is

$$y = h - x\frac{h}{l_1}. \tag{8-9}$$

Eliminating y between Eqs. (8-8) and (8-9) leads to the following quadratic.

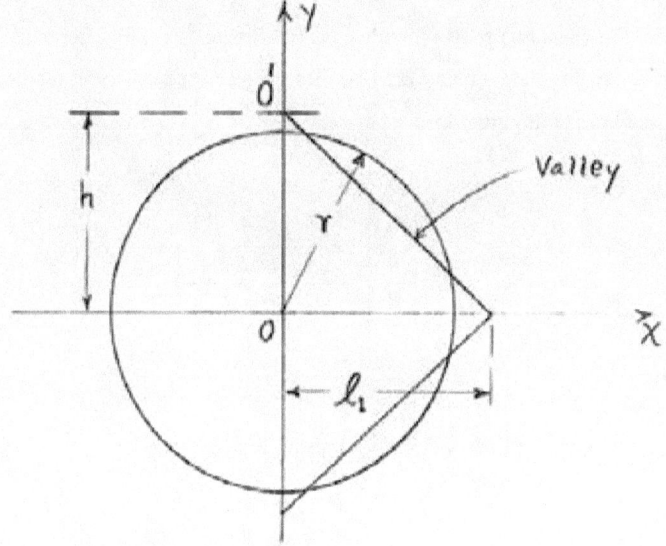

Fig. 8-2. The inscribed sphere of radius r in Fig. 8-1a. intersects each valley line in two points.

$$x^2\left(1+(h/l_1)^2\right)-2\frac{h^2}{l_1}x+h^2-r^2=0 \qquad (8\text{-}10)$$

This quadratic in x has two roots which we can designate as $x_\pm$ and after considerable but straightforward manipulation using Eq. (8-3) for the inscribed spherical radius r, the roots can be written in the following form.

$$x_\pm = h\left(\frac{h}{R}\right)\left[\frac{1\pm\left(\frac{1-a_1^2}{1+(h/R)^2}\right)^{\frac{1}{2}}}{a_1\left(1+(h/a_1R)^2\right)}\right] \qquad (8\text{-}11)$$

The corresponding y coordinates in Fig. 8-2, using Eq. (8-9) are

$$y_\pm = h - x_\pm\left(\frac{h}{a_1R}\right). \qquad (8\text{-}12)$$

We note from the latter that the coordinates of intersection of the inscribed sphere with a valley do not simply depend on the ratio of altitude to radius but also are proportional to the altitude itself.

From Eqs. (8-3) and (8-7), we can express the radius r in terms of the radius r_v through the relation

$$r = r_v\sqrt{\frac{1+(h/a_1R)^2}{1+(h/R)^2}}. \qquad (8\text{-}13)$$

It is interesting to note from Eq. (8-13) that if we construct a three-dimensional star with altitude related to the star radius, $h = R/\phi$ is the golden ratio, then

$$r = \phi r_v, \qquad (8\text{-}14)$$

that is, the radius r of the inscribed sphere tangent to the ridge lines is just ϕ times the radius of the inscribed sphere tangent to the valley lines! It is equally interesting in this regard to recall from Chapter 5 that the only way in which a three-dimensional star of altitude h can be folded from a plane figure is when the ratio of altitude to radius is $h/R = 1/\phi$.

8-2. Star altitudes for ridge and valley tangencies to a particular inscribed spherical surface

Consider again the base plane star as indicated in Figure 8-3 and note that the projection of the segment l_1 on the radius, that is, $l_1 \cos 36°$, lies on each of the five chordal lengths such as P_1P_3, P_2P_4, etc., that are used to construct the five-point mathematical star. Because of this, a circle of radius $l_1 \cos 36°$, drawn with center at O provides an additional centrally located feature of the plane star. Suppose we construct a sphere of radius $l_1 \cos 36°$ with center at O in Fig. 8-3. Now, what is the altitude of a three-dimensional star constructed on the base star such that all the ridge lines are tangent to this spherical surface? To determine the altitude h for which this is true, we first solve Eq. (8-3) for h in terms of the star radius R and radius r of inscribed sphere:

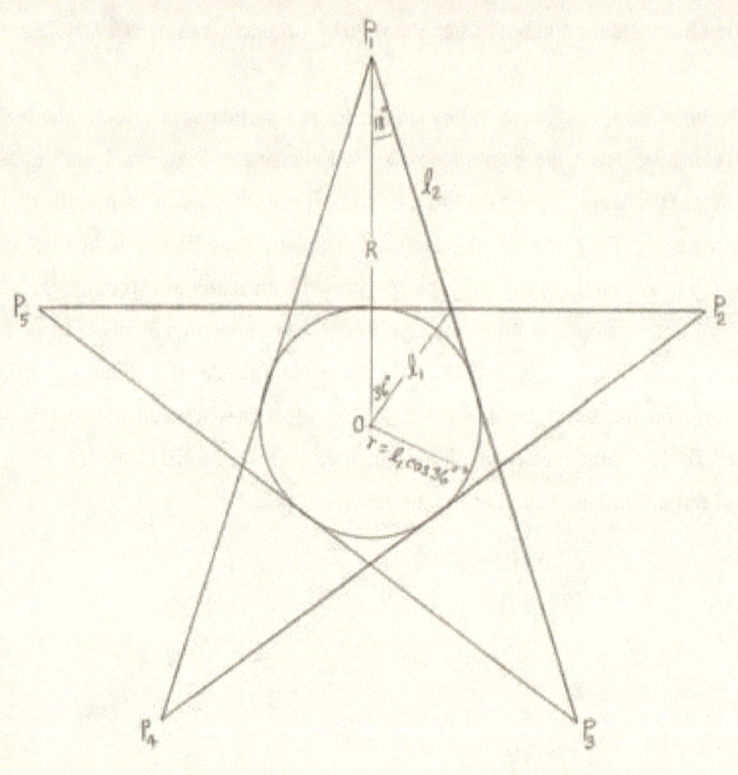

Fig. 8-3. A circle with center at O and radius $l_1 \cos 36°$ is tangent to each of the chordal lengths P_1P_3, P_2P_4, P_3P_5, P_4P_1 and P_5P_2 at the points where the radius R intersects them, in the five-point star [5, 2].

$$h = \frac{r}{\sqrt{1-(r/R)^2}} \qquad (8\text{-}15)$$

Substituting $r = l_1 \cos 36°$ and remembering that $l_1 = a_1 R$ given in Eq. (4-6), the latter gives, correct to nine decimal places,

$$h = 0.324919696\, R, \qquad (8\text{-}16)$$

which is the altitude in terms of the base star radius for which all the ridge lines are tangent to the inscribed sphere of radius $l_1 \cos 36°$ that intersects the base plane in the circle shown in Fig. 8-3.

In a similar manner, we can determine the altitude h_v for which an inscribed sphere of radius $r_v = l_1 \cos 36°$ is tangent to all ten of the valley lines in the three-dimensional star. To this end we solve Eq. (8-7) for h, designate it as h_v and substitute for r_v which gives

$$h_v = \frac{R a_1 \cos 36°}{\sqrt{1-\cos^2 36°}}, \qquad (8\text{-}17)$$

Using the numerical value for a_1, the altitude is found to be

$$h_v = 0.525731112\, R. \qquad (8\text{-}18)$$

The fact that $h_v > h$ from Eqs. (8-18) and (8-16) is consistent with the earlier analysis related to Eqs. (8-3) and (8-6) indicates that for an inscribed sphere of given radius, the altitude must be greater for tangency at the valley lines, compared to tangency at the ridge lines. But how much greater for the particular case above for the inscribed sphere of radius $l_1 \cos 36°$? From Eqs. (8-18) and (8-16), correct to nine decimal places, we see that the golden ratio appears!

$$\frac{h_v}{h} = \phi \qquad (8\text{-}19)$$

The corresponding angles β in Fig. 8-1 for the ridge tangency and valley tangency, in the case of the three-dimensional star of radius R with inscribed sphere of radius $l_1 \cos 36° \equiv$

$a_1 R \cos 36°$, can be found as follows. From Fig. 8-1a and Eq. (8-16), the angle β for ridge tangency at the inscribed spherical surface is

$$\beta = \arctan(h/R)$$
$$= \arctan(0.324919696)$$
$$= 18° \qquad (8\text{-}20)$$

A similar surprisingly simple result for the angle β_v in the case of the valley tangency at the inscribed spherical surface is obtained from Fig. 8-1b and Eq. (8-18).

$$\beta_v = \arctan(h_v/a_1 R)$$
$$= \arctan(1.376381921)$$
$$= 54° \qquad (8\text{-}21)$$

Consider now the area of the triangle formed by the altitude, the radius R, and the ridge in Fig. 8-1a for the case of the inscribed sphere of radius $l_1 \cos 36°$. The area of this triangle is

$$A_r = \frac{1}{2} h R, \qquad (8\text{-}22)$$

where h is given by Eq. (8-16). Next, for the valley tangency at the inscribed spherical surface of radius $l_1 \cos 36°$, the area of the triangle formed by the altitude, the base segment l_1. and the valley line in Fig. 8-1b is

$$A_v = \frac{1}{2} h_v l_1$$
$$\equiv \frac{1}{2} h_v a_1 R. \qquad (8\text{-}23)$$

From Eqs. (8-16) and (8-18) the ratio of the areas of the two triangles, for ridge tangency and valley tangency in Eqs. (8-23) and (8-22), is found to be just equal to the golden ratio:

$$\frac{A_r}{A_v} = \phi \qquad (8\text{-}24)$$

8-3. Two right circular cones related uniquely to the tangencies of the inscribed sphere in 8-2

An interesting relation can be found between two right circular cones, one with altitude equal to the radius of the star and the other with altitude equal to the segment l_1 in the base plane of the star. For the cones under consideration, their circular bases have radii given by h and h_v in Eqs. (8-16) and (8-18). Consider the plane perpendicular to the base plane, passing through the center O, and perpendicular to the radius R. The circle with radius equal to the altitude h, in this plane, forms a right circular cone of altitude R, with two ridge lines lying in the conical surface. The volume of this cone is

$$V_{rc} = \frac{1}{3}\pi h^2 R, \qquad (8\text{-}25)$$

where the altitude h under consideration is that in Eq. (8-16) for the ridge lines tangent to the inscribed sphere of radius $l_1 \cos 36°$. Now, the circle of radius h_v, in Eq. (8-18), in the plane perpendicular to the base plane through O oriented perpendicular to the segment of length l_1, forms the base of a right circular cone having altitude l_1 with two valleys lying in its conical surface. The volume of this cone is

$$V_{vc} = \frac{1}{3}\pi h_v^2 l_1. \qquad (8\text{-}26)$$

Knowing that $l_1 = a_1 R$ with a_1 given in Eq. (4-6), we obtain from Eqs. (8-25) and (8-26) the relation

$$\frac{V_{rc}}{V_{vc}} = \frac{h^2}{h_v^2 a_1}, \qquad (8\text{-}27)$$

and substituting the value for a_1 and the values for h and h_v from Eqs. (8-16) and (8-18) gives the following unexpected result.

$$V_{rc} = V_{vc}. \qquad (8\text{-}28)$$

The two cones are represented in the sketch of Fig. 8-4. So, for an inscribed sphere of radius $l_1 \cos 36°$, the right circular cone with altitude R and base circular radius equal to the star altitude for ridge-line tangency is equal in volume to the right circular cone with altitude l_1 having circular base radius equal to the star altitude for tangency on the valley lines.

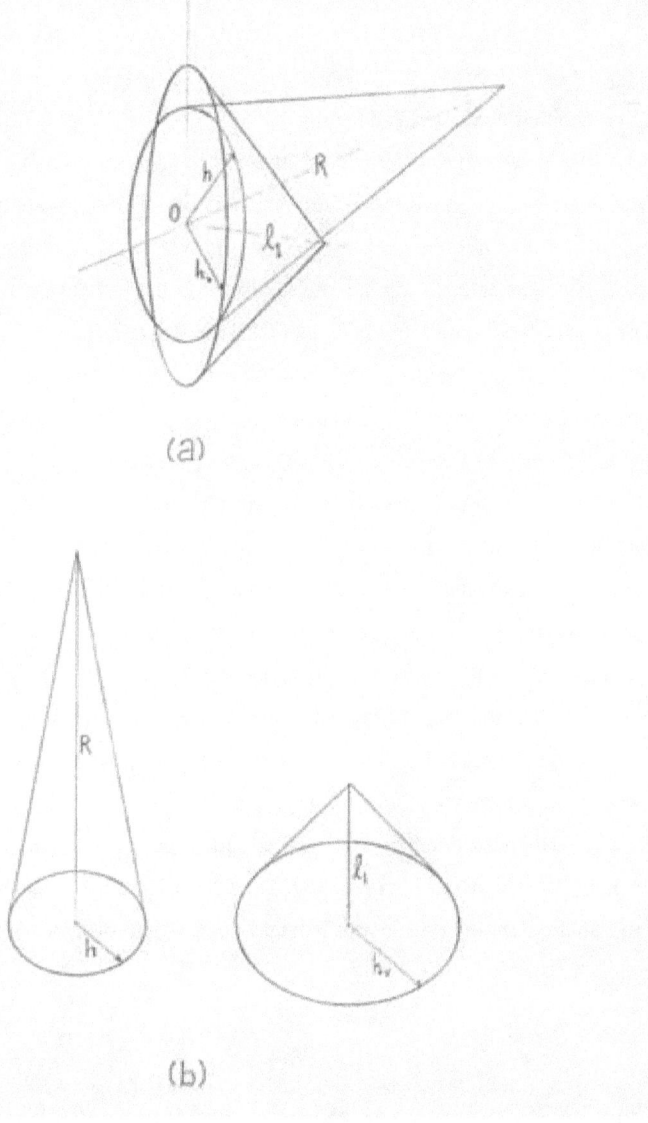

Fig. 8-4. (a) Two right circular cones with bases having common center O of base star of radius R. One cone has altitude R, base radius equal altitude h of three-dimensional star. The other cone has altitude l_1, inclined 36° to the first, and base radius h_v. In (b) the two cones are shown separately.

CHAPTER 9
FIVE-POINT STARS WITH VARIABLE TIP ANGLES

9-1. Star geometry with variable tip angle

To review briefly, the standard five-point mathematical star [5, 2] we have dealt with to this point is formed by constructing a circle of desired radius R, laying off five points on the circumference, each separated by 72° from an adjacent point, and then constructing straight lines joining each point with the second point from it. This was described earlier in relation to Fig. 2-1 of Chapter 2. As a result of this construction, each chordal line makes an angle of 18° with the radius at the point where they meet on the circumference. Suppose, instead, that we construct a five-point plane star on a circle of radius R by laying off five points on the circumference, each at 72° from an adjacent point, but then construct straight lines through each circumferential point at a desired angle φ relative to the radius at that point. This construction is shown in Fig. 9-1. The two lines from adjacent points meet at a point designated by B in the figure. A comparison of the shape of this star with the standard star is shown in Fig. 9-2. When the chosen angle φ is greater than 18°, we have what we may call a "thick" star as in Fig. 9-2a, while an angle φ < 18° results in a "thin" star of Fig. 9/2c. The standard star is shown in Fig. 9-2b.

Referring again to Fig. 9-1 we see, because of symmetry, that there are ten identical line segments like the one joining point P_1 to point B, and let the length P_1B be designated by L_2. Likewise, from symmetry there are ten line segments like the one joining the center O to point B, designated by L_1 in Fig. 9-1. We have chosen uppercase L_1 and L_2 to distinguish them from the analogous lengths l_1 and l_2 used earlier in the standard star. From the triangle OP_1B we can write

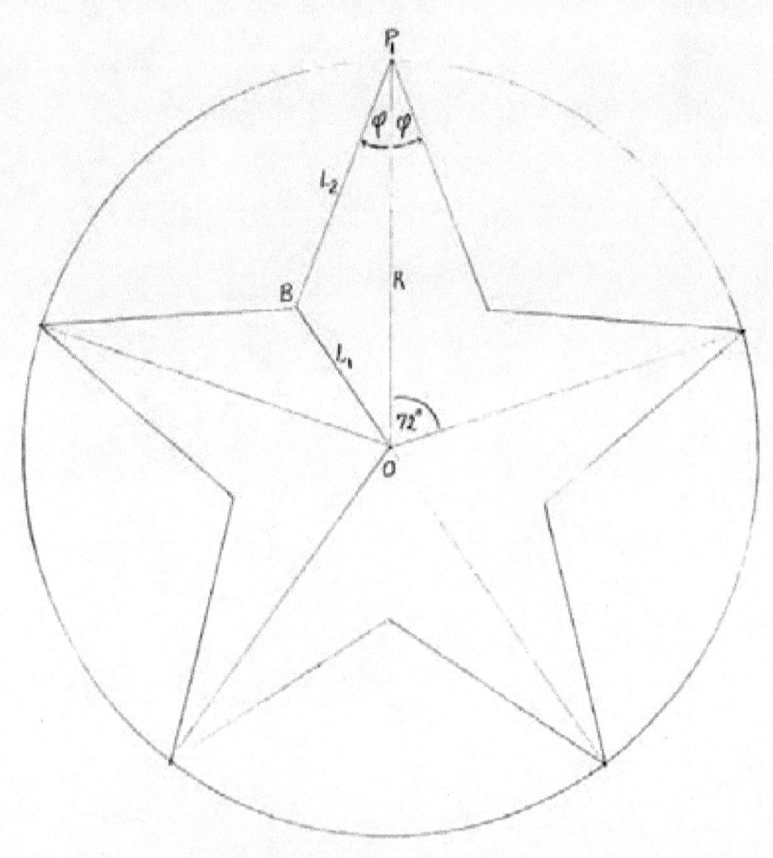

Fig. 9-1. A five-point star of radius R with variable tip angle φ.

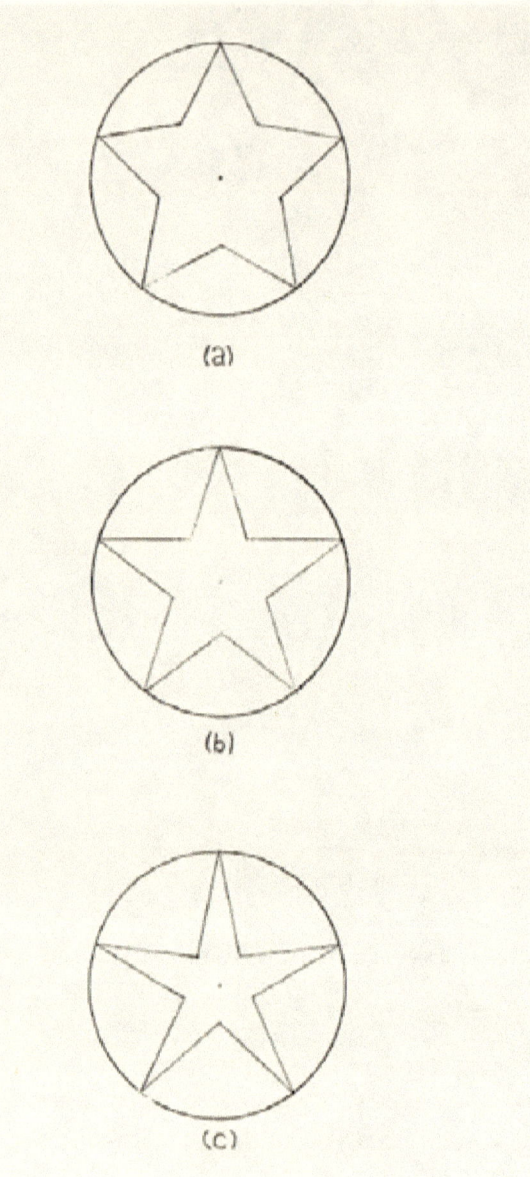

Fig. 9-2. When φ = 18° in Fig. 9-1 the [5, 2] star in (b) is obtained. In (a) φ > 18° and in (c) φ < 18°.

$$L_1 \sin 36° = L_2 \sin \varphi, \tag{9-1}$$

and applying the law of sines gives

$$\frac{R}{\sin[\pi-(\varphi+36°)]} = \frac{L_2}{\sin 36°}. \tag{9-2}$$

Using the fact that $\sin(\pi - z) = \sin z$, the latter two relations can be solved for L_1 and L_2 and written as follows.

$$L_1 = R\frac{\sin \varphi}{\sin(\varphi+36°)}$$

$$L_2 = R\frac{\sin 36°}{\sin(\varphi+36°)} \tag{9-3}$$

If numerical quantities A_1 and A_2 are defined, the relations in Eq. (9-3) can be written as

$$L_1 = A_1 R$$

$$L_2 = A_2 R \tag{9-4}$$

where A_1 and A_2 are defined in terms of the angles

$$A_1 = \frac{\sin \varphi}{\sin(\varphi+36°)} \qquad A_2 = \frac{\sin 36°}{\sin(\varphi+36°)} \tag{9-5}$$

The relations in Eqs. (9-3) – (9-5) for the plane star characterized by angle φ in Fig. 9-1 are analogous to those for the standard star in Eqs. (4-3) – (4-6) of Chapter 4. If the angle φ is set equal to 18°, then Eqs. (9-3) – (9-5) reduce to the corresponding relations in Chapter 4. Fig. 9-3 provides a plot of the lengths of sides L_1 and L_2 in relation to the star radius R, as a function of the angle φ, based on Eqs. (9-5). The maximum angle that φ can have is 54° because, as is obvious from Fig. 9-1, the star figure degenerates into a pentagon.

9-2. Three-dimensional star of altitude h formed on base star with tip angle φ, surface area

To form a three-dimensional star on the base plane star of radius R in Fig. 9-1, let us erect a perpendicular of length h called the altitude, passing through the center of the star. Next, straight lines called "ridges" are drawn connecting the altitude with each tip of the star at radius R. Then, the altitude is connected with straight lines called "valleys" to each point such as B in the plane of the star. There are thus five ridges and five valleys on each side of the base plane and so the distance from apex to apex through the symmetry plane at O is $2h$. One of these three-dimensional elements is shown in Fig. 9-4. The triangle OP_1B is in the plane of the base star, and the tilted triangle $O'BP_1$ is one of twenty identical triangular facets that comprise the surface area of the three-dimensional star, symmetric at altitude h either side of the base plane. We can find the angle θ between the ridge $O'P_1$ and the segment L_2 in the base plane by applying the law of cosines to the triangular facet, noting that the side $O'B = (h^2 + L^2_1)^{1/2}$ is opposite the angle θ. From this we get the following expression, realizing that the length of the ridge $O'P_1$ is $(h^2 + R^2)^{1/2}$.

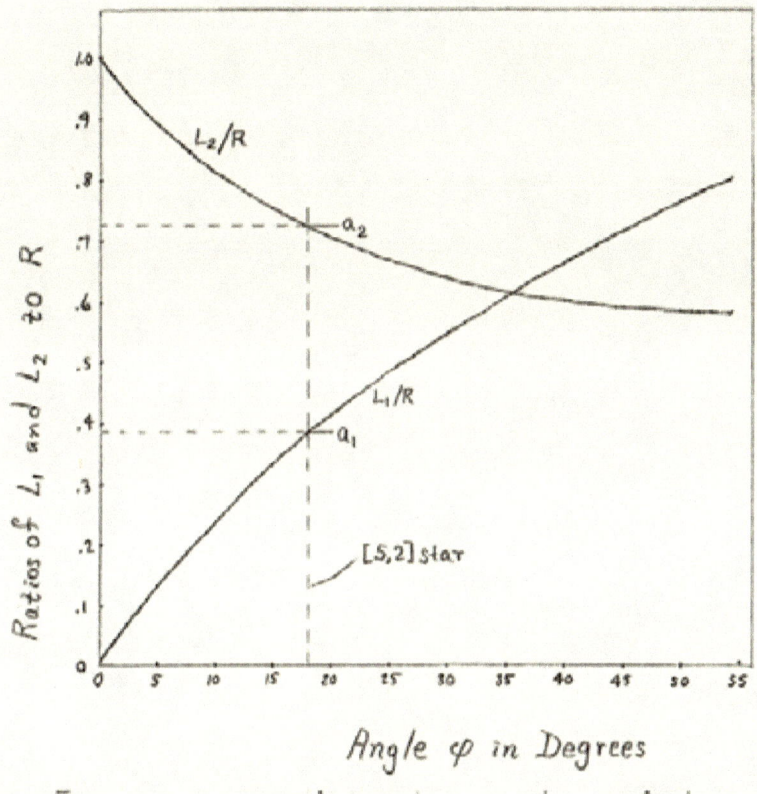

Fig. 9-3. Ratio of lengths L_1 and L_2 of the star in Fig. 9-1, to its radius, versus the tip angle φ. When φ = 18° the ratios are simply a_1 and a_2 of Chapter 4.

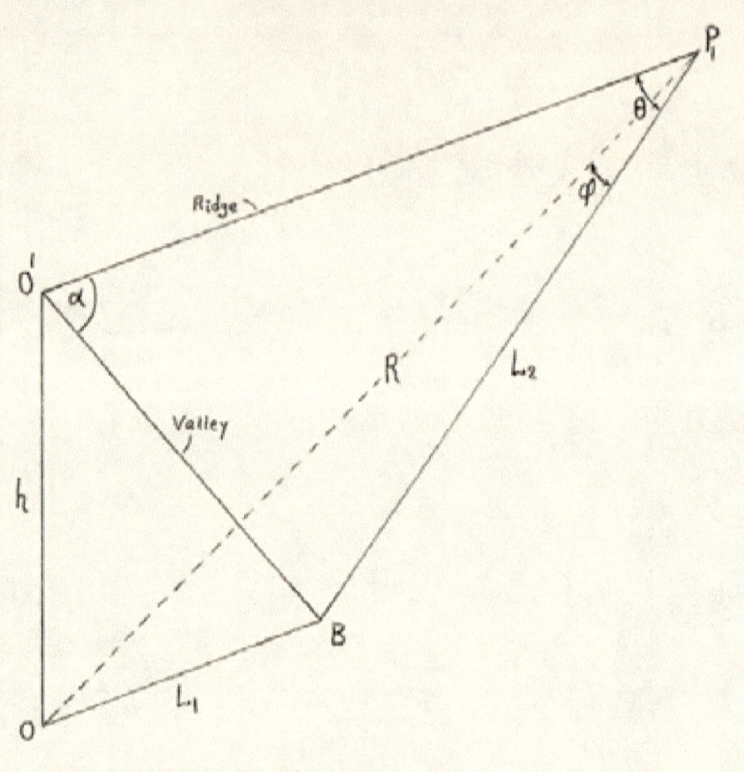

Fig. 9-4. One of ten identical pyramidal volume elements when a three-dimensional star of altitude h is constructed on one side of the five-point base plane star of radius R and tip angle φ.

$$\theta = \arccos\left(\frac{R^2 + L_2^2 - L_1^2}{2L_2\sqrt{h^2 + R^2}}\right) \qquad (9\text{-}6)$$

For a given angle φ, the lengths L_1 and L_2 are related to R through Eqs. (9-4) and (9-5), which allows the expression for angle θ to be put in the form

$$\theta = \arccos\left(\frac{1 + A_2^2 - A_1^2}{2A_2\sqrt{1 + (h/R)^2}}\right). \qquad (9\text{-}7)$$

Of course, A_1 and A_2 in Eq. (9-5) are functions of the angle φ in the base plane star and therefore the angle θ in Eq. (9-7) is also a function of φ, as well as h and R. The total surface area of the three-dimensional star is twenty times the area of one triangular facet $O'BP_1$, and therefore

$$A_\varphi = 20\left(\frac{1}{2}\right)\sqrt{R^2 + h^2}\, L_2 \sin\theta$$

$$= 10\, A_2 R^2 \sqrt{1 + (h/R)^2}\, \sin\theta, \qquad (9\text{-}8)$$

where the subscript "φ" emphasizes that the area is a function of the base plane star angle φ, as well as h and R. The angle θ can be eliminated between Eqs. (9-7) and (9-8), allowing A_φ, after some manipulative steps, to be expressed in the form

$$A_\varphi = 5R^2 \sqrt{4A_2^2\left(1 + \frac{h^2}{R^2}\right) - \left(1 + A_2^2 - A_1^2\right)^2}. \qquad (9\text{-}9)$$

The surface area of the star characterized by angle φ in Eq. (9-9) can be compared with that of the standard star derived earlier in Eq. (7-4) of Chapter 7 by evaluating the quotient A_φ/A_s, and this takes the form

$$\frac{A_\varphi}{A_s} = \left[\frac{4A_2^2(1 + h^2/R^2) - (1 + A_2^2 - A_1^2)^2}{4a_2^2(1 + h^2/R^2) - (1 + a_2^2 - a_1^2)^2}\right]^{\frac{1}{2}}. \qquad (9\text{-}10)$$

Remember that a_1 and a_2 for the standard star are constant numerical values from Eq. (4-6) of Chapter 4, whereas A_1 and A_2 are functions of the angle φ from Eq. (9-5). A plot of A_φ/A_s

calculated from Eq. (9-10) as a function of the angle φ in Fig. 9-1, for various ratios of altitude h to radius R, is given in Fig. 9-5. The value of $A_φ/A_s$ is unity for all values of h/R when the angle φ = 18°, because for this value of φ, the three-dimensional star shape is identical to the standard star shape. Note the shapes of the curves in Fig. 9-5. For $h/R > 1$ the area ratio is greater than unity for φ < 18°, and less than unity for φ > 18°. When $h/R = ½$, $A_φ/A_s > 1$ for small values of φ but decreases below unity for φ slightly less than 18°, but increases steadily above unity for φ > 18°. For $h/R ≥ ¼$ the value of $A_φ/A_s < 1$ for φ < 18°, but $A_φ/A_s ≥ 1$ for φ > 18°. The curves for small h/R, in particular those for $h/R = 0.1$ and 0.05, show evidence of an inflection point at φ = 18°, because the rate of increase of $A_φ/A_s$ over the range 0 < φ ≤ 18° is greater than the rate for φ > 18°.

As the angle φ in Fig. 9-1 becomes smaller, the plane star becomes thinner and in the limit φ = 0 the thin star degenerates to five lines. What happens to the surface area of the three-dimensional star built on the base star of Fig. 9-1 as φ becomes zero, compared to the area of the standard three-dimensional star, i.e., φ ≡ 18°? One insight can be obtained by asking what value

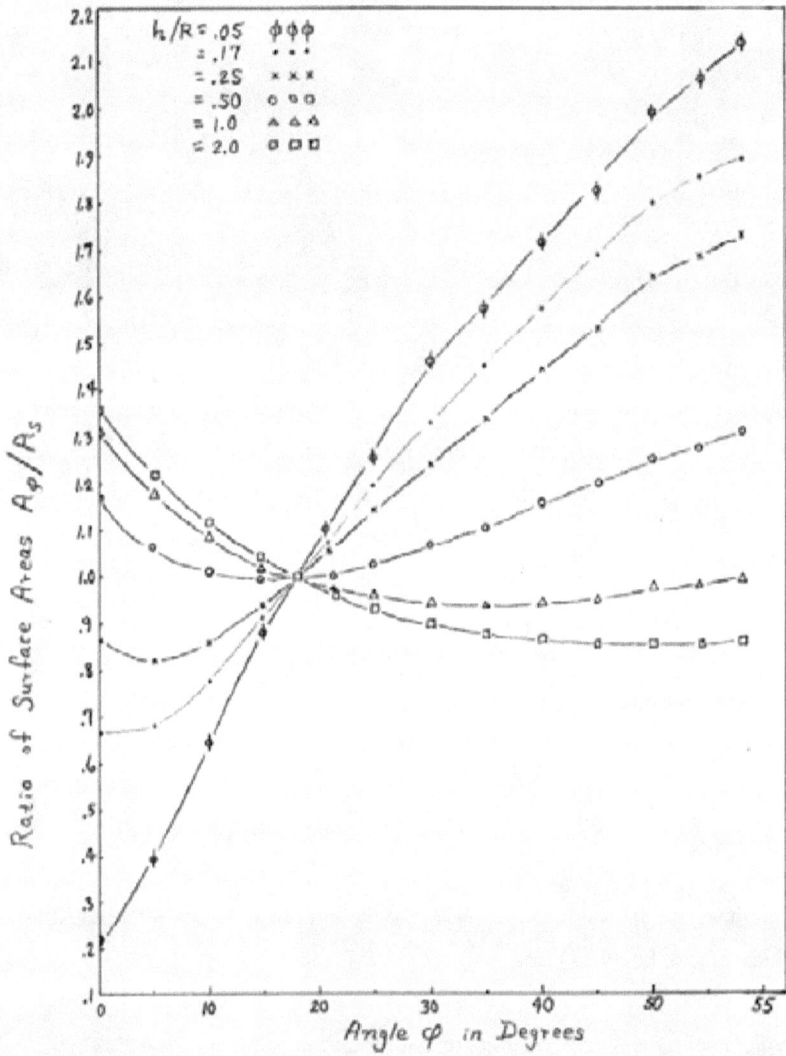

Fig. 9-5. Comparison of surface area A_φ of star formed on base star of tip angle φ to that formed on [5, 2] base star, versus angle φ, for various ratios of star altitude h to radius R.

of h/R will result in the two stars having equal surface area for $\varphi = 0$. To answer this, we set $A_\varphi = A_s$ in Eq. (9-10), square both sides and solve for the ratio of altitude h to radius R. Doing this gives

$$\left(\frac{A_\varphi}{A_s}\right)_{\varphi=0} = 1 \quad \Rightarrow \quad \frac{h}{R} = 0.326745687. \tag{9-11}$$

As a check, if we substitute the latter value into Eq. (9-9), along with $\varphi = 0$, we get

$$A_\varphi = 3.26745687\, R^2 \tag{9-12}$$

which agrees with the value of A_s at this value of h/R for the standard three-dimensional star in Fig. 7-2 of Chapter 7, and of course, with the value of A_s calculated from Eq. (7-4).

As pointed out earlier, the other limiting case for the plane star characterized by angle φ in Fig. 9-1 is when $\varphi = 54°$, because for this angle, the plane star degenerates to a regular pentagon. It is interesting to determine the ratio of altitude to radius for which the surface area A_φ equals the area A_s for the degenerate case of the base star becoming a pentagon. To this end we set $A_\varphi = A_s$ in Eq. (9-10), along with $\varphi = 54°$ in the expressions for A_1 and A_2, and then solve for h/R. The result is

$$\left(\frac{A_\varphi}{A_s}\right)_{\varphi=54°} = 1 \quad \Rightarrow \quad \frac{h}{R} = 0.981593348. \tag{9-13}$$

On a curious note, the value in Eq. (9-13) for the limiting case $\varphi = 54°$ is equal to three times the value in Eq. (9-11) for $\varphi = 0°$, to within 0.138%.

9-3. Volume of three-dimensional star on base star of tip angle φ

The volume of the three-dimensional star constructed on the plane star base characterized by angle φ in Fig. 9-1 can be determined by referring again to Fig. 9-4. The volumetric element is the pyramidal element $OO'P_1B$, with altitude h and base triangle OP_1B. The area of the base triangle is $½\, R\, L_2 \sin \varphi$. Now, the volume of the element $OO'P_1B$ is one-third the area of this base triangle times the altitude h. There are twenty identical elements like $OO'P_1B$ in the three-dimensional star figure symmetric on both sides of the base plane star, and therefore the volume of the star figure is

$$V_\varphi = \frac{10}{3} hRL_2 \sin\varphi, \qquad (9\text{-}14)$$

and from Eqs. (9-4) and (9-5), we can write this as

$$V_\varphi = \frac{10}{3} R^3 \left(\frac{h}{R}\right) \frac{\sin\varphi \sin 36°}{\sin(\varphi+36°)} \qquad (9\text{-}15)$$

So, the volume is proportional to the cube of the base star radius and the ratio of altitude to radius, as well as the angle factor $\sin\varphi / \sin(\varphi + 36°)$ involving the angle φ defining the base star geometry. Notice that for the special case $\varphi = 18°$, the latter reduces to the volume for the standard star in Eq. (7-6) of Chapter 7. The volume V_φ can be compared to the volume of the standard star, V_s, in Eq. (7-6) by dividing Eq. (9-15) by V_s to give

$$\frac{V_\varphi}{V_s} = \frac{\sin 54° \sin\varphi}{\sin 18° \sin(\varphi+36°)}, \qquad (9\text{-}16)$$

where the defining relation was used from Eqs. (4-4) – (4-5) for a_2 in Eq. (7-6). The comparison of volumes is displayed graphically in Fig. 9-6 as a function of the angle φ over its range from 0° to 54°.

9-4. Foldability of three-dimensional star on base star with tip angle φ

Earlier in Chapter 5, it was shown that a starlike figure could be constructed on a plane piece of paper, which could be folded alternately convex and concave to produce a three-dimensional star figure with the boundary of the original figure lying in the base plane and conforming to a standard mathematical star. According to Eq. (5-11), this operation of foldability was possible only for the unique relationship between star radius R and altitude in terms of the golden ratio, i.e., $R = h\phi$. So, given a base plane star characterized by a desired angle $\varphi \neq 18°$ as in Fig. 9-1, is it possible to construct a plane starlike figure that can be folded alternately convex and concave to provide a three-dimensional star shape with a plane base perimeter conforming exactly to the original star with angle φ? To find an answer to this question, we proceed with an analysis similar to that used in Chapter 5 in the case of the standard mathematical star. Consider the star characterized by angle φ at each tip such as point P_1 in Fig. 9-7. There are of course five points such as P_1 located symmetrically on the circle of radius R. The lines at angle φ with respect to the radius intersect at each of five inward points such as B, at distance L_1 from the center at O. L_2 denotes the length of each of the ten segments such as P_1B. Now, the starlike figure to be folded is constructed with circle at the same center O but with a radius greater than R so that its five tips such as P_1' lie farther from the center than P_1 and, likewise, its inward points such as B_1 lie at a greater distance than L_1 from the center O. The starlike figure to be folded has five ridge lines like OP_1' and five valley lines like OB_1. The intent is to fold it in convex fashion with the triangular facets like $OP_1'B_1$ bent downward from the reader about each ridge line OP_1', while at the same time folding it in concave fashion with each triangular facet bent upward about a valley line such as OB_1. Thus, when the center point O rises above the plane of Fig. 9-7 to altitude h, each tip point like P_1' will move inward to coincide with P_1, and each point like B_1 will move inward to coincide with corresponding point B. This means that the length $P_1'B_1$ in the foldable figure must be identical in length to P_1B, i.e., exactly equal to L_2, and it is labeled as such. Now, in Fig. 9-8a is shown a plane perpendicular to the plane of Fig. 9-7, containing the altitude h and radius R; the plane of Fig. 9-8b, also perpendicular to plane of Fig. 9-7, contains the altitude and base segment L_1. So, with convex folding about OP_1' and concave folding about OB_1, point P_1' moves in to point P_1 in Fig. 9-8a and point B_1 in Fig. 9-8b moves in to point B. The line OP_1' becomes a ridge in the three-dimensional figure of altitude h, and from Fig. 9-8a the ridge length is

$$OP_1' = \sqrt{h^2 + R^2}, \qquad (9\text{-}17)$$

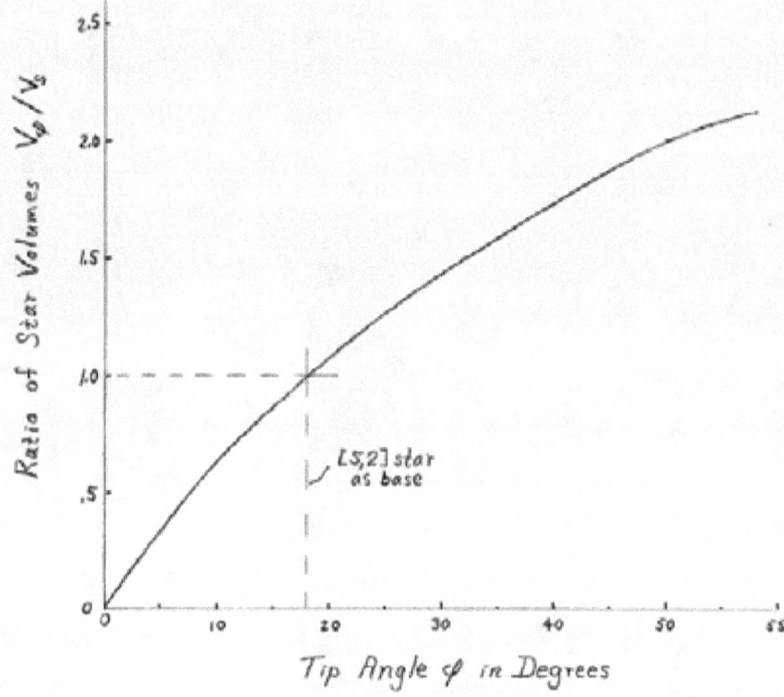

Fig. 9-6. Volume of three-dimensional star constructed on base star of tip angle φ, compared to volume on [5, 2] base star, versus tip angle φ.

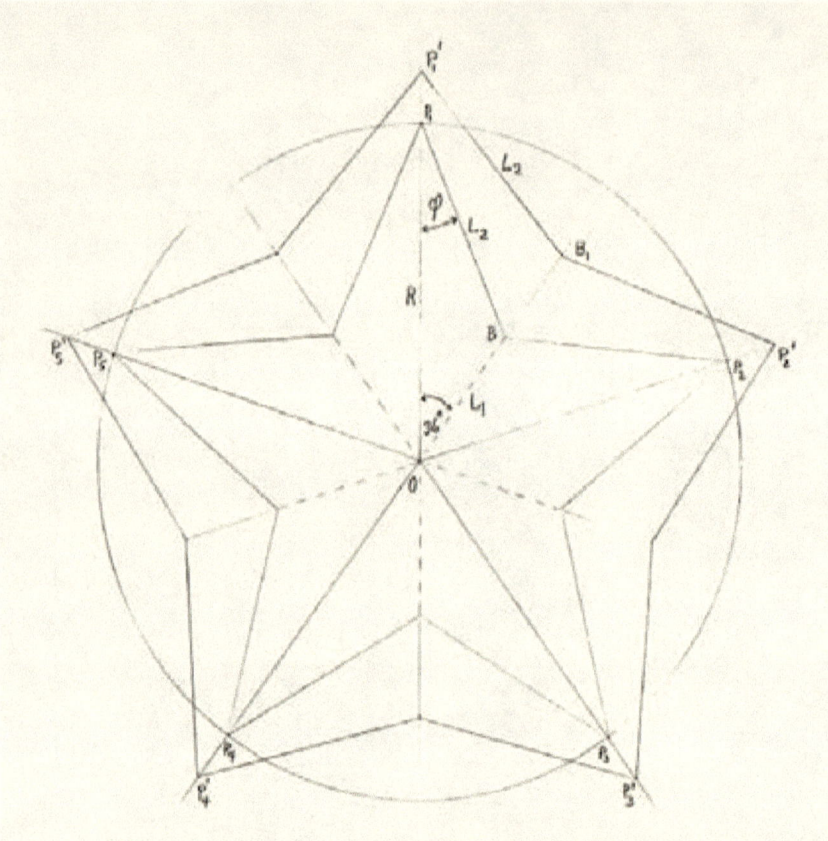

Fig. 9-7. Geometry used to investigate the conditions under which the star $P_1', \ldots P_5'$ can be folded to altitude h above point O, whereupon P_1', P_2', P_3', P_4', P_5' move inward to coincide with P_1, P_2, P_3, P_4, P_5, respectively, in the plane of the page.

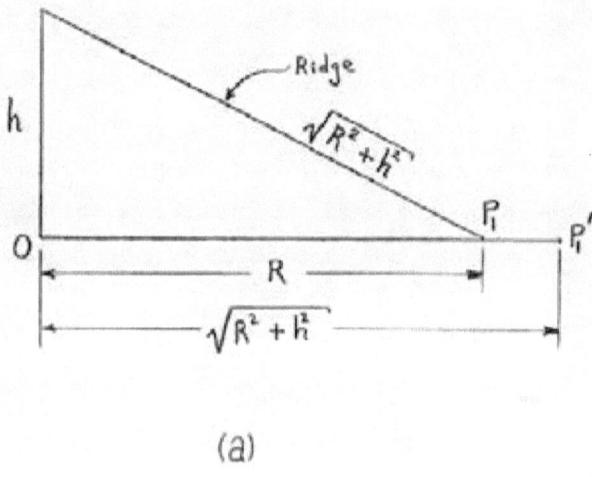

(a)

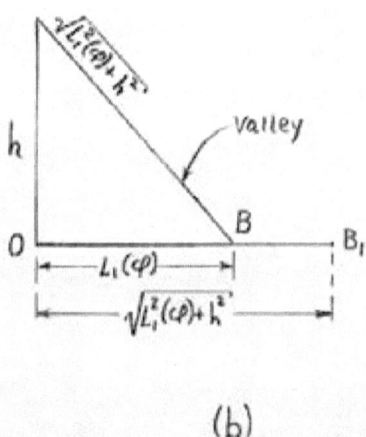

(b)

Fig. 9-8. After folding the $P_1'\ldots P_5'$ star in Fig. 9-7, (a) shows a plane perpendicular to the base star containing the altitude and a ridge, while (b) shows a plane perpendicular to the base star that contains the altitude and a valley.

while at the same time the line OB_1 becomes a valley, and from Fig. 9-8b the valley length is

$$OB_1 = \sqrt{h^2 + L_1^2}. \tag{9-18}$$

The two triangles OP_1B and $OP_1'B_1$ in Fig. 9-7 have the angle 36° in common and also the side opposite this angle has length L_2 in both triangles. Using Eqs. (9-17) and (9-18), along with the relations in Eq. (9-4), we consider the common angle, with side opposite, and apply the law of cosines to triangles OP_1B and $OP_1'B_1$ of Fig. 9-7 to obtain the following two equations, respectively.

$$A_1 \cos 36° = \frac{1}{2}\left(1 + A_1^2 - A_2^2\right) \tag{9-19}$$

$$A_2^2 = 1 + A_1^2 + 2(h/R)^2 - 2\sqrt{1 + (h/R)^2}\sqrt{A_1^2 + (h/R)^2} \cos 36° \tag{9-20}$$

If we move the radicals alone to one side in Eq. (9-20), and square both sides of the equation to remove them, and then combine the result with Eq. (9-19), we find after straightforward but lengthy manipulation that the ratio of altitude h to radius R for which the starlike figure in Fig. 9-7 can be folded as described above is

$$\frac{h}{R} = \sqrt{\frac{A_2^2}{\sin^2 36°} - 1 - A_1^2}. \tag{9-21}$$

The latter can be expressed explicitly in terms of the angle φ in Fig. 9-7 by substituting for A_1 and A_2 from Eq. (9-5) to give

$$\frac{h}{R} = \frac{\sqrt{1 - \sin^2 \varphi - \sin^2(\varphi + 36°)}}{\sin(\varphi + 36°)}. \tag{9-22}$$

Let θ' be the angle between the side L_2 and the ridge OP_1' in the triangular facet of the foldable starlike figure in Fig. 9-7. The angle θ', of course, is a function of the angle φ and θ' can be found using the law of sines applied to triangle $OP_1'B_1$ to give

$$\sin \theta' = \frac{\sqrt{L_1^2 + h^2}}{L_2} \sin 36°. \tag{9-23}$$

Using Eqs. (9-4) and (9-5), the latter can be expressed as

$$\theta' = \arcsin \sqrt{\sin^2 \varphi + (h/R)^2 \sin^2(\varphi + 36°)}. \tag{9-24}$$

Now, realizing that h/R obeys Eq. (9-22) for the case of foldability, we can for this case substitute from Eq. (9-22) and get the following simple relation.

$$\theta' = \arcsin [\cos (\varphi + 36°)] \tag{9-25}$$

As an example, suppose that we choose a base star with angle $\varphi = 25°$ in Fig. 9-7, and choose a radius $R = 3$ in. For foldability, according to Eq. (9-22), the ratio of altitude h to radius R must be $h/R = 0.271614$, and therefore the altitude must be $h = 0.814842$ in. This means that the ridge length in Figs. 9-7 and 9-8a must be $OP_1' = \sqrt{h^2 + R^2} = 3.108692$ in., from Eq. (9-17), and according to Eq. (9-18), the valley length is $OB_1 = \sqrt{h^2 + L_1^2} \equiv \sqrt{h^2 + A_1^2 R^2} = 1.662927$ in., where A_1 was calculated from Eq. (9-5) with φ set equal to 25°. From Eq. (9-25) the corresponding angle θ' in the triangular facet of the folded structure is $\theta' = 29.0°$.

9-5. Limiting relationships associated with foldability

Suppose we choose a base plane star in Fig. 9-7 characterized by angle $\varphi = 30°$. However, substitution of $\varphi = 30°$ into Eq. (9-22) results in a negative quantity under the radical, meaning that the value of h/R is imaginary. Therefore, foldability cannot be achieved for $\varphi = 30°$. However, we know that a base plane star can be constructed for any angle φ up to 54° and that a three-dimensional structure of triangular facets can be constructed on their base with a desired altitude. It follows, then, that a maximum angle φ must exist for which foldability is possible, that is, for which the quantity under the radical in Eq. (9-22) is positive. The limiting value of φ is thus the angle for which the quantity under the radical is zero and if we call this angle φ_L, then we must have

$$\sin^2 \varphi_L + \sin^2 (\varphi_L + 36°) = 1. \qquad (9\text{-}26)$$

To solve for φ_L, we note that $1 - \sin^2 \varphi_L = \cos^2 \varphi_L$, and therefore using the identity for the sine of the sum of two angles Eq. (9-26) reduces to

$$(1 - \sin 36°) \cos \varphi_L = \sin \varphi_L \cos 36°,$$

from which we get

$$\varphi_L = \arctan \left(\frac{1 - \sin 36°}{\cos 36°} \right)$$

$$= 27°. \qquad (9\text{-}27)$$

This result is remarkable in the sense that the limiting angle is exactly equal to 27°, without nonzero decimal places. So, from a mathematical viewpoint, foldability is possible for all angles in the interval $\varphi = 0°$ to 27°.

We note that the limiting value of h/R in Eq. (9-22) for $\varphi = 27°$ is zero, that is,

$$\left(\frac{h}{R} \right)_{\varphi = \varphi_L} = 0. \qquad (9\text{-}28)$$

Now, we note a very curious relationship at the other limit when $\varphi = 0$, because in Eq. (9-22), we have

$$\left(\frac{h}{R} \right)_{\varphi=0} = \cot 36°$$

$$= 1.37638192. \qquad (9\text{-}29)$$

However, referring to Eqs. (4-5) and (4-6) of Chapter 4 for the standard mathematical star, i.e., with $\varphi = 18°$, we see that the result in Eq. (9-29) is just the reciprocal of l_2/R in the length relationship of side l_2 to the radius of the star. So,

$$\left(\frac{h}{R} \right)_{\varphi=0} = \frac{1}{\left(\frac{l_2}{R} \right)_{\varphi=18°}}, \qquad (9\text{-}30)$$

where the subscript φ = 18 refers to the standard star geometry. The curious aspect of Eq. (9-30) is that the limiting ratio of altitude to radius for foldability on a plane base star characterized by angle φ, when φ goes to zero, is just equal to the ratio of radius R to side l_2 in the standard plane mathematical star.

A plot of the ratio of altitude h to radius R for foldability on a base star of angle φ, versus the angle φ, is given in Fig. 9-9. These results were calculated from Eq. (9-22). Note the limiting value of h/R at φ = 0, reflecting the value arrived at in Eq. (9-29). Also, it can be seen that h/R approaches zero rapidly within a small angular interval as the limiting angle $φ_L$ = 27° is approached. When φ = 18°, the value of h/R = 0.618034 as seen in Fig. 9-9, and this is true

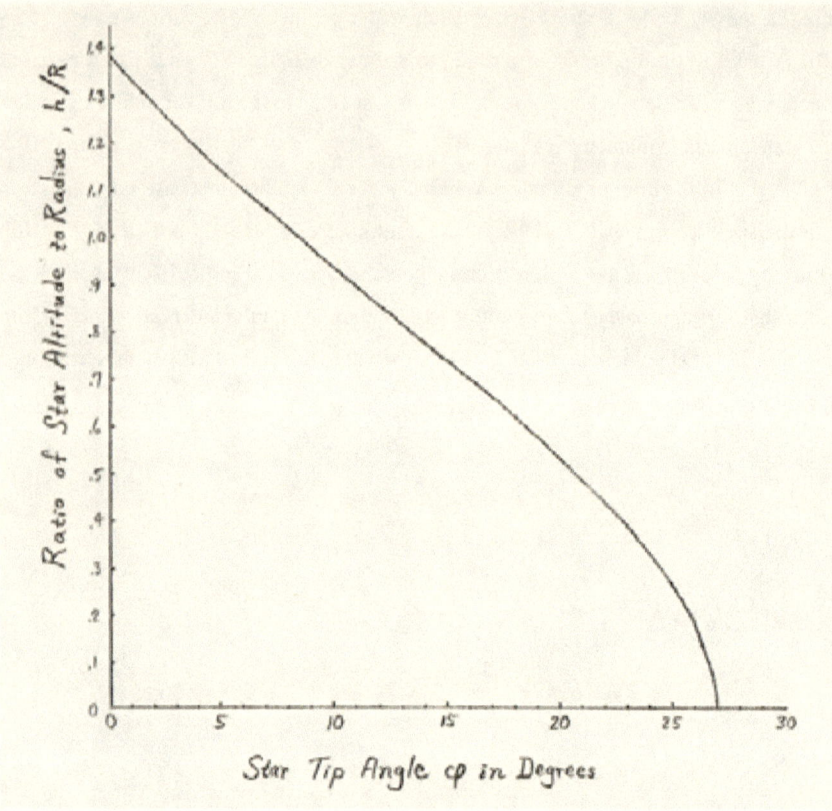

Fig. 9-9. Ratio of altitude h to base star radius R, versus base star tip angle φ, for which foldability of the star $P_1' \ldots P_5'$ in Fig. 9-7 is possible.

because the special case $\varphi = 18°$ is the standard star for which it was shown in Eq. (5-10) of Chapter 5 that foldability is possible there only when $h/R = 0.618034$.

According to Eq. (9-25), the angle θ' between a ridge and the line L_2 in the base decreases linearly from $\theta' = 54°$ at $\varphi = 0$ to $27°$ at $\varphi = 27°$. This at first seems unusual because sine and cosine functions have their familiar non-linear shapes. However, taking the derivative of the arc sine function in Eq. (9-25) shows that the slope of θ' is independent of φ.

$$\frac{d\theta'}{d\varphi} = -1 \qquad (9\text{-}31)$$

9-6. Angles in triangular facet of solid star on base star with tip angle φ.

Having investigated the conditions for foldability, we set that aside and return to Fig. 9-4 and examine the variation of the angles in a triangular facet as a function of altitude h when the three-dimensional star is constructed on the base plane star characterized by the angle φ. Earlier in Eq. (9-7), the angle θ between a ridge and the segment L_2 in the base was expressed in terms of the angle φ and h and R. Referring again to the triangular facet $O'P_1B$, we see that the law of sines makes it possible to determine the angle α between the ridge and valley through the relation

$$\frac{\sin \alpha}{L_2} = \frac{\sin \theta}{\sqrt{h^2 + L_1^2}}, \qquad (9\text{-}32)$$

and combining Eqs. (9-4) and (9-7) with the latter leads to the following.

$$\alpha = \arcsin\left[\frac{A_2}{\sqrt{A_1^2 + (h/R)^2}}\sqrt{1 - \frac{(1+A_2^2-A_1^2)^2}{4A_2^2\left(1+(h/R)^2\right)}}\right] \qquad (9\text{-}33)$$

So, for given values of h, R, and the angle φ, the two angles in a triangular facet are determined by Eqs. (9-7) and (9-33), and it follows that the third angle, i.e., the angle between the valley and the segment L_2, is merely $\pi-\theta-\alpha$. Now, for a given angle φ, it is seen from Eq. (9-7) that the angle θ between ridge and L_2 steadily decreases with increasing value of h/R. However, because h/R is present in two places in Eq. (9-33), the dependence of the angle α, between the ridge and valley, on h/R is more complicated. To examine the dependence of α on h/R, we first define a quantity A_{12} in terms of the quantities A_1 and A_2 as

$$A_{12} = \frac{1 + A_2^2 - A_1^2}{2A_2}, \tag{9-34}$$

and then re-write Eq. (9-33) in the form

$$\alpha = \arcsin \sqrt{\frac{(1 + h^2/R^2 - A_{12}^2)A_2^2}{(1 + h^2/R^2)(A_1^2 + h^2/R^2)}}. \tag{9-35}$$

To test for possible maxima or minima in the curve of α versus h/R, we calculate the first derivative, set it equal to zero, and solve for possible values of h/R that cause it to vanish. Letting W be the radical function in Eq. (9-35), the first derivative of the arc sin of W is

$$\frac{d\alpha}{dx} = \frac{xA_2^2}{\sqrt{1 - w^2}\,w} \left[\frac{(1 + x^2)(A_1^2 + x^2) - (1 + x^2 - A_{12}^2)(1 + 2x^2 + A_1^2)}{(1 + x^2)^2 (A_1^2 + x^2)^2} \right], \tag{9-36}$$

where $x \equiv h/R$. The first derivative will vanish provided the numerator inside the square brackets is equal to zero, and this will be true for

$$x \equiv \frac{h}{R} = \sqrt{u} \tag{9-37}$$

where u^2 satisfies the quadratic

$$u^2 + 2u(1 - A_{12}^2) + 1 - (1 + A_1^2)A_{12}^2 = 0. \tag{9-38}$$

The solution for u, and therefore $x \equiv h/R$, depends on the angle φ because A_{12} is defined in terms of A_1 and A_2, which in turn are dependent on φ through Eq. (9-5). So, Eqs. (9-5), (9-34), and (9-38) and (9-37) were used to calculate the ratio of altitude to radius, h/R, as a function of angle φ in the base star for which the angle α in the triangular facet of Fig. 9-4 is a maximum. The results are given in Fig. 9-10. For example, if we choose a base star in Fig. 9-1 with φ = 5°, then from Fig. 9-10, we see that $h/R = 0.304$ is the ratio of altitude to radius for which the angle α between a ridge and a valley is a maximum, while a choice of

$\varphi = 25°$, for example, leads to $h/R = 0.184$ for a maximum angle α in the triangular facet. Note from Fig. 9-10 that no value of h/R

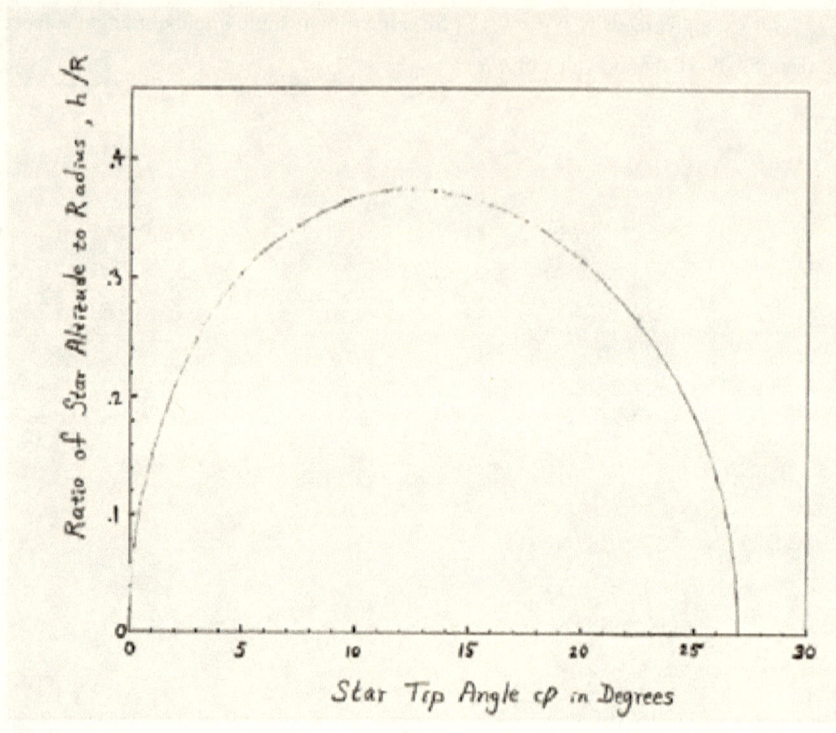

Fig. 9-10. Ratio of altitude h to base star radius R, versus base star tip angle φ, for which the angle α between a ridge and valley (Fig. 9-4) is a maximum.

exists for which the angle α has a maximum when the angle φ is equal to or greater than 27°. Also, from Fig. 9-10 it is seen that a given value of h/R corresponds to two values of the angle φ; for example, the value $h/R = 0.25$ will give a maximum for angle α when the base star angle φ = 3° is chosen, while the same value of h/R will cause α to be a maximum when φ = 23° is chosen. It is important to note, however, that the actual maximum value of α for φ = 3° is different from the maximum value when φ = 23°, as will be seen in the following.

Eq. (9-33) was used to calculate the angle α in the triangular facet as a function of h/R, for each of several different values of the angle φ in the base star. The results are provided in Fig. 9-11. For φ < 27°, each curve exhibits a maximum value of angle α at the corresponding value of h/R as predicted in the calculations leading to Fig. 9-10. For example, the curve labeled φ = 12.5° in Fig. 9-11 exhibits a maximum α = 42.223° at h/R = 0.368, which is the value of h/R for which α is predicted to be a maximum when φ = 12.5° in Fig. 9-10. Finally, it can be seen that the special case φ = 18° corresponds to the standard mathematical star dealt with in the previous chapters. When φ = 18°, the results in Figs. 9-10 and 9-11 are consistent with earlier results for the standard star. That is, the value of h/R for φ = 18° in Fig. 9-10 is 0.344, but this is the value obtained earlier in Eq. (4-23) of Chapter 4 for the standard star. The curve of α versus h/R in Fig. 4-7 of Chapter 4 for the standard star, if superimposed on Fig. 9-11, lies within the region between the two curves labeled φ = 12.5° and φ = 25°, as it should.

9-7. Examples of folded stars

A photograph of a folded star constructed on a star base with tip angle φ = 12° and radius $R = 3$ in. is shown in Fig. 9-12. For this case the ratio of h/R calculated from Eq. (9-22) is 0.8558 and the angle θ' in the triangular facets is 42°, calculated from Eq. (9-25). The length of

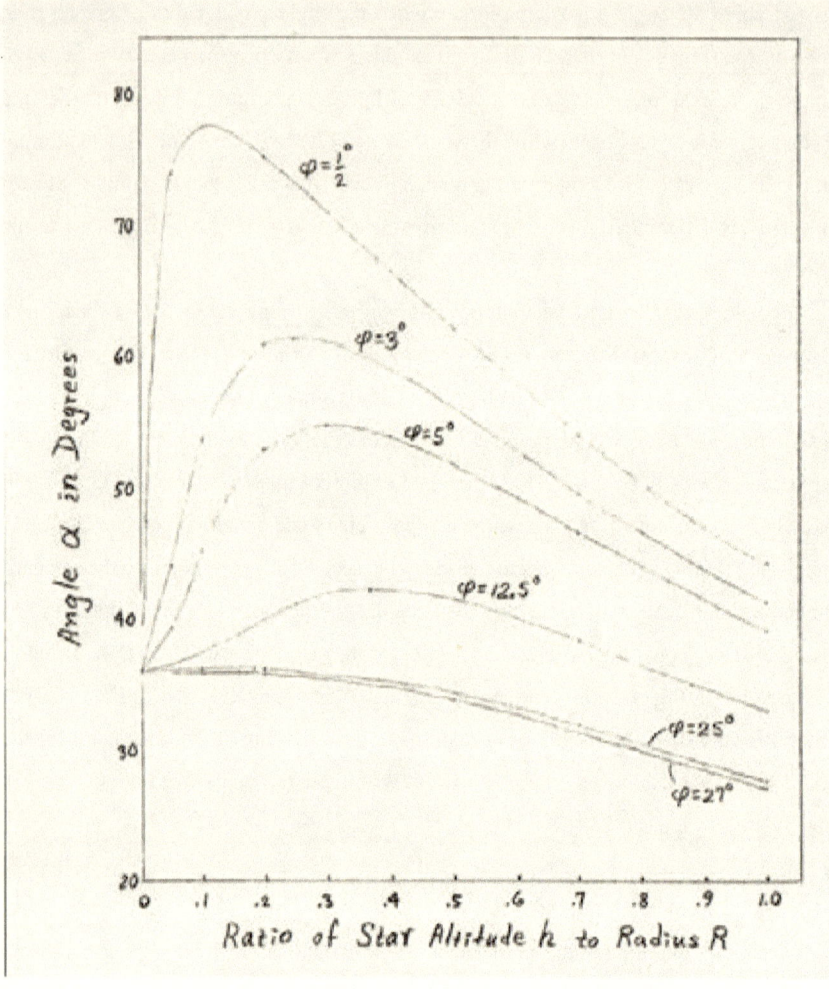

Fig. 9-11. Angle α between a ridge and a valley in a triangular facet, versus the ratio of altitude h to base star radius R, for each of several different tip angles φ in the base plane star.

a ridge line calculated from Eq. (9-17) is 3.9487 in. In section 9-4 above, just after Eq. (9-25), some details were given concerning the construction of a foldable star on a base star of radius $R = 3$ in., with tip angle $\varphi = 25°$.

Fig. 9-12. Examples of three-dimensional stars folded on five-point base star of radius $R=2$. Left: Tip angle $\varphi = 12°$, $h/R = .8558$. Right: $\varphi = 25°$, $h/R = .2716$.

CHAPTER 10
N-POINT STARS

10-1. Geometry and surface area of N-point stars

All the plane star figures dealt with in previous chapters have been the five-point type. As explained earlier, the mathematical five-point star is also known as the pentagram and often denoted by the symbol [5,2] meaning that each of five equally spaced points on a circle is connected by a straight line to the second point from it on the circle, thus forming the star figure. In this standard figure, each external line of the star makes an angle 18° or $\pi/10$ radian with the radius drawn from the circle center to the tip. In Chapter 9, we considered five-point stars in which the angle between the radius and an external line in the star could be less than or greater than $\pi/10$. In all these five-point stars, the angle subtended between two radii joining two adjacent tips was $2\pi/5$ radians, or 72°.

Consider now a higher-order star with N points formed by joining each point on the circle with its second nearest neighbor. Following notation referred to above, this is represented by [N,2]. In the case of $N = 6$, shown in Fig. 10-1a, the angle between the radii joining the center with two adjacent tips is $2\pi/6$ or 60°, while the seven-point star with $N = 7$ in Fig. 10-1b has a corresponding angle $2\pi/7 \cong 51.42857°$.

For the N-point star in which each tip is formed by the intersecting lines that connect each point on the circle to its second nearest-neighbor point, the relationships among the angles and sides can be understood with reference to Fig. 10-2. The circle of radius R with center at point O contains N equally spaced points P_j where j = 1, 2, ... N. Therefore, the angle subtended at the center by the two adjacent points P_j and P_{j+1}, is $2\pi/N$. The triangle OP_jP_{j+1} is isosceles and as a

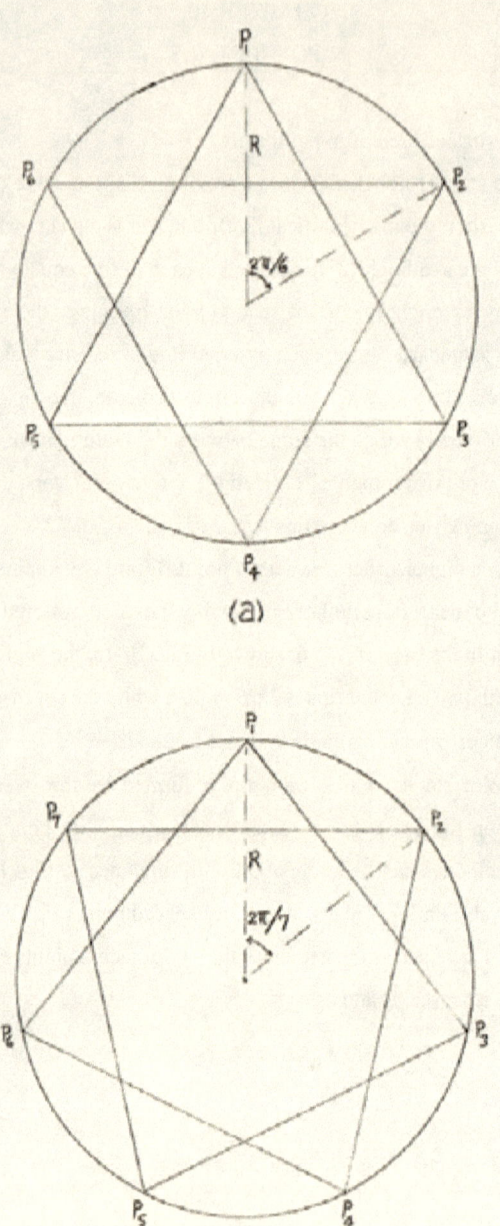

Fig. 10-1. (a) A [6, 2] star and (b) a [7,2] star.

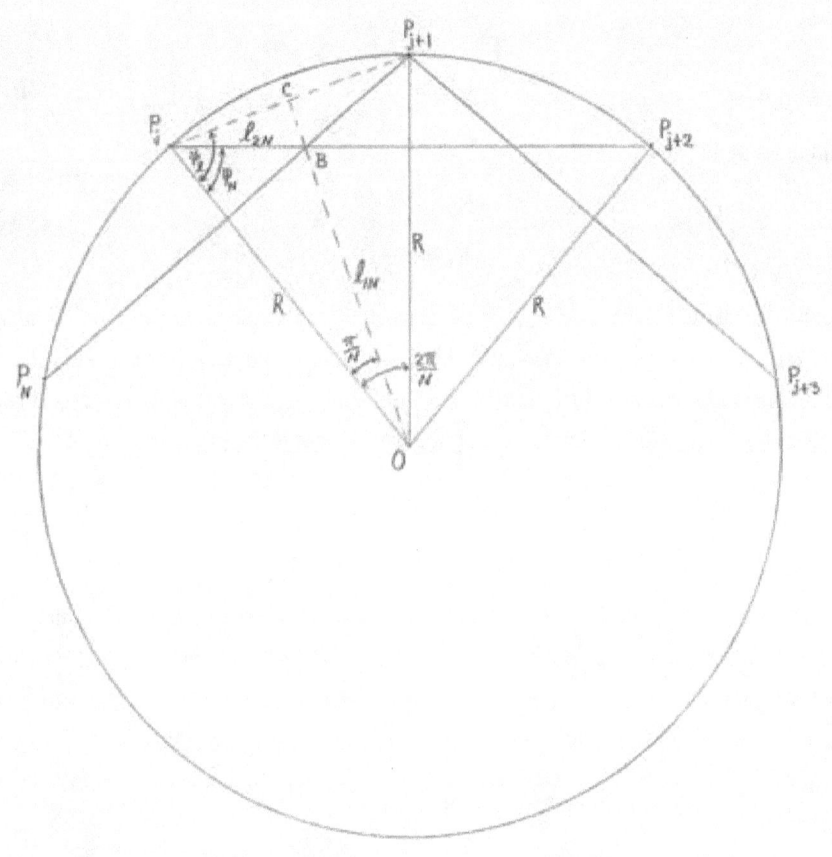

Fig. 10-2. Geometry of the [N, 2] star.

result the line *OBC* drawn perpendicular to the base P_jP_{j+1} bisects the angle P_jOP_{j+1}, which means that

$$\angle P_jOC = \frac{\pi}{N}, \qquad (10\text{-}1)$$

and in the right triangle P_jCO, the angle OP_jC, which we shall designate as ψ_I, is

$$\psi_I = \frac{\pi}{2} - \frac{\pi}{N}. \qquad (10\text{-}2)$$

Each chordal line, such as P_jP_{j+2}, is perpendicular to the radius drawn from *O* to the intermediate point P_{j+1}, which follows from the symmetry and the geometric properties of the circle. The triangle OP_jP_{j+2} is isosceles with vertex angle at *O* equal to $2(2\pi/N)$, and therefore each base angle OP_jP_{j+2}, which is designated as Ψ_N in Fig. 10-2, is

$$\psi_N = \pi\left(\frac{N-4}{2N}\right). \qquad (10\text{-}3)$$

By virtue of the symmetries of the isosceles triangles, two chords such as P_NP_{j+1} and P_jP_{j+2} intersect at a point *B* lying on the perpendicular bisector *OC* of chord P_jP_{j+1}, and it follows that there are 2*N* identical triangles like OP_jB in the N-point star of Fig. 10-2. Let l_{1N} and l_{2N} represent the two sides *OB* and BP_j, respectively, in triangle OP_jB. Therefore, we can write

$$l_{1N} \sin \pi/N = l_{2N} \sin \psi_N \qquad (10\text{-}4)$$

$$l_{1N} \cos \pi/N + l_{2N} \cos \psi_N = R. \qquad (10\text{-}5)$$

Using the trigonometric identity for the sum of two angles, Eqs. (10-4) and (10-5) can be solved for l_{1N} and l_{2N} and expressed as

$$l_{1N} = \frac{R \sin \psi_N}{\sin\left(\psi_N + \frac{\pi}{N}\right)} \qquad (10\text{-}6)$$

$$l_{2N} = \frac{R \sin \frac{\pi}{N}}{\sin\left(\psi_N + \frac{\pi}{N}\right)} \qquad (10\text{-}7)$$

If we define quantities a_{1N} and a_{2N} such that

$$l_{1N} = a_{1N} R \qquad (10\text{-}8)$$

$$l_{2N} = a_{2N} R,$$

then from Eqs. (10-6) and (10-7), with use of Eq. (10-3), we have

$$a_{1N} = \frac{\sin \psi_N}{\sin\left(\psi_N + \frac{\pi}{N}\right)} = \frac{\cos \frac{2\pi}{N}}{\cos \frac{\pi}{N}}$$

$$a_{2N} = \frac{\sin \frac{\pi}{N}}{\sin\left(\psi_N + \frac{\pi}{N}\right)} = \tan \frac{\pi}{N}. \qquad (10\text{-}9)$$

For the special case of $N = 5$ it is easily seen that Eqs. (10-3) through (10-9) reduce to those for the standard five-pointed star in Eqs. (4-3) through (4-6) in Chapter 4.

Because of symmetry, the area of the N-point star in Fig. 10-2 is simply $2N$ times the area of triangle OP_jB, and so the total area A_N is

$$A_N = 2N \cdot \frac{1}{2} \cdot R\, l_{1N} \sin \frac{\pi}{N} . \qquad (10\text{-}10)$$

Now, by combining Eqs. (10-6), (10-8) and (10-9) with Eq. (10-10), we can express A_N in the following form:

$$A_N = NR^2 \cdot \tan\frac{\pi}{N} \cos\frac{2\pi}{N} \tag{10-11}$$

Intuitively, as the number N of tips in the N-point star becomes large, the area A_N of the star would be expected to approach that of the circle of radius R because for larger and larger N, the adjacent points such as P_j and P_{j+1} become closer and closer together on the circle and points of intersection B become closer to the circle as well. This is in fact the case because in the limit as N becomes very large, the quantity multiplying R^2 on the right in Eq. (10-11) approaches π.

$$\underset{N \to \infty}{\text{Limit}} \left(N \tan\frac{\pi}{N} \cos\frac{2\pi}{N} \right) = \pi \tag{10-12}$$

For example, use of a simple calculator shows that $N \tan \pi/N \cos 2\pi/N$ differs from π by only 0.00518 for $N = 100$, and when $N = 1000$, the difference is only 5.16×10^{-5}, while for $N = 100{,}000$ the difference is only 2×10^{-9}.

It is interesting to compare the area of the N-point star to that of the standard five-point star. From Eq. (10-11) the area ratio is

$$\frac{A_N}{A_5} = \frac{N \tan\dfrac{\pi}{N} \cos\dfrac{2\pi}{N}}{5 \tan\dfrac{\pi}{5} \cos\dfrac{2\pi}{5}}. \tag{10-13}$$

A graph of A_N/A_5 versus the number of points N, calculated from Eq. (10-13), is given in Fig. 10-3.

10-2. Three-dimensional star of altitude h on N-point base star, surface area and volume

Let a perpendicular of height h be erected at the center of O of the N-point star in Fig. 10-2, and let straight lines, called ridges, be drawn from the altitude h to each of the N points P_j on the base star. Similarly, let straight lines called valleys be drawn from the altitude h to each of the intersecting points such as B in the base star figure of Fig. 10-2. The result is a three-

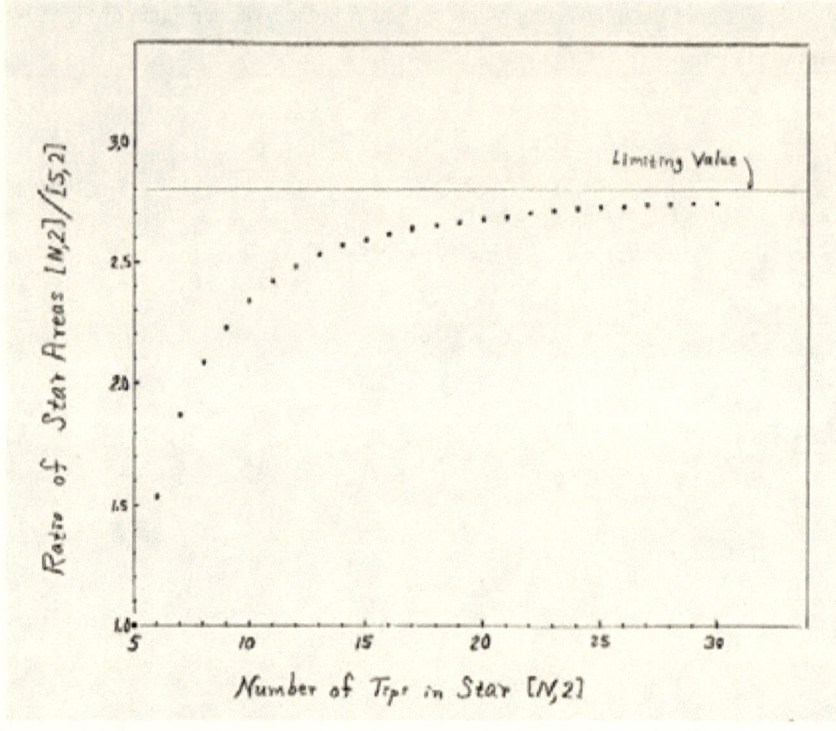

Fig. 10-3. Ratio of N-point star area to the area of the five-point star, versus number of tips N.

dimensional star of altitude h at the center with a N-point base star. Making up the solid star on one side of the base star plane are $2N$ of the volumetric elements shown in Fig. 10-4. The prismatic volume element OBP_jO' has base area equal to that of the triangle OBP_j and therefore the volume is 1/3 times the area of OBP_j times the altitude h. Using Eqs. (10-8) and (10-9), the volume of $2N$ elements is

$$V_N = 2N \frac{1}{3}\left(\frac{1}{2}l_{1N} \sin \frac{\pi}{N}\right)hR$$

$$= \frac{1}{3}R^2 h N \tan \frac{\pi}{N} \cos \frac{2\pi}{N}. \qquad (10\text{-}14)$$

The latter is the volume of the three-dimensional N-point star of altitude h on one side of the base plane star. Intuitively, as the number of points N increases, the volume of the solid star should approach that of a right circular cone of altitude h with circular base of radius R. That this is true can be seen by noting that, from Eq. (10-12), the factor multiplying $(1/3)R^2h$ in Eq. (10-14) approaches π as N becomes very large and therefore Eq. (10-14) leads to

$$\underset{N\to\infty}{\text{Limit }} V_N = \frac{1}{3}\pi R^2 h, \qquad (10\text{-}15)$$

which is just the volume of a right circular cone of base radius R with altitude h.

It is to be noted that the volume of a full three-dimensional N-point star with altitude h on both sides of the base star plane of symmetry is just twice the value given in Eq. (10-14). Now, the total surface area of this solid star is $2N$ times the area of the triangular facet $O'BP_j$ in Fig. 10-4, on each side of the base plane of symmetry, and therefore

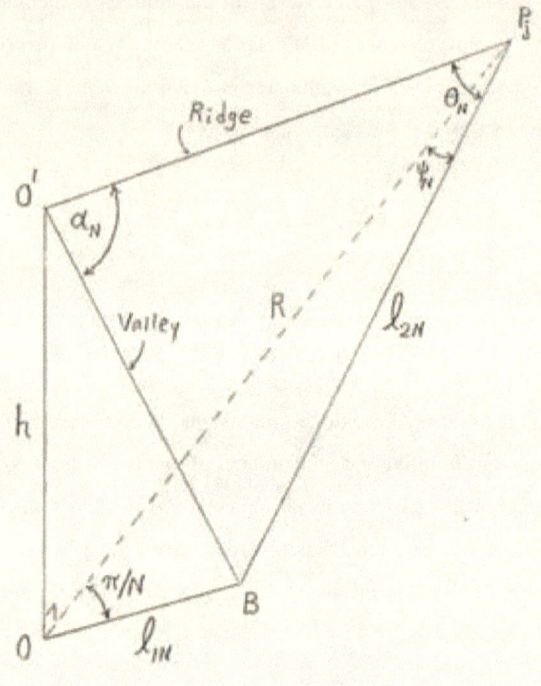

Fig. 10-4. One of $2N$ pyramidal volume elements of a three-dimensional star constructed on one side of a base plane $[N, 2]$ star.

$$A_{NT} = 4N \cdot \frac{1}{2}\sqrt{h^2 + R^2}\, l_{2N} \sin \theta_N, \qquad (10\text{-}16)$$

where the radical is the length of a ridge line $O'P_j$ and θ_N is the angle between the ridge and the line segment l_{2N} in the base star. Making use of the law of cosines and Eq. (10-8) makes it possible to express θ_N as

$$\theta_N = \arccos\left(\frac{1 + a_{2N}^2 - a_{1N}^2}{2a_{2N}\sqrt{1 + h^2/R^2}}\right). \qquad (10\text{-}17)$$

Eliminating θ_N between Eqs. (10-16) and (10-17), and using Eq. (10-9), gives the following expression for total surface area

$$A_{NT} = 2R\sqrt{h^2 + R^2}\, N \left(\tan^2 \frac{\pi}{N} - \frac{4\sin^4 \frac{\pi}{N}}{(1 + h^2/R^2)}\right)^{\frac{1}{2}} \qquad (10\text{-}18)$$

In the limit as the number of points N in the base star becomes very large, we would expect the total surface area of the three-dimensional star to approach twice the conical surface area of a right circular cone of altitude h and circular base radius R. That this is true can be seen as follows. As the number N becomes large, the tangent and sine functions are very nearly equal to their arguments in radians, so that $\tan^2 \pi/N \cong (\pi/N)^2$ and $\sin^4 \pi/N \cong (\pi/N)^4$. For large N, the factor $(\pi/N)^4$ can be neglected relative to $(\pi/N)^2$. Furthermore, the quantity $1 + h^2/R^2$ in the denominator of the term involving $(\pi/N)^4$ is always greater than unity. Under these approximations for large N, Eq. (10-18) becomes

$$A_{NT} \cong 2R\sqrt{h^2 + R^2}\, N(\pi/N)$$
$$\cong 2\pi R\sqrt{h^2 + R^2}, \qquad (10\text{-}19)$$

but $\pi R\sqrt{h^2 + R^2}$ is just the curved surface area of a right circular cone.

10-3. Angle between ridge and valley in triangular facet of solid star

The angle α_N between a ridge line and a valley line in the triangular facet $O'BP_j$ of Fig. 10-4 can be found by applying the law of sines and using Eqs. (10-8), (10-9), and (10-17). After considerable manipulation, the following expression for α_N is obtained:

$$\alpha_N = \arcsin\left[\tan\frac{\pi}{N}\sqrt{\frac{(h/R)^2 + \cos^2 2\pi/N}{\left(1 + h^2/R^2\right)\left(h^2/R^2 + \frac{\cos^2 2\pi/N}{\cos^2 \pi/N}\right)}}\right] \quad (10\text{-}20)$$

As the altitude of the three-dimensional star with N-points is increased, the angle α_N between a ridge and a valley in the surface of the star varies with the radius and altitude according to Eq. (10-20). To test if α_N versus h/R exhibits a maximum or minimum for some value of h/R, we take the first derivative of α_N with respect to the variable h/R, set it equal to zero, and solve for critical values, if any, that cause the derivative to vanish. Taking the first derivative of the arcsine function in Eq. (10-20), we get after straightforward but lengthy manipulation that the critical value of h/R is

$$\left(\frac{h}{R}\right)_c = \sqrt{u}, \quad (10\text{-}21)$$

where u is a root of the quadratic

$$u^2 + 2u\cos^2\frac{2\pi}{N} + \left(1 + a_{1N}^2\right)\cos^2\frac{2\pi}{N} - a_{1N}^2 = 0, \quad (10\text{-}22)$$

and where a_{1N} is given in Eq. (10-9). As a check, if we set $N = 5$, corresponding to the standard five-point star, then the value of h/R calculated from Eqs. (10-22) and (10-21) is identical to the value obtained in Eq. (4-23) of Chapter 4, as it should be. However, if we take $N = 6$ for a six-point star then $h/R = 0$, and for $N = 7, 8 \ldots$ there are no real solutions because $u < 0$, which means that h/R is an imaginary number. So, it is only for the case of a three-dimensional star constructed on the base plane five-point star of Fig. 4-2 in Chapter 4 that the angle α between a ridge and a valley in the surface exhibits the peculiar maximum as the ratio of altitude to radius, h/R, is increased from zero as shown earlier in Fig. 4-7.

10-4. Foldability of [N, 2] star

Earlier in Chapter 4, it was shown that a solid star could be formed by alternately folding in convex and concave fashion a plane five-point star constructed under certain conditions. We now inquire if a similar condition of foldability exists for the N-point star of Fig. 10-2. To determine if an N-point star can be constructed on a plane and then alternately folded convex about ridge lines and concave about valley lines to form a three-dimensional star of altitude h with its base an N-point star of radius R, consider Fig. 10-5. Two adjacent tips P'_j and P'_{j+1} in the outer star figure are shown and OP_j' and OB' are ridge and valley lines, respectively, in this figure. When the figure is folded convex about OP_j' and concave about OB', the intent is that point O will rise to altitude $OO' = h$, perpendicular to the plane at O, while points P_j' and B' move inward to reside at P_j and B, respectively, which are adjacent points on the plane N-point star that is to be the base of the solid star. That is, if foldability is possible, then a segment such as P'_jB' in the starlike figure must coincide with P_jB in the base star when point O' rises to altitude h directly above O. These conditions are shown graphically in Fig. 10-6, where Fig. 10-6a is in a plane perpendicular to the plane of Fig. 10-5 containing the altitude h and a ridge line, while a plane perpendicular to Fig. 10-5 and containing a valley and the altitude is given in Fig. 10-6b. Applying the law of cosines to the two triangles in Fig. 10-5 that have angle π/N common, with sides l_{2N} opposite it, we find after lengthy algebraic manipulation that foldability will be possible provided the ratio of the altitude h to radius R of the base star satisfies the equation

$$\frac{h}{R} = \sqrt{\frac{1 + a_{1N}^2 - \dfrac{1 + a_{1N}^2 - a_{2N}^2}{\cos^2 \pi/N}}{\tan^2 \dfrac{\pi}{N}}} \qquad (10\text{-}23)$$

where a_{1N} and a_{2N} are given in Eqs. (10-9). After further lengthy simplification using the relations for a_{1N} and a_{2N}, the foregoing expression for h/R becomes

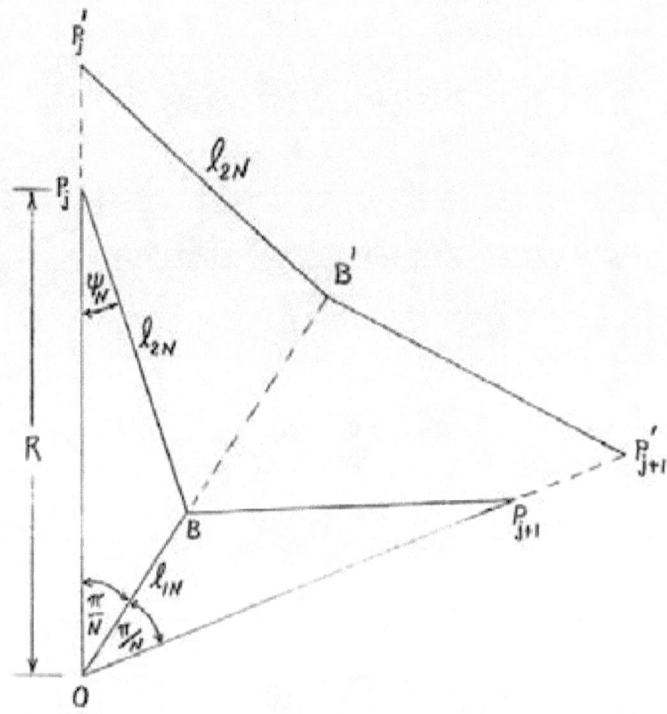

Fig. 10-5. Geometry used in determining the conditions under which a star figure can be folded on a [N, 2] base plane star.

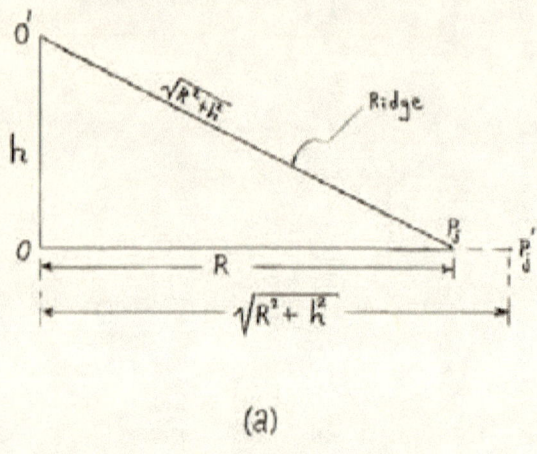

(a)

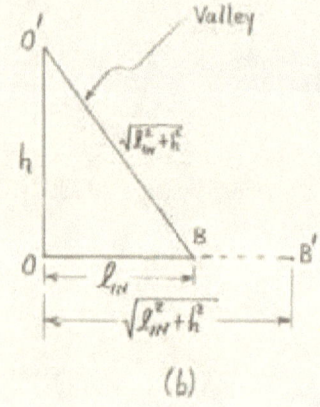

(b)

Fig. 10-6. Conditions that must be obtained in planes perpendicular to base containing a ridge (a) and a valley (b) if foldability exists of an N-point star on a $[N, 2]$ base plane star.

$$\frac{h}{R} = \sqrt{3 - 4\cos^2 \frac{\pi}{N}}. \qquad (10\text{-}24)$$

In the special case for $N = 5$, the latter gives $h/R = 0.618033989$, which is identical to the result found for foldability of a five-point star figure in Eq. (5-10) of Chapter 5. Substitution of $N = 6$ in Eq. (10-24) yields $h/R = 0$, which does not allow foldability for the six-point star. Furthermore, for $N = 7, 8, \ldots$ it is found that the quantity under the radical in Eq. (10-24) is negative, which means that the values for h/R are imaginary. Therefore, a plane star figure can be folded into a three-dimensional shape on a plane star base only for the mathematical five-point star. Recall from Chapter 2 that the adjective "mathematical" here refers to the star construction in which each point on the underlying circle is connected to the second point from it, i.e., the star is often designated by $[N,2]$.

10-5. Foldability of N-point star on base star with tip angle φ

Earlier in Chapter 9, the conditions for foldability of a five-point star were investigated for the case in which the angle between the radius and side l_2 was allowed to have a value less than or greater than the angle 18°, which is standard when each point on the circle is connected to its second nearest neighbor. There it was found that foldability was possible for these "thinner" and "thicker" five-point stars provided the angle between a radius and side l_2 did not exceed 27°. It is logical to ask if foldability is possible in the case of an N-point star when the angle between radius R and the side l_2 in Fig. 10-2 is allowed to be different from the value $\Psi_N = \pi[(N-4)/2N]$ arrived at in Eq. (10-3) when each point P_j on the circle is connected to point P_{j+2}. (Remember that in the special case $N = 5$, the angle Ψ_N is $\pi/10$, or 18°.) So, for this more general case of the N point star, we will replace the angle Ψ_N by φ and allow φ to take on other values below and above those given by Ψ_N in Eq. (10-3). This means that l_{1N} and l_{2N} will no longer be given by Eqs. (10-6)-(10-9). To distinguish, we shall refer to sides l_{1N} and l_{2N} by L_{1N} and L_{2N}, respectively, and Fig. 10-7 can be used to determine their relations to R, φ and N. So, analogous to the earlier case in Eqs. (10-4)-(10-5), we now get

$$L_{1N} \sin \frac{\pi}{N} = L_{2N} \sin \varphi \qquad (10\text{-}25)$$

$$L_{1N} \cos \frac{\pi}{N} + L_{2N} \cos \varphi = R. \qquad (10\text{-}26)$$

The latter two equations can be solved for L_{1N} and L_{2N}, and they can be written in the form

$$L_{1N} = \frac{R \sin \varphi}{\sin\left(\varphi + \dfrac{\pi}{N}\right)} \qquad (10\text{-}27)$$

$$L_{2N} = \frac{R \sin \dfrac{\pi}{N}}{\sin\left(\varphi + \dfrac{\pi}{N}\right)}. \qquad (10\text{-}28)$$

By defining quantities

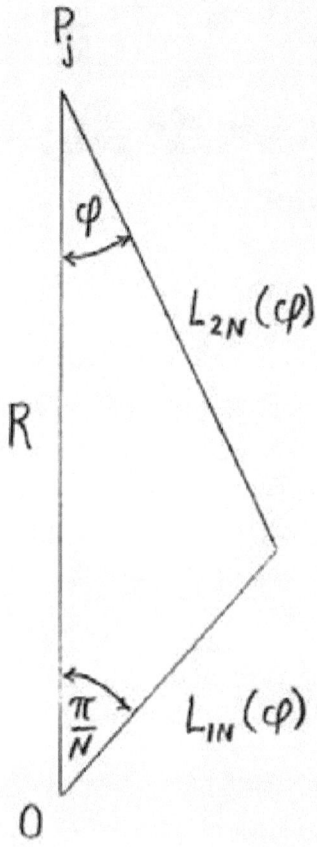

Fig. 10-7. One of $2N$ identical triangles in an N-point star characterized by a tip angle φ.

$$A_{1N} = \frac{\sin \varphi}{\sin\left(\varphi + \frac{\pi}{N}\right)}$$

$$A_{2N} = \frac{\sin \frac{\pi}{N}}{\sin\left(\varphi + \frac{\pi}{N}\right)}, \quad (10\text{-}29)$$

the lengths L_{1N} and L_{2N} in Fig. 10-7 can be expressed as

$$L_{1N} = A_{1N} R$$
$$L_{2N} = A_{2N} R. \quad (10\text{-}30)$$

We now refer to Fig. 10-8 to examine the conditions under which the N-point star with arbitrary angle φ between a radius and side L_{2N} is foldable into solid shape with altitude h at center of the base plane star. Proceeding as before in regard to Fig. 10-5, we apply the law of cosines to the two triangles that share the common angle π/N, each with side L_{2N} opposite it, in Fig. 10-8, and find, after very lengthy but straightforward algebraic operations, that the ratio of altitude to base star radius for foldability is

$$\frac{h}{R} = \sqrt{\frac{\cos^2 \varphi}{\sin^2\left(\varphi + \frac{\pi}{N}\right)} - 1}. \quad (10\text{-}31)$$

In obtaining the latter, all four relations in Eqs. (10-29) and (10-30) were used to arrive at a result containing only the number of points N in the base star and the angle φ. Just as a check, suppose we take the special case of the five-point star dealt with in Chapter 5. For this case, $N = 5$ and $\varphi = 18°$, for which we find $h/R = 0.618033989$ for the condition of foldability, agreeing with Eq. (5-10).

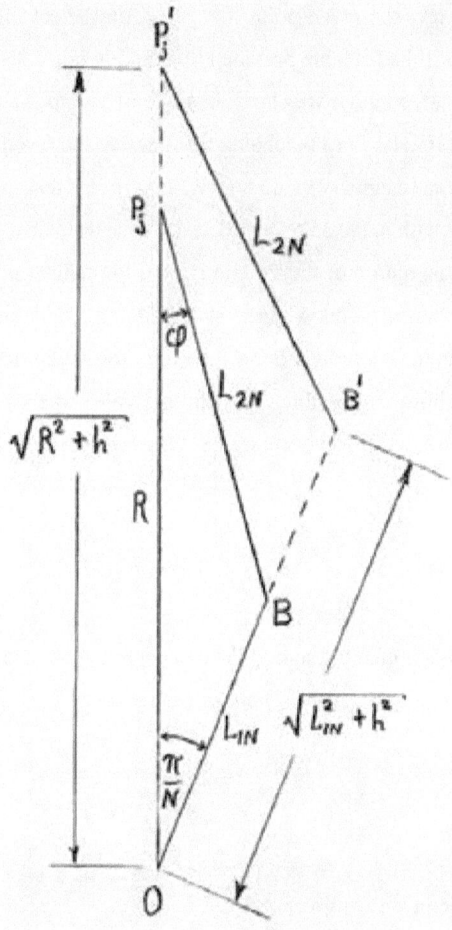

Fig. 10-8. Geometry used in deriving Eq. (10-31), giving the conditions under which an N-point star figure is foldable into a three-dimensional figure of altitude h on a base plane N-point star with radius R and tip angle φ.

Suppose we take the angle φ = 15° in the six-point star with $N = 6$. Then according to Eq. (10-31), foldability is possible for an altitude h that is 0.930605 times the radius R. As another example, take the seven-point star, $N = 7$, and select angle φ = 20°; then, from Eq. (10-31) the star will be foldable provided the altitude h is 0.85035 times the radius R. For the seven-point star, suppose we chose an angle of 35° and substitute this for φ along with $N = 7$ into Eq. (10-31). For this choice we find that the quantity under the radical is negative, resulting in an imaginary value for h/R. This means that foldability is not possible for a seven-point star with angle 35° between a radius and side L_{2N} in Fig. 10-8.

By virtue of the nature of the function under the radical in Eq. (10-31), it is seen that, for a given number of points N in the star, a limiting value of the angle φ exists for which the quantity under the radical is positive, i.e., for which h/R is a real number, not imaginary, and foldability is possible. The limiting value of the angle $φ_L$ for which the radicand is positive in Eq. (10-31) occurs for

$$\cos^2 φ_L = \sin^2\left(φ_L + \frac{\pi}{N}\right). \tag{10-32}$$

Expanding the sine function of the sum of the two angles, we find, after tedious operations, that the limiting angle $φ_L$ in Eq. (10-32) obeys the equation

$$\sin^4 φ_L - \sin^2 φ_L + \frac{1}{4} \cos^2 \frac{\pi}{N} = 0. \tag{10-33}$$

Solving this quadratic in $\sin^2 φ_L$ gives

$$\sin^2 φ_L = \frac{1 \pm \sin\frac{\pi}{N}}{2},$$

from which the angle $φ_L$ is found to be

$$\varphi_L = \arcsin \sqrt{\frac{1 \pm \sin \pi/N}{2}}. \qquad (10\text{-}34)$$

As with any quadratic, there are two roots, and the one that applies depends on the application. In this case the positive sign in Eq. (10-34) gives a value of φ_L for a given N that results in a negative value under the radical in Eq. (10-31). Therefore, the negative sign in Eq. (10-34) is the one that applies. Using the negative sign in Eq. (10-34), the limiting value of angle φ in Fig. 10-8 for foldability was calculated as a function of the number N of points in the star, and the results are shown as solid dots in the graph of Fig. 10-9. Also shown in Fig. 10-9, for comparison, are the values of angle Ψ_N versus N calculated from Eq. (10-3). The latter are designated by crosses, and these are simply the values of the angle between a radius R and a side l_{2N} in the standard N-point star in Fig. 10-2 when each point on the circle is joined by a straight line to its second nearest neighbor. Finally, the open circles in Fig. 10-9 give the maximum value or angle Ψ_N versus N corresponding to the case in which the N-point star degenerates into an N-point polygon, and these were calculated from Eq. (10-2) in reference to Fig. 10-2.

Referring again to the solid dots in Fig. 10-9, we note these are the limiting values of angle Ψ, for a given N, for which foldability can occur. For example, for a thirteen-point star, $N = 13$, foldability is possible for $\Psi < 38$ as seen from the graph. For a thirteen-point star constructed in the standard manner, [13, 2], the corresponding angle is $\Psi_N \cong 62.3°$, and so foldability can occur only when Ψ is considerably less than this value.

For a given value of N, the ratio of altitude to radius, h/R, for which foldability is possible, can be calculated as a function of the angle φ from Eq. (10-31) over the range of allowable values of φ for which the radical remains positive. This was done and the results are given in the graph of Fig. 10-10. Each curve corresponds to a fixed value of N as labeled. For example, if an angle $\varphi = 11°$ is chosen for a seven-point star ($N = 7$), then foldability is possible for $h/R = 1.3$. Only five curves, each corresponding to a given value of N, are displayed in Fig. 10-10, but the shape of curves for higher values of N can easily be inferred and, of course, calculated from Eq. (10-31). As a final note, if N is set equal to 5, then the curve of h/R calculated as a function of angle φ from Eq. (10-31) is identical to that of Fig. 9-9 in Chapter 9 where the five-point star was allowed to have an angle between the radius and side l_2 different from 18° for the standard star.

For a given N, as smaller and smaller angles φ are chosen, the difficulty of folding increases because of the finite thickness, approximately 0.003 in., of typical media such as paper on which the plane star is constructed. However, mathematically, as angle φ approaches zero, the limiting value of h/R exists from Eq. (10-31) and this is $(h/R)_{φ=0} = \cot π/N$. At the other extreme, for a given angle φ, when the number N of tips becomes very large, folding of the star constructed on typical media such as paper is not too practical. Nonetheless, mathematically, the

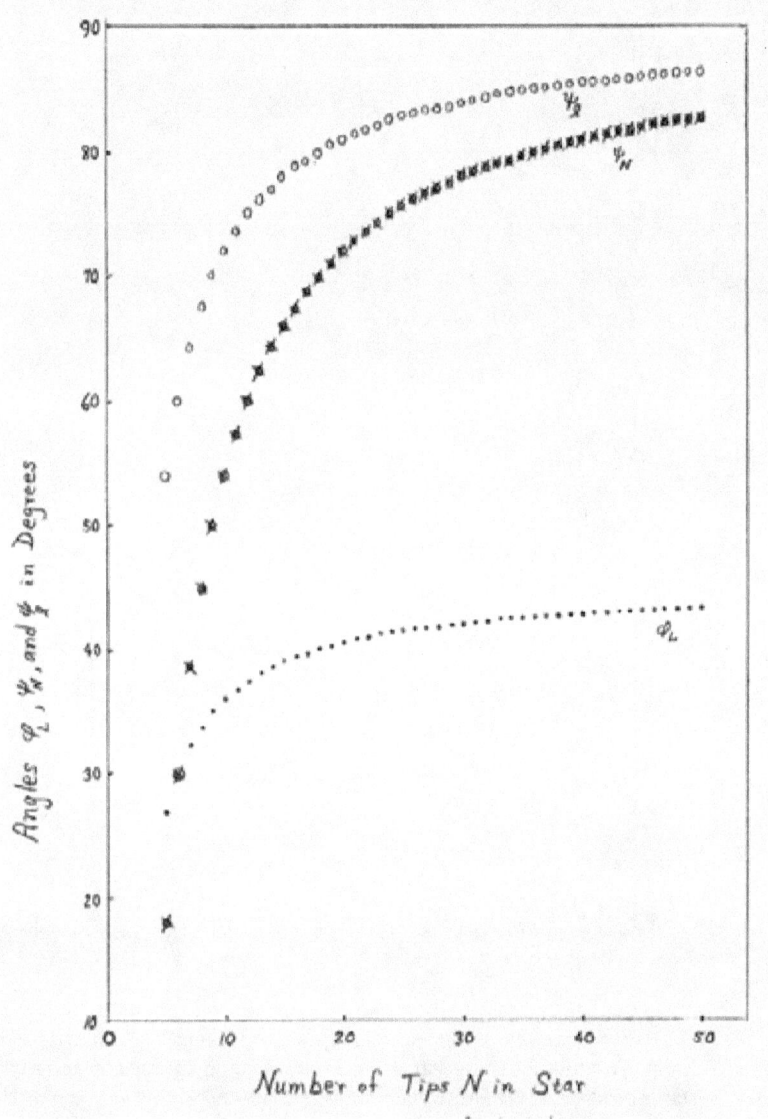

Fig. 10-9. Limiting angle φ_L for foldability, angle Ψ_N between radius and side l_{2N}, and angle Ψ_I for degeneracy to regular polygon, all versus number N of tips in star.

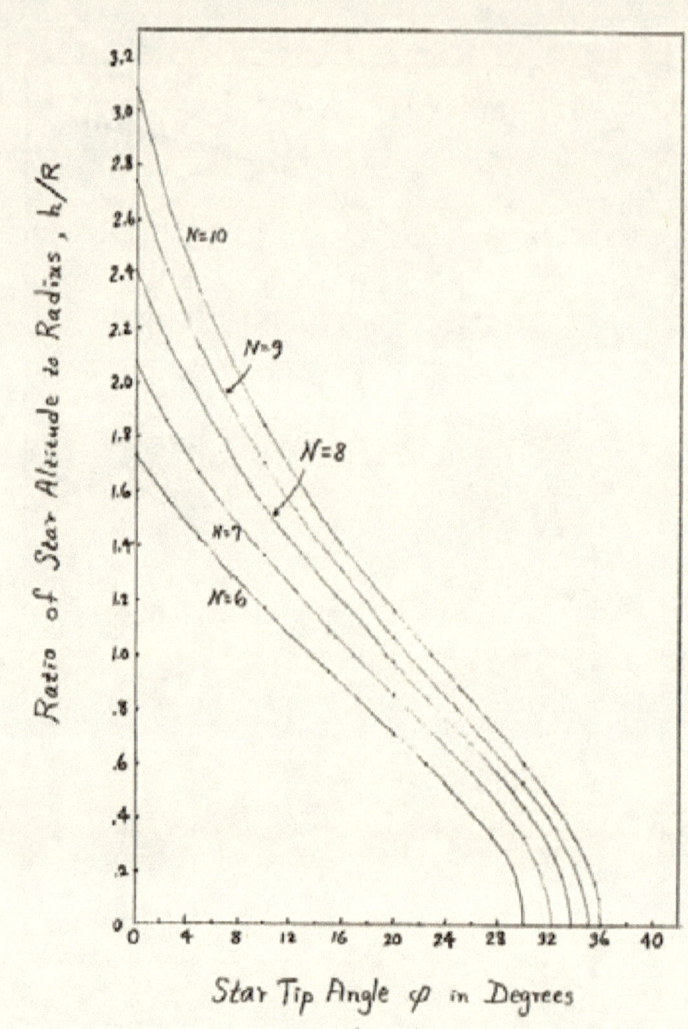

Fig.10-10. Ratio of altitude h to base star radius R for foldability, versus tip angle φ in base star for each of several different numbers of tips N.

Ch.10. Examples of three-dimensional stars folded on six-point base stars of radius $R = $ 3in. Left: Tip angle $\varphi = 20°$, $h/R = .7105$. Right = Tip angle $\varphi = 28°$, $h/R = .2898$.

Ch.10. Examples of three-dimensional stars folded on seven-point base stars. Upper left: tip angle $\varphi = 24°$, radius $R = 3$ in., $h/R = .6589$. Lower left: Tip angle $\varphi = 12°$, radius $R = 2$ in., $h/R = 1.207$. Right: Tip angle $\varphi = 30°$, radius $R = 3$ in., $h/R = .314$.

Ch.10. Examples of three-dimensional stars folded on eight-point base stars of radius R = 3in. Left: Tip angle $\varphi = 27°$, $h/R = .6107$. Right: Tip angle $\varphi = 33°$, $h/R = .1887$.

limit for $N \to \infty$ from Eq. (10-31) is $(h/R)_{N=\infty} = (\cot^2\varphi - 1)^{1/2}$. From the latter, it is seen that angle φ must be less than $\pi/4$ radians to avoid an imaginary value of h/R.

10-6. Angle α_N in N-point star with tip angle φ

We now inquire in the general case of the N-point star with arbitrary angle φ between radius and side L_{2N} whether the angle α_N between a ridge line and valley line in a triangular facet exhibits a maximum for some value of altitude h. Referring to Fig. 10-11, the triangular facet in the three-dimensional shape of altitude h is $O'BP_j$, with angle α_N opposite the side L_{2N} in the plane star and θ_N, is the angle opposite the valley of length $\sqrt{h^2 + L_{1N}^2}$. So, the angle α_N is

$$\sin \alpha_N = \frac{L_{2N}}{\sqrt{h^2 + L_{1N}^2}} \sin \theta_N, \qquad (10\text{-}35)$$

where angle θ_N can be expressed as

$$\theta_N = \arccos \left(\frac{R^2 + L_{2N}^2 - L_{1N}^2}{2 L_{2N} \sqrt{h^2 + R^2}} \right). \qquad (10\text{-}36)$$

Making use of the relations in Eq. (10-30), Eqs. (10-36) and (10-35) can be combined to express the angle α_N as

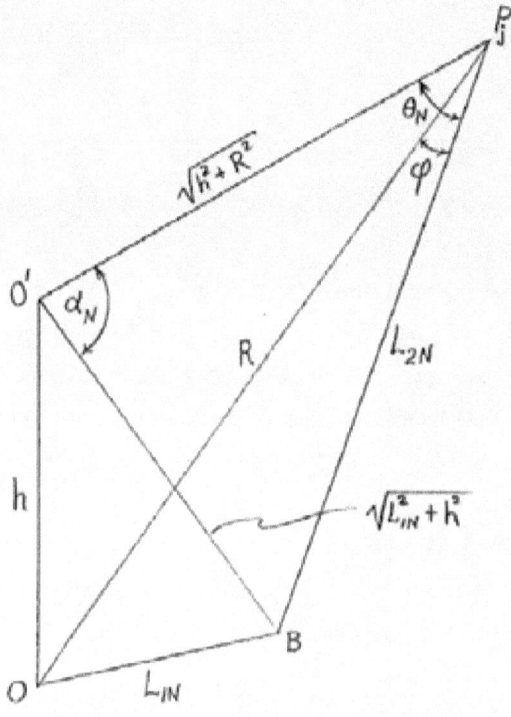

Fig. 10-11. Angle α_N between a ridge and valley in one of $2N$ identical triangular facets of a three-dimensional star formed on one side of an N-point base star characterized by tip angle φ.

$$\alpha_N = \arcsin\left[A_{2N}\sqrt{\frac{1+(h/R)^2 - A_{12N}^2}{\left(A_{1N}^2 + h^2/R^2\right)\left(1 + h^2/R^2\right)}}\right], \qquad (10\text{-}37)$$

where

$$A_{12N} = \frac{1 + A_{2N}^2 - A_{1N}^2}{2A_{2N}}, \qquad (10\text{-}38)$$

and A_{1N} and A_{2N} are given in terms of φ and N in Eq. (10-29).

For a given choice of N, radius R, and angle φ the argument of the arccosine in Eq. (10-36) steadily becomes smaller as the altitude h is increased, and therefore the angle θ_N steadily increases as h increases. However, the dependence of angle α_N, between ridge and valley is more involved because of the appearance of the factor h/R in three places in the argument of arcsine in Eq. (10-37). So, to test for a possible maximum in the dependence of angle α_N on the variable h/R, we calculate the first derivative of the arcsine function in Eq. (10-37) with respect to h/R, set the resulting function equal to zero, and solve for the critical value of h/R that causes the first derivative to vanish. This leads to the following equation to be solved for h/R.

$$\left(\frac{h}{R}\right)^4 + 2\left(\frac{h}{R}\right)^2 \left(1 - A_{12N}^2\right) + 1 - A_{12N}^2 - A_{1N}^2 A_{12N}^2 = 0 \qquad (10\text{-}39)$$

To solve the latter, we let $u = \left(\dfrac{h}{R}\right)^2$ and this gives the quadratic

$$u^2 + ub' + c' = 0, \qquad (10\text{-}40)$$

where

$$b' = 2\left(1 - A_{12N}^2\right)$$

$$c' = 1 - A_{12N}^2 - A_{1N}^2 A_{12N}^2. \qquad (10\text{-}41)$$

Upon solving the quadratic in u^2 from Eq. (10-40), the desired value of h/R is

$$\frac{h}{R} = \sqrt{u} \qquad (10\text{-}42)$$

As an example, consider a seven-point star with $N = 7$ and choose angle $\varphi = 25°$. The two roots to the quadratic in Eq. (10-40) are $u_+ = 0.1347344$ and $u_- = -0.4919468$. Now, the root u_- gives an imaginary value for h/R when substituted into Eq. (10-42), and so we ignore u_-. Substitution of the other root u_+ into Eq. (10-42) gives the following value for h/R corresponding to a possible maximum in the value of angle α_N.

$$\frac{h}{R} = 0.3670619 \qquad (10\text{-}43)$$

That this value of h/R does in fact result in a maximum angle α_N can be seen by substituting $\varphi = 25°$ and $N = 7$ into Eq. (10-37), which gives $\alpha_N = 26.598°$, but substituting values of h/R slightly less or greater than that of Eq. (10-43) yields values of α less than the value for h/R in Eq. (10-43).

Allowable solutions of h/R from Eq. (10-39), for which angle α_N in the triangular facet has a maximum, were calculated as a function of tip angle φ for a $N=9$ point star and the results are presented in Fig. 10-12. Eqs. (10-37) and (10-38) were used to calculate the variation of angle α_N as a function of h/R for the nine-point star with tip angle $\varphi = 10°$, and these results are given in Fig. 10-13 from which it can be seen that the value of h/R, for which angle α_N is a maximum, agrees with Fig. 10-12.

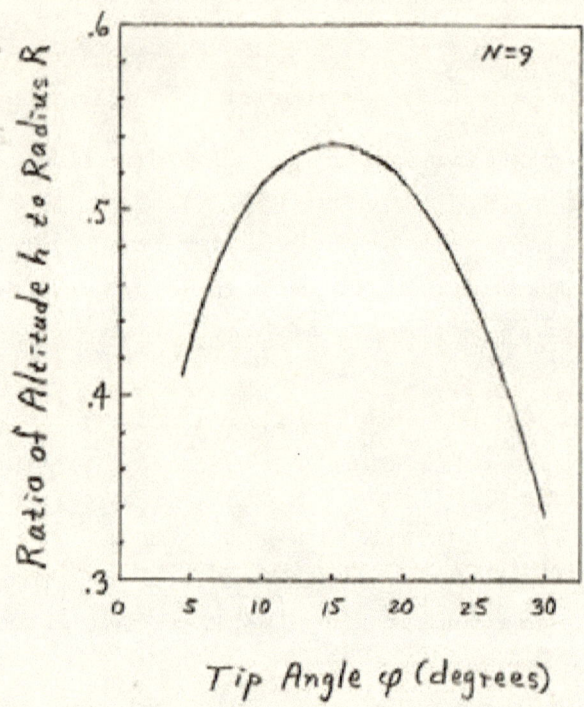

Fig. 10-12. Ratio of altitude to radius h/R for which the angle α_N between a ridge and valley is a maximum, versus the tip angle φ of the nine-point base plane star.

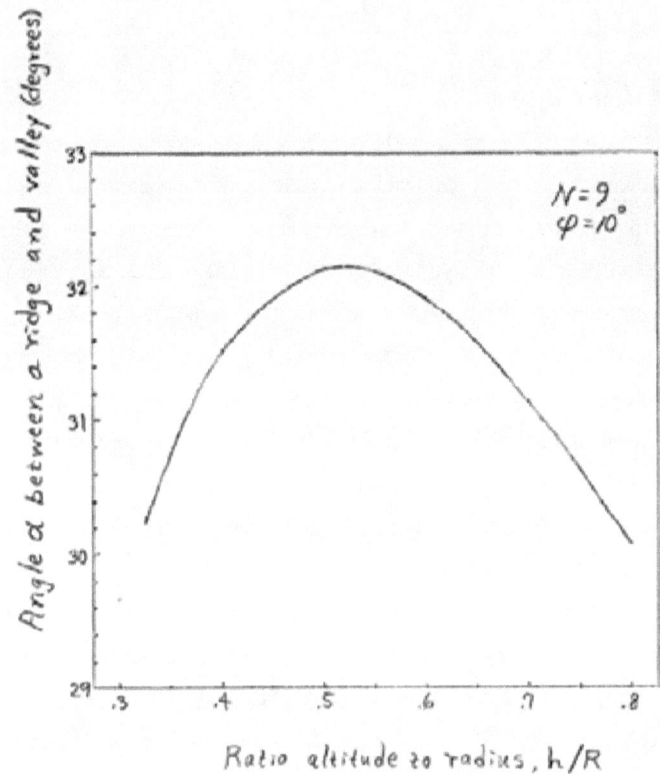

Fig. 10-13. Angle α between a ridge and valley in a triangular facet of a three-dimensional star formed on a nine-point base star of tip angle 10°, versus ratio of altitude to radius, h/R. Note that α is a maximum at the value of h/R corresponding to $\varphi = 10°$ in Fig. 10-12.

CHAPTER 11
STARS OF THE TYPE [N, J]

11-1. The [N, J] symbology

In all the analyses to this point, we have dealt with stars formed by connecting each point on a circle with the second point from it. In the case of the pentagram designated by [5, 2], there are five points equally spaced on the circle while in the case of the higher-order star, [N, 2], there are N points equally spaced on the circle. But in either case, each point on the circle was connected to the second point from it as designated by the number "2" appearing as the second number in the designators [5, 2] and [N, 2]. In this chapter, consideration will be given to stars formed by connecting each point on the circle with the third, or fourth, or fifth, etc., point from it. As such, these stars are designated by [N, J], where N is the number of equally spaced points on a circle of radius R, and J is an integer representing the number of intervals between each point and the point to which it is connected to form the N-point star figure.

Beginning with the five-point star, [5, 2], we note that the five-point star is also obtained if each point on the circle is connected with a straight line to the third point from it, so that we have [5, 3] = [5, 2]. Of course, connecting each point to the point nearest it on the circle results in a pentagon, [5, 1], and it easy to see that this is equivalent to [5, 4].

Taking $N = 6$ we get a hexagon when each of six equally spaced points on a circle is connected to the point nearest it, [6, 1] and we note that this is equivalent to [6, 5] which also gives a hexagon. The mathematical six-point star [6, 2] is also obtained when each point on the circle is connected to the fourth point from it, [6, 4]. When each point is connected to the third point from it the symbol representing this is [6, 3] and the resultant figure is a six-point degenerate "line star."

Going next to the case of seven points equally spaced on a circle, we see that [7, 1] is equivalent to [7, 6], each resulting in the heptagon, a regular seven-sided polygon. Now, the standard seven-point star, [7, 2], is also obtained by connecting each point with the fifth point from it, so that [7, 5] = [7, 2]. Likewise, it is easy to see that [7, 3] and [7, 4] are equivalent.

When $N = 8$, we see that [8, 1] and [8, 7] are equivalent, each resulting in a regular octagon. The "standard" eight-point star [8, 2] is also obtained from [8, 6]. Similarly, [8, 3] and [8, 5] are equivalent, while [8, 4] results in a degenerate eight-point "line star."

A number of these stars are illustrated in Fig. 11-1. Some generalizations can be made as follows, for stars generated from N equally spaced point on a circle.

[N, J = 1] ≡ [N, J = N - 1] N-sided polygons
[N, J] ≡ [N, J']   provided $J + J' = N$

For a given odd $N > 5$ the "thinnest" stars are for

$$[N, J = \frac{N+1}{2}] \equiv [N, J = \frac{N-1}{2}],$$

and for N even, "line" stars are obtained for

$$[N, J = N/2].$$

11-2. Angles and sides in a [N, J] star

Next we consider the relationships between angles and sides in stars of the general type [N, J]. In Fig. 11-2, a circle of radius R has been drawn containing N equally spaced points located on it. Let P_1 designate one of the points and P_2 a point adjacent to it. Then, the angle subtended between radii drawn to P_1 and P_2 is $2\pi/N$ expressed in radians. Now, the designation

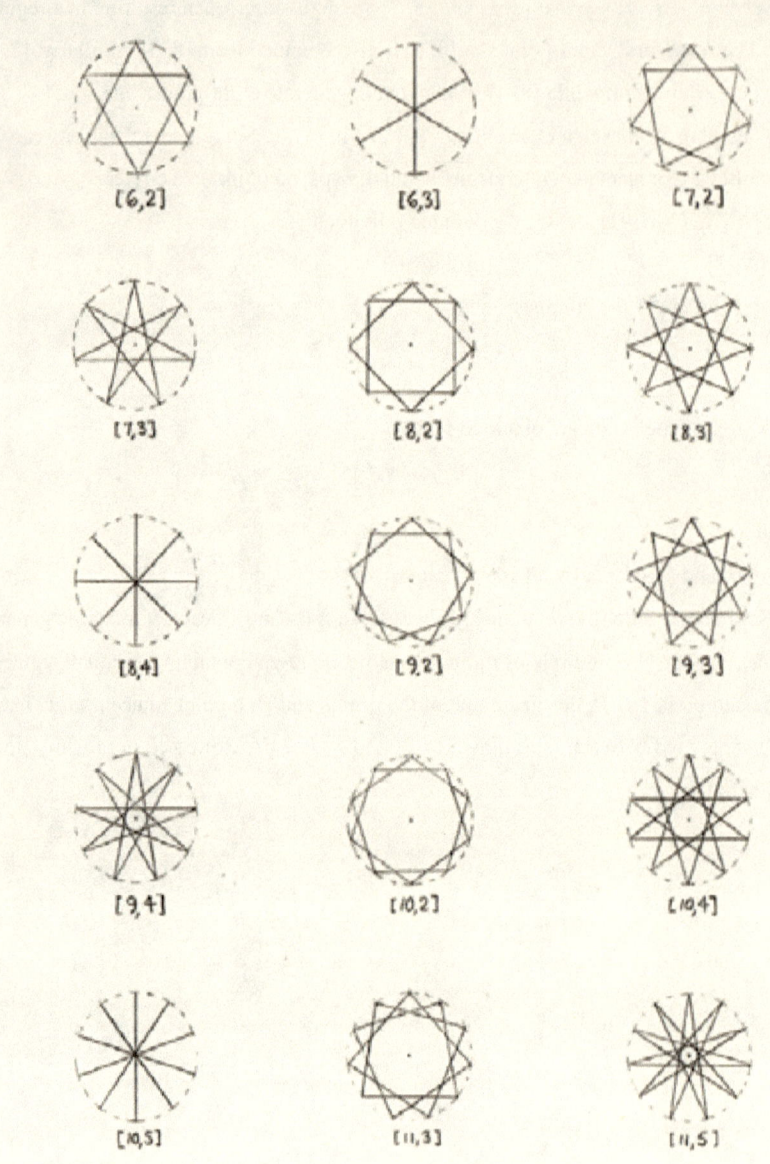

Fig. 11-1.   Some examples of [*N*, *J*] stars.

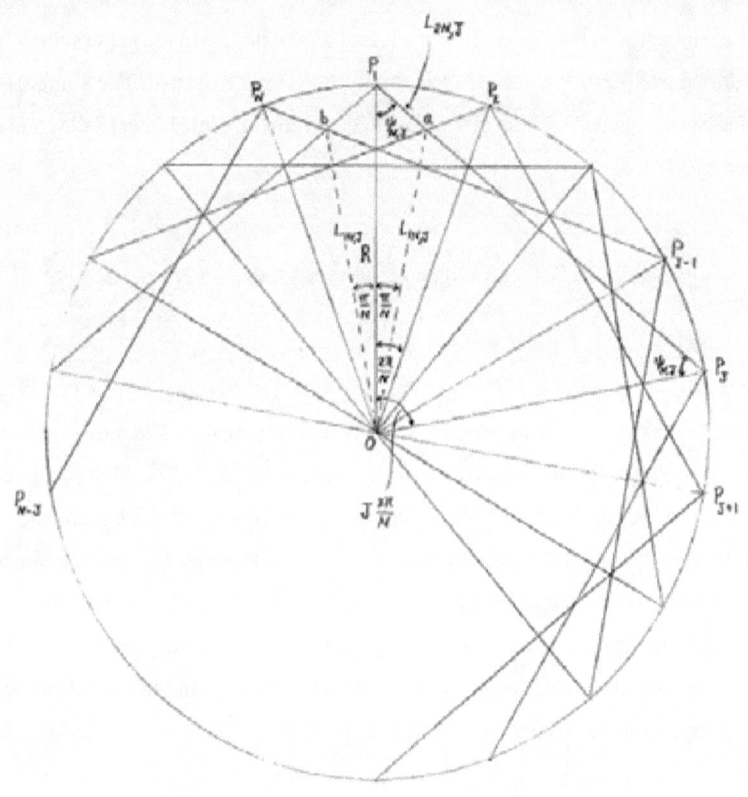

Fig. 11-2. Angles and sides in a [N, J] star of radius R.

[N, J] means that the Jth point is joined to P_1 by a straight line, and so also P_2 is joined to P_{J+1}, etc., as indicated in the figure. Therefore, in the triangle OP_1P_J the angle subtended by the radii drawn from O to P_1 and O to P_J is simply $J(2\pi/N)$ as indicated. The triangle OP_1P_J is isosceles because two of its sides are radii and therefore the angle between OP_1 and P_1P_J, designated by $\psi_{N,J}$, is

$$\psi_{N,J} = \pi\left(\frac{1}{2} - \frac{J}{N}\right)$$ (11-1)

Let a be the point at which P_1P_J intersects the line connecting P_2 with the Jth point counterclockwise from it. Then, in keeping with line segment designations in previous chapters regarding [N, 2], star figures, we designate the line Oa in Fig. 11-2 by L_1 and the line P_1a by L_2, but to emphasize that these depend on both N and J we shall place subscripts on them, thereby calling these segments $L_{1N,J}$ and $L_{2N,J}$. The line $L_{1N,J}$ bisects the angle P_1OP_2 because of symmetry associated with the N equally spaced points and the fact that each point is joined symmetrically with the Jth point from it measured in both clockwise and counterclockwise senses. Therefore, the angle P_1Oa is π/N, and using this along with Eq. (11-1) applied to the triangle OaP_1 in Fig. 11-2, the following two relations can be written.

$$L_{1N,J}\sin\frac{\pi}{N} = L_{2N,J}\sin\left[\pi\left(\frac{1}{2} - \frac{J}{N}\right)\right]$$

$$L_{1N,J}\cos\frac{\pi}{N} + L_{2N,J}\cos\left[\pi\left(\frac{1}{2} - \frac{J}{N}\right)\right] = R$$ (11-2)

After some manipulations of trigonometric functions, the latter can be solved for the distances $L_{1N,J}$ and $L_{2N,J}$, and expressed as

$$L_{1N,J} = A_{1N,J}\, R$$
$$L_{2N,J} = A_{2N,J}\, R$$ (11-3)

where

$$A_{1N,J} = \frac{\cos\frac{J}{N}\pi}{\cos\pi\left(\frac{J-1}{N}\right)}$$

$$A_{2N,J} = \frac{\sin\pi/N}{\cos\pi\left(\frac{J-1}{N}\right)}$$

(11-4)

For the special case $N = 5$ and $J = 2$ corresponding to the five-point star [5, 2], it is easy to show that Eqs. (11-3) and (11-4) reduce to Eqs. (4-5) and (4-6) of Chapter 4.

11-3. Surface area of $[N, J]$ star

Referring again to Fig. 11-2, consider the straight line connecting point P_N, adjacent to P_1, to the Jth point clockwise from it, namely, P_{J-1}, and let b be the intersecting point of line $P_N P_{J-1}$ with the line joining P_1 to the Jth point counterclockwise from P_1. Appealing again to the symmetry referred to above, it is seen that Ob is equal to $Oa \equiv L_{1N,J}$ and, likewise, $bP_1 = P_1a \equiv L_{2N,J}$. So, triangle OaP_1 and ObP_1 are congruent. The quadrilateral OaP_1b is the basic unit of symmetry comprising the $[N, J]$ star figure and it follows that the area of the star $[N, J]$ is simply N times the area of quadrilateral OaP_1b. Equivalently, the area $A_{N,J}$ of the star $[N, J]$ is just $2N$ times the area of triangle OaP_1, and referring to Fig. 11-2 and using Eqs. (11-3) and (11-4), the area of the star $[N, J]$ can be expressed as

$$A_{N,J} = NR^2 \frac{\sin\frac{\pi}{N}\cos J\frac{\pi}{N}}{\cos\pi\left(\frac{J-1}{N}\right)}$$

(11-5)

A graph of the area of [N, J] stars calculated from Eq. (11-5) for each of several different values of N, as a function of J, is given in Fig. 11-3. The graph of course consists of discrete dots because both N and J are integers.

11-4. Three-dimensional star of altitude h on base star [N, J]. Volume

Next, suppose a segment of length h is erected perpendicular to the plane of the star in Fig. 11-2, passing through the center O. Let straight lines be drawn, connecting the tip of this altitude segment to each of the N points on the circle and also to each of the N points of intersection such as point a. Doing likewise with a segment through O of length h on the opposite side of the plane of Fig. 11-2 thus provides a three-dimensional solid star figure of double altitude thickness $2h$ along the line perpendicular to the base plane star at its center. The volume of this solid star can be determined by considering the elemental pyramidal shape shown in Fig. 11-4, which has a base triangle equal to that of triangle OaP_1 in Fig. 11-2 and an altitude h through point O. It is seen that there are $2N$ identical pyramidal solids of this size comprising the solid star of altitude h on one side of the base plane star, and also $2N$ of the identical pyramidal elements on the other side of the plane. So, based on a theorem from solid geometry the total volume $V_{N,J}$ of the solid star of altitude h on either side of the base is

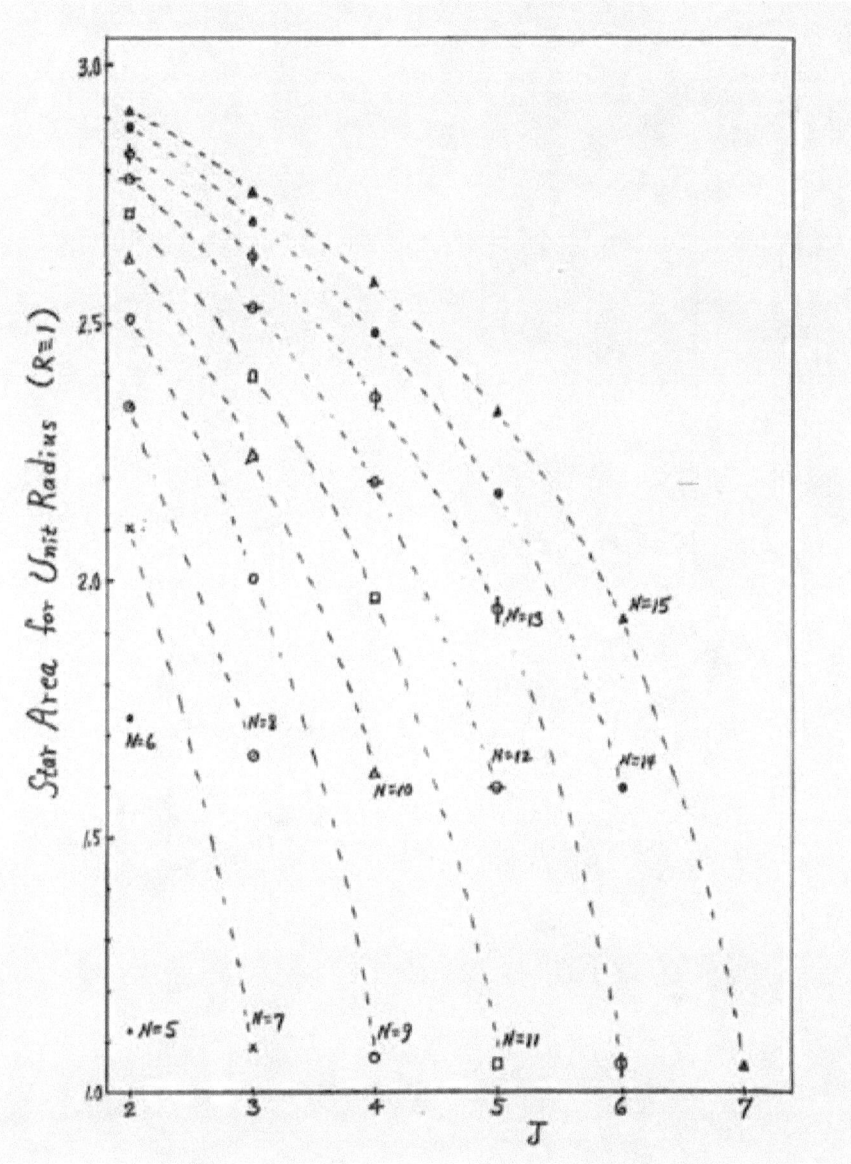

Fig. 11-3. Area of [N, J] stars versus J, for each of several values of N, calculated from Eq. (11-5) for unit radius, $R \equiv 1$. For any other value of radius the area is merely R^2 times the value given.

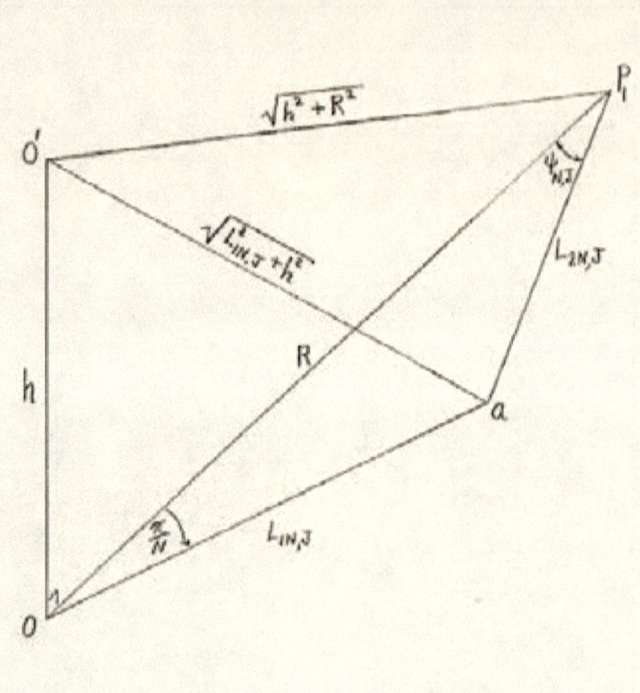

Fig. 11-4. There are 2N pyramidal volume elements identical to OaP_1O' when an altitude $h = OO'$ is erected at point O of the plane star $[N, J]$ in Fig. 11-2 and the point O' is connected with each of the N points like P_1 and each of the points like a in that figure.

$$V_{N,J} = 4N \cdot \frac{1}{3} A_{O_aP_1} \cdot h \qquad (11\text{-}6)$$

where A_{OaP_1} is the area of the base triangle formed by the center O of the star, point P_1 on the circle of radius R, and point a. Now, the area of the base triangle OaP_1 is

$$\frac{1}{2} RL_{1N,J} \sin\frac{\pi}{N} \qquad (11\text{-}7)$$

and therefore from Eqs. (11-3) and (11-4), the expression for the volume in Eq. (11-6) becomes

$$V_{N,J} = \frac{2}{3} NR^2 h \frac{\sin\frac{\pi}{N} \cos J \frac{\pi}{N}}{\cos \pi \left(\frac{J-1}{N}\right)} \qquad (11\text{-}8)$$

Eq. (11-8) was used to calculate the volume of $[N, J]$ stars for each of several values of the number N of tips, and for each of various J values for each N. These results are displayed in Fig. 11-5.

11-5. Foldability

It will now be shown that, for certain combinations of N and J, an N-point starlike figure constructed in the plane can be folded into a solid star of altitude h with base conforming to a $[N, J]$ star. The outer figure in Fig. 11-6 is the starlike figure with tips at P_1', P_2' etc. and inward

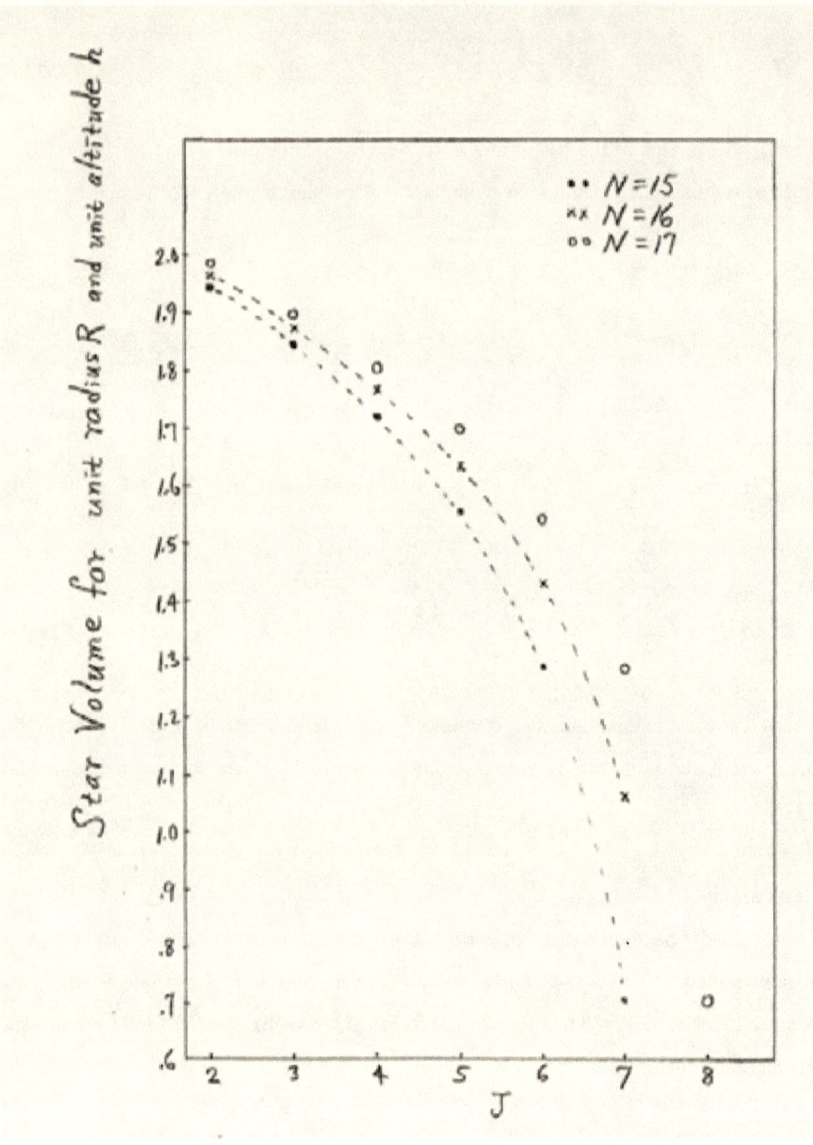

Fig. 11-5. Volume of three-dimensional star of altitude h either side of a $[N, J]$ base plane star in Fig. 11-2, versus J, for three different values of N, for unit radius and unit altitude. For $R = 3$ cm and $h = 2$ cm, for example, the volume of a $[15, 5]$ solid star is $(3)^2 \cdot 2 \cdot 1.553 = 27.95$ cm^3.

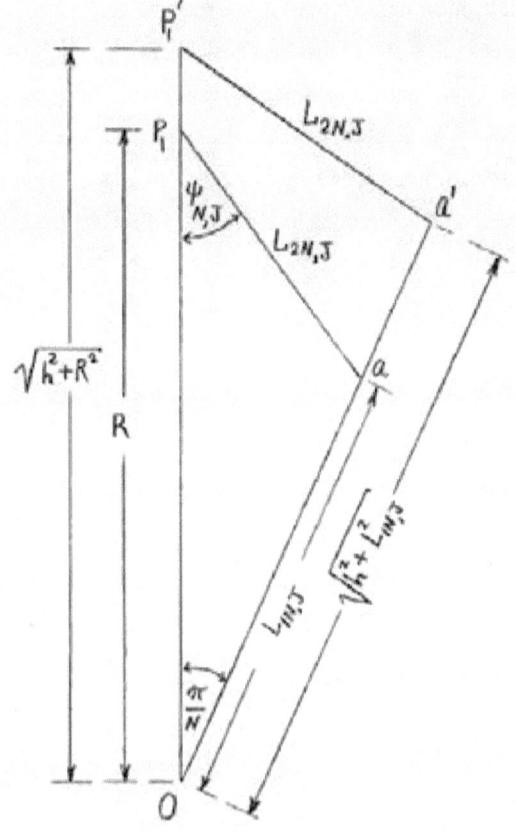

Fig. 11-6. Foldable N-point star contains $2N$ identical triangles like $Oa'P_1'$ and when it is folded convex about N lines like OP_1' and concave about Oa', point O will be at altitude h above plane of the page and $P_1'a'$ will coincide with P_1a of the base plane star $[N, J]$.

points a', b', etc. For foldability of this figure to altitude h, with resulting plane base coincident with the star of radius R with tips at P_1, etc., and inward points at a, etc., points P_1' and a', for example, must move inward in the plane to coincide with points P_1 and a, respectively. This means that $P_1'a'$ must be equal in length to P_1a, but P_1a have been labeled to reflect this. After folding to altitude h at the center O, the length OP_1' becomes a ridge with length $(h^2 + R^2)^{\frac{1}{2}}$ and the length Oa' becomes a valley with length $(L^2_{1N,J} + h^2)^{\frac{1}{2}}$. In triangle OP_1a and $OP_1'a'$, the sides $P_1a \equiv L_{2N,J}$ and $P_1'a' \equiv L_{2N,J}$ are each opposite the common angle π/N at O and therefore applying the law of cosines leads to the equality

$$2h^2 + R^2 + L^2_{1N,J} - 2\left(R^2 + h^2\right)^{\frac{1}{2}}\left(L^2_{1N,J} + h^2\right)^{\frac{1}{2}} \cos\frac{\pi}{N} = R^2 + L^2_{1N,J} - 2RL_{1N,J} \cos\frac{\pi}{N}. \qquad (11\text{-}9)$$

Moving the radicals to one side, squaring both sides, and using Eqs. (11-3) and (11-4) allows the latter to be expressed as

$$\left(\frac{h}{R}\right)^4 \left(\cos^2\frac{\pi}{N} - 1\right) + \left(\frac{h}{R}\right)^2 \left[\cos^2\frac{\pi}{N} + A^2_{1N,J} \cos^2\frac{\pi}{N} - 2A_{1N,J} \cos\frac{\pi}{N}\right] = 0. \qquad (11\text{-}10)$$

Solving for the ratio of altitude h to radius R gives

$$\frac{h}{R} = \frac{1}{\sin\frac{\pi}{N}} \sqrt{\cos^2\frac{\pi}{N}\left[1 + \frac{\cos^2 J\frac{\pi}{N}}{\cos^2 \pi\left(\frac{J-1}{N}\right)}\right] - 2\frac{\cos\frac{\pi}{N}\cos J\frac{\pi}{N}}{\cos\pi\left(\frac{J-1}{N}\right)}}. \qquad (11\text{-}12)$$

Eq. (11-12) was used to calculate the ratio h/R for each of several values of N, with different values of J at each N, and the results are tabulated in Table 11-1. The number of tips N is listed at the left, and the second column gives the values of J. Inspection of Eq. (11-12) shows that it may be possible for some combinations of N and J that the radical is negative, thereby giving an imaginary number for h/R. The third column in Table 11-1 gives the calculated values of h/R, and in those instances in which the quantity under the radical is negative, the result is listed as imaginary.

Table 11-1. Calculated values of altitude-to-radius ratio, Eq. (11-12), for which a solid star is foldable on a base plane star [N, J].

Number of Tips N	Number of Angular Intervals Between Adjacent Tips J	Altitude to Radius h/R
6	2	0
7	2	Imaginary
	3	1.2311
8	2	Imaginary
	3	0.8409
9	2	Imaginary
	3	0.5273
	4	1.6969
10	2	Imaginary
	3	0
	4	1.2720
11	2	Imaginary
	3	Imaginary
	4	0.9641
	5	2.1627
12	2	Imaginary
	3	Imaginary
	4	0.7071
	5	1.6529
13	2	Imaginary
	3	Imaginary
	4	0.4570
	5	1.3074
	6	2.6148
14	2	Imaginary
	3	Imaginary
	4	0
	5	1.0431
	6	2.0122

15	2	Imaginary
	3	Imaginary
	4	Imaginary
	5	0.8216
	6	1.618033989
	7	3.0590

    All the calculated entries for h/R in Table 11-1 have been rounded to four decimal places except for the entry for [15, 6], which is given to nine decimal places and it is immediately seen that this is simply ϕ, the golden ratio, in Eq. (3-5) of Chapter 3. Now, we recall from Eq. (5-11) of Chapter 5 and the associated discussion that the [5, 2] star is foldable only if altitude and radius satisfy the relation $R = h\phi$. Remarkably, we see from Table 11-1 that the [15, 6] star is foldable if $h = R\phi$!

    Some photographs of stars constructed in the plane and folded to three-dimensional shapes of altitude h on base plane [N, J] stars are shown in Fig. 11-7.

Fig. 11-7. Examples of folded three-dimensional stars with [N, J] bases. Upper left: [10, 4] star of radius R = 2 in., h/R = 1.272. Lower left: [12, 4] star of radius R = 3 in., h/R = 0.7071. Upper right: [9, 3] star, radius 3 in., h/R = .5273.

CHAPTER 12
MOMENTS OF INERTIA OF SOLID STARS

12-1. Solid stars with flat, parallel faces

Perhaps the simplest solid shape star is that shown in Fig. 12-1 in which the plane five-point mathematical star [5, 2] is displaced in a direction perpendicular to its plane, without rotation, and through distance t. The volume of this solid star is

$$V = 10\left(\frac{1}{2} R l_1 \sin\frac{\pi}{5}\right) t, \qquad (12\text{-}1)$$

and remembering that l_1 is related to R through Eq. (4-5) of Chapter 4, the latter becomes

$$V = 5R^2 t\, a_1 \sin\frac{\pi}{5}, \qquad (12\text{-}2)$$

where the numerical value of a_1 is given in Eq. (4-6). Let the solid star be composed of a medium such as metal or glass that has a uniform density ρ throughout. Then, the mass of this solid star is

$$m = \rho V. \qquad (12\text{-}3)$$

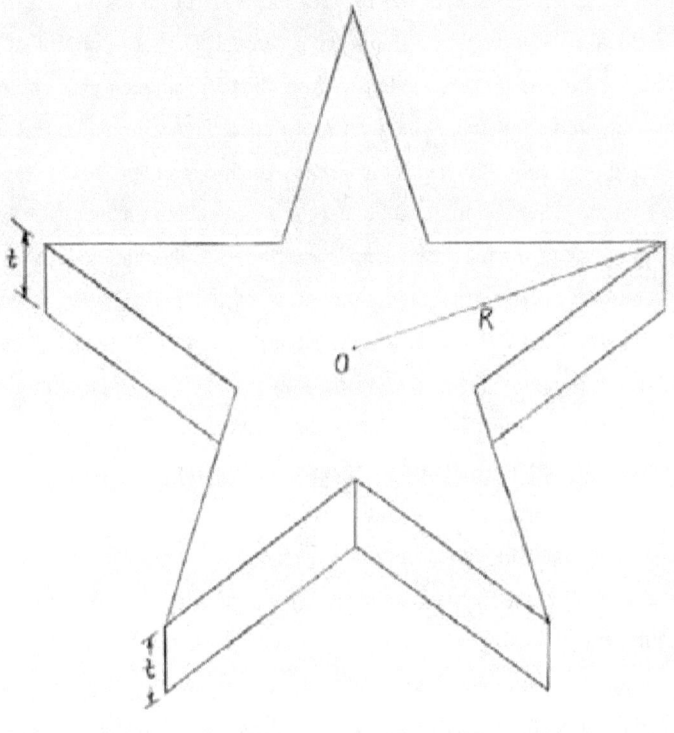

Fig. 12-1. A simple solid star formed by two [5, 2] parallel star faces separated by distance t.

Imagine an axis perpendicular to the plane of the star in Fig. 12-1 passing through the center point O. Portions of the mass near the center lie near the axis; some near B are farther from the axis, while those in the tips are farthest from the axis. If we imagine rotating this solid star about the perpendicular axis through O, those portions of its mass near the axis do not move as far as those farther from the perpendicular axis, and of course those portions in the outer tips move the greatest distance. The combined effect of all the mass elements and their various distances from the axis through O provide a resistance to motion when a torque is applied to the solid star to rotate it about the axis. The combined resistance to motion of all the mass elements is referred to as the "moment of inertia." In the case of rotational motion, the inertial moment of the body is the property that determines the magnitude of torque necessary to set the body into motion at a given angular rate about an axis of rotation. Conversely, if the body is in uniform angular motion about the axis, its moment of inertia is the property that determines the magnitude of torque required to decrease its rotation and bring it to rest.

The moment of inertia of a body about a given axis is defined as the sum of the products of each small mass element times the square of its distance from the axis. So, it is easy to see that a small mass element in the region of a tip of a solid star contributes far more to the moment of inertia about the axis through O than the same mass element located, for example, near the intersection of two sides of the star periphery. Mathematically, the moment of inertia can be determined through a process of integration to sum up all the mass elements times the square of their respective distances from the axis. To apply this process to the solid star body in Fig. 12-1, refer to Fig. 12-2, which shows one of five identical segments comprising the solid star, with center at O and radius R. The sides l_1 and l_2 make angles $\pi/5$ and $\pi/10$, respectively, with the radius because this is the standard mathematical star [5,2] under consideration. To carry out the

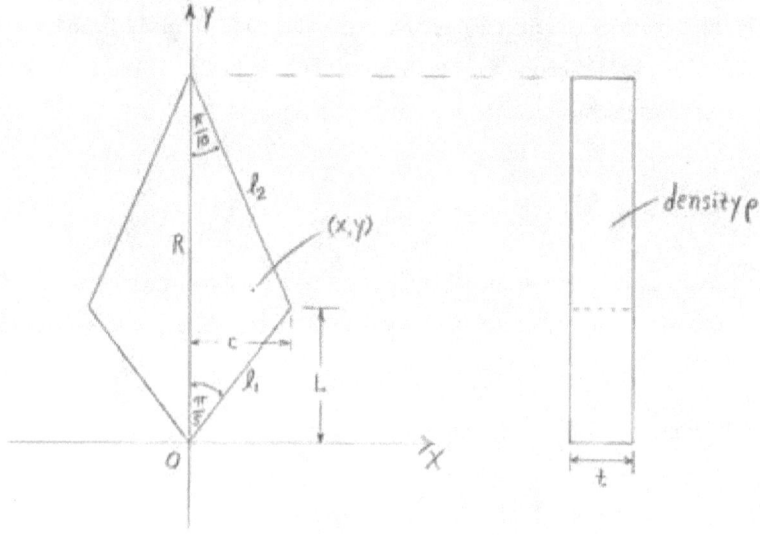

Fig. 12-2. One of five identical elements comprising the solid star figure in Fig. 12-1.

integration to determine the moment of inertia, let an x-y coordinate system be oriented with its center at point O and y-axis lying along the radius R as shown. Now, the segment in Fig. 12-2 has thickness t in the direction perpendicular to the plane of the figure because it is one of five identical portions of the solid star body in Fig. 12-1. Therefore, a very small differential mass element located at point (x, y) has mass:

$$dm = \rho dx dy t, \tag{12-4}$$

where $dxdy$ is the cross-sectional differential area of the element and its differential volume is $dxdy \cdot t$. The distance of this mass element from the axis through the center at O is $\sqrt{x^2 + y^2}$, and so the square of its distance from O is simply $x^2 + y^2$. Therefore, the moment of inertia of the body in Fig. 12-2 is

$$\begin{aligned} I &= \iint (x^2 + y^2) dm \\ &= \iint (x^2 + y^2) dx dy \rho t. \end{aligned} \tag{12-5}$$

Suppose that we integrate with respect to y first in Eq. (12-5). Referring to Fig. 12-2, we see that for a fixed value of $x \leq l_1 \sin \pi/5$, the value of y ranges from a point on the side l_1 to the point vertically above it on the side l_2. So, the limits on y are from the equation of the line representing l_1, i.e.,

$$y = x \frac{L}{l_1 \sin \frac{\pi}{5}} \tag{12-6}$$

to the equation representing l_2, which is:

$$y = R - x \cot \frac{\pi}{10} \tag{12-7}$$

Letting $c = l_1 \sin \pi/5$, the limits on x are $\pm c$. Taking into account symmetry about the y-axis in Fig. 12-2, we can integrate from $x = 0$ to $x = +c$ in Eq. (12-5) and multiply the result by two, giving us:

$$I = 2\rho t \int_0^c dx \int_{xL/c}^{R-x \cot \pi/10} (x^2 + y^2) dy, \qquad (12\text{-}8)$$

in which the density and thickness have been removed from inside the integrals because they are assumed to be independent of both x and y. Now, carrying out the integrations in Eq. (12-8) and realizing that because of symmetry, the total moment of inertia I_f of the solid star in Fig. 12-1 is five times that represented by Eq. (12-8), we get:

$$I_f = 10\rho t \left[\frac{c^3}{3} \left(R - \frac{3L}{4} \right) + \frac{c}{3} \left(R^3 - \frac{L^3}{4} \right) - \frac{c^4}{4} \left(\cot \frac{\pi}{10} + \frac{1}{3} \cot^3 \frac{\pi}{10} \right) + \frac{1}{3} R c^3 \cot^2 \frac{\pi}{10} - \frac{1}{2} c^2 R^2 \cot \frac{\pi}{10} \right],$$

$$(12\text{-}9)$$

where:

$$c = l_1 \sin \pi/5$$
$$L = l_1 \cos \pi/5. \qquad (12\text{-}10)$$

Remembering that $l_1 = a_1 R$ where the numerical factor a_1 is given in Eq. (4-6) of Chapter 4, we find, after evaluating all the factors in Eq. (12-10) and (12-9), the simple result for the moment of inertia of the star in Fig. 12-1 about the axis through O:

$$I_f = 0.2722073 \, R^4 \rho t \qquad (12\text{-}11)$$

We see that the moment of inertia of the solid star is proportional to the fourth power of its radius, and proportional to the product of its density and thickness.

12-2. Comparison of solid star moment of inertia with that of common geometric solids

The moments of inertia of various common bodies are often expressed in terms of the masses of the bodies. We can do this for the solid star of Fig. 12-1, and then compare the result with those for other bodies. In combining Eqs. (12-2) and (12-3) and evaluating the numerical factors, we find the following for the mass of the solid star of Fig. (12-1):

$$m = 1.12257 \, \rho t \, R^2 \tag{12-12}$$

Therefore, the moment of inertia of the star from Eq. (12-11) can be expressed in terms of its mass from Eq. (12-12) as follows:

$$I_f = 0.2424858 \, mR^2, \tag{12-13}$$

and we see that the moment of inertia of the solid star is simply proportional to the product of its mass times the square of its radius.

A comparison of the moment of inertia of the solid star, expressed in Eq. (12-13), with that of other common bodies is given in Table 12-1. In this tabulation, a sketch of each body is provided along with the axis about which its moment of inertia is given, and the quantity m in each case is the mass of the corresponding body shown.

Table 12-1. Comparison of the Moment of Inertia of the Solid Five-Point Star with the Moments of Inertia of Other Common Bodies.

Body / Axis	Moment of Inertia
Rectangular plate (sides a, b)	$1/12\,m\,(a^2 + b^2)$
Solid cylinder, axis through center	$\tfrac{1}{2}mR^2$
Cylindrical shell, axis through center	mR^2
Solid sphere	$2/5\,mR^2$
Solid five-point star	$0.24249\,mR^2$

12-3. Solid stars with flat, parallel faces but variable tip angle φ

Next, consider the moment of inertia of a five-point solid star of thickness t as shown in Fig. 12-3, in which we allow the angle between a radius R and side L_2 to have a value different from 18° for the standard [5, 2] star, i.e., we allow the angle to be represented by φ as we did earlier in Fig. 9-1 of Chapter 9. To determine the moment of inertia of the solid star in Fig. 12-3 about an axis perpendicular to its plane, passing through its center at O, we proceed in a manner similar to that above for the solid star in Fig. 12-1. Referring to Fig. 12-4 and remembering that the relation between side L_1, R and the angle φ is that obtained earlier in Eq. (9-3), we see that Eqs. (12-10) for Fig. 12-2 are to be replaced by the following for the star in Figs. 12-3 and 12-4.

$$C(\varphi) = L_1 \sin \pi/5 = R \frac{\sin \varphi \sin \pi/5}{\sin(\varphi + \pi/5)}$$

$$L(\varphi) = L_1 \cos \pi/5 = R \frac{\sin \varphi \cos \pi/5}{\sin(\varphi + \pi/5)} \qquad (12\text{-}14)$$

In the latter, C and L have been written as $C(\varphi)$ and $L(\varphi)$, respectively, to indicate explicitly that these variable dimensions in Fig. 12-4 depend on the angle φ between R and side L_2. To proceed with the integration over x and y to evaluate Eq. (12-5) for the case of Fig. 12-4, we note that the limits on x are from $-C(\varphi)$ to $+C(\varphi)$, and the limits on y (for $x \geq 0$) that replace those in Eqs. (12-6) and (12-7) are from:

$$y = x \frac{L(\varphi)}{L_1 \sin \pi/5} \qquad (12\text{-}15)$$

for side L_1 to the following for side L_2.

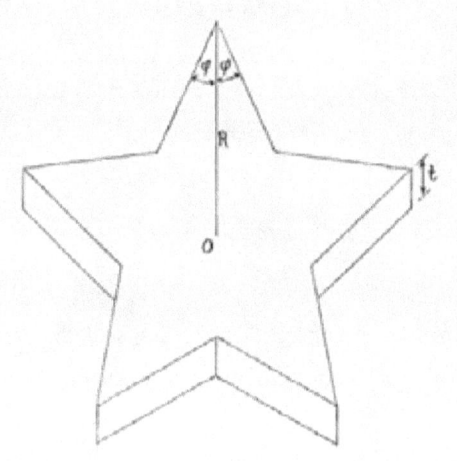

Fig. 12-3. A solid star formed by two parallel stars of tip angle φ separated by distance t.

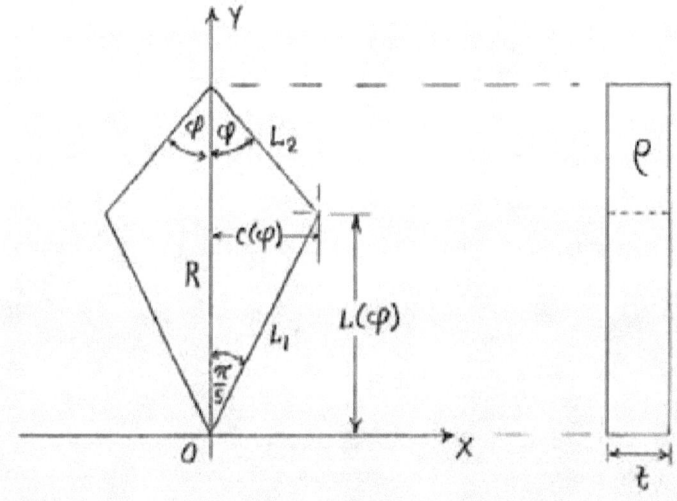

Fig. 12-4. Five volume segments like that shown comprise a solid star of the type in Fig. 12-3.

$$y = R - x \cot \varphi \qquad (12\text{-}16)$$

Because of symmetry, we can integrate from $x = 0$ to $x = +C(\varphi)$ and multiply the result by two. The double integral in Eq. (12-5) now becomes:

$$I = 2\rho t \int_0^{C(\varphi)} dx \int_{xL(\varphi)/C(\varphi)}^{R-x\cot\varphi} (x^2 + y^2) \, dy. \qquad (12\text{-}17)$$

Doing the integrations and evaluating them in terms of the parametric angle φ, and remembering that the moment of inertia of the solid star in Fig. 12-3 is five times the value in Eq. (12-17) for Fig. 12-4, we get:

$$I(\varphi) = 10\rho t \left[\frac{1}{3} C^3(\varphi) \left(R - \frac{3}{4} L(\varphi) \right) + \frac{1}{3} C(\varphi) \left(R^3 - \frac{1}{4} L^3(\varphi) \right) - \frac{C^4(\varphi)}{4} \left(\cot\varphi + \frac{1}{3}\cot^3\varphi \right) \right.$$
$$\left. + \frac{1}{3} RC^3(\varphi) \cot^2\varphi - \frac{1}{2} C^2(\varphi) R^2 \cot\varphi \right]. \qquad (12\text{-}18)$$

The quantities $C(\varphi)$ and $L(\varphi)$ in Eq. (12-14) are each proportional to R, and from the form of each term in the square brackets of Eq. (12-18), it can be seen that the moment of inertia $I(\varphi)$ is proportional to R^4 and, of course, to the product ρt. However, the proportionality factor depends on the angle φ chosen, and only for $\varphi = 18°$ does it have the value in Eq. (12-11) for the special case of solid star in Fig. 12-1.

By symmetry, the volume of the solid star in Fig. 12-3 is five times that of the volume of the segment in Fig. 12-4 and therefore:

$$V(\varphi) = 5 \cdot 2 \cdot \frac{1}{2} R L_1 (\sin \pi/5) t$$
$$= 5R^2 t \frac{\sin\varphi \sin\pi/5}{\sin(\varphi + \pi/5)}, \qquad (12\text{-}19)$$

from which we can express the mass in terms of the density ρ as:

$$m(\varphi) = \rho V(\varphi). \qquad (12\text{-}20)$$

The moment of inertia $I(\varphi)$ was calculated from Eqs. (12-18) and (12-14) as a function of angle φ for unit values of radius R, density ρ, and thickness t, and the results are presented in the graph of Fig. 12-5. Note that for $\varphi = 18°$, the value of $I(18°)$ is the same as the factor multiplying $R^4 \rho t$ in Eq. (12-11) for the standard star which has angle 18° between the radius and side l_2. It might be mentioned that the moment of inertia $I(\varphi)$ for values of R, ρ, and t differing from unity can be obtained from Fig. 12-5 simply by multiplying the value for a given angle φ by the appropriate values of R, ρ, t and taking into account that the dependence of $I(\varphi)$ on ρ and t is linear but varies as the fourth power of R. For example, for a star of radius 2 units, density 2.5 units, and thickness 1/8 unit, the value of $I(\varphi)$ for $\varphi = 10°$ is 2^4 x 2.5 x 1/8 times the value 0.148 read from the graph at $\varphi = 10°$, which yields $I(10°) = 0.74$. Now, in the commonly used MKS system of units, length, mass, and time are measured in meters, kilograms, and seconds. Referring to Eq. (12-11), we note that the numerical factor has no units because it is merely the number

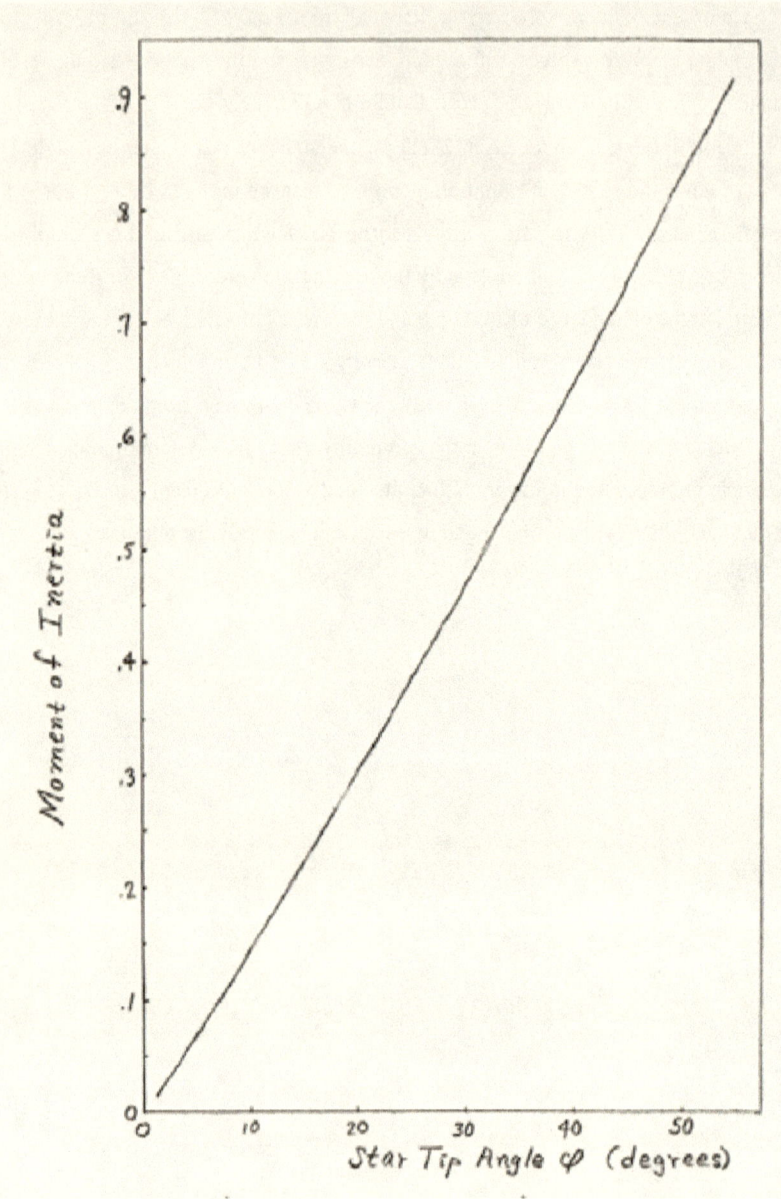

Fig. 12-5. Moment of inertia of star in Fig. 12-3 about axis perpendicular to its plane through center O, versus tip angle φ. The calculations are for unit radius, unit density, and unit thickness. For non-unit values, the moment is multiplied by $\rho t R^4$, at a given φ.

obtained upon evaluating all the numerical factors in Eq. (12-9). However, the moment of inertia I_f has units of length to the fifth power because of the product $R^4 \cdot t$, and units of mass per cubic length resulting from the density ρ. Therefore, the units of I_f in the MKS system are m^4(kg/m^3)m, or simply kg·m^2. So, in the example above, if MKS units are used, then $I(10°) = 0.74$ kg·m^2, remembering that "m" here stands for meter, not mass.

We see from Table 12-1 that the moment of inertia I of a given body divided by its mass m is just equal to a constant numerical factor times the square of its radius. In the case of the rectangular plate, it is the square of the diagonal that is multiplied by its corresponding numerical factor. Now, in the case of the solid star with arbitrary angle φ in its tip, as in Figs. 12-3 and 12-4, we note that from Eqs. (12-14) that a common factor, R^4, can be removed from each of the five terms inside the square brackets in Eq. (12-18) so that the factor multiplying the bracket is $10R^4 \rho t$. Combing Eqs. (12-19) and (12-20), it is seen that the mass $m(φ)$ is equal to $10R^2 \rho t$ times the trigonometric factor in Eq. (12-19), and if we divide the moment of inertia $I(φ)$ of the solid star in Fig. 12-3 by its mass $m(φ)$, the following is obtained:

$$\frac{I(\varphi)}{m(\varphi)} = \frac{R^2 \sin(\varphi + \pi/5)}{\sin\varphi \sin\pi/5} \left[\frac{C_R^3(\varphi)}{3}\left(1 - \frac{3L_R(\varphi)}{4}\right) + \frac{C_R(\varphi)}{3}\left(1 - \frac{L_R^3(\varphi)}{4}\right) \right.$$

$$\left. - \frac{C_R^4(\varphi)}{4}\left(\cot\varphi + \frac{1}{3}\cot^3\varphi\right) + \frac{1}{3}C_R^3(\varphi)\cot^2\varphi - \frac{1}{2}C_R^2(\varphi)\cot\varphi \right].$$

(12-21)

In the latter, the angular factors $C_R(\varphi)$ and $L_R(\varphi)$ are given in terms of Eqs. (12-14) as:

$$C_R(\varphi) = \frac{1}{R}C(\varphi) \equiv \frac{\sin\varphi \sin\pi/5}{\sin(\varphi + \pi/5)}$$

$$L_R(\varphi) = \frac{1}{R}L(\varphi) \equiv \frac{\sin\varphi \cos\pi/5}{\sin(\varphi + \pi/5)}.$$

(12-22)

So, the factor multiplying R^2 on the right side in Eq. (12-21) is dependent on the angle φ in the geometry of the solid star in Fig. 12-3. Eqs. (12-21) and (12-22) were used to calculate

$I(\varphi)/m(\varphi)$ as a function of the angle φ, and the results are given in the graph of Fig. 12-6. For the special case $\varphi = 18°$, the value of $I(18°)/m(18°)$ read from the graph is approximately 0.242, which agrees with the factor multiplying mR^2 in Eq. (12-13) for the standard star [5, 2].

It is interesting to note that as the angle φ becomes smaller and smaller, the volume of the star does likewise, as well as the mass. When $\varphi = 0$, the volume is zero and so is the mass, as seen from Eqs. (12-19) and (12-20). Furthermore, the moment of inertia calculated from Eq. (12-18) and plotted in Fig. 12-5 approaches zero as the angle φ approaches zero. However, from Fig. 12-6, the moment of inertia $I(\varphi)$ of the solid star divided by its mass $m(\varphi)$, as calculated from Eqs. (12-21) and (12-22), approaches a nonzero value slightly greater than $0.165R^2$ as φ approaches zero. So, even though the mass and the moment of inertia are independently zero for $\varphi = 0$, the quotient $I(\varphi)/m(\varphi)$ is not. We can find the limiting value of the quotient from Eqs. (12-21) and (12-22). First, note that as φ becomes very small, the factors $\sin(\varphi + \pi/5)$ in $C_R(\varphi)$ and $L_R(\varphi)$ approach $\sin \pi/5$ and in the limit, $\varphi = 0$, they equal $\sin \pi/5$. Using this applied to $\cos \varphi$ and $\sin \varphi$, each term in the square brackets can be expanded and a common factor $\sin \varphi$ removed from each to allow Eq. (12-21) to be written as follows.

$$\left(\frac{I(\varphi)}{m(\varphi)}\right)_{\varphi \cong 0} = 2\frac{R^2 \sin\varphi}{\sin\varphi}\left[\frac{1}{3}\sin^2\varphi - \frac{1}{4}\sin^3\varphi\cot\frac{\pi}{5} + \frac{1}{3} - \frac{1}{12}\sin^3\varphi\cot^3\frac{\pi}{5} - \frac{1}{4}\frac{\sin^3\varphi}{\sin\varphi}\cos\varphi \right.$$
$$\left. - \frac{1}{12}\frac{\sin^3\varphi\cos^3\varphi}{\sin^3\varphi} + \frac{1}{3}\frac{\sin^2\varphi\cos^2\varphi}{\sin^2\varphi} - \frac{1}{2}\frac{\sin\varphi\cos\varphi}{\sin\varphi}\right] \quad (12\text{-}23)$$

In the limit when $\varphi = 0$, the factor $\sin \varphi/\sin \varphi$ multiplying the brackets in Eq. (12-23) is indeterminate because $\sin 0 = 0$, but applying L'Hospital's rule shows that the limit of $\sin\varphi/\sin \varphi$

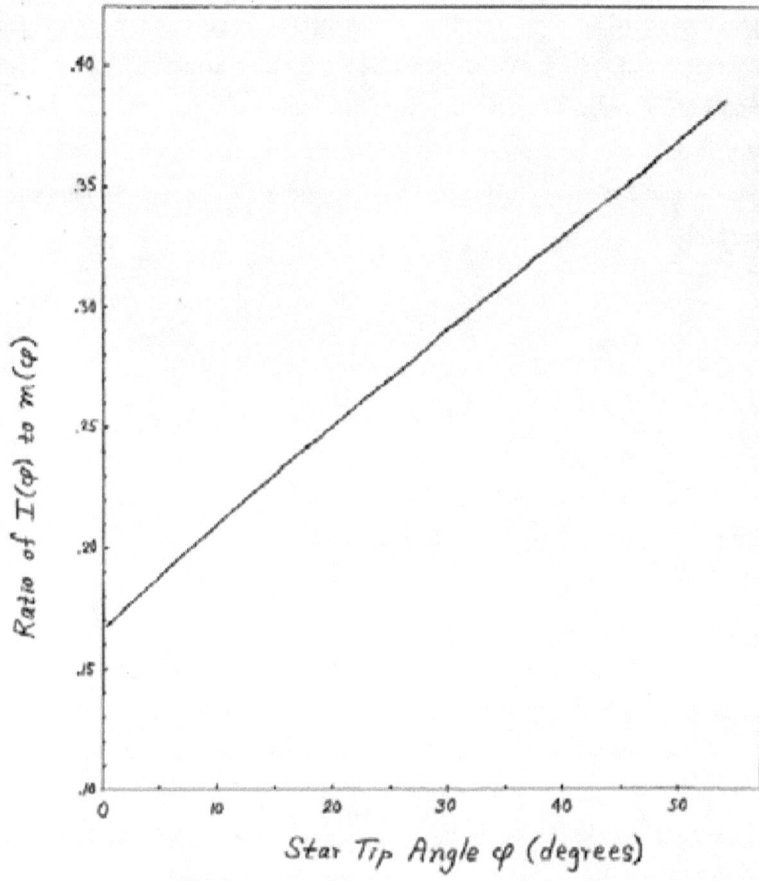

Fig. 12-6. Ratio of moment of inertia $I(\varphi)$ to mass $m(\varphi)$ for the solid star in Fig. 12-3, versus the tip angle φ.

when φ = 0 is 1.0. Inside the brackets, it is easy to see that the first, second, and fourth terms are simply zero for φ = 0. The third term is independent of φ, but the remaining four terms are indeterminate for φ = 0 because each involves sin φ to first or higher power in the numerator and in the denominator. However, L'Hospital's rule can be used repeatedly, as necessary, to differentiate the numerator and denominator of each term to obtain a quotient that is determinate for φ = 0. Carrying out these operations, we see that the limit when φ = 0 in Eq. (12-23) is:

$$\underset{\varphi \to 0}{\text{Limit}} \left(\frac{I(\varphi)}{m(\varphi)} \right) = 2R^2 \left(0 - 0 + \frac{1}{3} - 0 - 0 - \frac{1}{12} + \frac{1}{3} - \frac{1}{2} \right)$$

$$= (1/6) R^2. \tag{12-24}$$

The latter is the basis for the limiting value evident in Fig. 12-6 at φ = 0.

12-4. Solid stars with N tips, angle φ at each tip, and the altitude h at center

Next, we consider the moment of inertia of a solid star formed by erecting a perpendicular altitude of height h at the center of the N-point star shown in Fig. 12-7, and connecting the altitude with straight lines (ridges) to each tip at radius R and with straight lines (valleys) to each inward point such as B. We allow the general case in which the angle between a radius and side L_2 in the base plane is φ. Of course, in the final result, we can simply put $N = 5$ and φ = 18° for the case of standard [5, 2] star. The axis about which the moment of inertia is to be calculated is through the center O perpendicular to the base plane.

Consider the solid segment shown in Fig. 12-8a, of which there are N on one side of the base plane of symmetry. For a fully symmetric solid star at altitude h on both sides of the base plane, there are $2N$ of those elements. Let an x-y coordinate system with origin O be oriented

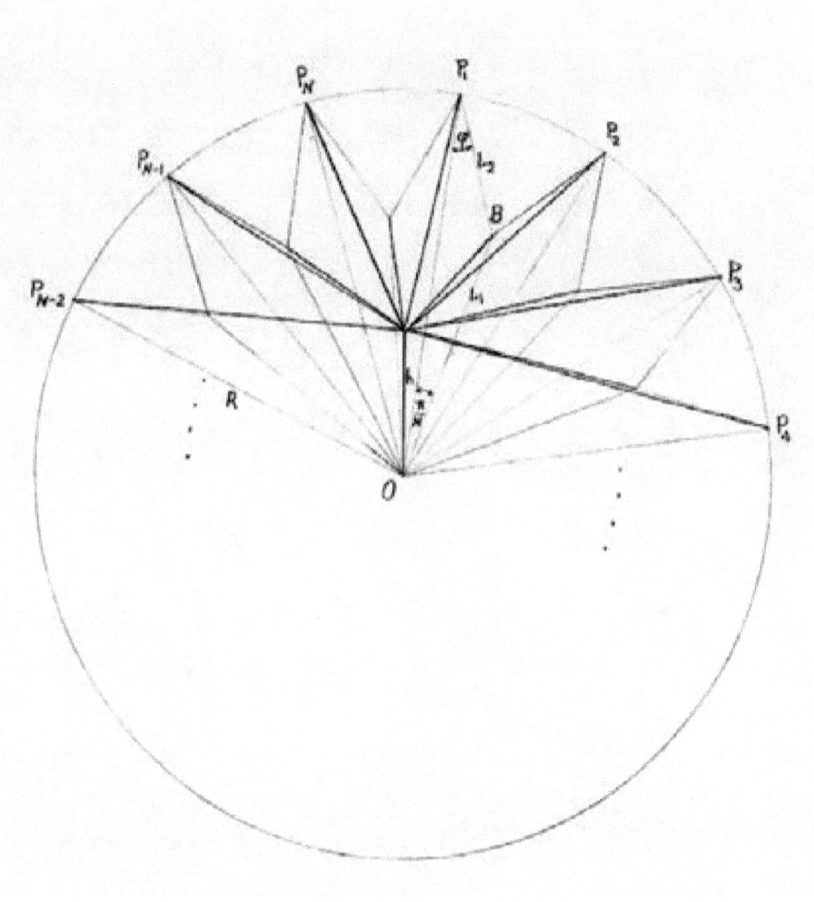

Fig. 12-7. Representation of a three-dimensional star of altitude h constructed on a N-point star of radius R, having tip angle φ.

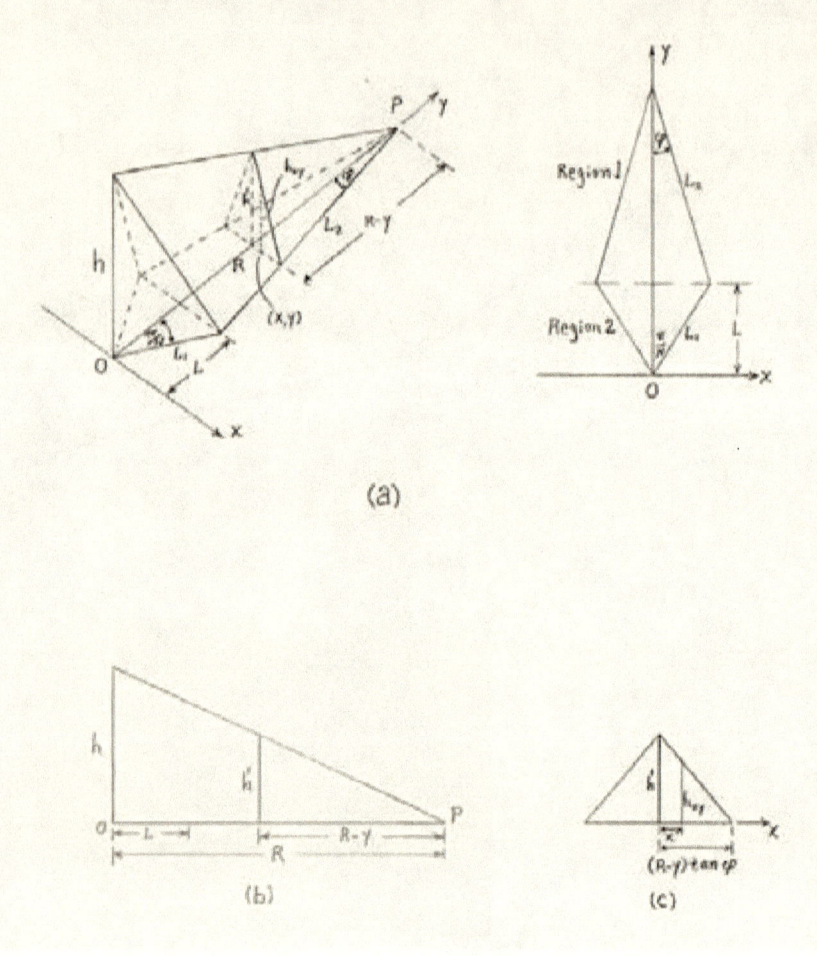

Fig. 12-8. (a) One of N identical volume elements of the three-dimensional star of altitude h constructed on one side of the base star plane of Fig. 12-7. (b) The two regions of integration in the (x, y) plane for calculating moment of inertia and (c) the height h_{xy} of differential volume element in Region 1.

with the y-axis along a radius as indicated. To determine the moment of inertia about an axis through the center O perpendicular to the base plane, we divide the solid segment of Fig. 12-8a into two regions, letting Region 1 extend from $y = L$ to $y = R$ and Region 2 extend from $y = 0$ to $y = L$, where:

$$L = L_1 \cos \pi/N \qquad (12\text{-}25)$$

Let the coordinates (x, y) represent the location of a point in the x-y plane in Region 1, and let h_{xy} be the perpendicular distance from this point to the surface of the triangular facet. Let the cross-sectional area of this element of height h_{xy} be $dxdy$. Then, the differential mass of the element is:

$$dm = \rho h_{xy}\, dxdy, \qquad (12\text{-}26)$$

where ρ is the density of the medium comprising the solid star, such as glass, metal, etc. The square of the distance of this mass element from the axis through point O is $x^2 + y^2$, and therefore the moment of inertia of Region 1 of the solid star is obtained by evaluating the following double integral over the appropriate limits on x and y.

$$\begin{aligned} I_1 &= \iint (x^2 + y^2)\, dm \\ &= \iint (x^2 + y^2)\, \rho h_{xy}\, dxdy \end{aligned} \qquad (12\text{-}27)$$

The plane perpendicular to the base plane and perpendicular to R, containing the height h_{xy}, is shown in Fig. 12-8b. This plane is at distance $R - y$ from the tip at P, and the height h' of the ridge line at the intersection with this plane is:

$$h' = \frac{h}{R}(R - y). \qquad (12\text{-}28)$$

The plane intersects the side L_2 at distance $(R - y) \tan \varphi$, from the foot of the perpendicular h', as shown in Fig. 12-8c, and the foot of h_{xy} is at distance x from this intersection of the plane with R, on the y axis. Therefore, from the right triangle, we have:

$$\frac{h_{xy}}{(R-y)\tan\varphi - x} = \frac{h'}{(R-y)\tan\varphi} \tag{12-29}$$

Eliminating h' between Eqs. (12-28) and (12-29) and solving for the height h_{xy} of the differential mass element, we substitute into Eq. (12-27) to get the following:

$$I_1 = \iint \rho(x^2 + y^2) \frac{h}{R} \frac{(R-y)\tan\varphi - x}{\tan\varphi} dx dy \tag{12-30}$$

We choose to integrate first with respect to y, and it is seen from Fig. 12-8a that the limits on y for Region 1 are from $y = L$, in Eq. (12-25), to the coordinate of y, as a function of x, on side L_2. The equation of the line representing L_2 in the x-y coordinate system is:

$$y = R - x \cot \varphi. \tag{12-31}$$

The volumetric element in Fig. 12-8a is symmetric with respect to the plane perpendicular to the base plane, containing R on the y-axis, and therefore we can integrate on x from $x = 0$ to $L_1 \cos \pi/N$ and multiply the result by two. This limit on x is designated by A and from Eq. (10-29), Chapter 10, it can be expressed as:

$$A = L_1 \sin \frac{\pi}{N} = \frac{R \sin\varphi \, \sin\pi/N}{\sin(\varphi + \pi/N)}. \tag{12-32}$$

In addition to the factor of two noted above, the double integral must be multiplied by N because there are N of the elements of Fig. 12-8a symmetrically located about the axis through O, and finally, another factor of two must multiply the integrals because of symmetry at altitude h on both sides of the base plane. So, taking into account the limits from Eqs. (12-25), (12-31), and (12-32), we write the expression for I_1 in Region 1, from Eq. (12-30) in the following form:

$$I_1 = 4N\rho \frac{h}{R} \int_{x=0}^{A} dx \int_{y=L}^{R-x\cot\varphi} (x^2 + y^2)\left(R - y - \frac{x}{\tan\varphi}\right) dy \qquad (12\text{-}33)$$

The density ρ was moved outside the integral because it, along with h and R, are parameters, independent of x and y. After integrating first with respect to y over the limits and then with respect to x over the limits shown, Eq. (12-33) yields the following result for the moment of inertia I_1 of Region 1 about the axis through the center O.

$$I_1 = 4N\rho\frac{h}{R}\left[A\left(\frac{R^4}{12} - \frac{1}{3}RL^3 + \frac{1}{4}L^4\right) + \frac{A^2}{6}(L^3 - R^3)\cot\varphi + \frac{A^3}{6}(R^2 + R^2\cot^2\varphi - 2RL + L^2) \right.$$

$$\left. + \frac{A^4}{4}\left(L - R - \frac{R}{3}\cot^2\varphi\right)\cot\varphi + \frac{A^5}{10}\left(1 + \frac{1}{6}\cot^2\varphi\right)\cot^2\varphi \right] \qquad (12\text{-}34)$$

Next, we evaluate the moment of inertia integral in Eq. (12-27) for Region 2, which extends from $y = 0$ to the lower boundary of Region 1 as seen in Fig. 12-8a. Let (x, y) be the coordinates of a mass element point within Region 1 as shown in Fig. 12-9a, and let h_{xy} be the height of this mass element, that is, the perpendicular distance from the base plane to the triangular facet. We erect a plane perpendicular to the radius R in the base plane positioned so that it includes h_{xy}. Now, from Fig. 12-9b, this perpendicular plane intersects the ridge line at distance h' from the base plane, and we can relate h' to R and y as in Region 1:

$$h' = \frac{h}{R}(R - y), \qquad (12\text{-}35)$$

except that, here, y is restricted to $0 \le y \le L$. As shown in Fig. 12-9c, the perpendicular plane that intersects the ridge line at height h' also intersects the valley at a height h_2 above the base plane, and h_2 can be found from Fig. 12-9d, which shows the plane perpendicular to the base plane containing the altitude h and the line segment L_1 of the base plane star. From the right triangles in Fig. 12-9d, the distance h_2 in Fig. 12-9c can be expressed as:

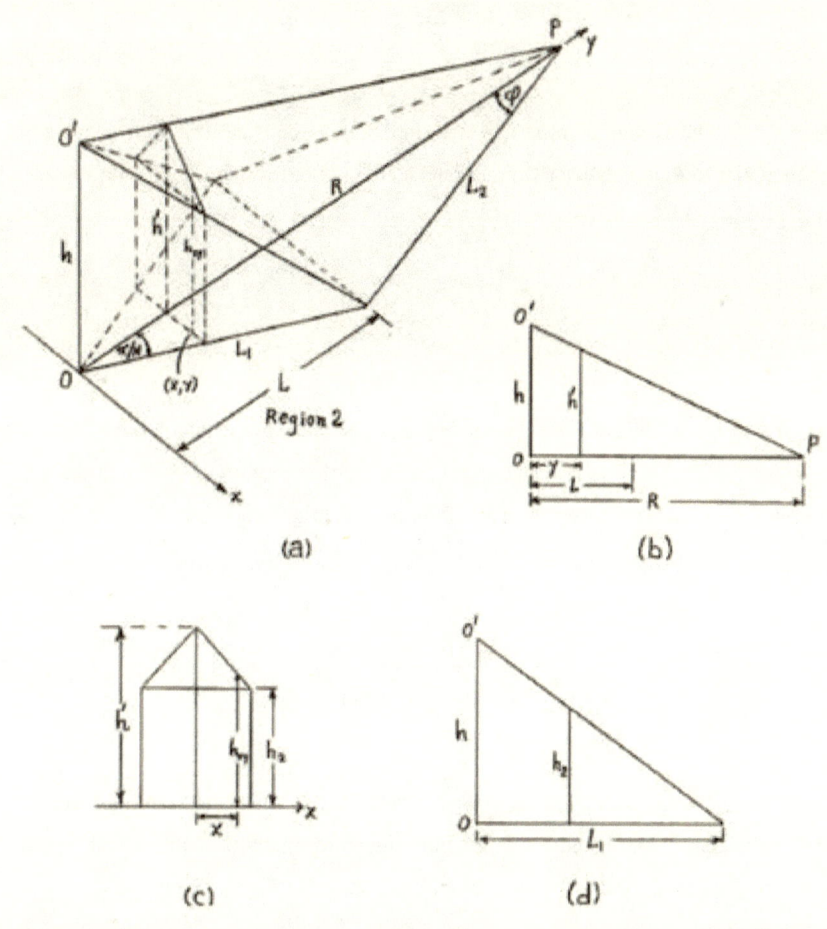

Fig. 12-9. (a) Geometry for determining height of differential mass element h_{xy} in Region 2 for moment of inertia integration. (b) Plane containing h_{xy} intersects $O'P$ at height h' above base plane, and (c) and (d) aid in relating h_{xy} to h, L_1, L and the angles.

$$h_2 = \frac{h}{L_1}(L_1 - L'_1), \tag{12-36}$$

where L'_1 is the distance from O, measured along the side L_1, at which the plane perpendicular to R at distance y from O intersects L_1. So, from Fig. 12-9a, the distance L'_1 in Eq. (12-36) is:

$$L'_1 = \frac{y}{\cos \pi/N}. \tag{12-37}$$

Now, from Figs. 12-9a and 12-9c, we note that in the plane perpendicular to R, the foot of the vertical segment h_2 is at distance $y\tan \pi/N$ from the radius R, and that the vertical height h_{xy} is at distance x from R. Therefore, from the right triangles in Fig. 12-9c, we can write:

$$\frac{h_{xy} - h_2}{y \tan \frac{\pi}{N} - x} = \frac{h' - h_2}{y \tan \frac{\pi}{N}}. \tag{12-38}$$

Remembering that L_1 in Eq. (12-36) is $R\sin \varphi/\sin(\varphi + \pi/N)$, we combine the results in Eqs. (12-35) through (12-38) and, after lengthy algebraic operations, the height h_{xy} of the differential mass element of cross-sectional area $dx \cdot dy$ in Region 2 can be written in the following form:

$$h_{xy} = \frac{h}{R}\left[R + x\left(\cot\frac{\pi}{N} - \frac{\sin(\varphi + \pi/N)}{\sin \varphi \sin \pi/N}\right) - y\right] \tag{12-39}$$

In Region 2, the limits on y are from a point on the line L_1 in Fig. 12-9a to the horizontal line $y = L \equiv L_1 \cos\pi/N$. The equation of the line representing the segment L_1 of the star is:

$$y = x \cot \pi/N. \tag{12-40}$$

The limits on x are from $x = -A$ to $x = +A$, the same as those for Region 1 in Eq. (12-32). Because of the symmetry, we can integrate from $x = 0$ to $x = +A$ and multiply the result by two, and again because of symmetry, the final result is $2N$ times this result because there are N tips and equal altitudes h on either side of the base plane. Therefore, substituting for h_{xy} from Eq. (12-39) into Eq. (12-27) applied to Region 2 and setting the limits for integrating first the respect to y, then for x, the expression for the moment of the inertia I_2 takes the form:

$$I_2 = 4N\rho \frac{h}{R} \int_{x=0}^{A} dx \int_{y=x\cot\pi/N}^{y=L} (x^2 + y^2)\left[R + x\left(\cot\frac{\pi}{N} - \frac{\sin(\varphi + \pi/N)}{\sin\varphi \sin\pi/N}\right) - y\right] dy. \tag{12-41}$$

Carrying out the integrations and collecting and combining all the terms leads ultimately to the following:

$$I_2 = 4N\rho \frac{h}{R}\left[\left(\frac{1}{20}LA^4 + \frac{1}{10}A^2L^3\right)\left(\cot\frac{\pi}{N} - \frac{\sin(\varphi + \pi/N)}{\sin\varphi \sin\pi/N}\right) \right.$$
$$\left. -A\left(\frac{1}{5}L^4 - \frac{1}{4}RL^3\right) + A^3\left(\frac{1}{12}RL - \frac{1}{15}L^2\right)\right] \tag{12-42}$$

Taking into account both Regions 1 and 2 in Fig. 12-8, the total moment of inertia of the solid star with N tips and altitude h, about the axis through its center perpendicular to the base plane, is the sum of I_1 and I_2 in Eqs. (12-34) and (12-42):

$$\mathcal{I} = I_1 + I_2 \tag{12-43}$$

We now apply Eq. (12-43) in conjunction with Eqs. (12-34) and (12-42) to calculate the moment of inertia for the special case of the five-point star, [5, 2] by substituting $N = 5$ and $\varphi = \pi/10 = 18°$. The result is:

$$(\mathcal{J})_{\substack{N=5 \\ \varphi=18°}} = 0.10888314\, \rho h R^4. \tag{12-44}$$

It is very interesting to compare the moment of inertia of the five-point solid star of altitude h in Fig. 12-7 with that of the flat solid star of thickness $t = h$ in Fig. 12-1. From Eqs. (12-44) and (12-11), we get the very simple numerical value:

$$\frac{\mathcal{J}_{5,18°}}{\mathcal{J}_f} = \frac{2}{5} \tag{12-45}$$

The result in Eq. (12-44) is for a solid star of altitude h either side of the base plane of symmetry, i.e., the on-axis thickness from apex to apex is $2h$, and this leads to the comparative factor 2/5 in Eq. (12-45). If we consider the solid star of altitude h, just one side of the plane of symmetry, and compare its moment of inertia with the flat solid star of thickness h, then the corresponding ratio in Eq. (12-45) would be merely 1/5.

Next, we express the moment of inertia of the solid five-point star, Eq. (12-44) in terms of its mass, and then compare with that of the solid, flat star. For the solid star in Fig. 12-8, the mass is ρV and the volume is ten times the volume of one of the volumetric elements $(1/3)(1/2)Rl_1 h \sin \pi/5$. Because the solid star is symmetric at altitude h on both sides of the base plane, the total volume is twice this, giving:

$$V = 2 \cdot 10 \cdot \frac{1}{3} \left(\frac{1}{2} Rl_1 h \sin \pi/5\right)$$

$$= \frac{10}{3} R^2 h\, a_1 \sin \pi/5. \tag{12-46}$$

Using the numerical value of a_1 from Eq. (4-6), Chapter 4 for the five-point star, we obtain the mass:

$$m = \rho V$$
$$= 0.74837996\, \rho R^2 h, \qquad (12\text{-}47)$$

and so the moment of inertia $\mathcal{J}$ in Eq. (12-44) can be expressed as follows in terms of the mass:

$$\mathcal{J}_{\substack{N=5 \\ \varphi=18°}} = 0.14549179\, mR^2 \qquad (12\text{-}48)$$

For the solid flat star of thickness $t = h$, the mass m_f from Eq. (12-12) is:

$$m_f = \rho V$$
$$= 1.12256994\, \rho R^2 h, \qquad (12\text{-}49)$$

and therefore from Eq. (12-13), its moment of inertia can be written as:

$$\mathcal{J}_f = 0.2424858\, m_f R^2. \qquad (12\text{-}50)$$

Now, consider two solid stars; one of the flat type in Fig. 12-1 and the other with central altitude as in Fig. 12-7, both having the same radius. If their masses are equal, $m_f = m$ in Eqs. (12-50) and (12-48), then their moments of inertia bear the simple relationship:

$$\mathcal{J}_{\substack{N=5 \\ \varphi=18°}} = \frac{3}{5}\, \mathcal{J}_f. \qquad (12\text{-}51)$$

Using Eq. (12-43) along with Eqs. (12-34) and (12-42), the moment of inertia of a three-dimensional star like that shown in Fig. 12-7 was calculated as a function of the angle φ at the tip for each of three different altitudes h, and the results are given in the graph of Fig. 12-10. These are for the five-point star with $N = 5$, and unit values of radius R and density ρ. For given values of radius R and density ρ, the moment of inertia increases linearly with altitude h as seen from the graph and is also evident from Eqs. (12-34) and (12-42). However, as the graph indicates, the moment of inertia increases at a slightly greater than linear rate with angle φ

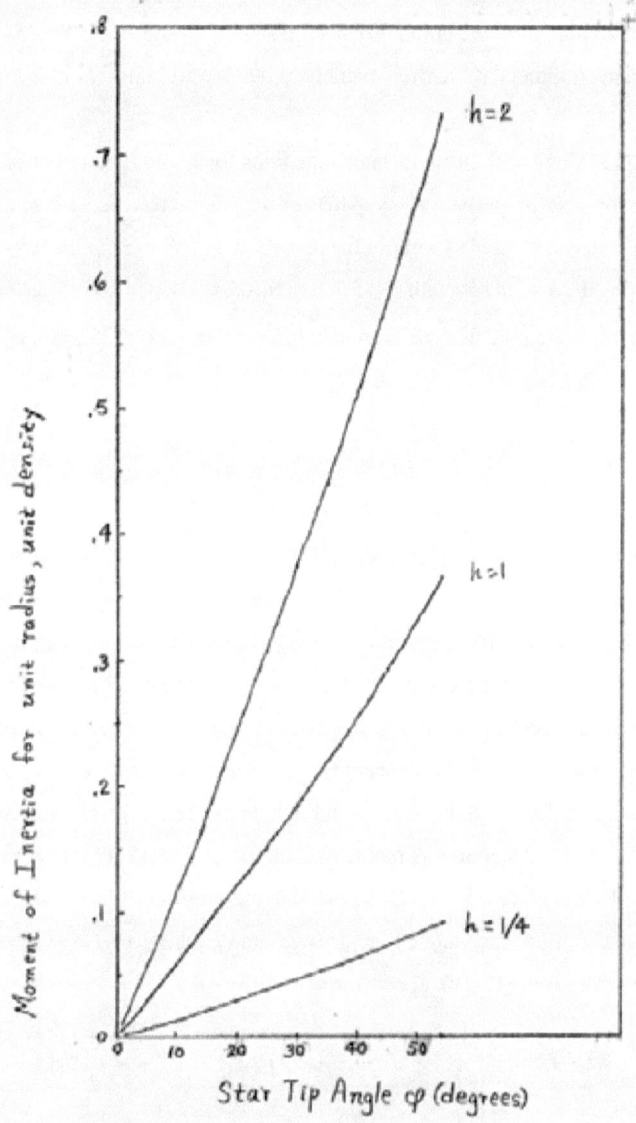

Fig. 12-10. Moment of inertia of five-point star versus tip angle φ, for each of three different altitudes h. Results are for unit values of radius R and density ρ.

because each of the three curves, for example, has increasing slope for increasing φ. An interesting thing to note from the graph is that solid stars with angles φ = 8°, 15° and 53.5° all have the same moment of inertia, namely 0.09, for altitudes h = 2,1 and 0.25, respectively.

Eq. (12-43) along with the associated equations for I_1 and I_2 can of course be used to calculate the moment of inertia for any values of the parameters N, R, h, and φ, but the curves in Fig. 12-10 can be used as well for the particular case N = 5 for the five-point star. For example, consider a solid star with N = 5 and radius R = 2.4, density = 3.2, and an angle φ = 25°, with h =1.7. We note that the curve labeled h = 1.0, for φ = 25°, gives $\mathcal{J}$ = 0.15. Therefore, assuming MKS units, we have:

$$\mathcal{J} = (0.15)(3.2)(1.7)(2.4)^4$$
$$= 27.073 \ kg \cdot m^2.$$

We return to the solid star with altitude h either side of the base plane, and angle φ at the tip, as in Fig. 12-7. For fixed values of radius R, altitude h, and number of tips N, we consider limiting values as the angle φ approaches zero. From Eqs. (12-19) and (12-20), it is seen that the mass is zero for φ = 0, and this is true because the volume is zero for φ = 0. Likewise, it can be seen that both components of the moment of inertia in Eqs. (12-34) and (12-42) approach zero for φ = 0, because L and A both are zero at φ = 0. So, as expected, both the mass of the solid star and its moment of inertia in Eq. (12-43) are zero when the angle φ is zero. However, it will now be shown that the moment of inertia divided by the mass has a nonzero value when angle φ approaches and equals zero. So, we examine the quantity formed from Eqs. (12-19), (12-20), and (12-43):

$$\frac{\mathcal{J}(\varphi)}{m(\varphi)} = \frac{I_1(\varphi) + I_2(\varphi)}{\frac{2}{3} N \rho R^2 h \frac{\sin \varphi \sin \pi / N}{\sin(\varphi + \pi / N)}} \qquad (12-52)$$

A plot of the ratio $\mathcal{J}(\varphi)/m(\varphi)$, versus angle φ, calculated from Eq. (12-52) is given in Fig. 12-11 from which it can be seen that the ratio does not approach zero for φ = 0. First, we note that as $\varphi \to 0$, $\sin(\varphi + \pi/N) \to \sin \pi/N$ because this quantity appears in both A and L in each of the terms of both I_1 and I_2. A common factor $R \sin \varphi$ can be factored from each term in I_1 and I_2, and both I_1 and I_2 contain the multiplicative factor $4N\rho h/R$. Many of the remaining terms inside the square brackets of I_1 and I_2 contain factors like $\sin^4\varphi/\sin^4\varphi$, $\sin^3\varphi/\sin^3\varphi$, $\sin^4\varphi/\sin\varphi$, etc., which are indeterminate when $\varphi = 0$ but can be evaluated at $\varphi = 0$ with the repeated use of L'Hospital's rule. Taking all this into account, we arrive at the following expression for Eq. (12-52):

$$\frac{\mathcal{I}(\varphi)}{m(\varphi)} = \frac{4N\rho \frac{h}{R} R \sin \varphi}{\frac{2}{3} N\rho R^2 h \sin \varphi} \left[\frac{R^4}{12} - \frac{R^4}{6} + \frac{R^4}{6} - \frac{R^4}{12} + \frac{R^4}{60} \right] \quad (12\text{-}53)$$

Again, using L'Hospital's rule, $\sin\varphi/\sin\varphi = 1$ when $\varphi = 0$ and therefore the latter reduces to

$$\underset{\varphi \to 0}{\text{Limit}} \left[\frac{\mathcal{I}(\varphi)}{m(\varphi)} \right] = \frac{1}{10} R^2 \quad (12\text{-}54)$$

We note that this limit holds for any values of N, R, h, and ρ. The result in Eq. (12-54) is analogous to the limiting result for $\varphi = 0$ in the case of the solid flat star, but in that case the

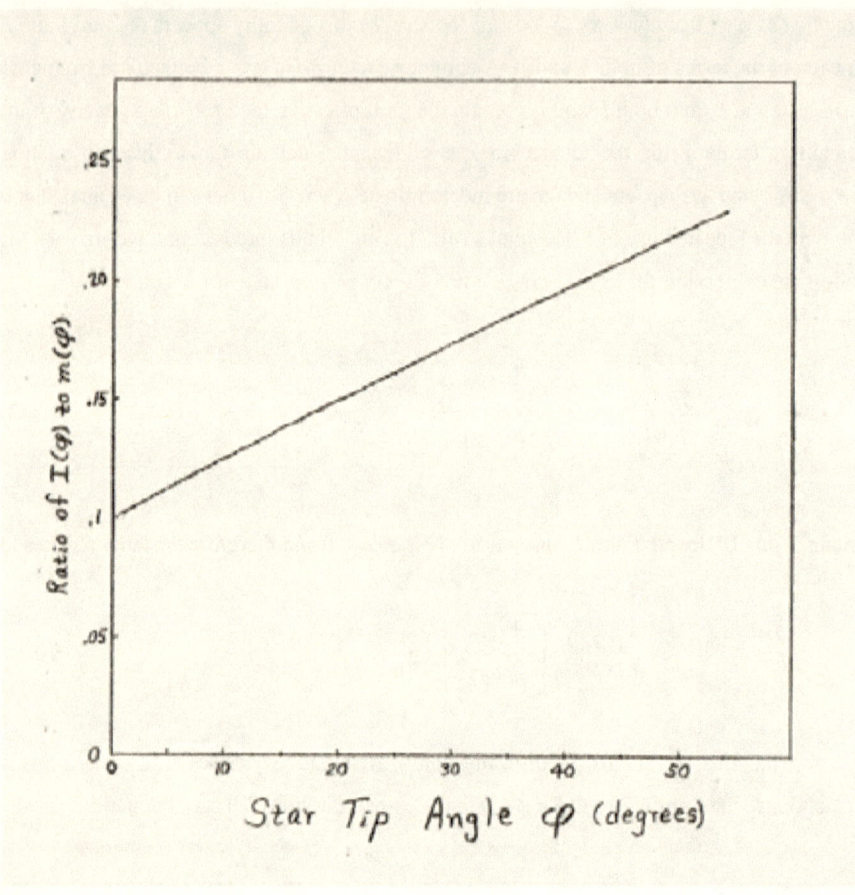

Fig. 12-11. Ratio of moment of inertia to mass of a three-dimensional, five-point solid star of altitude h, versus the tip angle φ.

factor multiplying R^2 in Eq. (12-24) is 1/6, which is simply 5/3 times the value of the result in Eq. (12-54) for the solid star with altitude h at its center.

CHAPTER 13

PASSAGE OF LIGHT THROUGH A SOLID STAR WITH FLAT PARALLEL FACES

13-1. Index of refraction

In Chapters 2 through 9, the solid star figures were treated as three-dimensional shapes. In Chapter 12, the three-dimensional volumes of the solid star were assumed to be occupied by homogeneous material of uniform density, and the resulting inertial properties were investigated. In this chapter, the solid mathematical star shapes will be assumed occupied by a uniform optical material such as glass, plastic, diamond, etc., that is transparent to light in the visible spectrum. Some very interesting properties of the solid star shape will be revealed when light is allowed to interact with it, as seen in the following analyses.

Consider the solid three-dimensional star with opposite plane faces parallel as indicated in Fig. 13-1 and let it be composed of a transparent optical material with uniform properties throughout. The star is assumed to be surrounded by air. Under these conditions, a ray of light oriented in a plane parallel to the plane faces of the star and incident at some angle on the face A will enter the star medium and travel in a redirected but straight line path within the star until it arrives internally at the face labeled B. As the ray passes out face B, it will in general change orientation relative to its path inside the star, but it will still travel in the plane parallel to that of the faces of the solid star. The path of the light inside the star and the position and angle at which it emerges from face B depend not only on the point and angle of incidence on face A but also on a property of the transparent medium known as its refractive index.

Some comments about the index of refraction are in order. Consider the simple case of light passing from air into an optical medium such as water or glass as indicated in Fig. 13-2. If

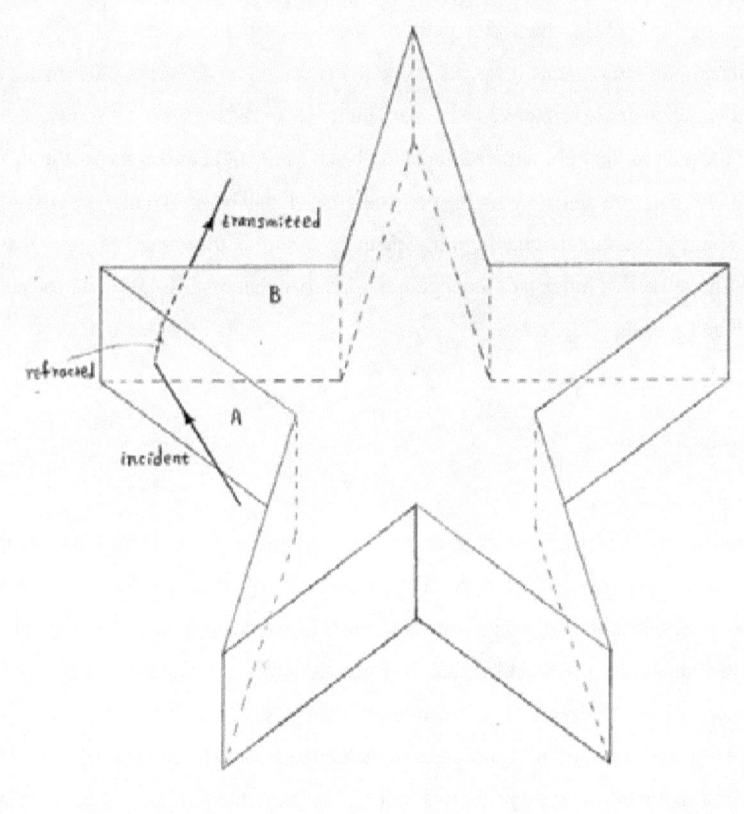

Fig. 13-1. A ray of light incident on face *A* of a solid star of optical medium is refracted internally and again refracted as it exits face *B*.

the light is incident in a direction perpendicular to the interface between air and the medium, as in Fig. 13-2a, then the path of the light is unaltered, i.e., it remains perpendicular to the interface as it travels in the lower medium. If, on the other hand, the light is incident at an angle θ relative to the perpendicular to the interface as shown in Fig. 13-2b, then the path of the light will be altered or "bent" as the light enters the medium, and its new path will make an angle r with the perpendicular. It can be shown that the alteration in path is a result of the fact that the light travels more slowly in the water (or glass) than it does in air. The refractive index n of the medium relative to that of air is defined in terms of the angles θ and r in Fig. 13-2b as:

$$n = \frac{\sin \theta}{\sin r}, \qquad (13\text{-}1)$$

and this is known as Snell's Law after its discoverer, Willebrord Snell, at the University of Leyden, Holland, in 1621. (Actually, Snell's geometrical construction required that the ratios of the cosecants of the angles be constant. It was Descartes who first used the ratio of sines, and in France, the law of refraction is generally known as Descartes's Law.) The refractive index of air is very nearly equal to unity, that is, the speed of light in air is very nearly equal to that in a vacuum. A more general situation is shown in Fig. 13-2c, in which light travelling in a medium with refractive index n_1 is incident at angle θ at the interface with a second medium of refractive index n_2. For this more general case, Snell's Law states that:

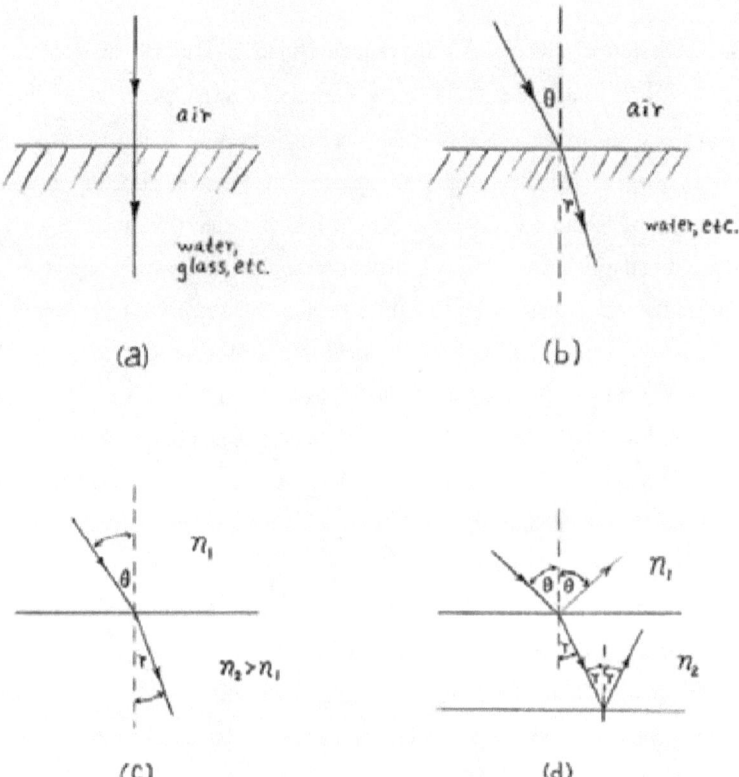

Fig. 13-2. Schematic representation of some aspects of refraction and reflection of light. (a) Light incident perpendicularly at the interface does not change direction. (b) When passing from air to water, for example, $\angle r < \angle \theta$. (c) Snell's Law embodied in Eq. (13-2). (d) Angle of reflection equals angle of incidence, but the magnitude reflected back into n_1 medium depends not only on θ but also n_1. Likewise, the amount reflected into n_2 depends on r, n_2, and the medium below n_2.

$$n_1 \sin \theta = n_2 \sin r. \qquad (13\text{-}2)$$

For the sketch shown in which $\theta > r$, the refractive index n_2 is greater than n_1. As a couple of examples, n for water is near 1.33, while for optical crown glass, it has a value near $n \cong$ 1.52. Another aspect of the path of light that we will make use of is illustrated in Fig. 13-2d, in which light again is incident from medium of index n_1 into medium of index n_2, but the lower portion of medium 2 is bounded by a horizontal surface, parallel to the n_1/n_2 interface. From the geometry, the ray is incident at angle r on the lower boundary, assumed to be reflective. According to the "law of reflection," the ray will be reflected from the lower boundary at the same angle as the incident angle, r in this case, and this is the familiar case of "angle of reflection equals the angle of incidence." Actually, although it is not shown in Fig. 13-2b, a small amount of light is reflected back into the air at angle θ relative to the perpendicular to the interface. Moreover, in Fig. 13-2a, a small portion of the light is reflected back into the air, in this case, the reflection is back along the incident path because the angle of incidence is zero.

13-2. Light incident perpendicular on an edge face

As a first example of the passage of light into a solid star of the type shown in Fig. 13-1, consider the view in Fig. 13-3 in the direction perpendicular to the face of the star. The star is composed of a uniform optical material, and light is incident on the edge face A. Let each of the remaining nine faces be designated by $B, C \ldots J$ as indicated, and let these be coated with a reflective coating for purposes of discussion. As we shall see later, the coating need not be present for the analysis to follow, but the arguments are easier to visualize with an assumed reflective coating in place. Consider four rays of light, each incident in a direction perpendicular to face A, but at difference distances from the tip P_1 as indicated in Fig. 13-3. It will now be

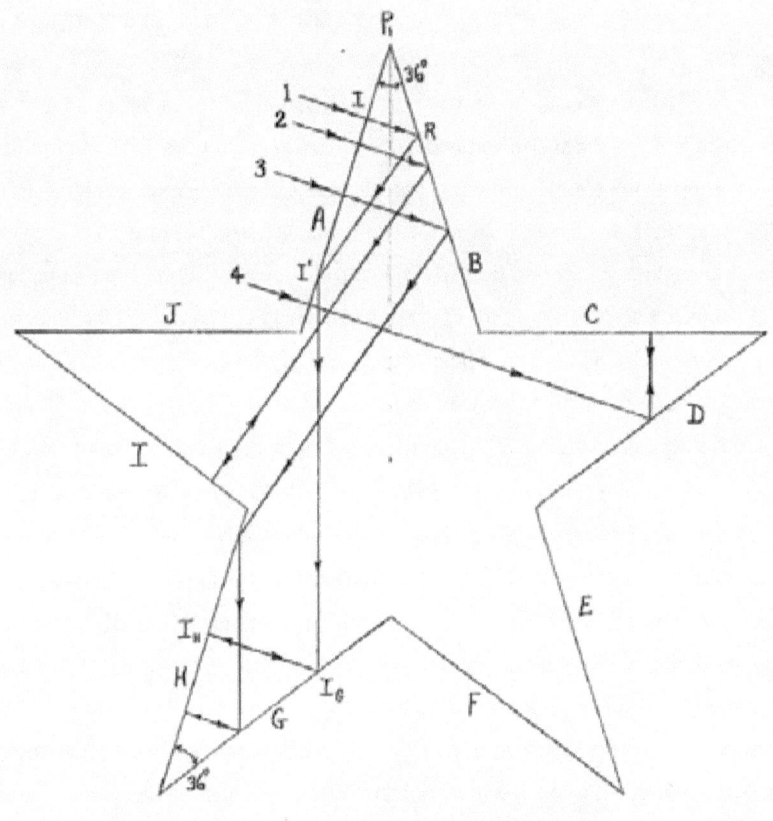

Fig. 13-3. Each of the four rays incident perpendicularly on face *A* ultimately will be retroreflected internally from the face shown, and therefore will retrace its path and exit face *A* along its original path of entry.

shown that each of these four rays enters the star, passes to one or more of the reflective faces, and eventually retraces its path and exits face A precisely on its particular path of entry.

Ray 1 is chosen near the tip, and it is incident at point I at 90° relative to face A, after which it enters the star in an undeviated direction and travels in a straight line inside the star, because the optical medium is assumed uniform, whereupon it is incident on face B at a point R. Now, triangle IP_1R is a right triangle, and because faces A and B are inclined at angle 2x18°, the angle P_1RI is 54°, which means that the angle of incidence of ray IR on face B is $\pi/2$ - 54° = 36°. This ray is reflected from point R on face B at the same angle, and it can been seen that if point I on face A is near enough to the tip, then the ray reflected from point R will be incident on face A at a point I', and the angle of incidence is $\pi/2$ - $\angle P_1I'R$, where angle $P_1I'R$ is in triangle $I'P_1R$. From the foregoing regarding the angles at point R, we can see that $\angle P_1I'R = \pi$ - (36° + 54° + 2x36°) = 18°, and therefore the angle of incidence of ray RI' on face A is $\pi/2$ - 18° = 72°. This means that ray RI' is reflected from face A at angle 72° relative to the perpendicular to face A; consequently, the reflected path makes angle $\pi/2$ - 72° = 18° with respect to the face A. However, from the geometry of the mathematical five-point star [5, 2], we know that face A makes angle 18° with radius OP_1, and therefore the reflected path of the ray from I' on face A is parallel to the radius. So, the ray reflected from I' will be incident on face G at some point I_G as indicated in Fig. 13-3, where it will be reflected and pass to face H, incident at a point I_H as shown. The incident and reflected paths $I'I_G$ and I_GI_H, respectively, are two sides of the triangle $I'I_GI_H$, because faces A and H are colinear by virtue of the construction of the mathematical star. Now, angle $I_HI'I_G$, which we have reasoned is 18°, is common to triangles $I'I_GI_H$ and $I'I_GP_4$; therefore, because faces G and H of the star are inclined at angle 36° at point P_4, the angle between the inclined path $I'I_G$ and side P_4I_G is π - 36° - 18° = 126°, and it follows that the ray $I'I_G$ is incident at angle 126° - $\pi/2$ = 36° on face G. Because the angle of reflection equals the angle of incidence, we see that angle $I'I_GI_H$ in triangle $I_HI'I_G$ is 72°, hence, angle $I_GI_HI' = \pi$ - 18° - 72° = 90°. That is, the ray $I'I_G$, after reflection from face G along path I_GI_H, is incident at angle 90° on face H, and therefore it is reflected directly back on its incident path and retraces its path at each point of reflection at I_G, I', and R, thence, it exits in direction perpendicular to face A along its initial path of entry. To summarize, a light ray incident at 90° on face A near the tip P_1 will be reflected internally from faces B, A, G, and H, and by virtue of retro-reflection, it will pass back out of the star following exactly its initial path.

Next, consider Ray 2 also incident at 90° on face A in Fig. 13-3, but farther from the tip P_1 than Ray 1. If Ray 2 is sufficiently far from point P_1, then upon internal reflection from face B, it will miss face A and, instead, be incident on face I as indicated. Now, making use of the angles and orientations of the sides in the mathematical five-point star [5, 2], an analysis similar to that above for Ray 1 shows that Ray 2 is retroreflected from face I, retraces its path, and exits from face A precisely on the path of entry.

Allowing a ray incident perpendicularly on face A to strike it at a point still farther from the tip point P_1, a region of incidence can be found in which the ray, after internal reflection from face B, will miss both faces A and I and instead will be incident on face H as indicated in Fig. 13-3. Following similar analysis to that for Rays 1 and 2, it can be shown that entry Ray 3 in Fig. 13-3 after reflection from face H will be incident on face G, and after reflection from face G, it is incident at 90° on face H again. By virtue of 90° incidence on face H, Ray 3 will retrace its path and exit face A directly on its initial path.

Finally, when the ray incident at 90° on face A is sufficiently far from the tip P_1 as indicated by Ray 4 in Fig. 13-3, the ray will travel directly to face D, whereupon it is reflected to face C. Analysis similar to the foregoing shows that this ray is incident on face C at 90°, and therefore it is retro-reflective and retraces its path back out through face A.

The boundaries of the regions of perpendicular incidence of light on face A for which the paths shown in Fig. 13-3 are realized will now be determined. In each case, let x be measured from tip P_1 along face A, but of course face A intersects the plane of the star in Fig. 13-3 in its side of length $l_2 = a_2 R$, where $a_2 = 0.726542528$ from Eq. 4-6, Chapter 4. So, in Fig. 13-4, x_1 is the limiting distance measured from P_1 for which Ray 1 will enter A, be reflected from face B, and be incident internally on face A. From the right triangles that have y_1 in common, we can write:

$$\tan 36° = y_1/x_1$$
$$\tan 18° = y_1/(l_2 - x_1), \tag{13-3}$$

from which we can solve for x_1.

$$x_1 = \frac{l_2 \tan 18°}{\tan 18° + \tan 36°}$$

$$= 0.309016994 \, l_2 \qquad (13\text{-}4)$$

The latter can be expressed as a fraction of the star radius R using $l_2 = a_2 R$, from which we get $x_1 = 0.224513989 \, R$. It follows that when Ray 1 is incident on face A for any distance along l_2 up to a maximum of 30.9% of l_2 measured from the tip of P_1, the path of the ray will be as shown in Fig. 13-3 in terms of the faces it will encounter in its overall transit.

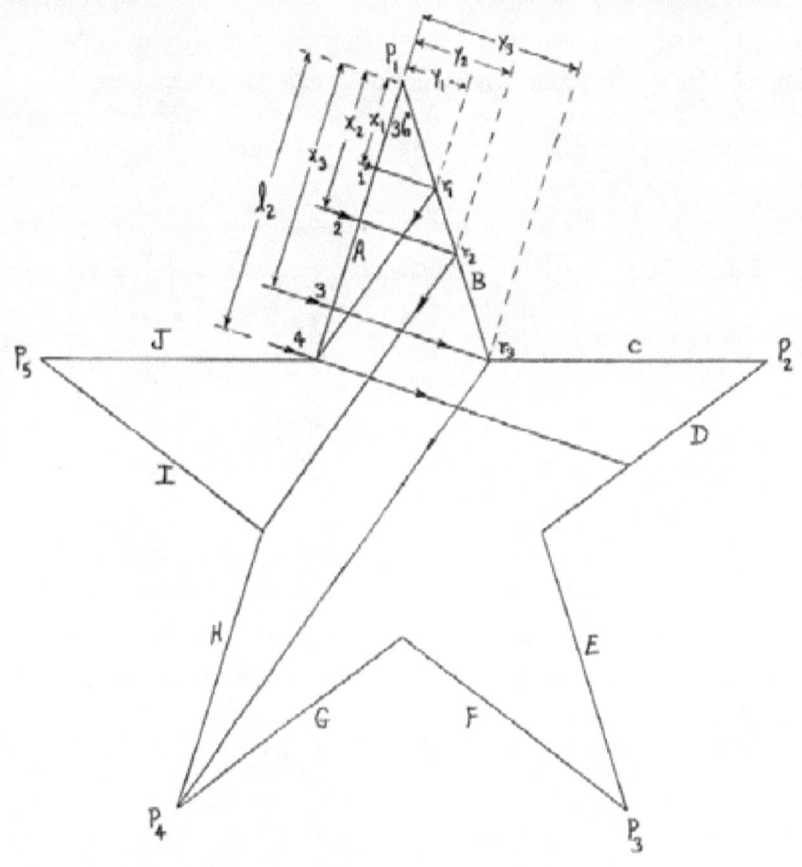

Fig. 13-4. Geometry used in determining the limiting points of incidence $X_1 \cdots X_4$ on Face A for which the light paths in Fig. 13-3 are obtained.

The path shown for Ray 2 in Fig. 13-3 will obtain for incident position on l_2 greater than x_1, up to a limiting value of x_2, which can be found by referring to the two right triangles having y_2 as a common side in Fig. 13-4. From these, we can write:

$$\tan 36° = y_2/x_2$$

$$\tan 18° = \frac{y_2}{l_2 - x_2 + 2l_2 \sin 18°}, \qquad (13\text{-}5)$$

and solving for x_2 gives:

$$x_2 = \frac{l_2(1 + 2\sin 18°)\tan 18°}{\tan 18° + \tan 36°}$$

$$= l_2/2. \qquad (13\text{-}6)$$

For Ray 3 to encounter faces as shown in Fig. 13-3, its distance along l_2 measured from P_1 in Fig. 13-4 must be greater than x_2, and its limiting distance is set by x_3, from which the length y_3 is common to the two right triangles shown, and we can write:

$$\tan 18° = \frac{y_3}{l_2 - x_3 + l_2 + 2l_2 \sin 18°}$$

$$\tan 36° = y_3/x_3. \qquad (13\text{-}7)$$

Solving for x_3 from the latter two relations gives:

$$x_3 = \left(\frac{2(1 + \sin 18°)\tan 18°}{\tan 36° + \tan 18°}\right) l_2$$

$$= 0.809016994\, l_2. \qquad (13\text{-}8)$$

Finally, the path taken by Ray 4 will encounter the faces shown in Fig. 13-3, provided its distance x from the tip in Fig. 13-4 exceeds x_3 in Eq. (13-8) but is less than l_2.

A summary of all these conditions and the features of the paths of the rays is given in Table 13-1.

Table 13-1. Description of Internal Light Paths for Light Incident Perpendicular on Face A of Solid Star, Figs. 13-3, 13-4.

Light Ray	Distance x^* of Incident Ray from Tip, Along Side l_2	Interval of x on l_2	Faces** Encountered by Light Ray	Face at Which Retro-reflection Occurs	Number of Reflections
1	$0 < x < 0.309 l_2$	0.30902	B, A, G, H	H	7
2	$0.309 l_2 < x < 0.5 l_2$	0.19098	B, I	I	3
3	$0.5 l_2 < x < 0.809 l_2$	0.30902	B, H, G, H	H	7
4	$0.809 l_2 < x < l_2$	0.19098	D, C	C	3

* Numerical values rounded to three decimal places.

** Excluding initial entry and final exit from Face A.

It is very interesting to note that the golden ratio appears in the comparative ratios of the limiting distances in Eqs. (13-4), (13-6), and (13-8), as shown below.

$$x_2/x_1 = x_3/x_2 = 1.618033989 \equiv \phi \tag{13-9}$$

$$x_1/(x_2 - x_1) = x_2/(x_3 - x_2) = \phi \tag{13-10}$$

We note from Figs. 13-3 and 13-4, along with the results in Eqs. (13-3) through (13-8), that light incident perpendicularly on face A never passes to faces E, F, and J. Stated another way, when light is incident at 90° on face A, it is impossible for it to reach any of the faces E, F, and J, although as has been amply demonstrated, the light can reach any of the faces B, C, D, G, H, and I depending on the position of incidence relative to the tip on face A. Of course, all these results are based on the assumption that the solid star has perfectly flat faces all oriented at precisely the angles governed by the mathematical star [5,

2]. In any actual case involving a solid star constructed from an optical material, very minor departures from flatness of the faces or minute deviations of the angles from their proper mathematical values could result in small amounts of stray light arriving at the three forbidden faces E, F, and J. However, these conditions represent only minor aberrations.

In all the foregoing analysis, it was assumed that, except for the entrance face A, the remaining faces were coated for perfect reflection. This assumption was made to aid in understanding the paths taken by the various light rays. However, it should be noted that in any actual case, reflection occurs even in the absence of a reflective coating, although the amount of reflection is considerably less than 100%. The fact that some reflection occurs in the absence of the coating is a consequence of the fact that light is an electromagnetic wave, and when it interacts with a transparent medium, such as glass, most of it is transmitted, but a small amount must be reflected. The simplest case is for light incident in a direction perpendicular at a boundary between air and, for example, glass. If n is the refractive index of the optical medium, then, according to electromagnetic theory, the fraction of incident reflected for 90° angle of incidence is $(n-1)^2/(n+1)^2$. A typical value of refractive index for visible light is $n = 1.5$, and so the fraction of light reflected is $(1.5-1)^2/(1.5+1)^2 = 0.04$, or 4%. For a glass solid star with $n = 1.5$ situated in air, 4% of the light incident perpendicularly on faces H, I, and C for the four rays as shown in Fig. 13-3 will be reflected back along the respective paths, in the absence of any coating on H, I, and C, and eventually exit through face A. At each of these points of incidence on H, I, and C, the balance of 96% of the incident light will be transmitted through the face and into the surrounding air. For other angles of incidence, the amount of light reflected depends not only on the angle of incidence but also on the state of polarization of the light, i.e., whether the light wave vibration is perpendicular to the plane of the incident light, or parallel to it. Now, in the above analysis related to Fig. 13-3, the only angles of incidence other than zero (incident ray, perpendicular to the surface) were 72° and 36°. Take first those cases in which the incident ray makes 36° with the perpendicular to the surface, that is, the face. In the absence of the coating, the light is incident inside the star optical medium at the interface with the surrounding air. The incident light will be split into the reflected portion internal to the star medium and the transmitted part that will travel into the air at an angle of refraction r that can be calculated from Snell's Law:

$$n \cdot \sin 36° = 1 \cdot \sin r. \tag{13-11}$$

Taking the refractive index of the star material to be $n = 1.5$ gives:

$$r = \arcsin(1.5 \cdot \sin 36°)$$
$$= 61.845°. \tag{13-12}$$

One polarization component of the light will be reflected internally, in the absence of the coating, with magnitude:

$$R_s = \left(\frac{\tan(36° - r)}{\tan(36° + r)}\right)^2 \tag{13-13}$$

and hence from Eq. (13-12), the amount of reflection is

$$R_s = 0.445\%. \tag{13-14}$$

For the other polarization component, the magnitude of the reflection is

$$R_p = \left(\frac{\sin(36° - r)}{\sin(36° + r)}\right)^2, \tag{13-15}$$

with the result:

$$R_p = 19.36\%. \tag{13-16}$$

Finally, consider the two cases in Fig. 13-4 in which the light ray is incident internally on the interface between the star medium and the surrounding air. Applying Snell's Law to this case gives:

$$n \cdot \sin 72° = 1 \cdot \sin r. \tag{13-17}$$

Substituting $n = 1.5$ leads to $r = \arcsin(1.42658)$, but this does not correspond to physical reality because the sine of an angle cannot exceed unity. This means that there is no light wave carrying energy transmitted into the air when the internal angle of incidence is 72°.

This situation is referred to as "total internal reflection," that is, all the light energy incident internally at 72° is reflected. So, the results of Eqs. (13-11) through (13-17) show that the analyses regarding Fig. 13-4 apply for a solid optical star medium located in air without any coating on the faces. Of course, the magnitude of reflection at the faces is different for the various angles of incidence. It should be noted, however, that total internal reflection will also occur for internal angles of incidence of 36° if the refractive index of the optical medium composing the star is equal to or greater than:

$$n = \frac{\sin 90°}{\sin 36°}$$

$$= 1.7013017.$$

Optical materials do exist for which this is true.

13-3. Splitting of a parallel light beam into seven individual beams

Now, let us consider the solid star comprised of refractive index n in Fig. 13-4 and examine the way in which it internally reflects, redirects, and transmits into air light rays from each of the four regions of incidence on face A when there are no coatings on the faces except for face B. A coating will be retained on face B to prevent light from being transmitted through B and refracted toward face C where under certain conditions, it can reenter the star medium and unnecessarily complicate the following analyses. First, we consider Fig. 13-5 and determine the boundaries of the incident light arriving at faces C, D, G, H, and I corresponding to the four regions of incidence on face A referred to in Eqs. (13-4) through (13-8) and in Table 13-1. To do this, we merely use the familiar geometric features of the five-point mathematical star [5, 2]. Each side, or "face" in this view, has length l_2 and makes angle 18° relative to the radius, so that the two faces meeting at a tip have an included angle of 36°. With the star oriented with radius R vertical, the line common to faces A and H, for example, is inclined at 72° to the horizontal, and the line common to faces D and G makes angle 36° with the horizontal.

Light following the path of Ray 1 is incident on face A over the distance range zero to $0.309\, l_2$ measured relative to the tip P_1, and this corresponds to distance l_2 measured from tip P_4 on face G to the distance:

$$l_2 - \frac{l_2 \sin 18°}{\cos 36°} = 0.618034\, l_2. \qquad (13\text{-}18)$$

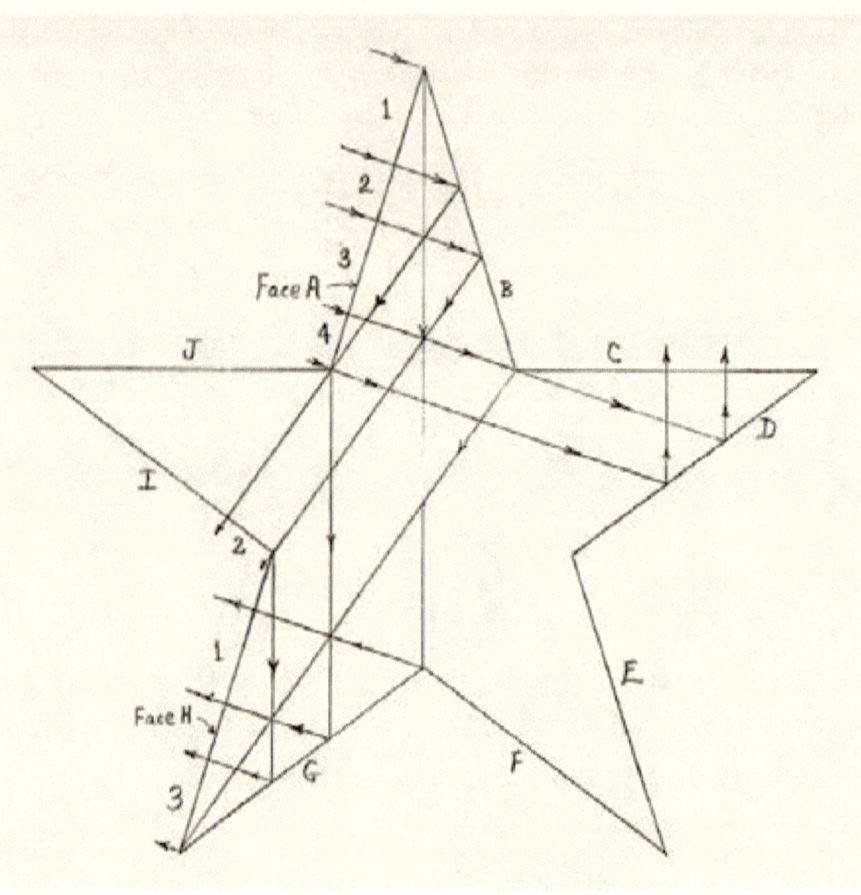

Fig. 13-5. The ranges 0° - incidence of the four rays on Face A (see Fig. 13-3) and the corresponding ranges of 0°-incidence of these four rays on Faces *H*, *I*, and *C*.

The corresponding distances of the light reflected from G to H measured from the tip P_4 on face H, are from:

$$l_2 \cos 36° = 0.809017\, l_2 \qquad (13\text{-}19)$$

to:

$$\left(l_2 - \frac{l_2 \sin 18°}{\cos 36°}\right) \cos 36° = \frac{1}{2} l_2. \qquad (13\text{-}20)$$

Ray 2 represents light incident in the region from $0.309\, l_2$ to $0.5\, l_2$ on face A, and the corresponding location on face I, measured from the tip P_5, is from:

$$l_2 \cos 36° = 0.809017\, l_2 \qquad (13\text{-}21)$$

to:

$$l_2. \qquad (13\text{-}22)$$

The range of incident light represented by Ray 3 on face A is from $0.5\, l_2$ to $0.809\, l_2$, measured from P_1. The corresponding range of Ray 3 on face G, measured from the tip P_4, is from:

$$\frac{l_2 \cos 72°}{\cos 36°} = 0.381966\, l_2 \qquad (13\text{-}23)$$

to:

$$0. \qquad (13\text{-}24)$$

The corresponding range of Ray 3 light arriving on face H is from:

$$l_2 \cos 72° = 0.309017\, l_2 \qquad (13\text{-}25)$$

to:

$$0. \qquad (13\text{-}26)$$

The range of Ray 4 light incident on face A is from x_3 in Eq. (13-8) to l_2. Therefore, from Fig. 13-5 the range of Ray 4 light arriving at face D is from:

$$\frac{\sin 18°}{\sin 126°} l_2 = 0.381966 \, l_2 \tag{13-27}$$

to:

$$\frac{\sin 18°}{\sin 126°} l_2 \, (1 + 2 \sin 18°) = 0.618034 \, l_2. \tag{13-28}$$

The corresponding range of Ray 4 light in its encounter with face C is from:

$$\frac{\sin 18°}{\sin 126°} l_2 \cos 36° = 0.309017 \, l_2 \tag{13-29}$$

to:

$$\frac{\sin 18° (1 + 2 \sin 18°)}{\sin 126°} l_2 \cos 36° = \frac{1}{2} l_2. \tag{13-30}$$

Finally, for completeness, we calculate the regions of incidence of the light rays on face B. Making use of the range on A for Ray 1 from Eq. (13-4), we find that Ray 1 is incident on face B, measured from its tip from zero to:

$$\frac{x_1}{\cos 36°} = 0.381966 \, l_2. \tag{13-31}$$

Using the result in Eq. (13-6) for the upper limit of the range of Ray 2 on face A, we see that the range on face B is from the distance in Eq. (13-31) to:

$$\frac{l_2 / 2}{\cos 36°} = 0.618034 \, l_2. \tag{13-32}$$

Knowing the upper limit of Ray 3 for incidence on face A, x_3 in Eq. (13-8), we find that the limit of Ray 3 on face B is from the distance in Eq. (13-32) to the distance:

$$\frac{x_3}{\cos 36°} = l_2. \tag{13-33}$$

For the case of light incident in a direction perpendicular to face A of the solid star, we can summarize the results of Eqs. (13-18) through (13-33) with the aid of the tabulation in Table 13-2.

Table 13-2. Ranges of Distances for Light Rays 1, 2, 3, 4 in Fig. 13-4 on the Faces Encountered by Each During Its Transit Through the Solid Star, After Initial Incidence in Direction Perpendicular to Face A.

Light Ray	Distance* on Face Indicated, as Fraction** of Face Length, l_2									
	A	B	C	D	E	F	G	H	I	J
1	0 – 0.309	0 – 0.382					1.0 – 0.618	0.809 – 0.5		
2	0.309 – 0.5	0.382 – 0.618							0.809 – 1.0	
3	0.5 – 0.809	0.618 – 1.0					0.382 – 0	0.309 – 0		
4	0.809 – 1.0		0.309 – 0.5	0.382 – 0.618						

* Measured from tip of star at each face.
** Values rounded to three decimal places.

We note that light is forbidden from arriving on faces E, F, and J for the case of light incident perpendicular to face A.

A graphical representation of these interesting results is given in Fig. 13-6 in which a beam of parallel light is incident in direction perpendicular to face A. We see that the single beam incident on face A gives rise to seven individual beams exiting various faces of the solid star. A single beam exits each of the faces C and I, and they each exit in a direction perpendicular to the face. Two beams exit face H, each in direction perpendicular to H. The reason that these four beams are transmitted into the air surrounding the star in direction perpendicular to the interface is because their directions internal the star are perpendicular to the respective faces so that, with zero angle of incidence, there is no deviation in path upon exit. The two beams that are transmitted into air from face H are parallel to the path of the original beam incident on face A, because all three beams are perpendicular to the common, co-linear line

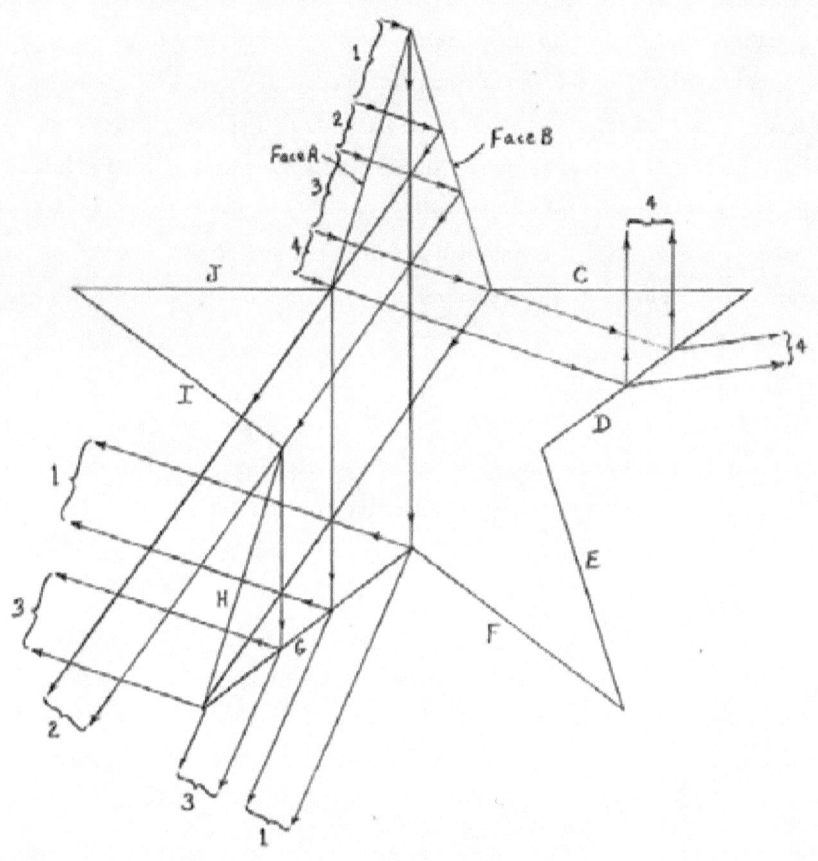

Fig. 13-6. Five-point [5, 2] solid star of thickness t, with Face B containing a reflective coating. Light incident at 0° (i.e., perpendicularly) along Face A gives rise to seven beams transmitted from Faces C, D, G, H, and I. The length of Face A is divided into four regions of 0°-incidence to show the contributions to the various seven transmitted beams.

represented by faces A and H. Although the two beams exiting face H are parallel to the path of the original incident beam, they are oppositely directed, i.e., they represent portions of the initial incident energy directed 180° from its path. Moreover, each of the two beams exiting face H is displaced laterally along the direction of faces A/H by the same distance relative to corresponding points on the initial beam incident on face A. Referring to Figs. (13-4) and (13-5) and measuring from the tip P_1 along the common line of faces A and H, we see that the lateral parallel displacement d of corresponding points on the two beams relative to the initial beam is:

$$d = l_2 + 2l_2 \sin 18° + (1 - \cos 36°) l_2, \qquad (13\text{-}34)$$

and upon evaluating the trigonometric factors, we can see that the resultant displacement can be expressed in terms of the golden ratio:

$$d = l_2 \left(1 + \frac{1}{2} \phi\right). \qquad (13\text{-}35)$$

As a final note regarding the two parallel beams exiting face H, we note intuitively from Fig. 13-6 and analytically from Eqs. (13-19), (13-20), (13-25), and (13-26) that the centers of these two beams are separated exactly by the lateral distance $l_2/2$.

The beam transmitted from face C into air in Fig. 13-6 is deviated angularly by $\pi/2 + 18° = 108°$ relative to the initial path of the beam incident on face A, and the sense of the angular deviation is counterclockwise. On the other hand, the beam transmitted into air in direction perpendicular to face I in Fig. 13-6 is deviated by 108° in a clockwise sense relative to the path of the initial beam incident on face A. These two beams transmitted from faces C and I into air are oppositely directed but not by 180°. Instead, their opposing paths are angularly separated by $2\pi - 2 \times 108° = 144°$.

The remaining three transmitted beams in Fig. 13-6, from faces D and G, make angles with their respective faces that depend on the refractive index of the medium from which the solid star is constructed. From the foregoing analysis related to the associated

Fig. 13-3, we see that the internal angle of incidence for each of these three beams is 36°. The refractive index of the solid star optical medium in Fig. 13-6 was assumed to be $n = 1.5$, and therefore, applying Snell's Law with internal angle of incidence gives:

$$n \cdot \sin 36° = 1 \cdot \sin r, \qquad (13\text{-}36)$$

and when this is solved for the angle of refraction that the transmitted rays make with the perpendiculars to faces D and G, the result is:

$$r = 61.845°. \qquad (13\text{-}37)$$

The angle r in Eq. (13-37) is the angle of refraction used to construct the three refracted transmitted beams in Fig. 13-6, based on the assumption $n = 1.5$.

The faces D and G are co-linear because they lie along the line joining P_2 and P_4 of the star. In general, the angular separation A_s between the paths of either transmitted beam from face G and the beam from face D can be determined from Eq. (13-36), with the result:

$$A_s = 2 \text{ arc sin } (n \sin 36°), \qquad (13\text{-}38)$$

and for the particular choice of $n = 1.5$ in Fig. 13-6, we find $A_s = 123.69°$. In the foregoing, use was made of the fact that the angles of internal incidence for the two beams transmitted from face G are both 36°, in general for the mathematical star, and therefore these two refracted beams are parallel.

13-4. The solid star as an optical device

In optics, numerous examples and applications exist in which a light beam is split or divided into two or three parts that travel in different directions. Most often, these involve optical cubes or prisms that split a single beam into two portions that travel in paths at 90° relative to each other. In reference to the analysis related to the solid optical star of refractive index n in Fig. 13-6, it would appear that this geometry possesses several unique features related to splitting and redirecting light beams. As we have seen, a single light beam incident perpendicularly on face A results in seven separate beams transmitted out of the solid star. Two of these beams, transmitted from a single face, are parallel and displaced laterally from the original beam, and travel in exact opposition at 180° relative to the original beam. Each of two other faces exhibits a transmitted beam perpendicular to its face; in relation to the original beam direction, one of these is deviated angularly in the clockwise sense by 108°, and from the other face, two parallel transmitted refracted beams occur at angle arcsin (n sin 36°) relative to the perpendicular to the face. A final face has a single, refracted, transmitted beam at the same angle relative to its face, but oriented such that its path relative to the paths of the other two refracted transmitted beams is simply twice the angle arcsin (n sin 36°).

Instead of directing a parallel beam of light on the entire length of face A in Fig. 13-6, we can choose a narrow beam and let it be incident in a perpendicular direction to face A, selectively, in each of the four regions referenced in Eqs. (13-4) to (13-8), and in Tables 13-1 and 13-2. This is shown in Figs. 13-7a to 13-7d. We see that selectively illuminating face A in this manner allows the beams to be "turned on" individually. In this capacity, the solid optical star can be said to function as a unique kind of optical switch.

13-5. Symmetric passage of light in the star, with two reflections in each tip

In all the foregoing, it has been shown that light incident at zero angle of incidence on a face of a solid star gives rise to some interesting features of the internally transmitted beams, but there are three faces of the star that the light cannot reach. Is it possible to introduce light on face A in Fig. 13-3 in such a way that the light enters the solid star and passes to all faces? Intuitively, the simplest condition that possibly can provide a positive answer to the question is to direct light on face A, so that when it enters the star medium, its refracted path is symmetric to the geometry of the star. To pursue this reasoning, consider the solid star in Fig. 13-8 and let a ray of light lying in a plane parallel to the plane of the figure be incident at angle θ at point P on face A as shown. It is assumed that the solid star is situated in air and, therefore, as light enters the star medium of refractive index n, it will be refracted toward the perpendicular to the surface,

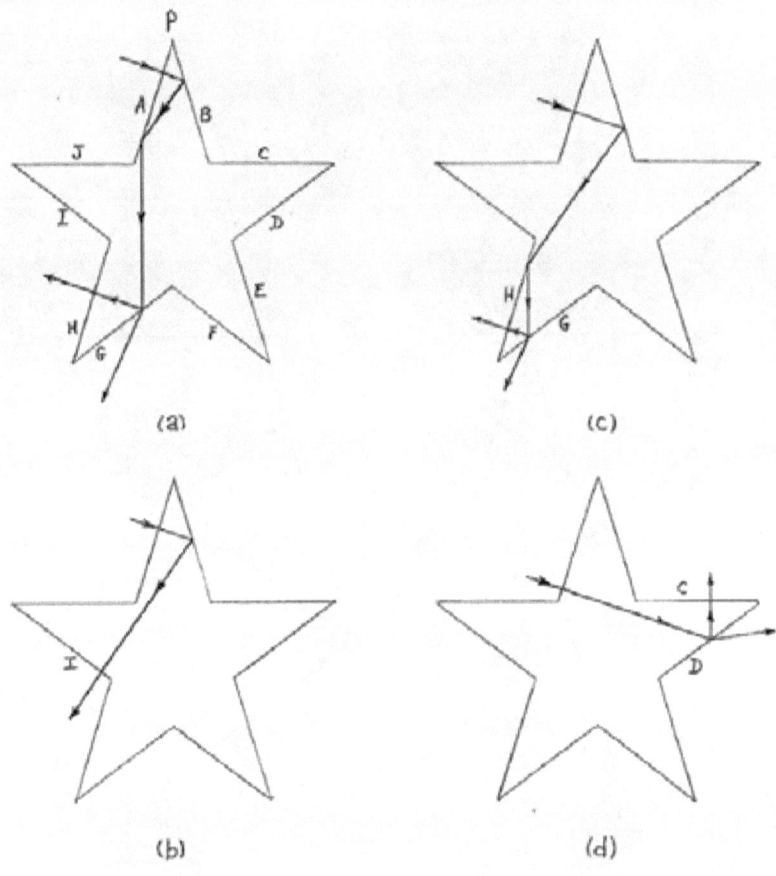

Fig. 13-7. When a narrow light beam is incident at 0° on Face *A* of a solid [5, 2] optical star, the various beams transmitted through Faces *C*, *D*, *G*, *H*, and *I* can be "switched on or off" depending on the location of the incident beam on Face *A*. As the distance from the tip *P* of the incident light on Face *A* becomes progressively greater, the passage of light is represented by (a), (b), (c), and (d), respectively.

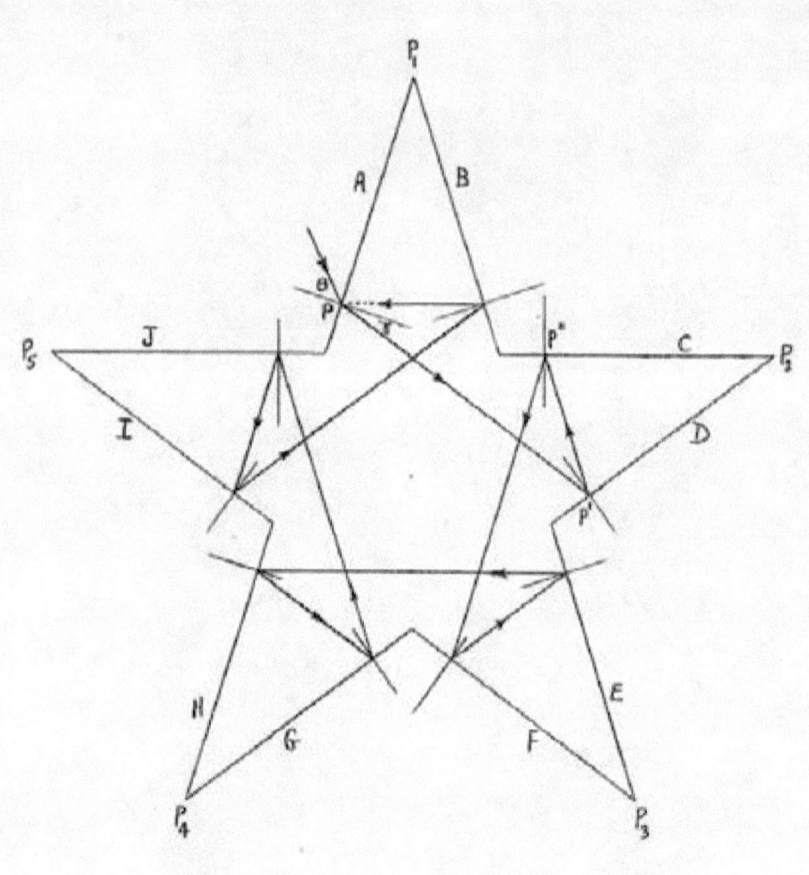

Fig. 13-8. When light is incident at angle θ on Face *A* such that the refracted ray travels at angle γ = 18°, then the light will traverse the symmetric path shown inside the solid optical star, making two reflections inside each tip region. If the star optical medium has refractive index *n* = 1.5, then θ must be ≅ 27.615° to cause angle γ to be 18°.

making an angle γ as indicated. We know from Snell's Law that the angle of refraction γ is related to n and θ through the relation:

$$r = \arcsin\left(\frac{\sin\theta}{n}\right). \tag{13-39}$$

So, to achieve symmetric passage of the refracted ray of light inside the star, let us choose angle θ for a given value of n to make angle γ, such that the path of the ray is parallel to the line joining P_3 and P_5 in Fig. 13-8. Letting P' be the point on face D at which the refracted ray intersects it; this means that γ must be such that PP' is parallel to P_3P_5. From the geometry of the mathematical five-point star, we know that faces H and G, each of length l_2 with included angle 36°, make angle of 72° with P_3P_5. Therefore, assuming the refracted ray path is parallel to P_3P_5, the triangle P_4PP' is isosceles. and the ray path PP' makes angle 72° with face A at P and 72° with face D at P'. The latter is true because the included vertex angle at each star tip such as P_4 is 36°. Now, because PP' makes angle 72° with face D, its angle of incidence at P' is π/2 - 72° = 18° and, of course, the same is true at point P, meaning that the refracted ray makes angle γ = 18° with the perpendicular to the surface. The angle of reflection at point P' on face D is equal to the angle of incidence, i.e., γ = 18° and the reflected ray intersects face C at point P''. This means that angle $P_2P'P''$ in triangle $P'P''P_2$ is π/2 - γ = 72°, but knowing that the vertex angle at P_2 in this triangle is 36° for the five-point star, it follows that triangle $P'P_2P''$ is isosceles and that angle $P'P''P_2$ is also 72°. So, we conclude that the ray reflected from P' is incident at angle π/2 - 72° = 18° on face C, and as a result, the ray is reflected at this angle at P'' and travels toward face F along a path parallel to P_1P_4. Appealing to the symmetry of the five-point star, we can continue this analysis to show that the path of the light inside the star is symmetric and that the angles of incidence and reflection at each of the ten faces are 18°. This is all true provided the initial condition holds, that is, light is incident on face A at angle θ such that the refracted light entering the star makes γ = 18° with the perpendicular to face A at point P in Fig. 13-8. For example, if the solid star is composed of an optical medium with refractive index $n = 1.5$

then knowing that angle γ must equal 18°, we solve for the necessary angle θ from Eq. (13-39):

$$\theta = \arcsin(n \sin \gamma)$$
$$= \arcsin(1.5 \cdot \sin 18°)$$
$$= 27.6148° \qquad (13\text{-}40)$$

A plot of the angle of incidence θ calculated from Eq. (13-40) as a function of the refractive index n of the star material is given in Fig. 13-9. For purposes of comparison, the refractive indexes of three familiar optical media are marked on the graph.

Limiting conditions exist on the point of incidence P in Fig. 13-8 in order for the internal pattern of light paths to be obtained. First, in order for the entering refracted ray to avoid being blocked by face B, the point of incidence P must be greater than $l_2 \sin 36°/\sin 108°$ measured from the tip P_1 on face A; on the other hand, of course, P must be just slightly less than l_2, measured from P_1, in order for the refracted ray to strike face D.

In Fig. 13-8, there are five segments such as PP' that are part of the overall path of the light within the star and, by condition, each of these is parallel to a line joining a tip on the star of radius R to the second tip from it. Therefore, by symmetry, if we extend these segments, they will meet in pairs at points that form a second star of radius R_1, as indicated in Fig. 13-10. This

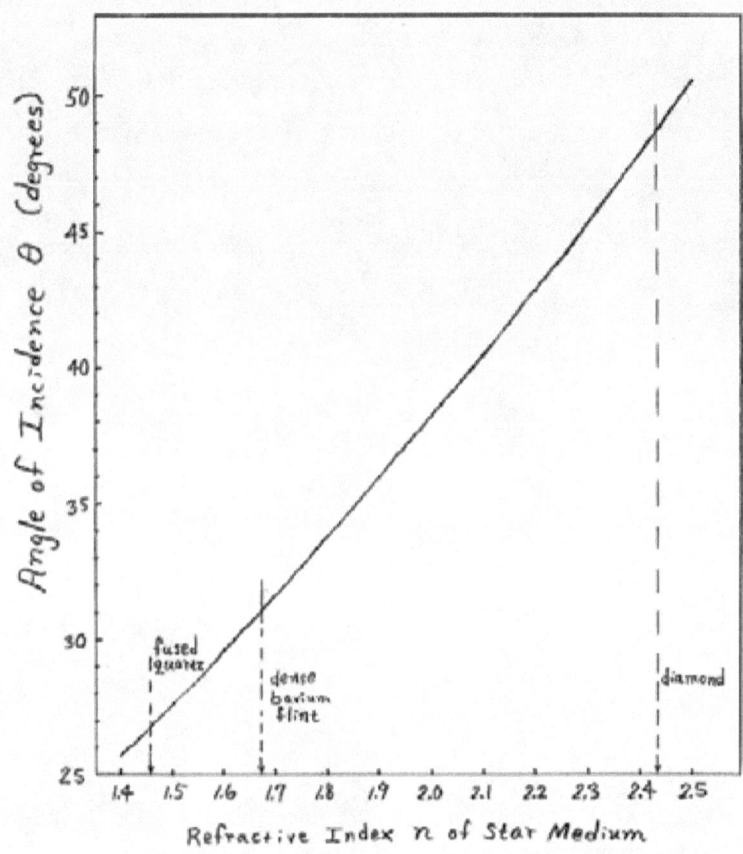

Fig. 13-9. Angle of incidence θ of light on Face *A* of the star in Fig. 13-8 versus refractive index n of the solid star medium to cause symmetric internal passage of the light. (The values of n for the media listed are for a wavelength $\cong$ 6,000 Angstroms.)

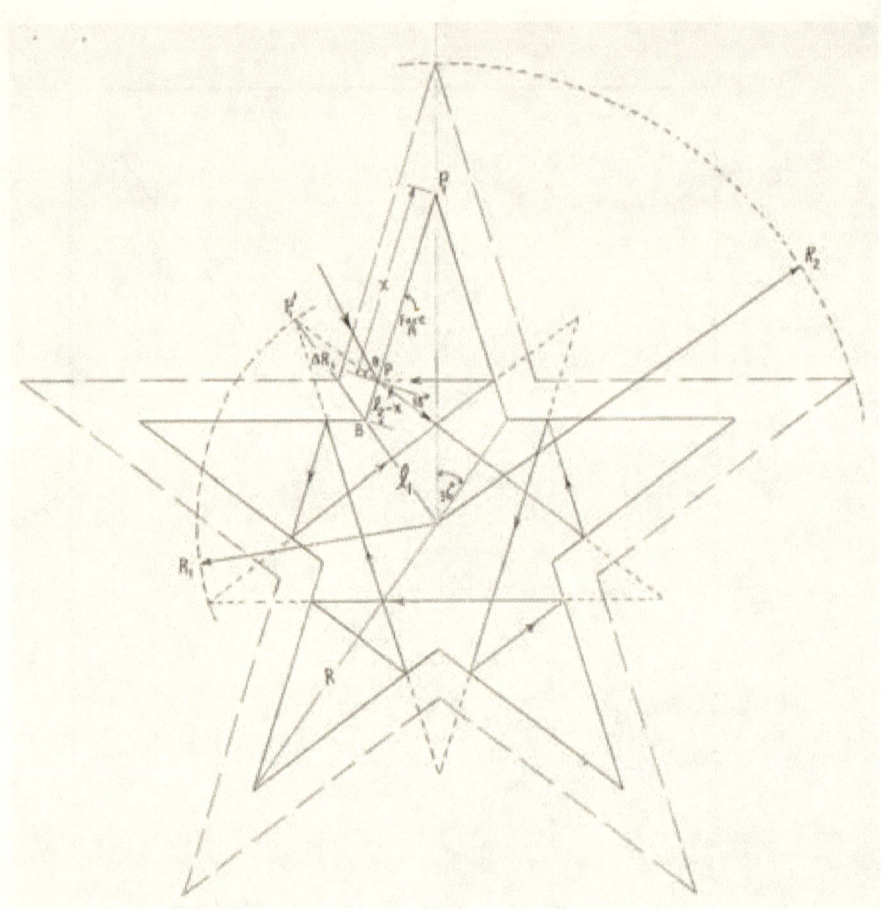

Fig. 13-10. When light is incident at ∠ θ on Face *A* of solid star of radius *R* such that the angle of refraction of the entering light is 18°, then an internal symmetric light path represented by the lines with arrows is obtained. Extensions of the latter lines in both directions give rise to two five-point stars, one of radius R_1 and one of radius R_2.

star of radius R_1 has the same center as the original star, but it is rotated through 36° relative to the original star. We also note that there is another set of five segments in Fig. 13-8 representing part of the overall path of the light, and that each of these segments, such as $P'P''$, intersects two adjacent faces of the original star symmetrically to form an isosceles triangle. These five segments like $P'P''$ can be extended to meet in pairs at points that, by symmetry in relation to the original star, form another star of radius R_2 as shown in Fig. 13-10. We see that this star of radius R_2 is aligned with the original star of radius R, because each radius R_2 is coincident with a radius R.

Using the symmetry properties of the five-point star as they transfer to each of the two additional stars in Fig. 13-10, the radii R_1 and R_2 of these stars can be determined in terms of the radius R of the original star into which light was introduced, forming internal light paths from which these stars were derived. Note from Fig. 13-10 that the radius R_1 is:

$$R_1 = l_1 + \Delta R_1 \tag{13-41}$$

where $l_1 = a_1 R$ is defined for the five-point star in Eq. (4-6) of Chapter 4, and the increment ΔR_1 can be obtained from the triangle $BP_1'P_1$, using the law of sines:

$$\Delta R_1 = \frac{\sin\left(\frac{\pi}{2} + 18°\right)}{\sin 18°}(l_2 - x), \tag{13-42}$$

where x is the distance measured from P_1 at which the light is incident on face A. Remembering that $l_2 = a_2 R$ with a_2 given in Eq. (4-6), the radius R_1 of the star is obtained from Eqs. (13-41) and (13-42).

$$R_1 = a_1 R + (a_2 R - x)\cot 18° \tag{13-43}$$

When the position of incident point P in Fig. 13-8 approaches $l_2 = a_2 R$, the radius R_1 is just equal to $l_1 = a_1 R$. It was mentioned earlier that the other limit on the distance x is $l_2 \sin 36°/\sin 108°$ and, as a result, the maximum value of the derived star radius R_1 is:

$$R_1 = R\left[a_1 + a_2\left(1 - \frac{\sin 36°}{\sin 108°}\right)\cot 18°\right]. \tag{13-44}$$

Evaluating the numerical factors, the latter gives:

$$R_1 = 2(\phi - 1)R. \tag{13-45}$$

Knowing that the golden ratio is 1.618033989, the maximum value of radius R_1 is approximately 1.236 times the radius R of the original star in Fig. 13-8.

For the other derived star of radius R_2, the use of similar right triangles in Fig. 13-10 allows the following relation to be written.

$$\frac{R_2 - l_1 \cos 36°}{l_1 \sin 36° + (l_2 - x)} = \frac{R - l_1 \cos 36°}{l_1 \sin 36°} \tag{13-46}$$

Solving for the latter for R_2 gives:

$$R_2 = a_1 R \cos 36° + \frac{1 - a_1 \cos 36°}{a_1 \sin 36°}(a_1 R \sin 36° + l_2 - x). \tag{13-47}$$

When the position x of the incident light point P in Fig. 13-8 is equal to l_2, we see from Eq. (13-47) that the radius R_2 of the derived star is just equal to the radius R of the original star. In the other limit when $x = l_2 \sin 36°/\sin 108°$, the value of R_2 becomes:

$$R_2 = R\left[a_1 \cos 36° + \frac{1 - a_1 \cos 36°}{a_1 \sin 36°}\left(a_1 \sin 36° + a_2\left(1 - \frac{\sin 36°}{\sin 108°}\right)\right)\right]$$

$$= 1.854101968\, R$$

$$= \frac{3}{\phi} R. \tag{13-48}$$

13-6. Symmetric passage of light in the star, with four reflections in each tip

In Fig. 13-8, it is seen that the light path within the solid star involves two reflections within the region of each of the five tips. It will now be shown that it is possible to introduce light into face A in such a way that the internally transmitted beam will undergo four reflections within the region of each tip and still pass into and out of all five tip regions. To accomplish this, we again consider a symmetrical condition in which the path of the beam innermost to the tip is perpendicular to the radius, that is, it forms the base of an isosceles triangle in which the vertex angle is the included angle at the tip, i.e., 36°, as shown in Fig. 13-11. Noting that the base angles of the isosceles triangle are 72°, it follows that the angle of incidence and angle of reflection are each equal to $\pi/2 - 72° = 18°$. We extend the paths of these rays back symmetrically to intersect the faces of the tip and label the angles of incidence and reflection as γ_1. We can determine angle γ_1 from either of the two triangles having two vertices formed at the two reflection points on one face, and the third vertex at the reflection point on the opposite face at the base of the isosceles triangle. Requiring the sum of the angles in either triangle to be π allows γ_1 to be determined. This gives $\pi/2 - \gamma_1 + \pi/2 + 18° + 36° = \pi$, or:

$$\gamma_1 = 54°. \qquad (13\text{-}49)$$

So, following the arguments of symmetry given earlier in relation to Fig. 13-8, it follows from the multiple-reflection light paths constructed in Fig. 13-11 that if light is incident on face A to make light enter the star medium at angle of refraction $\gamma_1 = 54°$, then the internal symmetric light paths shown in Fig. 13-12 will be obtained. There are some interesting differences in the light path in Fig. 13-12 compared to the path in Fig. 13-8. In Fig. 13-8, the refracted ray entering face *A* passes directly to face *D,* then to face *C,* thence into the interior, and so on, and the orientation of the ray in the interior rotates in a clockwise sense upon each entry from a tip region to the interior. In contrast, in Fig. 13-12, the refracted ray entering at face *A* proceeds directly to face *F,* then to face *E,* back to *F,* then to face *E* again, then to the interior region, over to face *J,* and so on. Upon each successive path from a tip region to the interior region, the orientation of the ray in the interior rotates in a counterclockwise sense. Other very intriguing comparisons

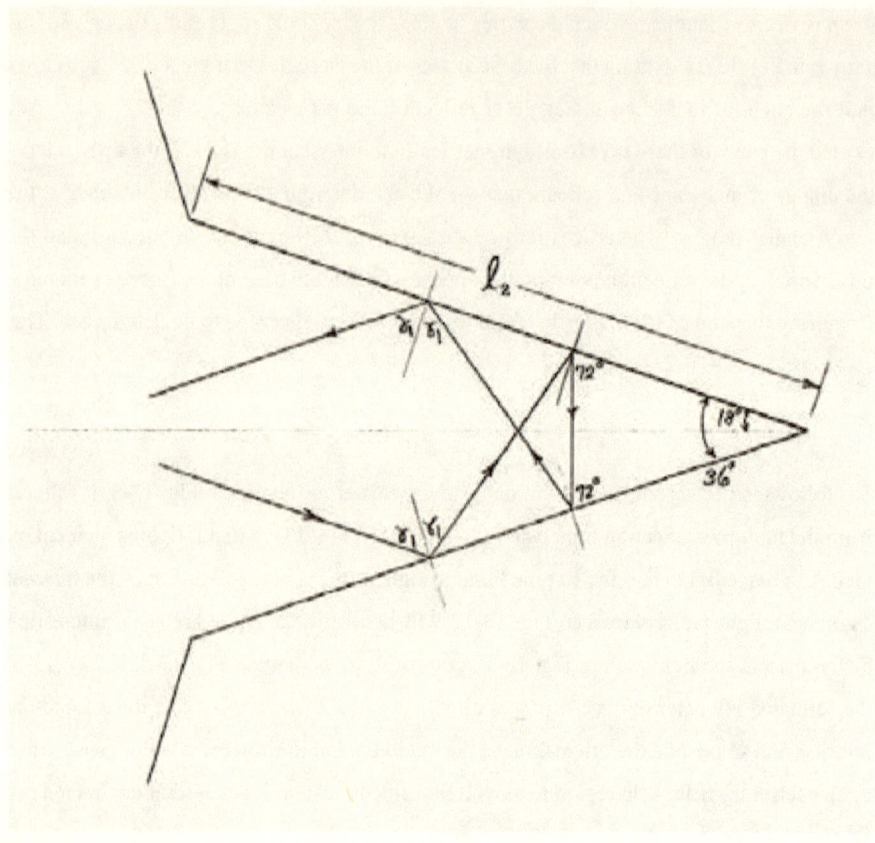

Fig. 13-11. When light enters the tip region of a solid [5, 2] star making angle of incidence $\gamma_1 = 54°$ with a face, it will be reflected to the other face, making angle of incidence 18° with that face, whereupon it is reflected to the first face, arriving at incident angle 18°, and thence reflected again from the second face at angle $\gamma_1 = 54°$, and finally exiting the tip region.

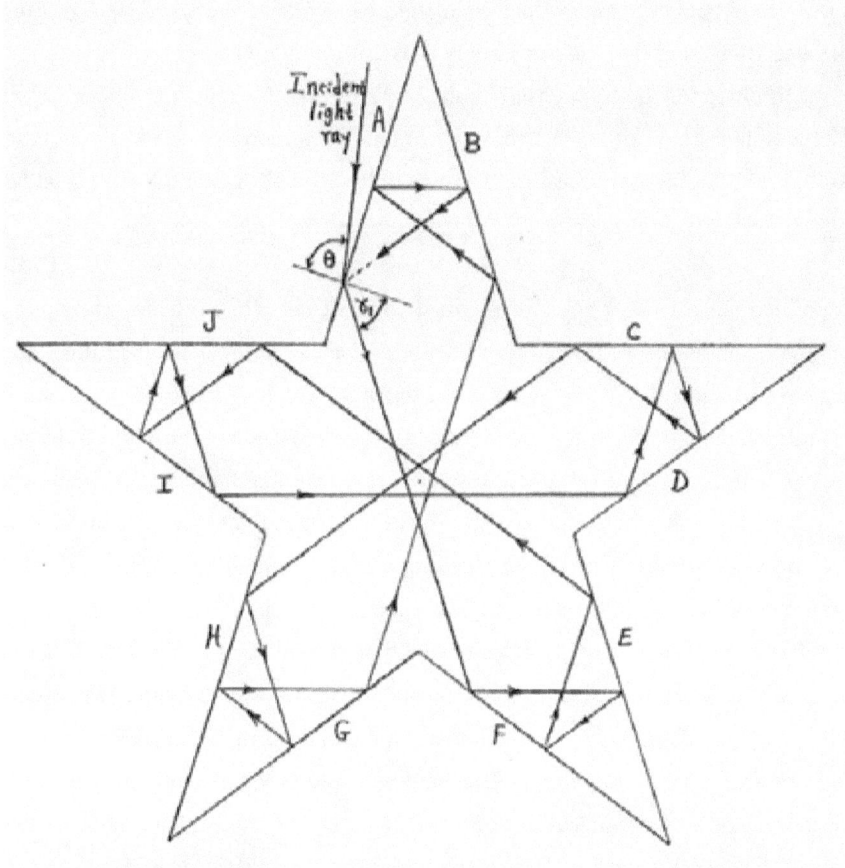

Fig. 13-12. When the angle of incidence θ of light on Face A of the solid [5, 2] star is such that the entering ray travels at the refraction angle $\gamma_1 = 54°$, then the symmetric light path is obtained in which four internal reflections occur within each tip region, two on each face.

can be made between the two different light paths inside the solid stars in Figs. 13-8 and 13-12, but these aspects are reserved for a later chapter.

In order for the light path of Fig. 13-12 to be achieved, it has been shown that the light beam must enter face A at the angle of refraction $\gamma_1 = 54°$ given in Eq. 13-49. From Snell's Law, we find that the angle of incidence θ on face A must be:

$$\theta = \text{arc sin}\,(n \sin \gamma_1). \tag{13-50}$$

As pointed out earlier, $n = 1.5$ is a typical value of refractive index for an optical medium, such as glass, from which the solid star can be made. Substituting this value of n along with $\gamma_1 = 54°$ leads to the result $\theta = \arcsin (1.2135)$, but the sine of an angle cannot exceed unity, and therefore it is not possible to introduce light into the star with $n = 1.5$ to achieve a refracted ray, making angle $\gamma_1 = 54°$ with the perpendicular to face A. For it to be possible to introduce light directly from air into the star to achieve a refracted path with angle $\gamma_1 = 54°$, Snell's Law shows that the maximum refractive index that the star material can have is $n_m = (\sin \gamma_1)^{-1} = 1.23607$. Even if an optical material existed with the value n_m or smaller, the angle of incidence is $\theta \cong 90°$, which is not practical. However, using simple auxiliary optical devices, it is possible to achieve the desired result for entry into face A. First, consider Fig. 13-13a in which a small rectangular vessel containing water of refractive index 1.33 is placed in contact with face A of the solid star. The contact plate of the vessel is optically transparent with the same reflective index as that of the star medium. A small beam of light inside the water making angle θ_w will enter the star at refraction angle $\gamma_1 = 54°$, provided θ_w has the value obtained from Snell's Law:

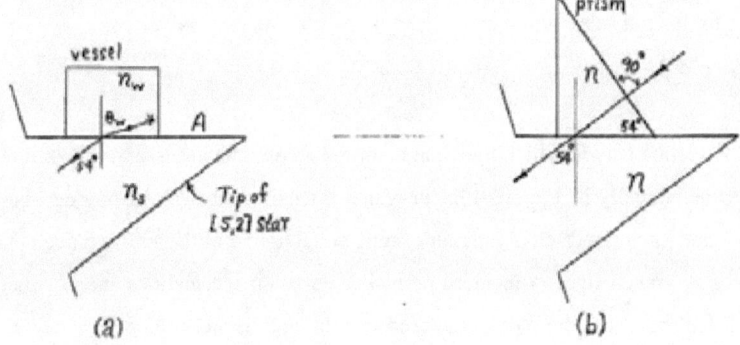
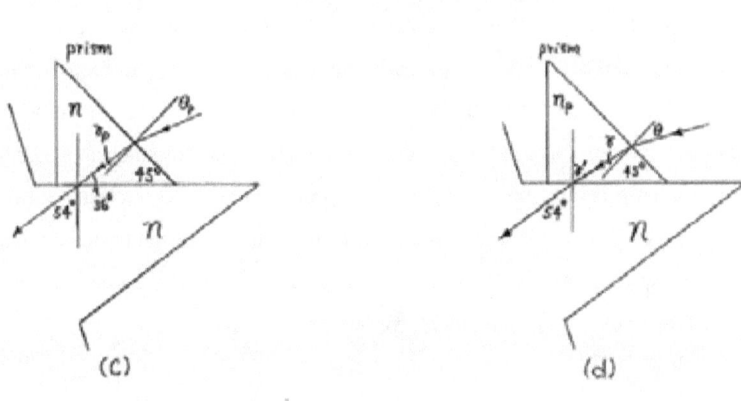

Fig. 13-13. Four techniques for introducing light into the [5, 2] star tip at angle 54°, required for the pattern in Fig. 13-12. In (a), light is incident from within a refractive medium contained in a small vessel. A prism with angle 54° and refractive index same as the star is used in (b), while a prism with 45° angle is used in (c). In (d), the prism has angle 45°, but its refractive index is different from that of the star medium.

$$n_w \sin \theta_w = n_s \sin \gamma_1. \tag{13-51}$$

Solving for θ_w and substituting $n_w = 1.33$, $n_s = 1.5$, and $\gamma_1 = 54°$ gives:

$$\theta_w \cong 65.84°. \tag{13-52}$$

A second way in which light can be introduced in the necessary way into face A is shown schematically in Fig. 13-13b, in which a small optical block having one face at angle γ_1, and having refractive index n exactly equal to that of the star, is placed in contact with face A. When light is incident perpendicularly on the inclined face of the optical block, it will pass into the block unaltered in path, and because the optical block has the same refractive index as the star, the light will pass undeviated from the block into the star, making the desired angle of entry $\gamma_1 = 54°$ into the star.

Optical prisms or blocks with one face inclined at $\gamma_1 = 54°$ to another are not nearly as commonly available as right angle prisms with a hypotenuse face, making angles of 45° with the two legs. So, a third way of properly introducing the light into face A is to place one of these prisms in contact with face A as shown in Fig. 13-13c. Assuming that the prism has the same refractive index n as the star, light will pass into the star at the desired angle γ_1 provided it is incident internally at this same angle at the interface between the prism and face A. This will be true if the angle of refraction γ_1 of the light as it enters the prism from air is $\gamma_p = \pi - 45° - 36° - 90° = 9°$. Therefore, the light must be incident on the hypotenuse face of the prism at angle θ_p given by Snell's Law:

$$\theta_p = \text{arc sin } (n \sin 9°), \tag{13-53}$$

and assuming both prism and star have refractive index $n = 1.5$, the resulting angle θ_p is:

$$\theta_p = 13.571°. \tag{13-54}$$

As shown in Fig. 13-13d, light can also be introduced properly into the star to achieve the results in Fig. 13-12 when the prism of Fig. 13-13c has a refractive index n_p, different from that of the star. If θ is the angle of incidence on the hypotenuse face of the prism and γ is the angle of refraction going into the prism, Snell's Law at the air-hypotenuse interface gives:

$$1 \cdot \sin \theta = n_p \cdot \sin \gamma, \tag{13-55}$$

If γ' is the angle of incidence of the light inside the prism at the prism-star interface, then knowing that the angle of refraction of the ray entering the star must be $\gamma_1 = 54°$, Snell's Law at this interface can be written as:

$$n_p \sin \gamma^1 = n \sin 54°. \qquad (13\text{-}56)$$

From Fig. 13-13d, it can be seen that angles γ and γ' are related by γ = γ' - 45°, and therefore Eqs. (13-55) and (13-56) can be combined and solved for the angle θ at which light must be incident on the prism face to obtain the light path in Fig. 13-12.

$$\theta = \arcsin\left\{n_p \sin\left[\arcsin\left(\frac{n}{n_p} \sin 54°\right) - \frac{\pi}{4}\right]\right\} \qquad (13\text{-}57)$$

For example, taking $n = 1.5$ for the star and $n_p = 1.45$ for the prism gives $\theta = 17.272°$ for the angle of incidence at the prism-air interface.

CHAPTER 14

PASSAGE OF LIGHT ALTERNATELY THROUGH TIPS OF A SOLID STAR AND SPACE BETWEEN

14-1. Refractive index for symmetric passage. Time of travel.

In Chapter 13, attention was given to the conditions under which light can be introduced into one face of a solid five-point star, such that the light successively travels into and out of each of the five tip regions without missing any, and in so doing, the light also crisscrosses the region interior to the tips. In this chapter, consideration will be given to conditions under which light can be introduced into a tip, pass through the tip into the air, and then pass into the adjacent tip, through it into the air, and to the next tip, and so on, until the light has successfully completed a complete pass through all the tips.

We begin with the solid star constructed on the mathematical five-point star [5, 2] and let a ray of light be incident at point P on face A as shown in Fig. 14-1. The simplest case to consider is a symmetrical light path around the solid star, both in the air between adjacent tips and through the tips as well. To meet these two conditions of symmetry, first the path PP' of the light through the tip must be perpendicular to the radius R of the star and, secondly, the path of the light in air must be perpendicular to the line joining the center O of the star with point B. The first condition implies that the path of the light inside the tip is the base of an isosceles triangle with vertex angle PP_1P', and the second condition implies that the path PP'' of the light in air between two adjacent tips is the base of an isosceles triangle $P''PB$. We see that the angle between line $B'BO$ and the face A, i.e., line BPP_1, is 54° because it is an exterior angle of triangle BOP_1 and therefore equal to the sum of the two alternate interior angles, 18° + 36°. Therefore, in

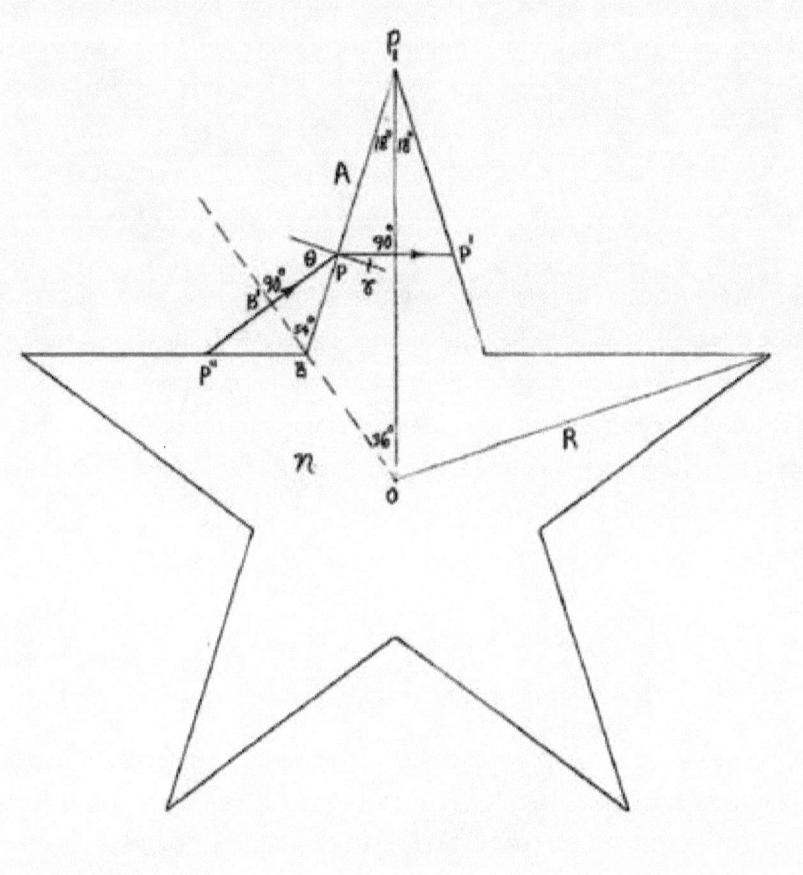

Fig. 14-1. Conditions for symmetric passage of light from air into a tip of a solid star [5, 2] at point P.

right triangle $BB'P$, the angle $B'PB$ is 36°, and it follows that the path of the light in air is incident at angle θ with respect to the perpendicular at point of incidence P on face A given by:

$$\theta = \frac{\pi}{2} - 36°$$
$$= 54°. \tag{14-1}$$

The optical medium from which the solid star is made is assumed to have uniform refractive index n throughout. So, the light enters at point P and is refracted at angle γ with respect to the perpendicular to the surface, and travels along the straight line path PP' which by our condition as stated above is the base of isosceles triangle $P'P_1P$. Because the vertex of this triangle is 36°, the base angles P_1PP' and $P_1P'P$ are each 72°, and it follows that the angle of refraction γ of the ray inside the tip is:

$$\gamma = \frac{\pi}{2} - 72°$$
$$= 18°. \tag{14-2}$$

We see that the conditions for symmetry of the light path in air and inside the tips in Fig. 14-1 require that the angle of incidence θ and the angle of refraction γ must have the values given in Eqs. (14-1) and (14-2). Therefore, from Snell's Law, we can find the corresponding refractive index n, and it is:

$$n = \frac{\sin \theta}{\sin \gamma} = \frac{\sin 54°}{\sin 18°}. \tag{14-3}$$

Evaluating the latter numerically leads to the very interesting result:

$$n = \phi^2, \tag{14-4}$$

where ϕ is the golden ratio.

To summarize, light can be made to pass alternately from air into a tip and back into air, symmetrically all the way around in Fig. 14-1 provided the refractive index of the solid star material is equal to the square of the golden ratio, i.e., $n = \phi^2 = 2.618033989$. This value of refractive index is relatively high compared with values of common optical media, i.e., most glasses are in the range 1.45 to 1.67. However, it is interesting to note that nature has provided us with rutile, a form of titanium dioxide, which has a refractive index $n = 2.618$ at a wavelength of 5850 Angstroms and therefore meets the condition very closely. However, rutile is a mineral, and as is the case with most minerals, the refractive index of its crystalline structure depends on the direction of the light passing through the structure. For rutile at wavelength 5850 Angstroms, the refractive index is 2.618 when light passes in the direction referred to as the "ordinary ray," but the refractive index is 2.915 for light passing through rutile in the direction referred to as the "extraordinary ray." So, the use of rutile as the solid star material for symmetric passage of light as indicated in Fig. 14-1 would require that all the tip regions be fabricated from rutile crystals cut with their axes oriented the same with respect to the center of the star, so that each path, such as PP' lies along the "ordinary ray" axis of the crystal for which $n = 2.618$.

We consider another aspect of the symmetric passage of light in Fig. 14-1, and that relates to the distance light travels in air related to the distance it travels in the star material. Obviously, these two distances depend on the location of the point of incidence P on face A. Let x be the distance of P from the vertex P_1 of the tip, and note the relative path distances in air and in the solid star for two different values of x as shown in Fig. 14-2. When the light is incident at point P at distance x from the vertex at P_1, let us determine the total time required for light to traverse the symmetric path all the way around. First, the distance $P''P$ of one of the five paths in air is:

$$P''P = 2(l_2 - x) \sin 54°, \qquad (14\text{-}5)$$

and therefore the time t_a for light to travel this distance is:

$$t_a = \frac{2(l_2 - x)\sin 54°}{c}, \qquad (14\text{-}6)$$

where c is the speed of light in air. Next, the corresponding distance PP' the light travels in traversing the tip is:

$$PP' = 2x \sin 18°. \qquad (14\text{-}7)$$

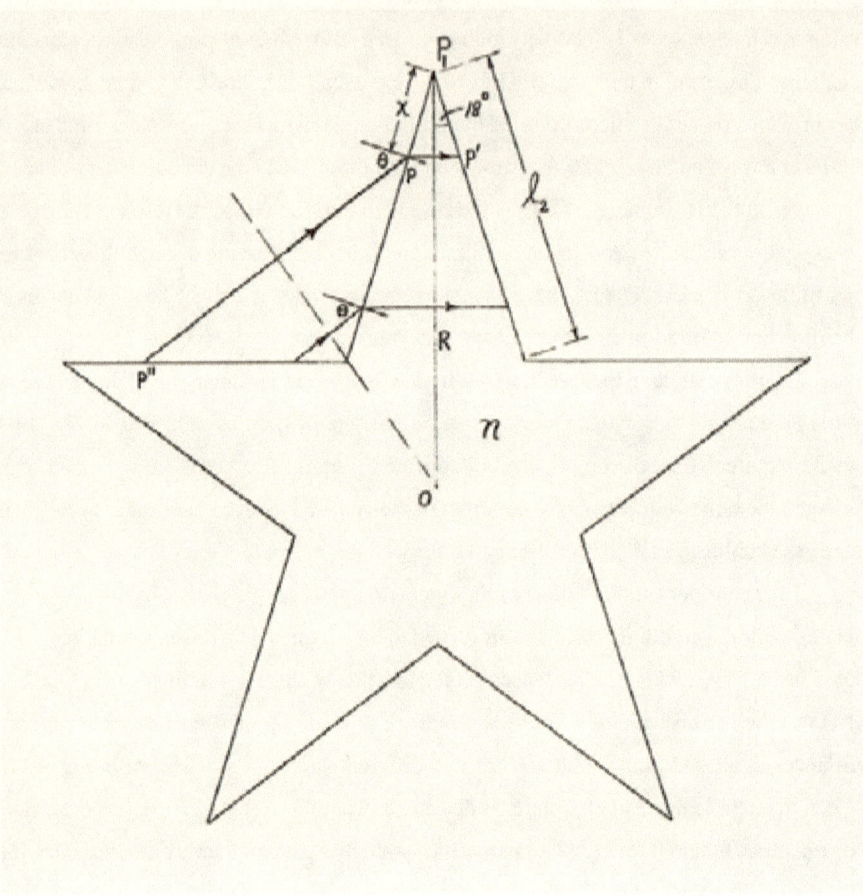

Fig. 14-2. For symmetric passage of light in the [5, 2] star tips and in the air between the tips, the physical distances travelled in air and in the star optical medium depend on the distance x from the tip P_1 at which light is incident at point P.

In an optical medium of refractive index n, such as the solid star material we are considering, light travels more slowly than in air and therefore a greater time is required to traverse a given distance in the medium than the same distance in air. The speed of light in the medium of refractive index n is c/n, and therefore the time t_s required for the light to traverse one tip at distance PP' in Eq. (14-7) is:

$$t_s = \frac{2x \sin 18°}{c/n}. \tag{14-8}$$

The total time t for the light to make one complete pass, alternately in air, and in the tips, is simply five times the sum of the two times t_a and t_s in Eqs. (14-6) and (14-8), which can be written as:

$$t = \frac{10}{c}\left[(l_2 - x)\sin 54° + nx \sin 18°\right]. \tag{14-9}$$

Now, from Eq. (14-3), we know that the refractive index $n = \sin 54°/\sin 18°$ in order to provide the symmetric path under consideration, and therefore substituting this for n into Eq. (14-9), we simply get:

$$t = \frac{10}{c} l_2 \sin 54°. \tag{14-10}$$

Note that the total time of transit, alternately in air and in the star material, for a compete pass all the way around is independent of the position of point P on face A in Fig. 14-2. When x is small, that is, P is near the vertex P_1, most of the light path is in air, very little in the star material. When x is nearly equal to l_2, very little of the light path is in air because most of it is in the star material. However, regardless of the distance x at which the light is incident on face A, the time for one complete pass around is independent of x as determined from Eq. (14-10). The total time t can be calculated from Eq. (14-10) merely by knowing the side l_2 of a particular star because the speed of light c and the trigonometric factor are independently known quantities.

14-2. Symmetric passage of light alternately through tips and space between, variable tip angle

In Chapter 9, a five-point star was constructed that contained the variable angle φ between the radius and side L_2 at each tip, in place of the fixed angle 18° in the case of the standard mathematical star [5, 2]. We now consider light incident on a face A of a solid star of this type as shown in Fig. 14-3. The solid star has uniform refractive index n, and it is surrounded by air. We consider a symmetric path of light both inside each tip and within the air between two adjacent tips. So, if light is incident on face A at point P at distance x from the vertex P_1 of the tip, then it must enter the tip and pass through in a path PP' that is perpendicular to the radius, therefore forming the base of isosceles triangle PP_1P'. Likewise, for a symmetric path in air, the path $P''P$ between two adjacent tips must be perpendicular to the line $B'BO$, joining the center of the star with the intersection of two adjacent faces. As a result, the triangle $P''PB$ is isosceles. In right triangle $BB'P$, the angle between side L_2 and the line OBB' is equal to the sum of φ and 36° in triangle OBP_1. Therefore, the angle of incidence θ between the path of the light in air, $P''P$, and the perpendicular to the face A at the point of incidence P is:

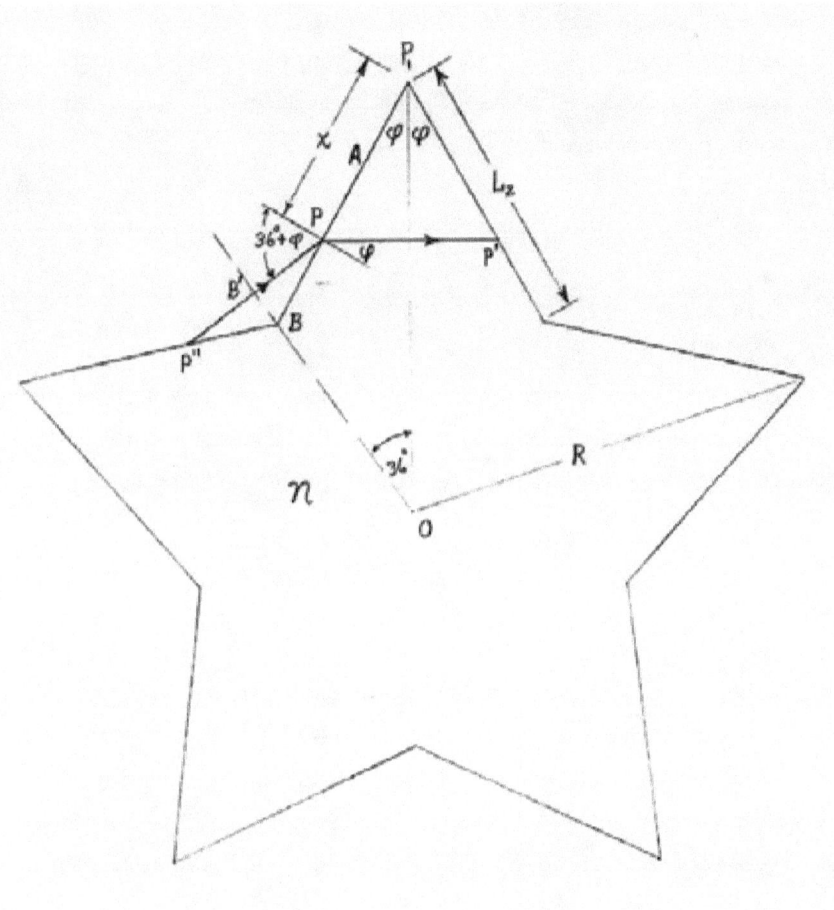

Fig. 14-3. Conditions for symmetric passage of light in air and through the tips of variable angle φ in a solid five-point star.

$$\theta = 36° + \varphi, \tag{14-11}$$

because angle $B'PB = \pi/2 - (\varphi + 36°)$. Remembering that the path PP' inside the tip is the base of the isosceles triangle PP_1P', the angle of refraction γ between the perpendicular at point P and the line PP' is simply:

$$\gamma = \pi/2 - \frac{1}{2}(\pi - 2\varphi)$$

$$= \varphi. \tag{14-12}$$

Now, from Snell's Law, in order to make these geometric conditions of a symmetric light path valid for any angle φ, the refractive index n of the solid star medium must be connected to angles θ and γ in Eqs. (14-11) and (14-12) through the relation:

$$n = \frac{\sin\theta}{\sin\gamma} = \frac{\sin(\varphi+36°)}{\sin\varphi} \tag{14-13}$$

For the special case of the mathematical five-point star for which $\varphi = 18°$, we see that Eq. (14-13) gives the earlier result for that case in Eq. (14-3).

The refractive index n of the solid star optical medium, required to achieve the symmetric light path in Fig. 14-3, was calculated from Eq. (14-13) as a function of the angle φ, and the results are given in the graph of Fig. 14-4. It is very interesting to note from the graph, and as

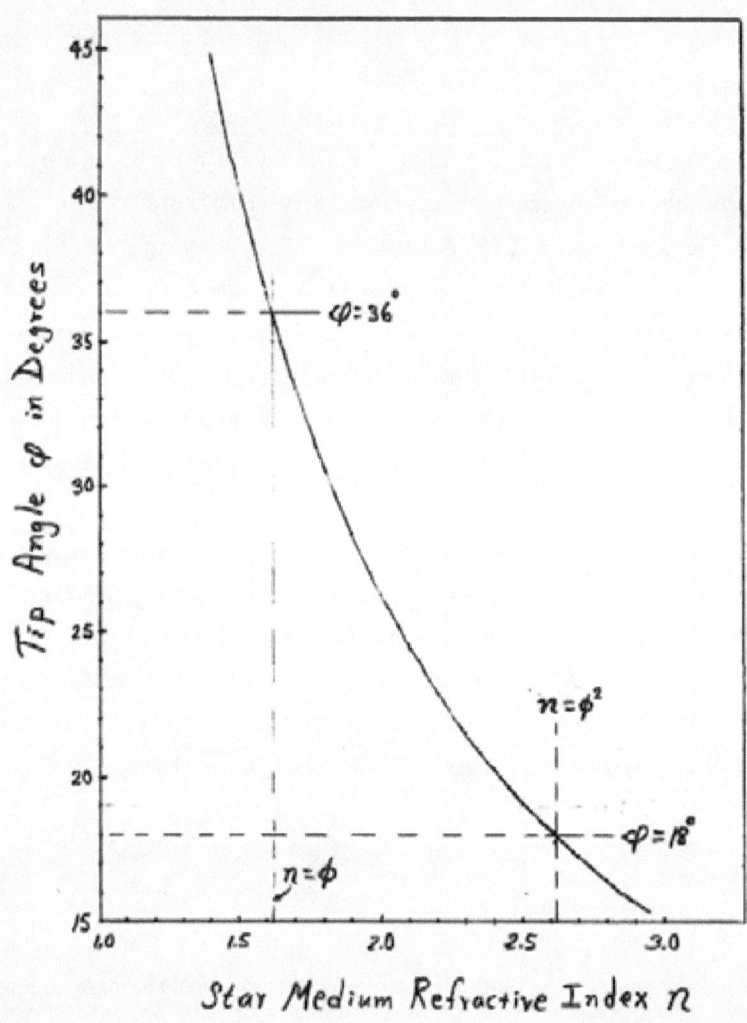

Fig. 14-4. Tip angle φ versus refractive index n of solid star medium for symmetric passage of light through the tips and intervening air in the geometric configuration of Fig. 14-3.

can be seen exactly in the numerical sense by substituting into Eq. (14-13), that the refractive index n for angle $\varphi = 36°$ is:

$$n = \phi. \qquad (14\text{-}14)$$

For $\varphi = 36°$, we see from Fig. 14-3 that the line joining the center O with a point such as B is parallel to two faces of length L_2 of the star, and from Eq. (14-14), it is seen that this will happen only if the refractive index n is equal to the golden ratio, 1.6180133989.

Calcite is a mineral with its refractive index very closely equal to 1.618 in one optical direction at the wavelength of light near 6500 Angstroms, but its refractive index is considerably higher in another direction. So, calcite with $n \cong \phi$ could serve as a solid star optical medium with angle $\varphi = 36°$, provided all the tips were fabricated in such a way that the axis along which light travels with $n = 1.618$ is oriented perpendicular to the radius. Another candidate optical medium for the solid star meeting the condition in Eq. (14-14) is KI, which has $n \cong 1.618$ at a wavelength 6500 Angstroms.

It is interesting to note that the refractive index required for symmetric passage of light through the standard star with $\varphi = 18°$ is $n = \phi^2$ in Eq. (14-4), but $n = \phi$ in Eq. (14-14) is the refractive index required when the angle φ is just twice that value.

When an optical medium of known refractive index n is desired, then the angle φ of the star in Fig. 14-3 for symmetric passage of light can be calculated by merely expanding the sine function, $\sin(\varphi + 36°)$, in Eq. (14-13) and solving for φ, which gives:

$$\varphi = \arctan\left(\frac{\sin 36°}{n - \cos 36°}\right). \qquad (14\text{-}15)$$

Possible optical media from which solid five-point stars could be made meeting the conditions for symmetric light passage are listed in the following table along with their reported refractive index values. Also listed are the corresponding angles φ calculated from Eq. (14-15).

Table 14-1. Refractive Index of Several Optical Media and Corresponding Calculated Angle φ for Symmetric Light Passage Through Five-Point Solid Star in Fig. 14-3.

Medium	n	Angle φ
Villiamunite	1.326	48.667°
Fused Quartz	1.458	42.167°
Crown Glass	1.517	39.700°
Cubic Zirconia	2.170	23.359°
Diamond	2.417	20.079°
Cuprite	2.848	16.081°

The relative shapes of solid stars with angle φ calculated for each of four different values of refractive index **n** are shown in Fig. 14-5.

14-3. Symmetric light passage through N-point solid star with variable tip angle. Time of travel.

Finally, we can generalize to the case of a solid star constructed on a plane star base having N points, equally spaced at angular intervals $2\pi/N$, with angle φ between the radius, and a side as shown in Fig. 14-6. The lengths of the sides L_2 and L_1 in relation to N and φ were

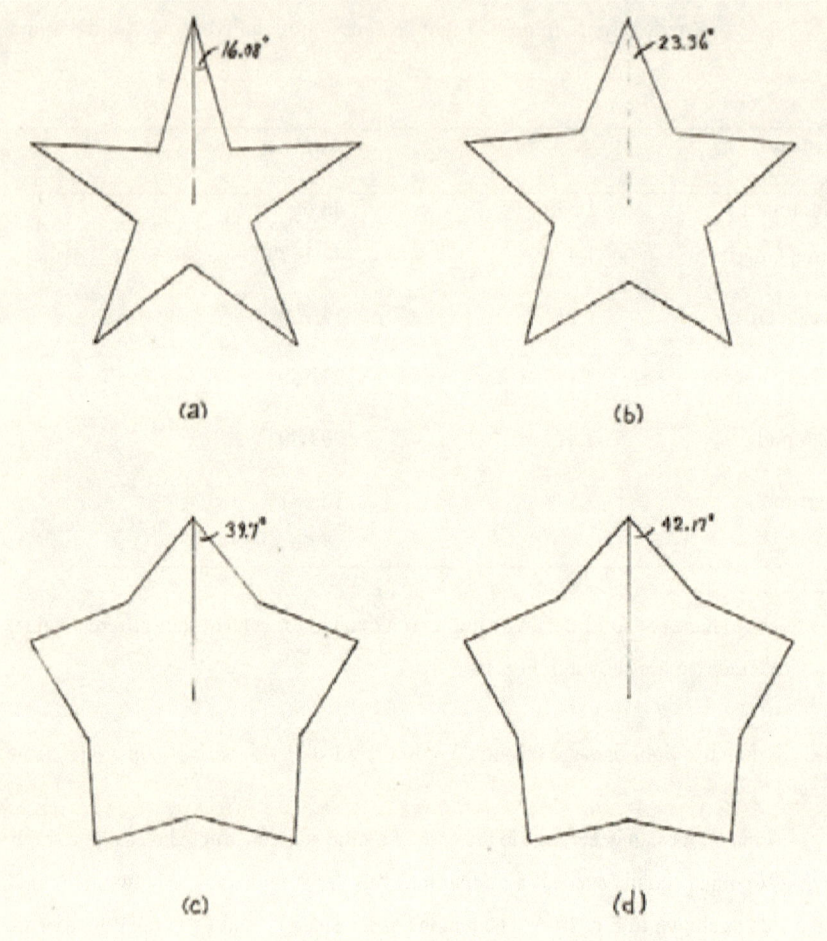

Fig. 14-5. Solid star shapes for symmetric passage of light through tips and air between for star media (a) Cuprite, (b) Cubic Zirconia, (c) Crown Glass, and (d) Fused Quartz.

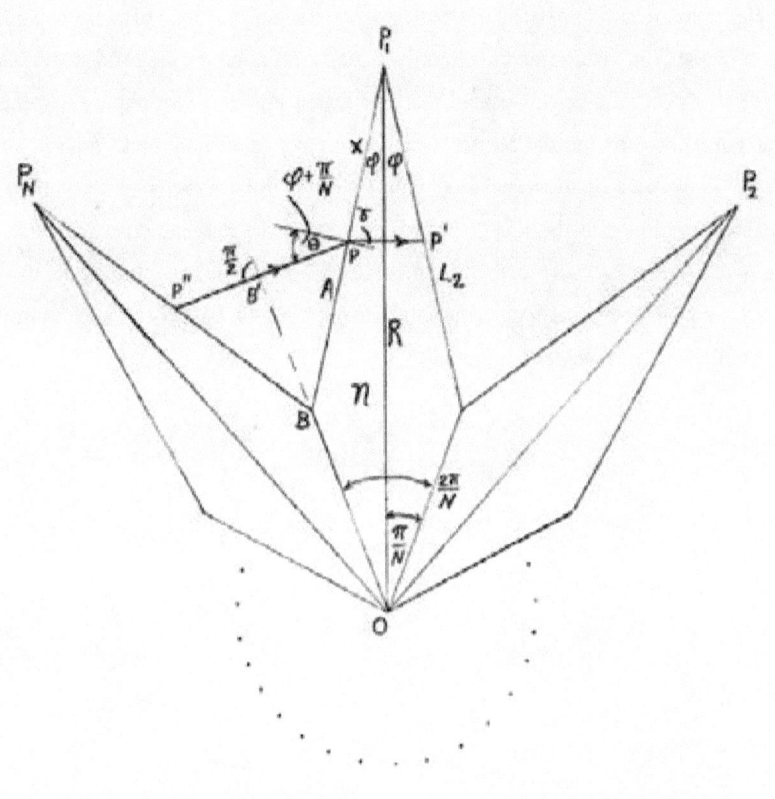

Fig. 14-6. Symmetric passage of light into and out the tips of a solid N-point star with variable tip angle φ, and refractive index n.

worked out earlier in Eqs. (10-3) through (10-9) of Chapter 10. The intent here is to impose the conditions of a symmetric light path alternately into and out of a tip and into the surrounding air, and determine the refractive index n required for the solid star medium to produce this path all the way around the star. So, in Fig. 14-6 we require that the light incident at point P on the star face at angle θ, be refracted into the tip at angle γ, and that this path be the base of an isosceles triangle PP_1P'. Furthermore, symmetry of the light path in air requires that the line $P''P$, representing it be perpendicular to OBB', thus making triangle PBP'' isosceles. Then, under these conditions, following the same analysis used earlier in reference to the solid stars in Figs. 14-1 and 14-3, we find from Fig. 14-6 that the angle of incidence at point P is:

$$\theta = \frac{\pi}{N} + \varphi, \qquad (14\text{-}16)$$

and the angle of refraction of the ray entering the star is:

$$\gamma = \varphi, \qquad (14\text{-}17)$$

from which Snell's Law shows us that the index of refraction n to meet those conditions must be:

$$n = \frac{\sin\left(\frac{\pi}{N} + \varphi\right)}{\sin \varphi}. \qquad (14\text{-}18)$$

Fig. 14-7 shows a graph of refractive index n versus angle φ for each of several different numbers N of tips in the solid star, calculated from Eq. (14-18).

For completeness, analogous to the form of Eq. (14-15), Eq. (14-18) can be solved for the angle φ and expressed as:

$$\varphi = \arctan\left(\frac{\sin \pi/N}{n - \cos \pi/N}\right), \qquad (14\text{-}19)$$

from which it is easy to calculate the angle φ of an *N*-point solid star of desired refractive index *n* for symmetric passage of light into and out of the tips all the way around.

It will now be shown that the time for light to make one complete symmetric path around the *N*-point solid star with angle φ at the tip in Fig. 14-6 is independent of the distance *x* at which the light is incident on the face *A*. First, the distance the light travels in one tip is the path PP', and this is:

$$PP' = 2x \sin \varphi. \tag{14-20}$$

The speed of light in the medium of the star is c/n, and therefore the time t_s to traverse the distance PP' is:

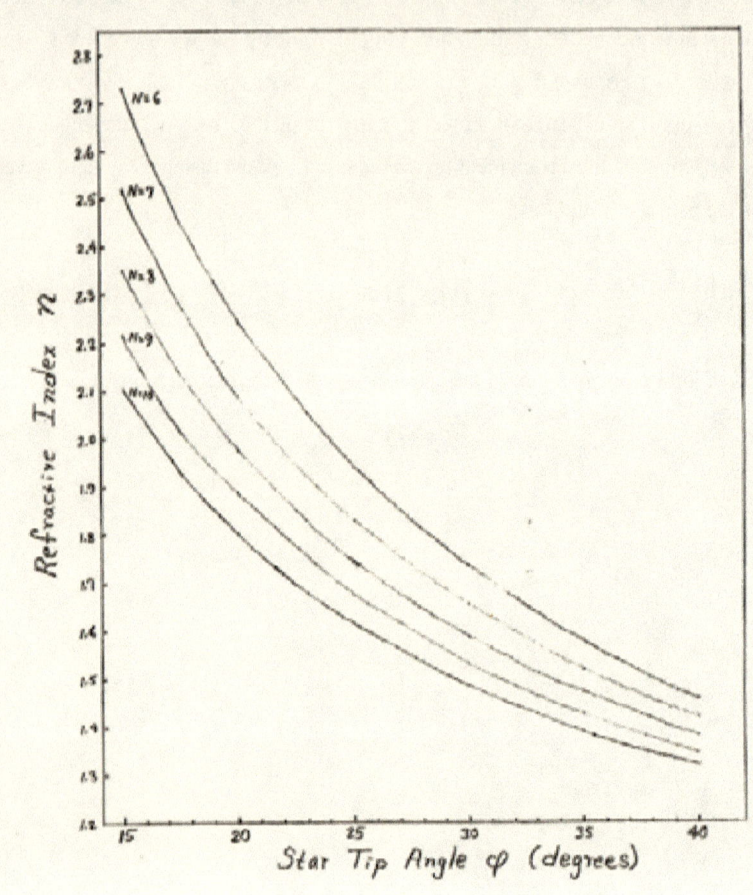

Fig. 14-7. Refractive index n versus tip angle φ for symmetric passage of light into and out the tips of solid N-point stars, for various values of N.

$$t_s = \frac{2x \sin\varphi}{c/n}. \tag{14-21}$$

The corresponding distance the light travels in air between two adjacent tips in Fig. 14-6 is:

$$P''P = 2(L_2 - x) \sin\left(\frac{\pi}{N} + \varphi\right), \tag{14-22}$$

hence, the time to travel this distance in air is:

$$t_a = \frac{2(L_2 - x)\sin\left(\frac{\pi}{N} + \varphi\right)}{c}. \tag{14-23}$$

The total time for one complete symmetric path is N times the sum of the two times in Eqs. (14-21) and (14-23).

$$t = \frac{2N}{c}\left[nx \sin\varphi + (L_2 - x)\sin\left(\frac{\pi}{N} + \varphi\right)\right] \tag{14-24}$$

The refractive index n is related to N and φ through Eq. (14-18), and therefore substituting for n in Eq. (14-24) leads to the result:

$$t = \frac{2N}{c} L_2 \sin\left(\frac{\pi}{N} + \varphi\right), \tag{14-25}$$

which shows that the total time of transit of the light around the solid star in Fig. 14-6 is independent of its symmetric path located with respect to the tip P_1, that is, relative to the center of the solid star.

14-4. Conditions for passage of white light through tips of a solid star and space between

In the foregoing discussions related to the symmetric passage of light through the tips and around the various solid stars, values of refractive index were calculated for making this possible. References were made to certain optical media, which possess refractive index values very close to those required mathematically, and it was stated that the values were for a particular wavelength of light. That is, at other wavelengths, the refractive index has a higher or lower value, and the mathematical condition for symmetric passage would not be satisfied. "White light" from the sun or from an incandescent source, such as an electric light, contains a range of wavelengths visible to the human eye. Almost everyone is familiar with the fact that light of this type, when passed through a prism, will be separated into individual colors, i.e., a "rainbow" spectrum consisting, in order of decreasing wavelength, of the colors red, orange, yellow, green, blue, indigo, and violet. The reason that these various colors are separated into space when "white light" is passed through a glass prism, for example, is that the refractive index of glass varies with the wavelength of the light, being approximately 1.520 for red and increasing steadily to approximately 1.534 for violet. Therefore, if a ray of white light is incident at point P in Fig. 14-1, each of the different wavelengths of light present will be refracted at a particular angle γ corresponding to the refractive index of the star optical medium for that particular wavelength. Actually, there is a continuum of wavelengths present in white light, but for purposes of discussion, it is convenient to think of seven different wavelengths, each associated with the seven colors of the rainbow spectrum. This is practical in a physiological sense because the typical human eye can discern these seven colors in a prismatic spectrum from white light, although to some extent gradations can be seen in between, as for example "yellow-green" or "blue-green." So, if a ray of white light is incident at angle θ in Fig. 14-1 and if the refractive index of the star material matches the value for the wavelength corresponding to "green" and obeys Eq. (14-3), then the green component of the white light will be transmitted symmetrically but the other colors will not. The colors red, orange, and yellow will be refracted at angles greater than γ as they enter the medium in Fig. 14-1, but the colors blue, indigo, and violet will each be refracted at angles smaller than γ. So, in general, symmetry will not exist when light of different wavelengths is incident on face *A* of the solid star, and as the light emerges from face *B* into air, the dispersion in paths of the different refracted beams will differ markedly from the angle θ at which the ray of white light was incident on face *A*. Proceeding then from face *B* to incidence on face C, the angles of refraction of the various colors are all different, entering this tip than they were entering face *A*. Intuitively, it thus appears difficult to pass an incident beam of white light alternately in and out of tips, all the way around the solid star as in the case of "monochromatic" or light of a single wavelength.

To analyze the non-symmetric case in which white light is incident on face A and each of the component wavelengths is refracted into the tip at various angles and these then are incident internally on face B after which each is refracted into air and then passes to face C where the process again repeats, we consider Fig. 14-8. The solid star is formed from a five-point star with

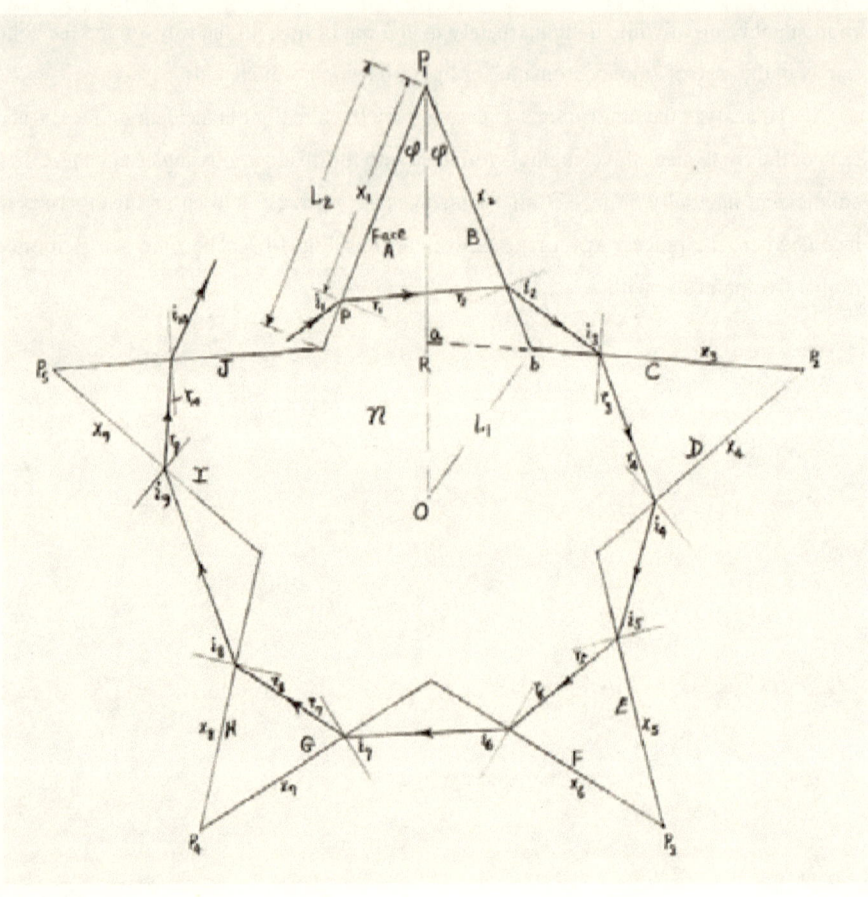

Fig. 14-8. Angles and distances used in deriving Eqs. (14-26)-(14-40) describing the passage of a ray of light incident at point P on Face A of a five-point solid star of refractive index n, with tip angle φ.

angle φ between the radius and a side, or face, at each tip, and the incident light ray lies in a plane parallel to the base plane star. Let a ray of light be incident at angle i_1 at distance x_1 from the tip P_1 on face A. As the ray enters the star medium of uniform refractive index n, it will undergo refraction, and its path relative to the perpendicular at P is measured by angle γ_1. When the refracted ray arrives at point P' on face B, at distance x_2 from P_1, it will be incident internally in the star medium at angle γ_2, and upon passing into the air, it will be refracted at angle i_2 relative to the perpendicular to face B. The ray will then encounter face C at distance x_3 from the tip at angle of incidence i_3 relative to face C.

In the triangle formed by the tip P_1 and the points of incidence of the refracted ray on faces A and B in Fig. 14-8, it follows that $\pi/2 - \gamma_1 + \pi/2 - \gamma_2 + 2\varphi = \pi$, from which we get:

$$\gamma_2 = 2\varphi - \gamma_1. \tag{14-26}$$

Now, we know that for a given angle of incidence i_1 on face A, the angle of refraction γ_1 and therefore angle γ_2 depend on the refractive index n of the star optical medium for the particular wavelength of light under consideration. Referring to the faces A and B in Fig. 14-8, Snell's Law gives:

$$1 \cdot \sin i_1 = n \cdot \sin \gamma_1 \tag{14-27}$$

$$n \cdot \sin \gamma_2 = 1 \cdot \sin i_2, \tag{14-28}$$

from which we get:

$$\gamma_1 = \arcsin\left(\frac{\sin i_1}{n}\right) \tag{14-29}$$

and:

$$i_2 = \arcsin(n \sin \gamma_2). \tag{14-30}$$

Knowing the angle of incidence i_1 and the value of n, the angles γ_1 and i_2 can be determined from Eqs. (14-29) and (14-30), realizing that γ_2 is related to γ_1 through Eq. (14-26).

Now, i_3 can be determined from γ_2 and ψ as follows. Let the extension of face C meet the radius in point a as shown. The angle $P_1 a P_2$ is equal to the sum of angles ψ and $2\pi/5$ in triangle aOP_2 because an exterior angle of a triangle is equal to the sum of the two alternate interior angles. If b is the point at which faces B and C meet, then angle $P_1 b a = \pi - \psi - \psi - 2\pi/5$, or $P_1 b a = 3\pi/5 - 2\psi$. However, angle $P_1 b a$ is an exterior angle to the triangle formed by point b, and the points of exit and incidence of the ray in air with faces B and C, hence:

$$\frac{3}{5}\pi - 2\varphi = \frac{\pi}{2} - i_2 + \frac{\pi}{2} - i_3, \qquad (14\text{-}31)$$

or:

$$i_3 = \frac{2}{5}\pi + 2\varphi - i_2. \qquad (14\text{-}32)$$

Then, from Snell's Law, the angle of refraction γ_3 of the ray as it enters the star medium through face C is:

$$\gamma_3 = \arc\sin\left(\frac{\sin i_3}{n}\right). \qquad (14\text{-}33)$$

Continuing around in Fig. 14-8, we see that γ_4 is the internal angle of incidence of the ray on face D and i_4 is the angle of refraction of the ray as it exits into air, and so on. Noting the form of Eqs. (14-26), (14-29), (14-30), (14-32), and (14-33), we can use an index j and express the jth angle internal to the tips as:

$$\gamma_j = \begin{cases} \arc\sin\left(\dfrac{\sin i_j}{n}\right) & \text{for } j = 1, 3, \cdots 9 \\ 2\varphi - \gamma_{j-1} & \text{for } j = 2, 4, \cdots 10 \end{cases} \qquad (14\text{-}34)$$

Likewise, the jth angle of incidence and exit on the tips can be written as:

$$i_j = \begin{cases} 2\varphi + \dfrac{2}{5}\pi - i_{j-1} & \text{for } j = 3, 5, \cdots 9 \\ \arcsin(n \sin \gamma_j) & \text{for } j = 2, 4, \cdots 10 \end{cases}. \quad (14\text{-}35)$$

The distance from the tips at which the rays are incident on the faces and exit from them can be found in terms of the angles of incidence and refraction as follows. In Fig. 14-8, let x_1 and x_2 be the distances from tip P_1, respectively, at which the ray is incident on face A and exits face B. Therefore, applying the law of sines to the triangle formed by P_1 and the incident and exits points on faces A and B allows us to write:

$$\frac{x_1}{\sin(\pi/2 - \gamma_2)} = \frac{x_2}{\sin(\pi/2 - \gamma_1)}, \quad (14\text{-}36)$$

from which we get for x_2:

$$x_2 = x_1 \frac{\cos \gamma_1}{\cos \gamma_2}. \quad (14\text{-}37)$$

Now, the distance x_3 from P_2 at which the ray is incident on face C can be related to the distance x_2 by applying the law of sines to the triangle formed by the exit points of the ray on face B, the incident point on face C, and the point of intersection of faces B and C with the result:

$$\frac{L_2 - x_3}{\sin(\pi/2 - i_2)} = \frac{L_2 - x_2}{\sin(\pi/2 - i_3)}, \quad (14\text{-}38)$$

where $L_2 = A_2 R$ with $A_2 = \sin(\pi/5)/\sin(\varphi + \pi/5)$ was derived earlier in Eqs. (9-4) and (9-5) of Chapter 9 for the type of star in Fig. 14-8. Solving Eq. (14-38) for x_3 gives the following:

$$x_3 = \left(1 - \frac{\cos i_2}{\cos i_3}\right) \frac{R \sin \pi/5}{\sin(\varphi + \pi/5)} + x_2 \frac{\cos i_2}{\cos i_3}. \quad (14\text{-}39)$$

Proceeding in this way, we see that for light passing through a tip the distances related to the points of incidence and exit are connected by an equation of the form for x_2 and x_1 in Eq. (14-37). However, for the light passing in air an equation of the type relating x_3, to x_2 in Eq. (14-39) is the corresponding expression. So, using an index j, we can express the jth distance depending on whether j is odd or even, as follows:

$$x_j = \begin{cases} x_{j-1} \dfrac{\cos \gamma_{j-1}}{\cos \gamma_j} & j = 2, 4, \cdots 10 \\ \left(1 - \dfrac{\cos i_{j-1}}{\cos i_j}\right) \dfrac{R \sin \pi/5}{\sin(\varphi + \pi/5)} + x_{j-1} \dfrac{\cos i_{j-1}}{\cos i_j} & j = 3, 5, \cdots 9 \end{cases} \quad (14\text{-}40)$$

Eqs. (14-34), (14-35), and (14-40) can be used to determine the path of a light ray that is incident at a known angle i_1 at distance x_1 from the tip P_1 of a solid star of known radius R, tip angle φ, and refractive index n in Fig. 14-8. Setting $j = 1$ in Eq. (14-34) gives γ_1 in terms of i_1, and setting $j = 2$ gives γ_2 in terms of γ_1. Angle i_2 is obtained in terms of γ_2 by setting $j = 2$ in Eq. (14-35) and then i_3 is obtained from i_2 with j set equal to 3. Distance x_2 is obtained from known distance x_1 by setting $j = 2$ in Eq. (14-40), using the previously calculated values of γ_1 and γ_2, and then setting $j = 3$ gives distance x_3 in terms of i_2 and i_3. Continuing this with $j = 4, 5, \ldots$ we eventually calculate all angles and distances up through i_{10} and x_{10} in Fig. 14-8. All of this is done for a particular value of n corresponding to the wavelength of light of interest. The process is then repeated for a different wavelength using the corresponding value of refractive index. This procedure was investigated to determine the conditions under which white light could be incident on face A such that all the refracted colors would pass through all the tips and air between, and make one complete pass around in a standard star with angle $\varphi = 18°$. No conditions could be found for a solid star medium with n in the range 1.5 to 2, because after passage through a couple of tips, the angles of refraction were such that some of the color components would not reenter the next tip. However, it was found that white light separated into its component colors could be made to pass all the way around through the tips provided the solid star is made from diamond. To make these calculations, the wavelengths corresponding to the seven colors of the white light spectrum were used and these are listed in the first column of Table 14-2. The refractive index of diamond corresponding to each of the wavelengths in Table 14-2 was found as follows. Some time ago, Edwards and Ochoa had measured the refractive index of diamond as a function of the wavelength of light. The second column in Table 14-2 gives the refractive index of diamond for each of the wavelengths of the seven colors based on the data of Edwards and Ochoa.

Table 14-2. Wavelengths and Corresponding Refractive Index of Diamond[1] for the Colors Associated with the White Light Spectrum.

Color	Wavelength	Refractive Index of Diamond
Red	0.65 μm	2.41
Orange	0.56	2.42
Yellow	0.50	2.43
Green	0.475	2.44
Blue	0.445	2.45
Indigo	0.425	2.46
Violet	0.395	2.475

Using a point of incidence x_1 equal to ¾ the length of l_2 on face A in Fig. 14-8, it was found from Eqs. (4-34), (4-35), and (4-40), using the data of Table 14-2, that each individual color of the incident white light could be transmitted all the way around for a particular angle of incidence ± 2°. However, only for the angle of incidence for $i_1 = 36°$ could all the colors be transmitted simultaneously, alternately in air and through the tips. The calculated angles i_j and distances x_j for unit radius R with initial angle of incidence $i_1 = 36°$ at $x_1 = 0.75 l_2$ are given in Table 14-3. The results drawn to scale for each color in the spectrum are shown in Fig. 14-9.

---

[1] Edwards, D.F. and Ochoa, E., J. Opt. Soc. Am., vol. 71, pp. 607-608, 1981.

Table 14-3. Points and angles of incidence for complete passage of white light component color wavelengths through all tips and spaces between in a five-point diamond star [5, 2]. White light is incident at angle 36.0° at distance .75 l_2 from tip on face A. The x_i are for unit radius R, for which $l_2 = a_2 R = 0.726543$.

Color	Diamond Refractive Index n	Face of Solid Star									
		A	B	C	D	E	F	G	H	I	J
		x_1/i_1	x_2/i_2	x_3/i_3	x_4/i_4	x_5/i_5	x_6/i_6	x_7/i_7	x_8/i_8	x_9/i_9	x_{10}/i_{10}
Red	2.41	.5449/ 36.0°	.5695/ 63.93°	.6305/ 44.07°	.6395/ 52.52°	.6325/ 55.48°	.6185/ 41.66°	.5258/ 66.35°	.5005/ 34.69°	.0795/ 73.30°	.0745/ 31.67°
Orange	2.42	.5449/ 36.0°	.5700/ 64.30°	.6345/ 43.27°	.6459/ 53.18°	.6465/ 53.94°	.6352/ 42.40°	.5715/ 64.63°	.5466/ 35.20°	.2575/ 71.94°	.2428/ 32.10°
Yellow	2.43	.5449/ 36.0°	.5705/ 64.60°	.6385/ 42.44°	.6527/ 53.60°	.6585/ 52.29°	.6510/ 42.90°	.6105/ 62.73°	.5871/ 35.60°	.3975/ 70.39°	.3762/ 32.30°
Green	2.44	.5449/ 36.0°	.5705/ 65.25°	.6435/ 41.59°	.6595/ 55.20°	.6695/ 50.53°	.6664/ 44.60°	.6435/ 60.61°	.6226/ 37.00°	.5065/ 68.60°	.4815/ 33.10°
Blue	2.45	.5449/ 36.0°	.5706/ 66.40°	.6475/ 40.71°	.6664/ 57.70°	.6805/ 48.63°	.6815/ 47.60°	.6715/ 58.21°	.6540/ 39.70°	.5905/ 66.47°	.5645/ 35.00°
Indigo	2.46	.5449/ 36.0°	.5710/ 67.50°	.6515/ 39.79°	.6735/ 60.00°	.6895/ 46.55°	.6963/ 50.30°	.6945/ 55.42°	.6820/ 42.20°	.6535/ 63.85°	.6293/ 36.90°
Violet	2.475	.5449/ 36.0°	.5715/ 68.90°	.6580/ 38.34°	.6845/ 63.10°	.7065/ 42.99°	.7185/ 54.90°	.7199/ 50.13°	.7194/ 46.50°	.7177/ 58.3°	.7007/ 40.00°

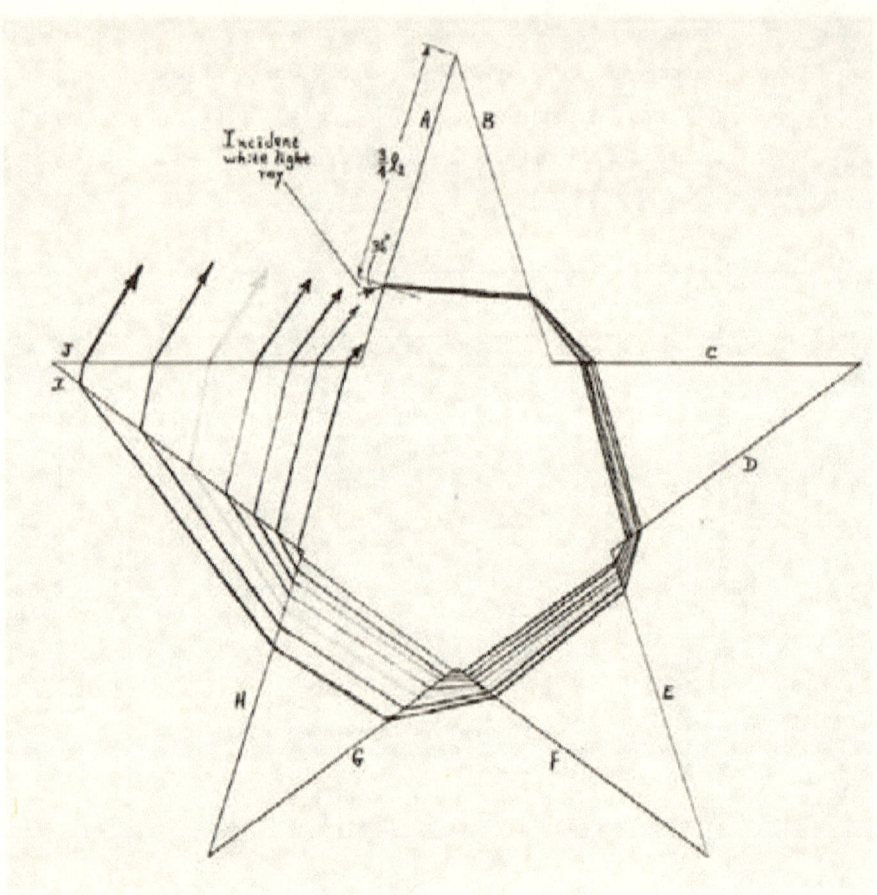

Fig. 14-9. A ray of white light in air incident at 36° on Face *A* at distance $0.75 l_2$ from the tip of a solid diamond [5, 2] star will travel alternately through the star tips and the intervening air, eventually exiting Face *J* where the component white light colors are distributed nearly over the entire length of *J* as seen from the scale drawing.

CHAPTER 15

STARS DERIVED FROM SYMMETRIC PASSAGE OF LIGHT IN SOLID [5, 2] STARS

15-1. Maximum number of reflections in each tip of [5, 2] star for symmetric light path

In Chapter 13, two cases of symmetric passage of light through a solid five-point star were studied. Before considering those in more detail, we begin by examining the passage of light into a tip of a mathematical N-point star $[N, 2]$ as shown in Fig. 15-1a. The angle between the radius of the tip and a side, according to Eq. 10-3 of Chapter 10, is

$$\varphi = \frac{\pi}{2} - \frac{2\pi}{N}. \tag{15-1}$$

We consider the condition of symmetric passage of light in which the portion of the light path innermost to the tip is perpendicular to the radius, and therefore this path, $B_1 B'_1$ is the base of an isosceles triangle with the tip T as vertex. The exterior angle formed by a side and the base equals the sum of the two opposite interior angles and therefore the angle of incidence i_1 at point B_1 can be found from the equality $\pi/2 + i_1 = 2\varphi + (\pi - 2\varphi)/2$, or:

$$i_1 = \varphi. \tag{15-2}$$

Upon reflection at this same angle from B_1, the ray will be incident at point B_2 on the opposite face with tip at T, and therefore the angle of incidence i_2 at B_2 can be found applying the same

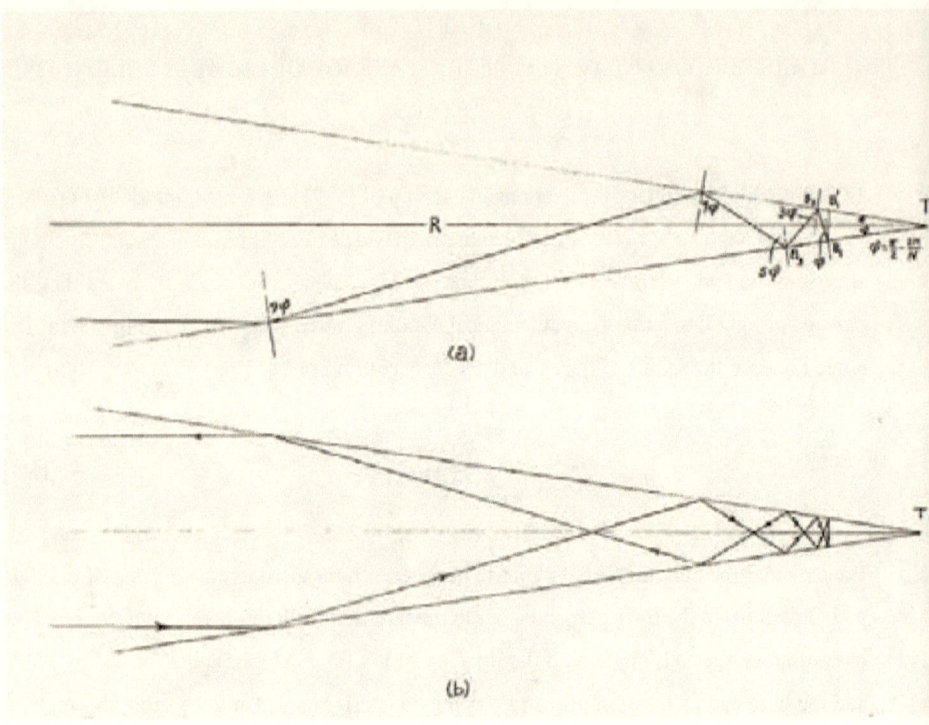

Fig. 15-1. (a) Passage of a light ray into the tip of a [N, 2] star, under the condition that the portion of the path innermost to T is perpendicular to the radius R, and by virtue of symmetry, an entering ray will depart from the tip as indicated in (b).

theorem, but to triangle B_2B_1T. Equating the exterior angle to the sum of opposite interior angles gives $\pi/2 + i_2 = 2\varphi + \pi/2 + i_1$, and using Eq. (15-2) we get:

$$i_2 = 3\varphi \qquad (15\text{-}3)$$

This ray will be reflected at angle i_2 from point B_2 and will arrive again at the opposite face, at angle of incidence at i_3 point B_3. Applying similar reasoning to that for i_2 and i_1, we find that:

$$i_3 = 5\varphi \qquad (15\text{-}4)$$

Letting j represent the number of the reflection, beginning with the first at point B_1, we can then express the angle of incidence i_j at the jth reflection as:

$$i_j = (2j - 1)\varphi \qquad j = 1, 2, \ldots \qquad (15\text{-}5)$$

For a star with N tips, the expression for angle φ in Eq. (15-1) allows i_j to be written as:

$$i_j = (2j - 1)\left(\frac{\pi}{2} - \frac{2\pi}{N}\right). \qquad (15\text{-}6)$$

Because of the symmetry associated with the innermost portion of the light path being perpendicular to the radius in Fig. 15-1a, all of the foregoing applies to light reflected from point B_1 to the opposite face, etc., and therefore we can construct the symmetric path of incident and reflected light as shown in Fig. 15-1b. Now, for the five-point star, we set $N = 5$ and letting $j = 1$ gives $i_1 = \pi/10$ or $18°$ from Eq. (15-6), which is the case of symmetry for the light path in Fig. 13-8, in which light is reflected only once from each face of a tip. Next, with $N = 5$, we set $j = 2$, and this gives $i_2 = 3\pi/10 = 54°$, but this is just the case for two reflections of the light from each face and corresponds to the symmetric light path in Fig. 13-12. If we set $j = 3$ in Eq. (15-6), we find that the angle of incidence is $i_3 = \pi/2 = 90°$, but this means that the reflected ray makes angle $90°$ with the face at the 3rd point of reflection. In other words, for $j = 3$, the reflected ray is either parallel to the opposite face or coincident with it. Therefore, for the symmetric passage of light within the tip of the five-point star, only the two patterns shown in Figs. 13-8 and 13-12 are possible, and these correspond, respectively, to $j = 1$ and $j = 2$ in Eq. (15-6).

15-2. Radii of stars formed from extensions of symmetric light path lines

Fig. 15-2a shows the symmetric light path corresponding to $j = 1$ when light is introduced on face A, so that it enters the solid five-point star at angle of refraction $\gamma = 18°$, which then becomes the same angle of incidence and reflection at each of the other faces. As shown in Chapter 13 in reference to Fig. 13-8, if we extend the lines representing the actual light paths, we then get two derived stars, one of radius R_1 that was given in Eq. (13-43) as:

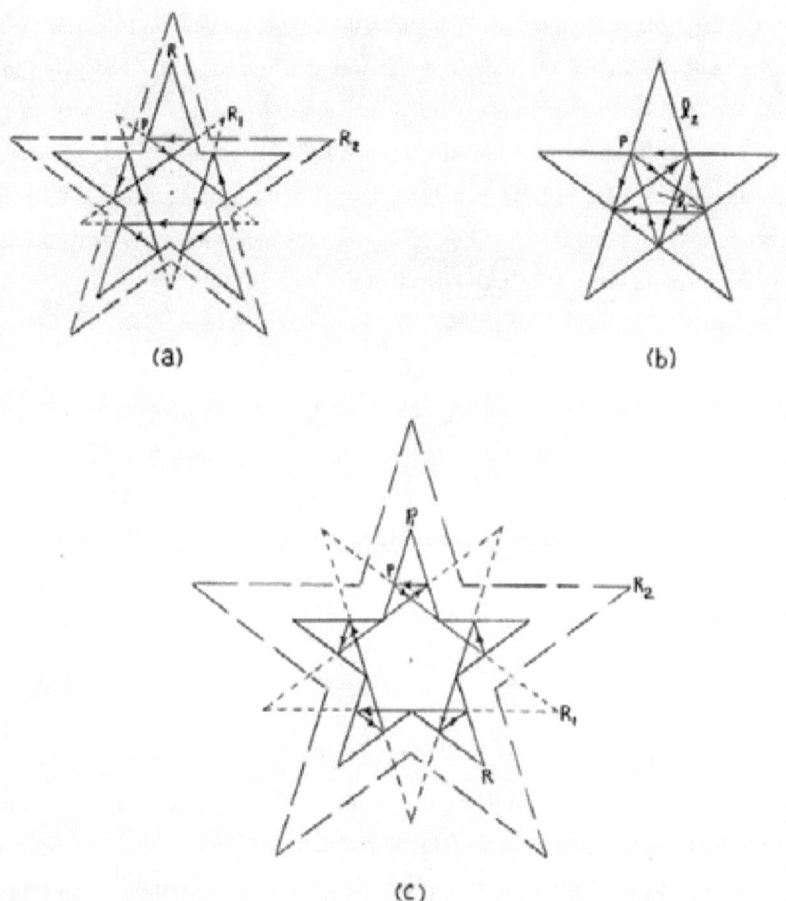

Fig. 15-2. (a) Light incident at P at the proper angle on solid star of radius R follows a symmetric path indicated by the arrows, and when these lines are extended in both directions, two stars are formed: one of radius R_1 and one of radius R_2. (b) With the point of incident light as indicated, the two stars have minimum radii, $R_1 = l_1$ and $R_2 = R$. (c) When P is at distance $l_2 \cos 36°$ from the tip P_1, the stars of radii R_1 and R_2 have maximum values.

$$R_1 = a_1R + (a_2 R - x) \cot 18°, \qquad (15\text{-}7)$$

where x is the distance from the tip P_1 at which the light is incident on face A of the solid star. The radius R_2 of the other derived star was determined earlier and given in Eq. (13-47). We recall that $l_1 = a_1R$ and $l_2 = a_2R$, where a_1 and a_2 are numerical constants given by Eqs. (4-6) of Chapter 4, and furthermore, that l_2 is the length of a side such as A. It follows that when x in Eq. (15-7) is equal to l_2, i.e., when the light is incident at the point of intersection of face A and face J in Fig. 15-2a, then the radius R_1 of the derived star is a minimum according to Eq. (15-7), and its value is:

$$(R_1)_{min} = a_1R. \qquad (15\text{-}8)$$

This is shown in Fig. 15-2b, and we note from Eq. (13-47) of Chapter 13 that the corresponding radius R_2 of the other derived star is simply equal to R. The minimum distance x can have is $l_2 \sin 36°/\sin 108°$, corresponding to the point of entry of the light for which the refracted ray just grazes the intersection of face B with face C. For this distance x the radius R_1 of the derived star has its maximum value shown in Fig. 15-2c, and from Eq. (15-7), this is:

$$(R_1)_{max} = a_1R + \left(a_2R - \frac{l_2 \sin 36°}{\sin 108°}\right)\cot 18°. \qquad (15\text{-}9)$$

Now, noting that $l_2 = a_2R$ and using the values of the numerical factors a_1 and a_2 from Eq. (4-6), and evaluating the sine and cotangent factors, we find from Eqs. (15-8) and (15-9) the following simple relationship involving the golden ratio:

$$\frac{R_{1\,max}}{2R_{1\,min}} = \phi. \qquad (15\text{-}10)$$

When R_1 is a maximum, we see from Eqs. (13-43) and (13-47) that R_2 is also a maximum, and this is portrayed in Fig. 15-2c.

15-3. Symmetric light path length for two reflections in each tip

We now make reference to Fig. 15-3 and consider the total path length traversed by the light for one complete passage in the symmetric case of Fig. 15-2.

The light is incident at point P on face A at distance x from the tip at P_1, and the incident angle θ is such that the refracted path makes angle $\gamma = 18°$ as it travels to face D where it is also incident at angle γ because of the symmetry, and therefore the path PP' is parallel to the line P_3P_5 joining opposite tips of the five-pointed star. Again, because of the symmetry, the distance of point P' from P_2 is also equal to x, as well the distance from the point of incidence P'' on face C, from point P_2. There are five identical path lengths PP' and five identical path lengths $P'P''$ for one complete traversal of the light in the solid five-point star, and as a result, the total path is:

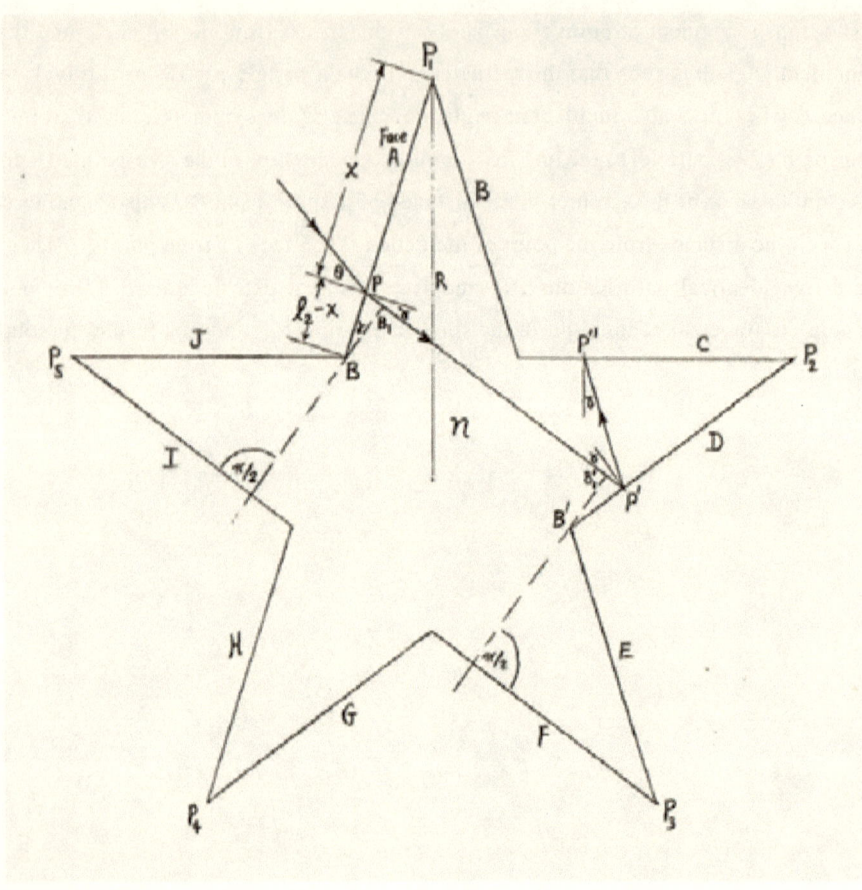

Fig. 15-3. Geometry used in deriving Eqs. (15-11) - (15-15) for total light path length when light is incident at point P on a solid star medium such that angle $\gamma = 18°$.

$$L_T = 5 (PP' + P'P'').\tag{15-11}$$

As a result of the symmetry, the path $P'P''$ is perpendicular to the radius, making triangle $P'P_2P''$ an isosceles triangle, and hence we can write:

$$P'P'' = 2x \sin 18°.\tag{15-12}$$

If we erect perpendiculars to the line P_3P_5, each passing through points B and B' which are the intersections of the faces A, J and D, E respectively, then the perpendiculars are parallel to the radius R and hence each makes angle $\gamma = 18°$ with the faces on which points P and P' lie. Letting B_1 and B_1' be the points at which the perpendiculars intersect the refracted ray path PP', we can express the length of PP' as:

$$PP' = 2l_2 + 2l_1 \sin 36° - 2l_2 \cos 36° + 2(l_2 - x) \sin 18°.\tag{15-13}$$

By substituting for the path lengths from Eqs. (15-12) and (15-13) into Eq. (15-11), we get for the total path length for one passage:

$$L_T = 10 (l_2 + l_1 \sin 36° - l_2 \cos 36° + l_2 \sin 18°).\tag{15-14}$$

Note that the total light path length in Eq. (15-14) is independent of the distance x, i.e., independent of the location of point P on face A at which the light is introduced. Remembering that $l_1 = a_1 R$ and $l_2 = a_2 R$ with numerical values of a_1 and a_2 given in Eq. (4-6), we can express L_T in Eq. (15-14) directly in terms of the radius R, and this gives:

$$L_T = 10 \sin 36° R$$
$$= 5.87785252 R.\tag{15-15}$$

The limits on the point of entry P for the symmetric path in Fig. 15-3 are $x \geq l_2 \sin 36°/ \sin 108°$ and $x \leq l_2$, or:

$$\frac{l_2}{\phi} \leq x \leq l_2,\tag{15-16}$$

but the total path traversed by the light has the single value given by Eq. (15-15), independent of the distance x. So, if light of a given wavelength, for which the solid star medium has refractive index n, is introduced at point P in Fig. 15-3, the time taken for the light to traverse one complete symmetric path is:

$$t_T = \frac{L_T}{c/n}, \qquad (15\text{-}17)$$

and this traversal time is independent of the location x of the point of entry.

It is interesting to compare the invariant light path length L_T in Eq. (15-15) with the periphery of the star of radius R. We know that each of the ten sides of the star has length $l_2 = a_2 R$, and therefore the periphery $P_S = 10 a_2 R$. From Eq. (15-15), we then get:

$$\frac{L_T}{P_S} = \frac{\phi}{2}. \qquad (15\text{-}18)$$

15-4. Stars formed by symmetric light paths with four reflections in each tip of star

We now turn to the case of symmetric light passage for $j = 2$, $N = 5$ in which the light makes two internal reflections from each face of the solid star, after having entered face A such that the angle of refraction is 54°. This symmetry, dealt with earlier in reference to Fig. 13-12 in Chapter 13, is shown here in Fig. 15-4. We begin by showing that the lines representing the symmetric intersecting light paths form a five-point star having a radius dependent on the distance x at which the light enters face A. Based on the arguments in Chapter 13, when light is incident at angle θ at point a in Fig. 15-4 such that the refracted ray makes angle 54° with the perpendicular to face A, then the path ab of the entering ray is parallel to the line joining tips P_1 and P_3 of the star. Likewise, following the path around, we see that the path segment cd is parallel to the line joining tips P_1 and P_4. But, the included angle between lines $P_1 P_3$ and $P_1 P_4$ of the star is 36°, and therefore the angle aed in Fig. 15-4 is also 36°. Continuing around the star of radius R in this way, it follows that the included angle at each of the other points of intersection f,

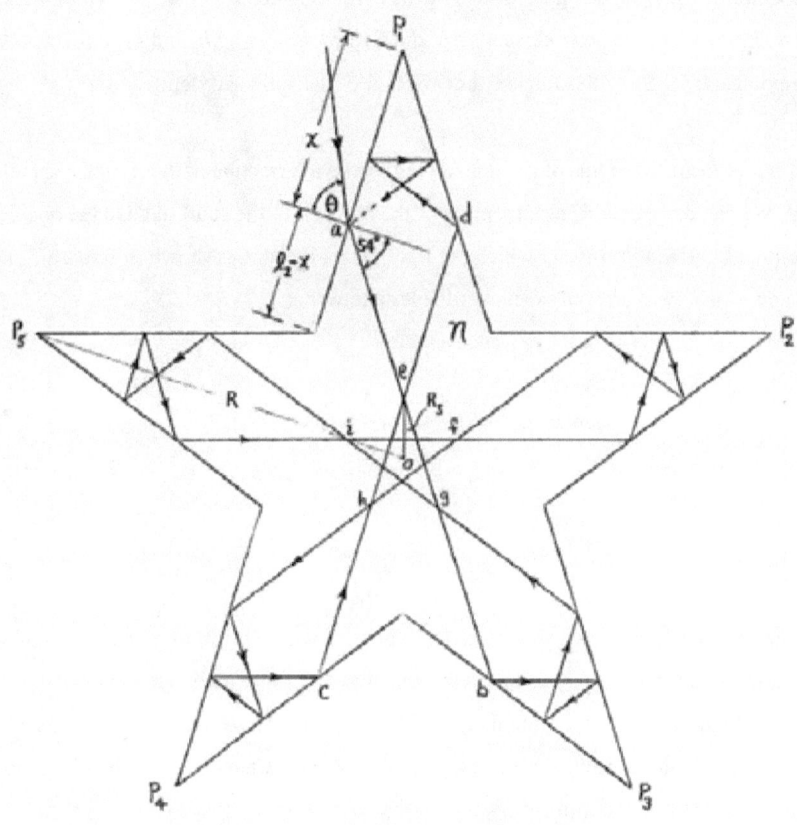

Fig. 15-4. Light incident at angle θ on the solid [5, 2] star, such that the refracted ray enters the medium at 54° as indicated, gives rise to the symmetric light path involving two internal reflections at each face, or four internal reflections within each tip region.

g, h, and i in the internal figure is also 36°. Therefore, because of all the symmetries, the figure defined by the lines intersecting at the five points e, f, g, h, and i is a mathematical five-point star [5, 2], with same center O as that of the solid star defined by P_1, P_2, P_3, P_4, and P_5.

Let R_S be the radius of the star formed by the intersection of the symmetric paths of light. We can determine R_S as a function of the radius R of the solid star and the position x, measured relative to tip P_1, at which the light enters the star as shown in Fig. 15-5. From triangle $P_1 a P_1'$, we can apply the law of sines and write:

$$\frac{R-R_s}{\sin(\pi/2+54°)} = \frac{x}{\sin(\pi-\pi/2-54°-18°)}, \qquad (15\text{-}19)$$

from which we obtain:

$$R_S = R - \frac{\cos 54°}{\sin 18°} x. \qquad (15\text{-}20)$$

It is interesting to note that the numerical value of the factor multiplying x in the latter equation is just equal to a_2/a_1 involving quantities defined earlier in Chapter 4 for the mathematical star. In fact, noting that $\cos 54° \equiv \sin 36°$, we see that the factor $\cos 54°/\sin 18°$ is just equal to the ratio l_2/l_1 in Eqs. (4-3) and (4-4) of Chapter 4, and therefore, we can write Eq. (15-20) in the form:

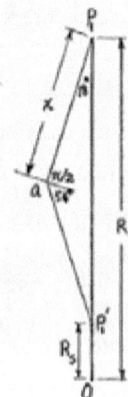

Fig. 15-5. Geometry relating radius R_S of efghi star in Fig. 15-4 to radius R of the solid star into which light is introduced, giving rise to the star of radius R_S.

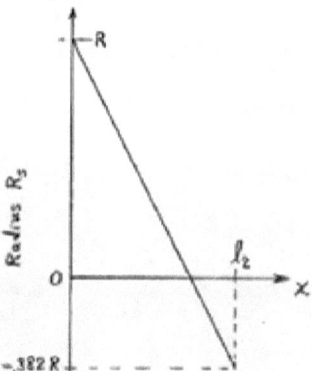

Fig. 15-6. Radius R_S of derived star efghi in Fig. 15-4 versus distance x from tip, of solid star of radius R, at which light ray is incident.

$$\frac{R_s}{R} = 1 - \frac{a_2}{a_1}\frac{x}{R}, \tag{15-21}$$

where $l_2 = a_2 R$ and $l_1 = a_1 R$ and the numerical factors a_1 and a_2 are given in Eq. (4-6).

A plot of the radius R_S of the star formed by the symmetric intersecting light paths in Fig. 15-3, versus the distance x at which light enters face A, is given in Fig. 15-6. Note that when x is zero, the radius R_S is just equal to the radius R of the five-point solid star. As x increases, the radius R_S decreases, and when $x = a_1 R/a_2$, the radius R_S is zero; further increase in x results in a negative value for the radius R_S. Fig. 15-7 is helpful in understanding this from a geometric perspective. A construction of the symmetric light path for a point of entry x close to the tip P_1 is shown in Fig. 15-7a. Next, we calculate the value of entry point x for which the entering ray ab in Fig. 15-4 just passes through the center O of the solid star; from triangle OaP_1 in Fig. 15-4, we can write:

$$\frac{R}{\sin(\pi/2 + 54°)} = \frac{x}{\sin 18°}, \tag{15-22}$$

but this can be expressed as:

$$x = \frac{\sin 18°}{\sin 36°} R, \tag{15-23}$$

and again, using the relations for the five-point star in Eqs. (4-3) through (4-6) of Chapter 4, the latter can be put in the following form:

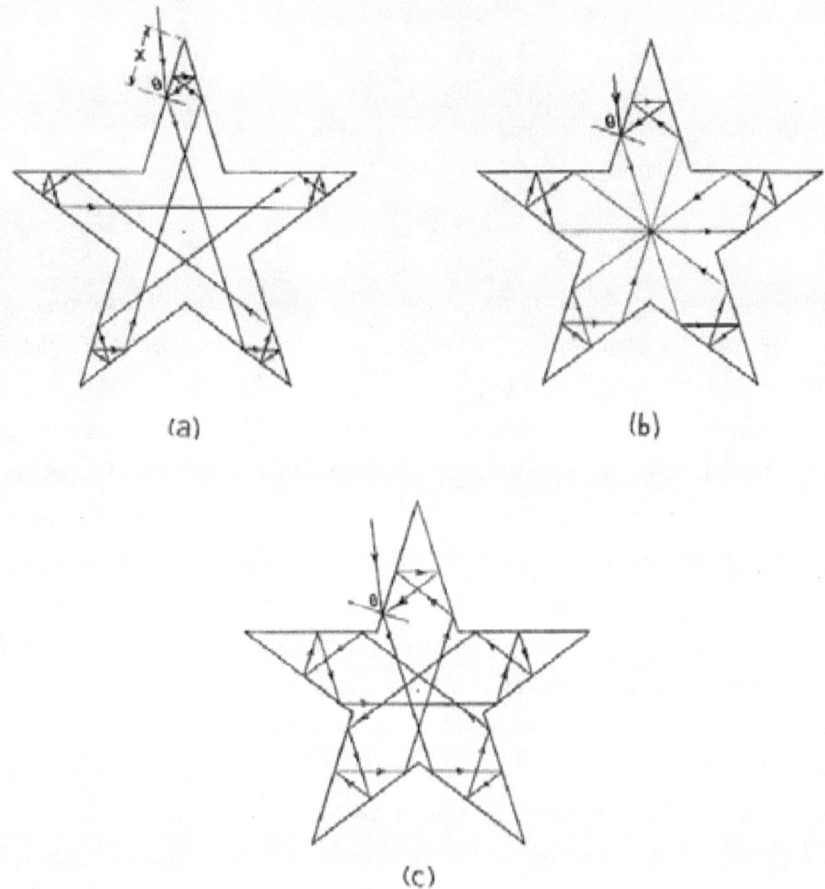

Fig. 15-7. Examples of size and orientation of the star formed by the intersecting light paths when a light ray is incident on a face of a solid star of radius R, at distance x from the tip. In (a) $x < (a_1/a_2) R$. When $x = (a_1/a_2) R$, the star coalesces to a point shown in (b), and in (c), the star orientation differs from (a) for $x > (a_1/a_2) R$.

$$x = \frac{l_1}{l_2}R = \frac{a_1}{a_2}R. \tag{15-24}$$

We see that Eq. (15-24) substituted for x into Eq. (15-21) gives:

$$R_S = 0, \tag{15-25}$$

and this is portrayed in the construction of Fig. 15-7b corresponding to the case in which all the light paths that are parallel to P_1P_3, P_2P_4 ... pass through the center O of the solid star.

A construction of the symmetric light path for an entry point x greater than the value in Eq. (15-24) is given in Fig. 15-7c. The value of R_S calculated from Eq. (15-21) for $x > a_1R/a_2$ is negative, but note that the tip e of the star figure is oriented 180° relative to the center O compared to its location in Fig. 15-7a for $x < a_1R/a_2$. That is, for $x < a_1R/a_2$, the light paths ab and cd intersect in point e on the line defined by radius R of the solid star, and point e lies "above" the center O, i.e., point e lies between O and P_1. However, for $x > a_1R/a_2$, the light paths ab and cd are oriented on opposite sides of O, and they intersect at a point e that is still on the line defined by radius R, but now e no longer lies between P_1 and O but instead it lies "below" O. This explains the significance of the negative values of radius R_S obtained from Eq. (15-21) when x is greater than a_1R/a_2. The maximum negative value of radius R_S is obtained when the point of entry x is at the intersection of faces A and J in Fig. 15-4, that is, when $x = l_2 = a_2R$. For this value of x, the radius R_S from Eq. (15-21) is:

$$R_S = -a_1R$$
$$= -0.381966\ R. \tag{15-26}$$

To summarize briefly, as the distance x of the point of entry of light on face A in Fig. 15-7 increases, the radius R_S of the internal star formed by the symmetric path intersections decreases, and when x reaches the value in Eq. (15-24), the star collapses to a point at the center O. As x increases further, the star appears again with increasing radius but the star is inverted because its tip that had been located between O, and P_1 is now located 180° in the opposite direction from O. That the star degenerates to a point when the entry point x has the value in Eq. (15-24), i.e., when the entering light ray passes through center O, is a very interesting and unusual aspect of the symmetric intersecting light paths. We have assumed that the refractive index of the solid star is perfectly uniform, so that light travels in perfectly straight lines between the points of internal reflection on the faces A through J and, furthermore, that the rays of light are simple lines and that the faces are perfect planes so that the conditions of equal angles of reflection and incidence are faithfully obeyed. These conditions can all be met to a high level of precision depending upon the degree of quality with which a solid star of this type could be made. To discuss further the collapse of the star, formed by intersecting light paths, into the "point star" when x has the value in Eq. (15-24), we will refer solely to the geometric aspects of the lines, without consideration of the degree to which the limiting point star could be achieved in reality. To this end, the following considerations will be made based purely on mathematical conditions of the intersecting lines that form the star.

First, we note that a mathematical point in the geometric sense has no width, no breadth, no thickness, and no size at all. Similarly, a straight line has no width and no thickness, only length. When two lines intersect in a plane, the point of intersection is merely a mathematical point. Contrast this with the tip of a well-sharpened pencil touched to a piece of paper to make a small dot that we refer to as a "point" in mathematical constructions. Assuming the dot is approximately hemispherical in shape with a diameter of only 0.005 inch in the plane of the paper, then it contains approximately 10^{16} molecules of pencil material. So, the mathematical points and lines are constructs of the mind, but important ones indeed. To consider further what is involved when the distance x becomes equal to the value in Eq. (15-24), thereby resulting in the degenerate "point star" of Fig. 15-7b, let us use "ε" to represent a number to which we are free to assign any value, however small we wish. We let x be:

$$x = \frac{a_1}{a_2}(1-\varepsilon)R, \qquad (15\text{-}27)$$

and we note that if $\varepsilon = 0$, then x in Eq. (15-27) is identical to that in Eq. (15-24), whereas we can choose a very small nonzero value for ε that makes x in Eq. (15-27) as close as we like to the value in Eq. (15-24), without actually being equal to it. So, substituting from Eq. (15-27) into Eq. (15-21) allows us to write the expression for the star radius R_S in terms of R simply as:

$$R_S = \epsilon R. \qquad (15\text{-}28)$$

Suppose we choose $\varepsilon = 10^{-12}$, then x in Eq. (15-27) is equal to the value in Eq. (15-24) multiplied by 0.999999999999, and if for example the radius R of the solid star is $R = 1.0$ inch, then the radius R_S of the star formed by the symmetric intersecting lines is one millionth of one millionth of an inch, i.e., $R_S = 10^{-12} R$. However, the exceedingly smaller star has all the properties of the mathematical star [5, 2]. If yet a smaller value of ε is chosen, for example $\varepsilon = 10^{-20}$, then x is even nearer the value in Eq. (15-24) and the radius $R_S = 10^{-20} R$. Although an incredibly small star, it still has all the properties of the mathematical star [5, 2]. Given any small nonzero value of ε, one can choose still a smaller value, meaning that x is even closer to the value in Eq. (15-24), but still we have a perfect although very, very small star. Only when we set ε equal to zero do we get $R_S = 0$, and the star coalesces into a single point which is the intersection point of the five lines passing through point O in Fig. 15-7b. As x increases steadily from zero, the radius R_S of the star in Fig. 15-7 decreases, and the star degenerates to a point when x passes through the value in Eq. (15-24), i.e., when $\varepsilon = 0$ in Eq. (15-28). However, the "point star" bears no features possessed by the star for values of x just smaller than or just greater than x in Eq. (15-24). That is, when $\varepsilon = 0$, the point at O in Fig. 15-7b is no different from the point of intersection of two arbitrary lines in a plane, neither of which had ever been associated with a star, because the mathematical point has no structure to it. In this regard, it is somewhat misleading to refer to it as a "point star," for $\varepsilon = 0$, although the usage is descriptive in relating it to the stars that exist for x less than or greater than the value in Eq. (15-24).

15-5. Light path length with four reflections in each tip of star

Next, we consider the total path length travelled by the light in one complete circuit for the symmetric case in Fig. 15-7. Referring to Fig. 15-8, we see that the light enters at point a at distance x from P_1, travels to point b where it is reflected to point b_1, and thence reflected to point b_2, and finally to point b'_2 on the opposite face. Note that this is exactly one-fifth the total path traversed in one complete circuit in Fig. 15-7 as a result of the symmetry. Recalling that the path ab is parallel to P_1P_3, we then know that bP_3 is just equal to x in Fig. 15-8, and we can express ab as:

$$ab = 2l_2 + 2l_1 \sin 36° - 2x \cos 36°. \tag{15-29}$$

Taking into account the angles in triangle bb_1P_3, we can express the light path segment bb_1 as:

$$bb_1 = x \frac{\sin 36°}{\sin 108°}. \tag{15-30}$$

Because the angles of incidence and reflection at point b are 54°, it follows that angle b_1bP_3 is 36°, and therefore triangle bb_1P_3 is isosceles with $b_1P_3 = bb_1$. Because of the symmetric condition that light path b_2b_1 is perpendicular to radius R, it follows that b_2b_1 is the base of isosceles triangle $b_1b_2P_3$ and hence the light path b_1b_2 is given by:

$$b_1b_2 = 2bb_1 \sin 18°. \tag{15-31}$$

The total light path is obtained from Eqs. (15-29) through (15-31), with the result:

$$L_{T2} = 5(ab + 2bb_1 + b_1b_2)$$
$$= 10\left[l_2 + l_1 \sin 36° + x\left(\frac{\sin 36°}{\sin 108°} - \cos 36° + \frac{\sin 36° \sin 18°}{\sin 108°} \right) \right].$$

$$\tag{15-32}$$

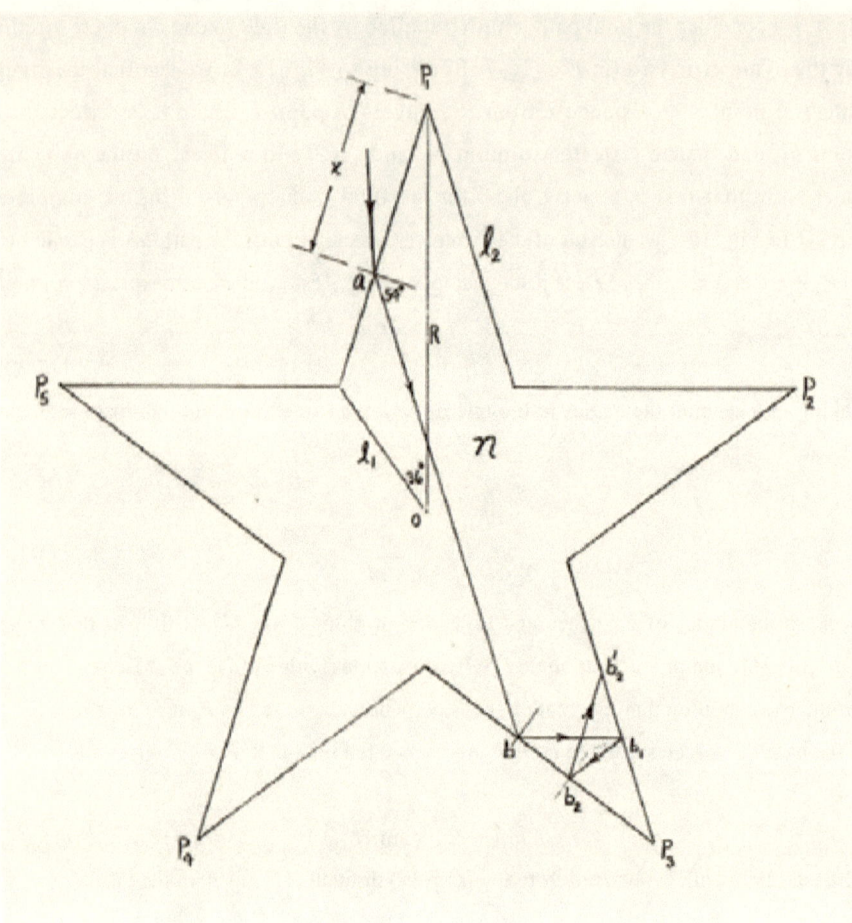

Fig. 15-8. Geometry used in deriving Eq. (15-32) for the total path travelled by light in one complete traversal, making four internal reflections within each tip region. The path shown is exactly one-fifth the total path distance.

Upon evaluating the trigonometric factors inside the parentheses multiplying the distance x in Eq. (15-32), we find that these combine identically to zero and therefore the total light path L_{T2} is simply:

$$L_{T2} = 10\,(l_2 + l_1 \sin 36°). \qquad (15\text{-}33)$$

So, the total light path for one complete pass from entry point back to the same point is independent of the position x of entry in Fig. 15-8, and this is true for any entry point along the face A of length l_2. It is interesting to note that the total light path in Eq. (15-33) is the sum of two parts. First, the quantity $10 l_2$ is simply the periphery of the star of radius R, because it contains ten sides, each of length l_2. Second, we note that $2 l_1 \sin 36°$ is the length of one side of the regular pentagon obtained by joining adjacent points of intersection of the sides of length l_2, and therefore $10 l_1 \sin 36°$ is the perimeter of the regular pentagon. As a result, the total light path L_{T2}, independent of entry point x, is the sum of the perimeters of the star of radius R and the regular pentagon defined by it. Viewed in another way, we see that $2 l_1 \sin 36°$ is the base of the isosceles triangle at each tip having sides of length l_2. In this view, we see that the total light path in Eq. (15-33) is simply the sum of the perimeters of these five isosceles triangles.

Using Eqs. (4-3) through (4-6) of Chapter 4 that relate l_2 and l_1 to the radius R of the five-point star, we can express the total light path L_{t2} in Eq. (15-33) in terms of the radius R of the solid star, and the result is:

$$L_{T2} = 9.510565161\,R. \qquad (15\text{-}34)$$

The quantity L_{T2} is the total symmetric path for one complete pass involving two reflections from each face of the solid star in Fig. 15-7. For the symmetric light path involving just one reflection from each face of the solid star, the total path for one complete pass is given by L_{T1} in Eq. (15-15). From Eqs. (15-15) and (15-34), we obtain the following unexpected and very intriguing result involving the golden ratio.

$$L_{T2} = \phi\,L_{T1}. \qquad (15\text{-}35)$$

The significance of the latter result is that if light is made to enter the face of the solid star with refraction angle 54°, then its symmetric path with two internal reflections at each face is just equal to the golden ratio times the symmetric light path obtained when light enters the face at refraction angle 18° and makes only one internal reflection at each face in its path around. Moreover, this ratio is independent of the points of entry on the star face in the two cases as shown in the derivation of Eqs. (15-14) and (15-33).

As pointed out earlier, a key aspect of the symmetry of the light path in Fig. 15-7 is that the portion of the path innermost to each tip is perpendicular to the radius R of the solid star. Referring to Fig. 15-8 and the arguments connected with Eqs. (15-30) and (15-31), we can express the perpendicular distance d of the path segment b_1b_2 from the tip as:

$$d = b_1P_3 \cos 18°$$
$$= x \sin 36°, \qquad (15\text{-}36)$$

where of course x is the distance from P_1 on face A at which the light is introduced. For any nonzero value of x, however small, the light path b_1b_2 does not reach the tip P_3. However, for any given distance d, we can choose a value of x calculated from Eq. (15-36) that will result in a smaller value of d, thereby closer to the tip, but only in the limit $x = 0$ does d also equal zero. These statements are true concerning the geometric aspects involved, but we must note that light can be represented as rays following geometric paths only for distances that are several times longer than the wavelength of the light itself. For light in the upper wavelength region of the visible spectrum, the wavelength is approximately 6500 Angstroms, or 25.6×10^{-6} inch. For any values of x that correspond to a distance b_1b_2 near this small magnitude the light paths no longer behave in a straight-line geometric sense, but instead the wave nature of light must be taken into account, and this invariably leads to spreading of the light referred to as diffraction.

CHAPTER 16

NON-SYMMETRIC FIVE-POINT STARS: THEIR ORIGINS AND PROPERTIES

16-1. Skewed stars formed from non-symmetric light paths

We now consider departures from the symmetric light path patterns dealt with in Chapters 13 and 15. To make the comparison, refer first to Fig. 16-1, which shows light incident on face A so that the entering refracted ray makes angle 18° with the perpendicular, thereby resulting in the symmetric light path in which the light is reflected internally once from each face of the solid star. We see that the intersecting light paths form a regular pentagon within the boundary of the star of radius R, and that the extensions of the sides of this pentagon result in a mathematical star [5, 2] as pointed out earlier in Chapter 13. Connecting each vertex of the regular pentagon with the second vertex from it in turn gives a mathematical star as shown in Fig. 16-1. As pointed out earlier, if the refractive index n of the solid star material is assumed to be 1.5, then the angle of incidence at which the light must be introduced on face A is, according to Snell's Law, θ = arcsin (1.5 sin 18°) = 27.615°.

Suppose we introduce light so that the entering refracted ray path makes angle γ = 17° with the perpendicular to the face A, instead of γ = 18°. According to Snell's Law, the angle of incidence must be θ = arcsin (1.5 sin 17°) = 26.012°. A drawing to scale for this small departure from the case of symmetry is shown in Fig. 16-2. Note that the intersecting light paths no longer form a regular pentagon as in Fig. 16-1, but now the pentagon is irregular with sides of unequal length. Furthermore, when the sides of the irregular pentagon are extended to meet, the resulting figure is a five-point star, but it is irregular as can be seen from Fig. 16-2. Finally, when each vertex of the irregular pentagon is connected to the second vertex, from it, a smaller irregular star

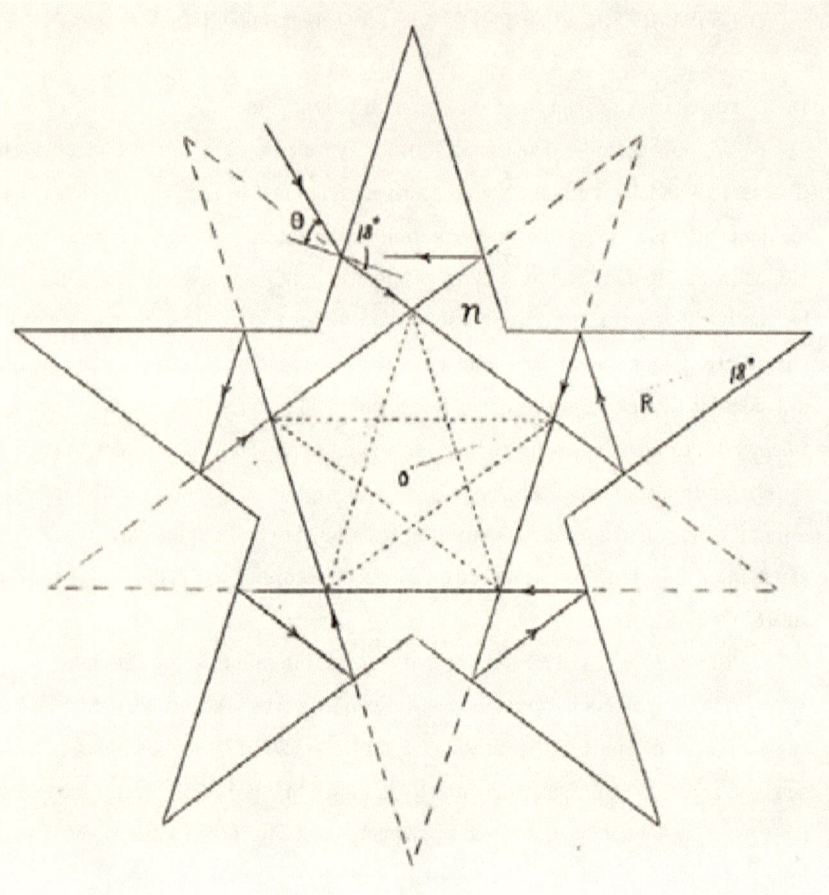

Fig. 16-1. Light entering a solid star [5, 2] at angle of refraction 18° will travel in the symmetric path indicated by the arrows, thus forming a pentagon the sides of which extended by long-dash lines give rise to another [5, 2] star. Further, connecting each vertex of the regular pentagon with the second vertex from it results in yet another [5, 2] star as shown by the short-dash lines.

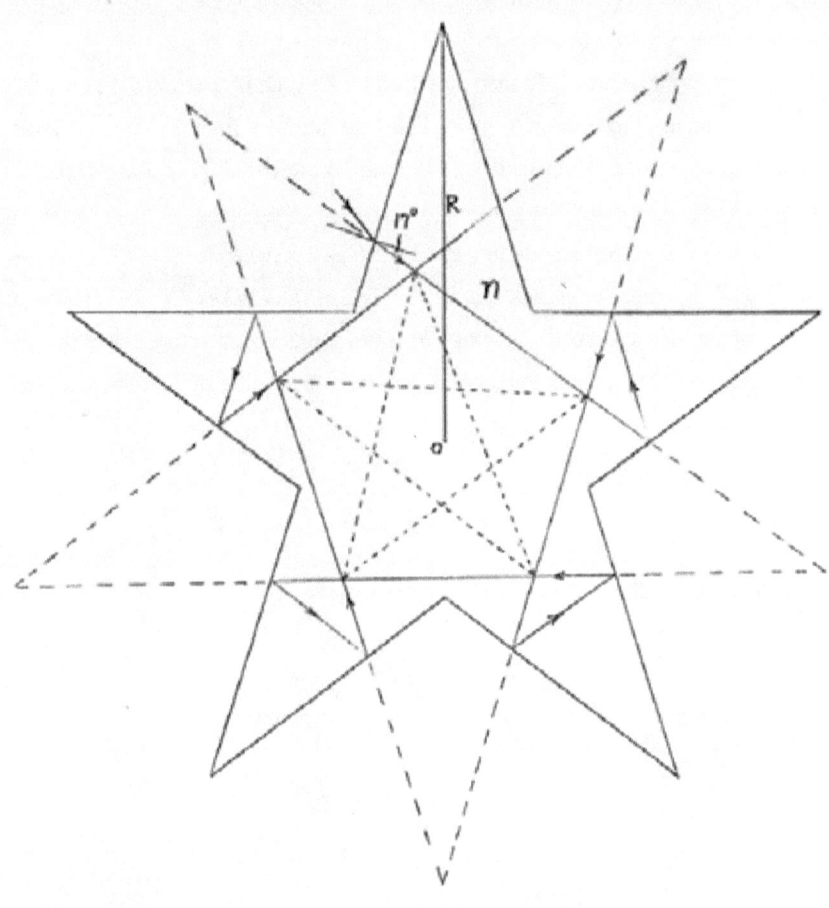

Fig. 16-2. Note the non-symmetric (skewed) star figures that are formed, compared to Fig. 16-1, when light enters the solid [5, 2] star of radius R at angle of refraction 17° instead of 18° as required for symmetric light path.

is formed. The effects of a small departure from the condition of symmetric light path are evident when Fig. 16-2 is compared with Fig. 16-1.

The asymmetric star formed by extending the sides of the irregular polygon formed when the angle of refraction γ in Fig. 16-2 is different from 18° does possess some interesting properties. To reveal these properties, we refer to Fig. 16-3 in which the angles of incidence and reflection are donated by i_1, i_2, i_3 . . . i_{10} at the internal faces of the solid star. Noting that each tip angle in the solid star is 2φ, where $\varphi = 18°$, we can see from triangle aP_1b that the angle abP_1 is $\pi - 2\varphi - (\pi/2 + \gamma)$, or $\pi/2 - 2\varphi - \gamma$. Each base angle in the tip of the solid star, such as angle cdb, is $(\pi - 2\varphi)/2$, and therefore noting that triangles abP_1 and cbd share a common angle because of intersecting straight lines, we find from triangle cbd that:

$$\frac{\pi}{2} - i_1 + (\pi - 2\varphi)/2 + \frac{\pi}{2} - 2\varphi - \gamma = \pi, \tag{16-1}$$

and remembering that $\varphi = \pi/10$ for the solid star, the latter can be solved for i_1, to give:

$$i_1 = 2\varphi - \gamma. \tag{16-2}$$

The sum of the angles in triangle cP_5e must equal π, giving us:

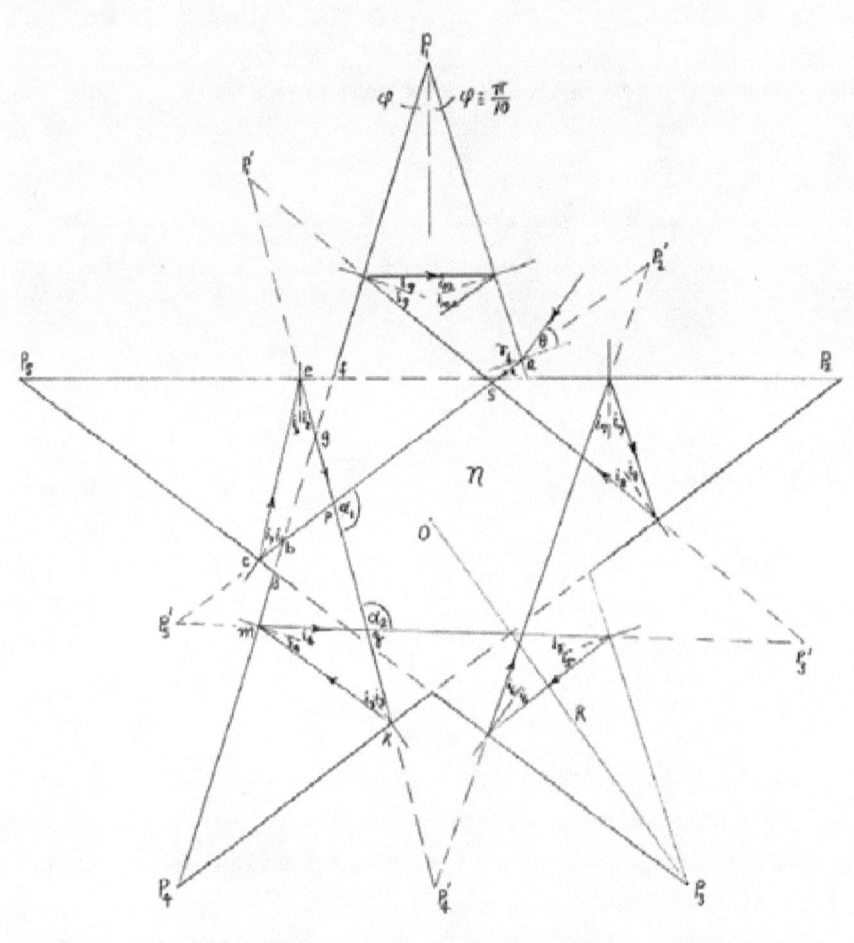

Fig. 16-3. Geometry used in showing that a light ray entering the solid star at refraction angle $\gamma \neq 18°$ gives rise to the irregular pentagon with all internal angles equal to 6φ, and to the non-symmetric star $P_1'P_2'P_3'P_4'P_5'$ with each tip angle equal to 2φ.

$$\frac{\pi}{2} - i_1 + 2\varphi + \frac{\pi}{2} - i_2 = \pi, \qquad (16\text{-}3)$$

and substituting for i_1 from Eq. (16-2) gives the following value for i_2.

$$i_2 = \gamma \qquad (16\text{-}4)$$

From triangle *feg*, the angle *fge* is $\pi - (\pi/2 - i_2) - 4\varphi$, or $\angle fge = \varphi + \gamma$. The latter is true because $\varphi \equiv 18°$. Now, triangles *feg* and *gkP$_4$* share the angle *fge* in common, hence, from triangle *gkP$_4$*, we can write:

$$\frac{\pi}{2} + i_3 + 2\varphi + \varphi + \gamma = \pi. \qquad (16\text{-}5)$$

Solving the latter for i_3 gives:

$$i_3 = 2\varphi - \gamma. \qquad (16\text{-}6)$$

In triangle *kP$_4$m*, we have $\pi/2 - i_3 + \pi/2 - i_4 + 2\varphi = \pi$, and solving for angle i_4, using Eq. (16-6), leads to:

$$i_4 = \gamma. \qquad (16\text{-}7)$$

Continuing this analysis in following the path of the light in Fig. 16-3, we see that the alternating pattern of the internal angles of incidence and reflection in Eqs. (16-2), (16-4), (16-6), and (16-7) is repeated at the other faces of the solid star. Using the index j to denote $i_1, i_2, \ldots$, we note that depending on whether j is odd or even the angles can be expressed as:

$$i_j = \begin{cases} 2\varphi - \gamma & \text{for } j = 1, 3, 5, \cdots 9 \\ \gamma & \text{for } j = 2, 4, \cdots 10. \end{cases} \qquad (16\text{-}8)$$

Referring to Fig. 16-3 and Eq. (16-8), it is seen that $i_{10} = \gamma$ which shows that after one complete traversal, the light is reflected internally at the same angle at which the refracted ray entered the solid star medium at point *a*.

In triangle *cep*, the angle *cpe* is:

$$\angle cpe = \pi - 2i_1 - 2i_2 \qquad (16\text{-}9)$$

and from Eq. (16-8), this is:

$$\angle cpe = \pi - 4\varphi + 2\gamma - 2\gamma. \qquad (16\text{-}10)$$

Remembering that $\varphi = \pi/10$, the latter can be written as:

$$\angle cpe = 6\varphi. \qquad (16\text{-}11)$$

Because of the intersecting straight lines *ac* and *ek*, the angle α_1 in the irregular pentagon in Fig. 16-3 is therefore:

$$\alpha_1 = \angle cpe = 6\varphi. \qquad (16\text{-}12)$$

Similarly, referring to triangle *mkg* and again using Eq. (16-8), the internal angle α_2 of the irregular pentagon is:

$$\alpha_2 = \pi - 2i_3 - 2i_4$$
$$= 6\varphi. \qquad (16\text{-}13)$$

Continuing in this fashion, it is seen that each of the remaining interior angles α_3, α_4, and α_5 is also equal to 6φ, i.e., 108°.

Now, consider the irregular star P_1', P_2', ... P_5' formed by extending lines *ac*, *ek*, etc. until they meet. In triangle $pP_1's$ the angle $P_1'ps$ is supplementary to α_1 of the irregular pentagon and, likewise, angle $P_1'sp$ is supplementary to α_2. However, $\alpha_1 = \alpha_2$, and therefore $\angle P_1'ps = \angle P_1'sp = \pi - 6\varphi = 4\varphi$. It follows that the tip angle at P_1' is equal to $\pi - 8\varphi = 2\varphi$, and that the tip triangle $pP_1's$ is isosceles with side pP_1' equal to side sP_1'. Using the same type analysis, it follows that each of the other tip triangles of the irregular star, with a base on the irregular pentagon, is isosceles with tip angle equal to 2φ.

In summary, when the ray enters the solid star at angle $\gamma \neq \varphi$ (18°), the intersecting light paths reflected internally from the faces form an irregular pentagon, and when its sides are extended to meet, an irregularly-shaped five-point star is formed. However, each internal angle of the irregular pentagon is equal to $6\varphi \equiv 108°$, and each tip angle of the irregular star is equal to $2\varphi \equiv 36°$, which is the same as for the mathematical star [5, 2]. Moreover, each triangular tip of the irregular star is an isosceles triangle with its base as one of the sides of the irregular pentagon.

So, we see that consideration of the non-symmetric light paths inside the solid star has led in a natural way to the geometric shape of a skewed or non-symmetric five-point star. It is obvious that we can omit the reference to light paths and, based on the foregoing analysis, simply state the geometric results as a theorem regarding the skewed star shape.

In Fig. 16-4

Given: Straight lines *ab* and *ac* intersect at point *a* with included angle $\alpha_1 = 36°$.

Straight line *de* intersects *ab* and *ac* so that *af* = *ag*.

Straight lines *eb* and *dc* each make angle 36° with *de*.

Then: The non-symmetric star *aecbd* has all tip angles $\alpha_2 = \alpha_3 = \alpha_1 = 36°$ and all triangles *geh, hcm, mbk,* and *kdf* are isosceles, in addition to given isosceles triangle *agf*.

It is interesting that the particular type of skewed or irregular five-point star represented in Figs. 16-4 and 16-3 has all ten sides of unequal length but, still, like the standard mathematical

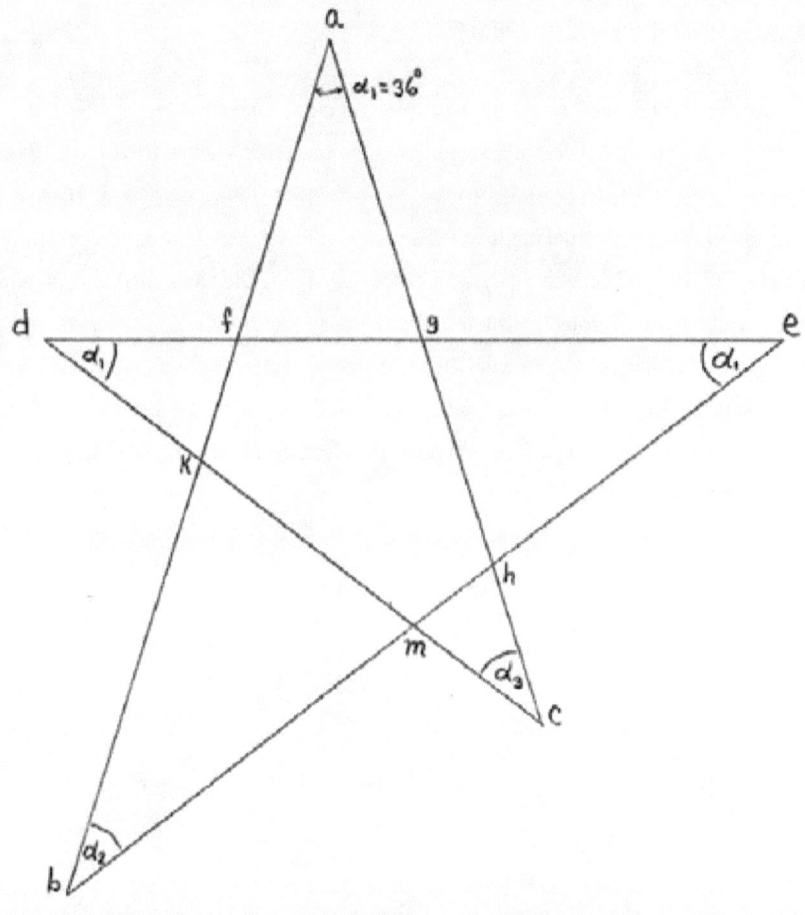

Fig. 16-4. A non-symmetric five-point star representing the theorem stated in the text, which is based on the analysis of the non-symmetric light paths in Fig. 16-3.

star [5, 2], the tip angles of the irregular star are all equal to 36°, and each triangle formed by a tip and intersection of two adjacent sides is isosceles.

16-2. Skewed stars formed on the basis of irregular pentagons

Next, consider the irregular star figure obtained when each vertex of the irregular pentagon in Fig. 16-3 is connected to the second vertex from it as in Fig. 16-5. It was shown earlier that the internal angle at each vertex of this pentagon is $6\varphi \equiv 108°$, per Eqs. (16-11) – (16-13) and related analysis. Let the lengths of the sides of this pentagon be represented by $l_1, l_2, \ldots l_5$ as indicated in Fig. 16-5, and let $L_1, L_2, \ldots L_5$ be the lengths defining the irregular star when each vertex of the irregular pentagon is joined with the second from it. (Note that the lengths l_1, l_2 and L_1, L_2 are not to be confused with these symbols used extensively in earlier chapters in reference to two segment lengths in the standard mathematical star [5, 2]). Consider the triangle formed by L_1, l_1, and l_2 in which the interior angle $6\varphi \equiv 108°$ is opposite side L_1. Using the law of cosines allows L_1 to be expressed as follows:

$$L_1 = \left(l_1^2 + l_2^2 - 2l_1 l_2 \cos 108°\right)^{\frac{1}{2}}. \qquad (16\text{-}14)$$

Similar relations hold for $L_2, L_3, \ldots$ and if we use the index j, we can write:

$$L_j = \left(l_j^2 + l_{j+1}^2 - 2l_j l_{j+1} \cos 108°\right)^{\frac{1}{2}}, \qquad (16\text{-}15)$$

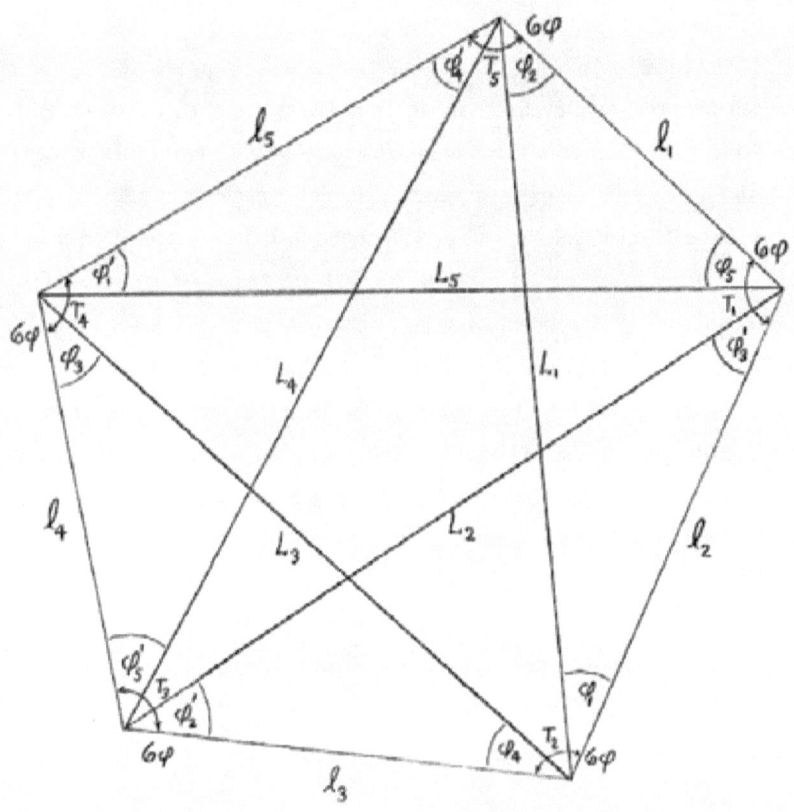

Fig. 16-5. An irregular pentagon having unequal sides $l_1, \ldots l_5$ but all internal vertex angles equal to $6\varphi \equiv 108°$ is the basis for forming a class of non-symmetric stars by connecting each vertex with the second vertex from it. The tip-to-tip lengths of the star sides are $L_1, \ldots L_5$, and the star tip angles are $T_1, \ldots T_5$.

where $j = 1, 2, \ldots 5$, and where it is understood of course that for $j = 5$ the length $l_{j+1} = l_6 \equiv l_1$.

In the triangle defined by L_1, l_1, and l_2, the angles opposite sides l_1 and l_2 are designated by φ_1 and φ_2, respectively, in Fig. 16-5. The angles φ_3, φ_4, and φ_5 are defined as shown. Now, it is also seen that side l_1 of the irregular pentagon forms a triangle along with side l_5 and the line L_5 joining two vertexes. In this triangle, the angle opposite l_1 is designated by φ_1' to distinguish it from φ_1 that is opposite l_1 in the triangle formed by L_1, l_1, and l_2. Following this pattern, it is understood how the angles φ_2', φ_3', φ_4', and φ_5' are defined in relation to their counterparts φ_2, φ_3, φ_4, and φ_5 in Fig. 16-5. Knowing $l_1, l_2, \ldots l_5$ of the pentagon, the lengths $L_1, L_2, \ldots L_5$, characterizing the irregular star can be determined from Eq. (16-15). Then, the angles $\varphi_1, \varphi_2, \ldots \varphi_5$ and $\varphi_1', \varphi_2', \ldots \varphi_5'$ can be determined by applying the law of sines to the particular triangle in which the angles appear. For example, in the triangle formed by L_1, l_1, and l_2, the angle φ_1 can be found in terms of l_1, and L_1 through the following:

$$\varphi_1 = \arcsin\left(\frac{l_1}{L_1}\sin 108°\right) \qquad (16\text{-}16)$$

Employing the index j, as in Eq. (16-15), the angles φ_j in Fig. 16-5 can be expressed in the following form.

$$\varphi_j = \begin{cases} \arcsin\left(\dfrac{l_j}{L_j}\sin 108°\right) & j = 1, 3, 5 \\[2mm] \arcsin\left(\dfrac{l_j}{L_{j-1}}\sin 108°\right) & j = 2, 4 \end{cases} \qquad (16\text{-}17)$$

For the angles φ_j', if we define $L_0 \equiv L_5$, then relations analogous to Eq. (16-17) can be written as:

$$\varphi'_j = \begin{cases} \arc\sin\left(\dfrac{l_j}{L_{j-1}}\sin 108°\right) & j=1,3,5 \\ \arc\sin\left(\dfrac{l_j}{L_j}\sin 108°\right) & j=2,4 \end{cases} \qquad (16\text{-}18)$$

The angle at each tip of the irregular star of Fig. 16-5 can be found from the angles φ_j and φ_j' according to the following.

$$T_1 = 6\varphi - \varphi'_3 - \varphi'_5$$
$$T_2 = 6\varphi - \varphi_1 - \varphi_4$$
$$T_3 = 6\varphi - \varphi'_2 - \varphi'_5$$
$$T_4 = 6\varphi - \varphi'_1 - \varphi'_3$$
$$T_5 = 6\varphi - \varphi'_2 - \varphi'_4 \qquad (16\text{-}19)$$

In Fig. 16-5, the line segments L_2 and L_5 meet at a common vertex of the pentagon, and they have the included tip angle T_1. The line segment L_1 intersects L_2 and L_5, and a portion of L_1 serves as the side opposite the tip angle T_1. One of the sides adjacent to tip T_1 in this small tip triangle is opposite angle φ_1 and the other side adjacent to T_1 is opposite angle φ_2. Noting that $\sin(\pi - x) = \sin x$, and applying the law of sines shows that the side adjacent to T_1 in the tip triangle and opposite φ_1 has length:

$$L'_2 = l_2 \frac{\sin \varphi_1}{\sin(\varphi_1 + \varphi'_3)}, \qquad (16\text{-}20)$$

and the other side adjacent to T_1 in the tip triangle and opposite angle φ_2 has length:

$$L'_5 = l_1 \frac{\sin \varphi_2}{\sin(\varphi_2 + \varphi'_5)}. \qquad (16\text{-}21)$$

Similarly, the tip angle T_2 of the irregular star is included between the segments L_1 and L_3, and segment L_2 intersects L_1 and L_3 to form the small tip triangle with T_2. In this tip triangle, the two sides adjacent to T_2 are opposite angles φ_2' and φ_3' contained in the triangle formed by L_2, l_2, and l_3. So, the lengths of the two sides adjacent to tip angle T_2 in the tip triangle are:

$$L_3' = l_3 \frac{\sin \varphi_2'}{\sin(\varphi_2' + \varphi_4')}, \qquad (16\text{-}22)$$

and:

$$L_1' = l_2 \frac{\sin \varphi_3'}{\sin(\varphi_1' + \varphi_3')}, \qquad (16\text{-}23)$$

Continuing the analysis, it is seen that the small tip triangle with tip angle T_3 is the result of intersecting lines L_2 and L_4, meeting at a vertex of the pentagon, with line L_3 intersecting L_2 and L_4. The two sides adjacent to T_3 are opposite angles φ_3 and φ_4 in the triangle formed by lines l_3, l_4, and L_3. The lengths of the two sides adjacent to tip angle T_3 are found to be:

$$L_4' = l_4 \frac{\sin \varphi_3}{\sin(\varphi_3' + \varphi_5')}, \qquad (16\text{-}24)$$

and:

$$L_2'' = l_3 \frac{\sin \varphi_4}{\sin(\varphi_2' + \varphi_4)}. \qquad (16\text{-}25)$$

For the small tip triangle containing tip angle T_4, its adjacent sides are opposite angles φ_5' and φ_4' in the triangle formed by lines L_4, l_4, and l_5. So, the lengths of the sides adjacent to tip angle T_4 are:

$$L_3'' = l_4 \frac{\sin \varphi_5'}{\sin(\varphi_3' + \varphi_5')}, \tag{16-26}$$

and:

$$L_5'' = l_5 \frac{\sin \varphi_4'}{\sin(\varphi_1' + \varphi_4')}. \tag{16-27}$$

Finally, the tip angle T_5 in the tip triangle formed by intersecting lines L_1, L_4, and L_5 has adjacent sides that are opposite the angles φ_1' and φ_5. These two sides adjacent to the tip angle T_5 are of length:

$$L_4'' = l_5 \frac{\sin \varphi_1'}{\sin(\varphi_1' + \varphi_4')}, \tag{16-28}$$

and:

$$L_1'' = l_1 \frac{\sin \varphi_5}{\sin(\varphi_2' + \varphi_5')}. \tag{16-29}$$

In summary, we have seen that departure from the symmetric internal light path in the solid star of Fig. 16-1 leads to light paths that intersect to form an irregular pentagon as shown in Fig. 16-2 and, although the sides of the pentagon are all of different length, the internal angles at the vertexes are all equal to 108°. This particular irregular pentagon becomes the generator of an irregular five-point star when each of its vertexes is joined to the second vertex from it. All the angles and sides of this particular class of irregular stars can be found in terms of the lengths of the five sides of the irregular pentagon through Eqs. (16-15) through (16-29).

Although the irregular pentagon used to generate the irregular star came about through consideration of non-symmetric intersecting light paths in Fig. 16-2, it is clear that from a mathematical standpoint, we can treat the method of generating irregular stars without reference to the asymmetric light paths. So, the two key features of the irregular pentagon used to generate this class of irregular stars are that the internal angles at each vertex are all equal to 108°, but that all five sides of the pentagon are of unequal length. In general, to construct an irregular star of this class, we begin by constructing the irregular pentagon. Beginning with a straight line of desired length l_1, one end of a second line of length l_2 is joined to l_1 but with the direction of l_2 making an angle of 108° with the direction of l_1. Next, one end of a third line of length l_3 is joined to the free end of l_2, with the direction of l_3 making angle 108° with that of l_2, being concave inward in the same sense as l_2 is with respect to l_1. Now, straight lines are constructed through the free ends of lines l_1 and l_3, each making an internal angle of 108° with the particular line through which it is constructed, and these two lines are extended to meet at a point. The length of the line from this point to the end of l_3 is designated l_4, and the distance from the point of intersection to the end of l_1 is designated as l_5. How do we know that the angle between l_4 and l_5 is 108°, per condition of the irregular polygon? The answer lies in the fact that four internal angles were constructed at 108° each, and we note the theorem, which states that the total of the internal angles of a polygon N sides is $(N - 2)$ 180°, which for a pentagon is 540°. Therefore, the angle between l_4 and l_5 is 540° - 4 (108°) = 108°. It is therefore seen that l_1, l_2, and l_3 can be chosen arbitrarily but that the lengths of l_4 and l_5 are determined by the requirement that l_4 is inclined to l_3 at 108°, and l_5 is inclined at the same angle to l_1. Finally, the irregular star is constructed by joining each vertex with the second vertex from it. Having done this, all the angles and segments of the star can be determined from Eqs. (16-15) through (16-29), based on knowledge of the lengths $l_1, l_2, \ldots l_5$.

In regard to the case in which not all the l_j are known in advance, but only l_1, l_2, l_3 as discussed above, use of the following relations:

$$L_4 = \left[l_1^2 + L_2^2 - 2l_1 L_2 \cos\left(108° - \varphi_3'\right) \right]^{\frac{1}{2}} \tag{16-30}$$

$$\varphi_4' = 108° - T_5 - \varphi_2 \tag{16-31}$$

$$\varphi_4' = \pi - 108° - \varphi_5' \qquad (16\text{-}32)$$

are helpful because they allow l_4 and l_5 to be determined from:

$$l_4 = L_4 \, \frac{\sin \varphi_4'}{\sin 108°} \qquad (16\text{-}33)$$

$$l_5 = L_4 \, \frac{\sin \varphi_5'}{\sin 108°}, \qquad (16\text{-}34)$$

as can be seen from reference to Fig. 16-5.

Two examples of skewed stars formed from irregular pentagons are characterized by the calculated values listed in Table 16-1. The corresponding skewed star figures are drawn to scale in Fig. 16-6. In Table 16-1, the first column gives the arbitrarily chosen values of l_1, l_2, and l_3 along with the calculated l_4 and l_5 values for compatibility, for each star displayed in Fig. 16-6. The second and third columns give the corresponding calculated lengths L_j, and tip angles.

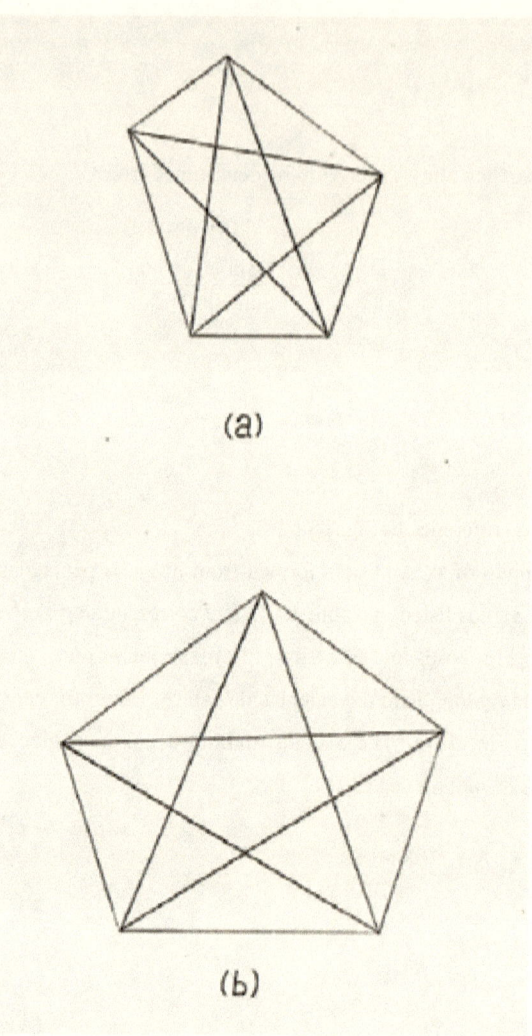

Fig. 16-6. Examples of non-symmetric five-point stars formed from irregular pentagons. In (a), the pentagon sides are 1, 1.2, 1.4, 0.876, and 1.524 units, and in (b), the sides are 1.5, 1.65, 1.815, 1.398, and 1.908 units. All internal vertex angles of the pentagons are 108°.

Table 16-1. Examples of Skewed Five-Point Stars Formed from an Irregular Pentagon that has all Internal Angles Equal.

Example	Given	Calculated Lengths, Angles		
		Remaining Two Sides of Irregular Pentagon	Distance from a Tip to a Second Tip from It	Tip Angle
I	$l_1 = 1.0$		$L_1 = 1.7837$	$T_1 = 24.229°$ $T_1: L'_2 = .6750$
	$l_2 = 1.2$		$L_2 = 2.1067$	$T_2 = 49.266°$ $L'_5 = .6429$
	$l_3 = 1.4$		$L_3 = 1.8672$	$T_3 = 28.113°$ $T_2: L'_3 = .8819$
		$l_4 = 0.8764$	$L_4 = 1.9786$	$T_4 = 35.085°$ $L'_1 = .8001$
		$l_5 = 1.5236$	$L_5 = 2.0647$	$T_5 = 43.307°$ $T_3: L'_4 = .6256$
				$L''_2 = .7267$
				$T_4: L''_3 = .6425$
				$L''_5 = .8107$
				$T_5: L''_4 = .8865$
				$L''_1 = .7052$
II	$l_1 = 1.5$			
	$l_2 = 1.65$			
	$l_3 = 1.815$			
		$l_4 = 1.3980$	$L_1 = 2.5499$	$T_1 = 29.050°$ $T_1: L'_2 = .9706$
		$l_5 = 1.9077$	$L_2 = 2.8049$	$T_2 = 43.368°$ $L'_5 = .9405$
			$L_3 = 2.6109$	$T_3 = 31.590°$ $T_2: L'_3 = 1.1238$
			$L_4 = 2.6911$	$T_4 = 35.582°$ $L'_1 = 1.0677$
			$L_5 = 2.7673$	$T_5 = 40.410°$ $T_3: L'_4 = .9297$
				$L''_2 = 1.0229$
				$T_4: L''_3 = .9481$
				$L''_5 = 1.0814$
				$T_5: L''_4 = 1.1284$
				$L''_1 = 1.0020$

We note that skewed five-point stars can of course be drawn without use of an auxiliary irregular pentagon. However, the skewed stars described by Eqs. (16-15) – (16-34) represent a particular class of skewness embodied in the condition that all interior angles of the irregular pentagon are equal in value to 108°. All the more interesting is the fact that this unexpected condition arose in the optical setting in which light was allowed to enter the solid star of Fig. 16-1 at an angle of refraction different from the value $\gamma = 18°$ corresponding to symmetric internal reflections.

16-3. A class of skewed stars formed with five non-uniformly spaced points on a circle

Another class of skewed five-point stars can be generated by constructing a circle of radius R, designating five randomly located points on the circle, and then connecting each point with the second point from it on the circle, as shown in Fig. 16-7. Let the angles subtended at the center of the circle by radii drawn from adjacent points on the circumference be designated by $\varphi_1, \varphi_2, \ldots \varphi_5$. These angles along with the radius R are the "given" or known values for generating this particular class of skewed stars that are formed by connecting each point on the circle with the second point from it. All the lengths of the sides of the star and all the angles associated with it can be determined from the given angles $\varphi_1, \ldots \varphi_5$ and the radius R as follows. An isosceles triangle is formed when radii are drawn from the center of the circle to opposite ends of the line connecting a point on the circle with the second point from it. Let L_1 designate the length of this line joining points P_2 and P_5. Then this line is the base of an isosceles triangle containing the vertex angle $\varphi_1 + \varphi_2$, and so each base angle in this isosceles triangle is simply $(\pi - \varphi_1 - \varphi_2)/2$. Therefore, using the law of sines, the length L_1 can be expressed as:

$$L_1 = R \frac{\sin(\varphi_1 + \varphi_2)}{\cos\left(\frac{\varphi_1 + \varphi_2}{2}\right)}. \tag{16-35}$$

Continuing the analysis and letting the index $j = 1, \ldots 5$ be used to designate the given angles $\varphi_1, \ldots \varphi_5$, we can see that the lengths L_j can be expressed in the form:

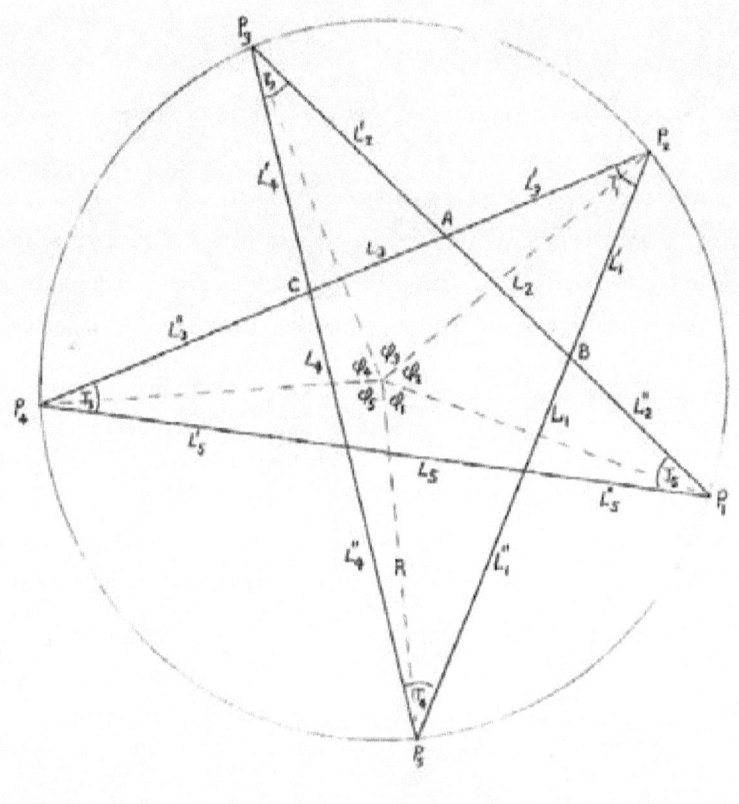

Fig. 16-7. A class of non-symmetric five-point stars formed by constructing five unequally spaced points $P_1 \ldots P_5$ on a circle of radius R and connecting each point to the second point from it, e.g., L_1 is the length of P_2P_5. Lengths of sides of tip triangles are designated by primes, e.g., $L_1^{''}$ and $L_4^{''}$ are the legs of the triangle containing tip angle T_4.

$$L_j = R \frac{\sin(\varphi_j + \varphi_{j+1})}{\cos\left(\dfrac{\varphi_j + \varphi_{j+1}}{2}\right)}. \tag{16-36}$$

In the latter, when $j = 5$, it is clear that $\varphi_{j+1} = \varphi_6$ is merely φ_1, as can be seen referring to Fig. 16-7.

The angles T_j in the tips of the skewed star can be found as follows. It is seen that T_1 is the sum of a base angle of the isosceles triangle having L_1 as base, plus a base angle of the isosceles triangle with L_3 as base. Therefore, because $\varphi_1 + \varphi_2$ is the vertex angle of one of these isosceles triangles, and $\varphi_3 + \varphi_4$ is the vertex angle of the other, it follows that:

$$\begin{aligned} T_1 &= (\pi - \varphi_1 - \varphi_2)/2 + (\pi - \varphi_3 - \varphi_4)/2 \\ &= \pi - (\varphi_1 + \varphi_2 + \varphi_3 + \varphi_4)/2. \end{aligned} \tag{16-37}$$

Similarly, it is seen that the tip angle T_2 is the angle included between the lines L_2 and L_4, and as such, it is the sum of a base angle of each of the isosceles triangles having L_2 and L_4 as bases, so that:

$$\begin{aligned} T_2 &= (\pi - \varphi_2 - \varphi_3)/2 + (\pi - \varphi_4 - \varphi_5)/2 \\ &= \pi - (\varphi_2 + \varphi_3 + \varphi_4 + \varphi_5)/2. \end{aligned} \tag{16-38}$$

Continuing this analysis with reference to Fig. 16-7 shows that the remaining tip angles of the skewed star are:

$$\begin{aligned} T_3 &= \pi - (\varphi_3 + \varphi_4 + \varphi_5 + \varphi_1)/2 \\ T_4 &= \pi - (\varphi_4 + \varphi_5 + \varphi_1 + \varphi_2)/2 \\ T_5 &= \pi - (\varphi_5 + \varphi_1 + \varphi_2 + \varphi_3)/2. \end{aligned} \tag{16-39}$$

Next, consider the "tip triangle" containing the tip angle T_1 and base AB defined by the points A and B where P_2P_4 and P_2P_5 intersect P_1P_3, respectively, in Fig. 16-7. The angle P_2AB is a base angle of the tip triangle P_2AB, and $\angle P_2AB$ is also an exterior angle of triangle P_1AP_4, which contains the alternate interior angles AP_4P_1 and AP_1P_4. However, the latter angles are just the tip angles T_3 and T_5, respectively, and so the base angle P_2AB of the triangle containing the tip T_1 is simply:

$$\angle P_2AB = T_3 + T_5. \tag{16-40}$$

Now, the other base angle, P_2BA, of the triangle with tip angle T_1, is an exterior angle to triangle BP_3P_5 that contains alternate interior tip angles T_2 and T_4, hence:

$$\angle P_2BA = T_2 + T_4. \tag{16-41}$$

Now, let the legs AP_2 and BP_2 of the triangle with tip T_1 be designated by L'_3 and L'_1, respectively, to emphasize that these are partial segments of L_3 and L_1. Then, applying the law of sines to triangle P_4AP_1 gives:

$$\frac{L_3 - L'_3}{\sin T_5} = \frac{L_5}{\sin(\pi - T_3 - T_5)}, \tag{16-42}$$

from which we obtain the length of one of the legs of tip triangle T_1.

$$L'_3 = L_3 - L_5 \frac{\sin T_5}{\sin(T_3 + T_5)}. \tag{16-43}$$

Then, using Eq. (16-41) and applying the law of sines to the tip triangle P_2AB allows the other leg L'_1 of this triangle to be expressed in terms of L'_3 from Eq. (16-43).

$$L'_1 = L'_3 \frac{\sin(T_3 + T_5)}{\sin(T_2 + T_4)} \tag{16-44}$$

Next, concerning the "tip triangle" with angle T_2 as the tip angle, it is seen that the line P_2P_4 forms the base because it intersects the two lines P_3P_5 and P_3P_1 that form the included tip angle. So, from the figure, it is easily seen that the base angles are exterior angles to the triangles CP_2P_5 and AP_4P_1. Hence the base angles opposite the legs L'_2 and L'_4 in the tip triangle are $T_4 + T_1$ and $T_3 + T_5$, respectively. Following the approach that led to Eq. (16-43) for the tip triangle T_1, we see that the leg L'_2 in triangle CP_3A obeys the relationship:

$$\frac{L_2 - L'_2}{\sin T_3} = \frac{L_5}{\sin(\pi - T_3 - T_5)}, \qquad (16\text{-}45)$$

and solving for L'_2 gives:

$$L'_2 = L_2 - L_5 \frac{\sin T_3}{\sin(T_3 + T_5)}. \qquad (16\text{-}46)$$

The other leg L'_4 in the tip triangle can therefore be expressed in terms of L'_2 with the aid of the law of sines, with the result:

$$L'_4 = L'_2 \frac{\sin(T_3 + T_5)}{\sin(T_4 + T_1)}. \qquad (16\text{-}47)$$

Following the same type of analysis to the tip triangle containing tip angle T_3, it is seen that the base angles of this triangle are $T_2 + T_5$ and $T_1 + T_4$, and the legs L''_3 and L'_5 are:

$$L''_3 = L_3 - L_1 \frac{\sin T_4}{\sin(T_1 + T_4)}$$

$$L'_5 = L''_3 \frac{\sin(T_1 + T_4)}{\sin(T_2 + T_5)}. \qquad (16\text{-}48)$$

Again, using the foregoing type of analysis applied to the tip triangle containing tip angle T_4, it can be shown that the lengths of the legs of this tip triangle are:

$$L_4'' = L_4 - L_2 \frac{\sin T_5}{\sin(T_2 + T_5)}$$

(16-49)

$$L_1'' = L_4'' \frac{\sin(T_2 + T_5)}{\sin(T_1 + T_3)}.$$

Finally, applying the analysis to the tip triangle containing the tip angle T_5 shows that the lengths of the two legs in this triangle are given by the following.

$$L_5'' = L_5 - L_3 \frac{\sin T_1}{\sin(T_1 + T_3)}$$

(16-50)

$$L_2'' = L_5'' \frac{\sin(T_1 + T_3)}{\sin(T_2 + T_4)}.$$

The calculated results using the Eqs. (16-36) through (16-50) for two examples are given in Table 16-2. The corresponding skewed stars drawn to scale are shown in Fig. 16-8.

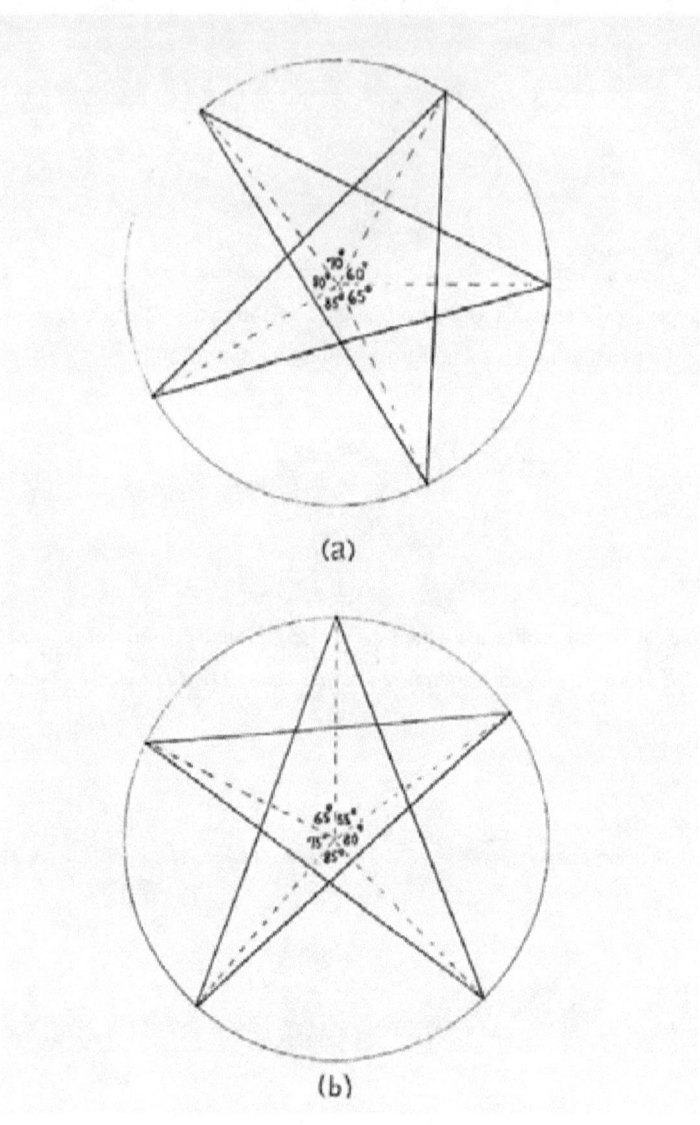

Fig. 16-8. Two examples of non-symmetric five-point stars formed on the basis of unequal arcs constructed on a circle.

Table 16-2. Examples of Skewed Five-Point Stars formed on a Circle with Adjacent Tips Subtending Unequal Angles at Center of Circle.

Example	Given	Calculated* Lengths, Angles		
		Distance from Point to Second Point on Circle	Tip Angle	Leg Lengths of Tip Triangle
I	$\varphi_1 = 60°$	$L_1 = 1.8126$	$T_1 = 32.5°$	$T_1: L'_1 = .7847$
	$\varphi_2 = 70°$	$L_2 = 1.9319$	$T_2 = 30.0°$	$L'_3 = .7553$
	$\varphi_3 = 80°$	$L_3 = 1.9829$	$T_3 = 35.0°$	$T_2: L'_2 = .8896$
	$\varphi_4 = 85°$	$L_4 = 1.9318$	$T_4 = 40.0°$	$L'_4 = .9107$
	$\varphi_5 = 65°$	$L_5 = 1.7740$	$T_5 = 42.5°$	$T_3: L''_3 = .7612$
				$L'_5 = .7612$
				$T_4: L''_4 = .5634$
				$L''_1 = .5816$
				$T_5: L''_5 = .6208$
				$L''_2 = .6104$
II	$\varphi_1 = 55°$	$L_1 = 1.7320$	$T_1 = 40°$	$T_1: L'_1 = .6962$
	$\varphi_2 = 65°$	$L_2 = 1.8794$	$T_2 = 27.5°$	$L'_3 = .6773$
	$\varphi_3 = 75°$	$L_3 = 1.9696$	$T_3 = 32.5°$	$T_2: L'_2 = .8516$
	$\varphi_4 = 85°$	$L_4 = 1.9829$	$T_4 = 37.5°$	$L'_4 = .8425$
	$\varphi_5 = 80°$	$L_5 = 1.8477$	$T_5 = 42.5°$	$T_3: L''_3 = .8896$
				$L'_5 = .9243$
				$T_4: L''_4 = .6317$
				$L''_1 = .6224$
				$T_5: L''_5 = .5203$
				$L''_2 = .5475$

*Without loss of generality the value of R was taken as unity in these calculations. For other values of R, the lengths in table are simply multiplied by the value of R because R appears to the first power in Eqs. (16-36) – (16-50). The calculated angles are independent of R as can be seen from the equations.

16-4. Unusual angle relations in arbitrary non-symmetric five-point stars

It will now be shown that the sum of the angles in each of the five triangular tips is equal to the sum of the angles in the five tips of a skewed star. Consider the arbitrary skewed star shape of Fig. 16-9 in which the points defining the tips are designated by P_1, $P_2, \ldots P_5$, with corresponding internal tip angles given by $T_1, T_2, \ldots T_5$. For example, the angle T_1 is the included angle between straight lines P_1P_4 and P_1P_3, and the tip triangle of which T_1 is a part is defined by P_1, and the two points a and b where line P_2P_5 intersects P_1P_4 and P_1P_3, respectively. The angles α_1 and α_2 are the base angles of the tip triangle P_1ab. Similarly, remarks apply to the other four tip triangles P_2bc, P_3cd, P_4de, and P_5ea. Now, in tip triangle P_1ab, we see that α_1 is an exterior angle to triangle aP_4P_2 and therefore is equal to the sum of the two opposite interior angles of triangle aP_4P_2, which means that:

$$\alpha_1 = T_2 + T_4. \tag{16-51}$$

Similarly, the other angle α_2 in the triangle P_1ab is an exterior angle of triangle P_5bP_3, and as such, it is equal to the sum of the opposite interior angles in triangle P_5bP_3, so that:

$$\alpha_2 = T_5 + T_3. \tag{16-52}$$

The sum S_{A1} of the angles in the tip triangle containing tip angle T_1 is therefore:

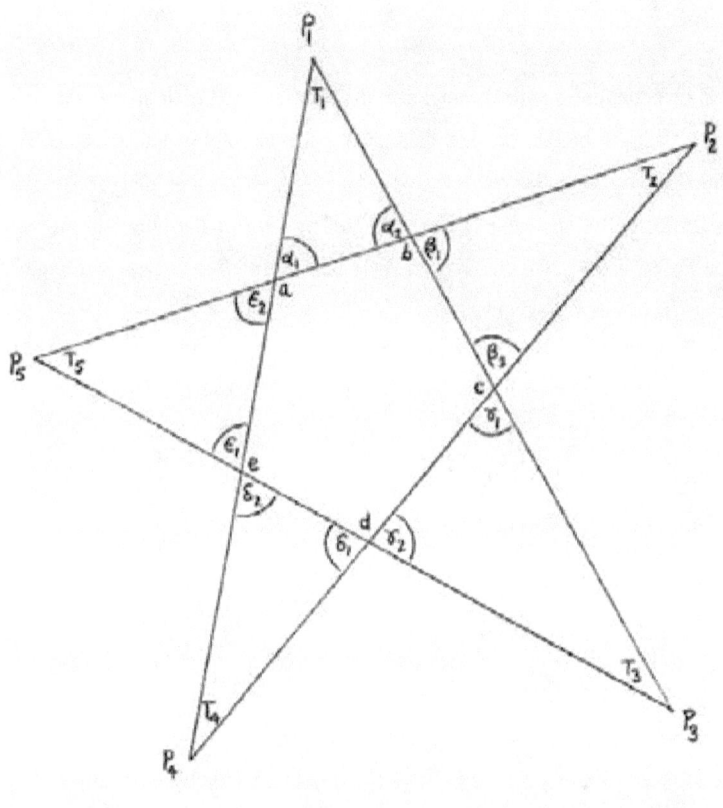

Fig. 16-9. Geometry used in proving that the sum of the angles in each triangular tip of an arbitrary non-symmetric star of this type is equal to the sum of the tip angles T_j.

$$S_{A1} = T_1 + \alpha_1 + \alpha_2$$
$$= T_1 + T_2 + T_3 + T_4 + T_5, \tag{16-53}$$

which shows that the sum of the angles in the tip triangle P_1ab is simply the sum of all five of the tip angles in the skewed star. Next, for example, consider the triangle P_4de containing the tip angle T_4. We note that ς_1 and ς_2 are exterior angles to triangles P_5dP_2 and P_1eP_3, respectively, and hence ς_1 is equal to the sum of the alternate interior angles in triangle P_5dP_2, while ς_2 is the sum of the alternate interior angles in triangle P_1eP_3. So, from Fig. 16-9, it is seen that:

$$\varsigma_1 = T_5 + T_2$$
$$\varsigma_2 = T_1 + T_3, \tag{16-54}$$

and it follows that the sum of the angles in tip triangle P_4de is:

$$S_{A4} = T_4 + \varsigma_1 + \varsigma_2$$
$$= T_4 + T_5 + T_2 + T_1 + T_3. \tag{16-55}$$

It is easily shown that identical results are obtained for the other three tip triangles P_2bc, P_3cd, and P_5ea. Therefore, in any skewed five-point star such as that in Fig. 16-9, the sum of the angles in each tip triangle is equal to the sum of the angles in the tips, and it also follows that:

$$T_1 + T_2 + T_3 + T_4 + T_5 = \pi, \tag{16-56}$$

because the sum of the angles in any triangle must be π.

Now, the mathematical star [5, 2] has each tip angle equal 36°, so we automatically get 180° or π for their sum. It seems remarkable that, as we have shown above, in an arbitrary skewed star with all five tip angles unequal the sum of these five tip angles is still equal to π. Using the calculated results for the four skewed five-point stars given in Tables 16-1 and 16-2, it is readily verified that the tip angles obey Eq. (16-56).

16-5. Skewed stars from non-symmetric light paths with four reflections in each tip of solid [5, 2] star

Consider again the arrangement dealt with in Chapter 15 in which light was introduced on face A of a solid star at an angle of incidence that resulted in the refracted light path entering at angle 54° with respect to the perpendicular to face A. It was shown that this gave rise to symmetric light paths within the solid star, and that the portion of the light path innermost to each tip is perpendicular to the star radius, and two reflections are made from each face as shown in Fig. 16-10. It was shown that these conditions of symmetry resulted in a standard five-point star formed by the intersecting lines representing the light paths. To consider the effects of small departures from symmetry, let the light be incident on face A so that the angle of refraction γ, as the light enters the star is slightly different from the value $\gamma = 54°$ for symmetric light paths, as shown in Fig. 16-11. The condition of small departure from symmetry is invoked so that the light entering face A will still pass to face F for its first internal reflection. So, light entering face A at point P, at distance x from point P_1, is refracted at angle γ and passes to point c on face F where it is incident at an angle i_1 and reflected at this same angle, thereby passing to face E. The

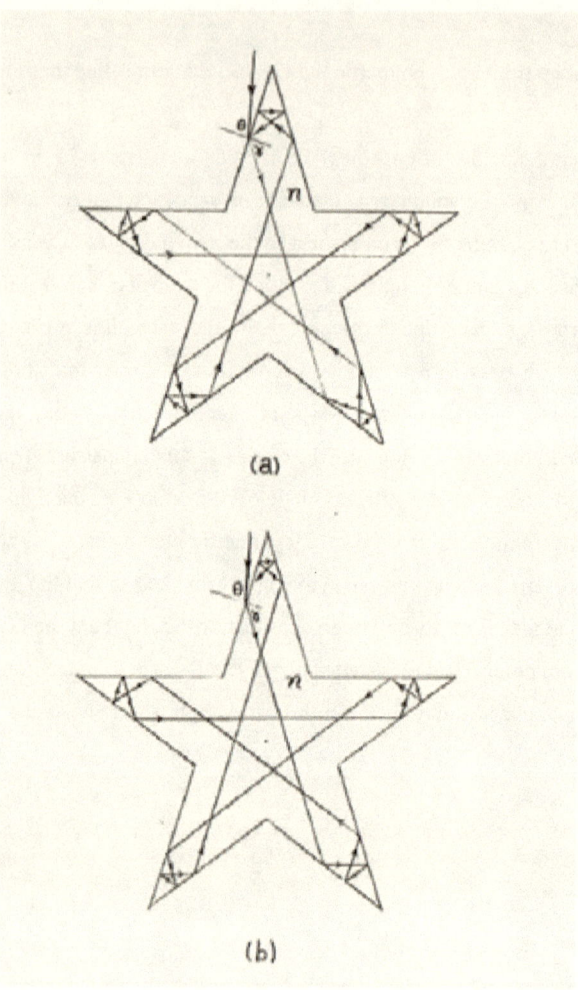

Fig. 16-10. (a) Light entering the [5, 2] solid star at refraction angle γ = 54° results in the symmetric light path with a [5, 2] star formed by intersections of the paths. (b) A small departure from the required angle γ for symmetry, in this case γ = 54.5° causes the non-symmetric intersecting light paths to produce a skewed star.

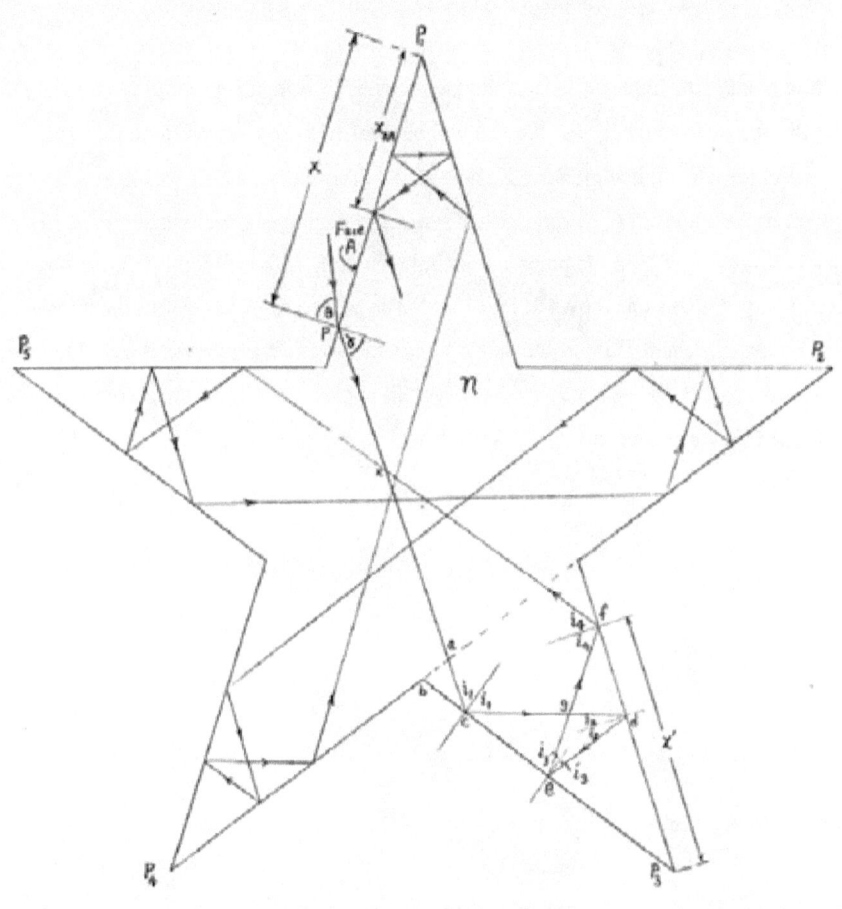

Fig. 16-11. Path of light in a solid [5, 2] star when the refractive angle γ at entry is different from 54°. After one complete path, the ray arrives at distance X_{AA} from the tip P_1. If γ = 54°, then X_{AA} = X and the ray arrives back at the point of entry P on Face A. Following earlier designations in Chapter 13, beginning with Face A, going clockwise, the remaining faces are B, C, D, E, F, G, H, and I. The length where each face intersects the plane of the figure is l_2, defined in Eqns. 4-4 to 4-6 of Chapter 4.

light is incident at angle i_2 at point d on face E where it is then reflected at this same angle, and passes again to face F where it is incident at angle i_3 at point e. After reflection at angle i_3 from point e, the light travels again to face E where it is incident at angle i_4 at point f that is at distance x' from the tip P_3. Now, it will be recalled from Chapter 15 that $i_4 = i_1$ and $i_2 = i_3$, and $x' = x$ when the angle of refraction $\gamma = 54°$ for the symmetric passage of the light. However, the angles i_1, i_2, i_3, and i_4, when symmetry no longer exists, can be found in terms of γ as follows. Let a be the point at which the entering refracted light path intersects the line joining P_2 and P_4 as shown in Fig. 16-11. The point designated by b is the intersection of the lines P_2P_4 and P_3P_5 in the star figure, and therefore angle abc is 72°. In triangle PP_4a, the angle PaP_4 is $\pi - (\pi/2 - \gamma + 36°)$, but this angle is an exterior angle to triangle abc, and therefore we can write:

$$\pi - \left(\frac{\pi}{2} - \gamma + 36°\right) = 72° + \frac{\pi}{2} - i_1, \qquad (16\text{-}57)$$

and solving for i_1 gives:

$$i_1 = 108 - \gamma. \qquad (16\text{-}58)$$

Now, in triangle cdP_3, we have:

$$\frac{\pi}{2} - i_1 + \frac{\pi}{2} + i_2 + 36° = \pi, \qquad (16\text{-}59)$$

and using Eq. (16-58), the angle i_2 is found to be:

$$i_2 = 72° - \gamma \qquad (16\text{-}60)$$

The angle i_3 can be found by summing the angles in triangle edP_3, which gives:

$$\frac{\pi}{2} - i_3 + \frac{\pi}{2} - i_2 + 36° = \pi, \tag{16-61}$$

and substituting for i_2 from Eq. (16-60) leads to the following for angle i_3.

$$i_3 = \gamma - 36° \tag{16-62}$$

Finally, the angle i_4 can be determined through summation of angles in triangle eP_3f, and this gives:

$$\frac{\pi}{2} - i_4 + \frac{\pi}{2} + i_3 + 36° = \pi, \tag{16-63}$$

which, after substituting for i_3 from Eq. (16-62) and solving for i_4 gives:

$$i_4 = \gamma. \tag{16-64}$$

The result in Eq. (16-64) is interesting because it shows that light entering face A at refraction angle γ will be reflected internally from face F, then from face E back to face F, and finally it is reflected again from face E, but at the same angle γ at which it entered face A, even though γ is different from the value of 54° for symmetry. Because of this result, the angles i_1, i_2, i_3, and i_4 will be the same in the other tips as the light passes from face E around, into and out of the remaining four tips in Fig. 16-11. That is, the light reflected from face E at point f will pass to face J, where it is incident at angle i_1, reflected at this angle, and passes to face I, arriving at angle of incidence i_2 and reflected back to face J, arriving at incident angle i_3 and finally reflected again to face I, incident at angle $i_4 = \gamma$, whereupon it is reflected at angle γ from I and passes to faces D and C, where the multiple incident and reflected angles again obey i_1, i_2, i_3, and i_4 in Eqs. (16-58), (16-60), (16-62), and (16-64).

Next, the distance x' at which the light is incident on face E, measured from the tip P_3, can be determined in terms of the distance x at which the light is initially incident at point P on face A, measured from tip P_1. This relationship is necessary to construct the star shape resulting from the departure from symmetry. The distance *bc* at which the light is incident on face *F* can be found by first determining distance *ab* through application of the law of sines to triangle PaP_4, which gives:

$$\frac{l_2 + 2l_2 \sin 18° + l_2 - x}{\sin\left[\pi - \left(\frac{\pi}{2} - \gamma\right) - 36°\right]} = \frac{l_2 + ab}{\sin\left(\frac{\pi}{2} - \gamma\right)}, \qquad (16\text{-}65)$$

from which *ab* is obtained:

$$ab = \left(\frac{2l_2(1 + \sin 18°) - x}{\cos(\gamma - 36°)}\right)\cos\gamma - l_2 . \qquad (16\text{-}66)$$

Then, applying the law of sines to triangle *abc* gives the distance *bc* in terms of *ab*.

$$bc = \frac{\cos(36° - \gamma)}{\cos i_1} ab \qquad (16\text{-}67)$$

Now, with the law of sines, the distance P_3d in triangle edP_3 can be expressed in terms of distance *bc*, with the result:

$$P_3d = \frac{\cos i_1}{\cos i_2}(l_2 - bc). \qquad (16\text{-}68)$$

Using the law of sines applied to triangle eP_3d, the distance eP_3 can be found as follows in terms of distance P_3d in Eq. (16-68).

$$eP_3 = \frac{\cos i_2}{\cos i_3} P_3d \qquad (16\text{-}69)$$

Then, the distance x' in triangle eP_3f can be expressed in terms of distance eP_3 through application of the law of sines, which gives:

$$x' = \frac{\cos i_3}{\cos i_4} eP_3. \tag{16-70}$$

In obtaining the foregoing relations, frequent use was made of the fact that sin $(\pi/2 + \theta)$ = cos θ. Combining Eqs. (16-66) through (16-70) and using Eq. (16-58) allow the distance x' at which the light is incident on face E in Fig. 16-11 to be expressed in the following form:

$$x' = x + l_2 \left[\frac{\cos(108° - \gamma) + \cos(\gamma - 36°)}{\cos \gamma} - 2(1 + \sin 18°) \right]. \tag{16-71}$$

As a check on Eq. (16-71), take the value of angle γ to be 54° corresponding to the case of symmetry of light paths. For $\gamma = 54°$, Eq. (16-71) gives $x' = x$ in Fig. 16-11, as should be the case.

Because of the fact that the second reflection of the light from face E occurs at the same angle γ as the angle at which the light enters at point P on face A, it was mentioned above that angles $i_1, \ldots i_4$ given in Eqs. (16-58) – (16-64) also apply for incidence and reflection at the other faces. Therefore, the relation in Eq. (16-71) giving the position of x' of reflection point f on face E in terms of the entry position x at point P on face A also applies in the appropriate combination of other faces as the light traverse its non-symmetric path around the star, in and out of the tips. For example, the distance of the second reflection from face I measured from P_5 can be found by substituting distance x' on face E for x in Eq. (16-71) and calculating the resultant new value of x'. The use of Eq. (16-71) in determining the positions of the second reflections on the various faces can be more readily followed by changing notation on x and x'. First, let the factor depending on angle γ that multiplies l_2 in Eq. (16-71) be denoted by $f(\gamma)$. Then, using subscript "A" on x will denote that it is the distance from P_1 on face A at which light enters the star at point P, and the prime on x' can be omitted and replaced with subscript "E" to indicate the distance from P_3 on face E at which the light is reflected and leaves the tip region. So, Eq. (16-71) becomes:

$$X_E = X_A + l_2 f(\gamma). \tag{16-72}$$

Using the latter, it is then seen that the distance x_1 on face I, measured from P_5, at which the light leaves the tip region is:

$$X_I = X_E + l_2 f(\gamma). \tag{16-73}$$

Similarly, the distance on face C measured from P_2 at which the light is reflected and leaves this tip region is:

$$X_C = X_I + l_2 f(\gamma), \tag{16-74}$$

and then the distance measured from P_4 on the second reflection from face G is

$$X_G = X_C + l_2 f(\gamma). \tag{16-75}$$

Finally, the light returns to face A and now the distance from P_1 at which the second reflection occurs is:

$$X_{AA} = X_G + l_2 f(\gamma). \tag{16-76}$$

where the double-A subscript is used to distinguish this distance from the initial entry point at distance x_A from P_1.

Combining Eqs. (16-72) through (16-75) with Eq. (16-76), it is seen that x_{AA} can be expressed as:

$$X_{AA} = X_A + 5l_2 f(\gamma), \tag{16-77}$$

and therefore the light upon returning to face A after one complete trip in and out of the tips is displaced relative to its initial entry point by the distance:

$$X_{AA} - X_A = 5l_2 f(\gamma). \tag{16-78}$$

Now, $f(\gamma)$ is the quantity in square brackets multiplying l_2 in Eq. (16-71) and for the condition of symmetry substituting $\gamma = 54°$ shows that $f(\gamma) = 0$, and therefore $x_{AA} = x_A$, i.e., the light returns to its original entry point on face A. The factor $f(\gamma)$ can be positive or negative, depending on whether $\gamma < 54°$ or $\gamma > 54°$. For example, if light enters face A at the refraction angle $\gamma = 55°$, then $x_{AA} - x_A = 0.3983 l_2$, from Eq. (16-78), while if $\gamma = 53°$, $x_{AA} - x_A = -0.3796 l_2$. In the latter case, the negative sign shows that for $\gamma = 53°$, the light returning after one complete passage undergoes its second reflection from face A at a distance closer to the tip P_1 than the distance of the initial entry point. It is to be noted that the light returning to face A upon its second reflection from A travels parallel to its initial refracted path when it entered at angle γ. This is true because of the result in Eq. (16-64) and the related discussion following it.

Returning to Fig. 16-11, we see that the angle ckf in the quadrilateral $gckf$ is a tip angle in the skewed star formed when angle γ is different from 54°. Now, the angle cgf of the quadrilateral can be found from triangle egd, and this gives $cgf = \pi - 2i_3 - 2i_2$. Knowing that the sum of the interior angles of a quadrilateral is 2π, the tip angle ckf in the skewed star is therefore:

$$\angle ckf = 2\pi - 2i_1 - (\pi - 2i_3 - 2i_2) - 2i_4, \qquad (16\text{-}79)$$

And substituting for angles i_1, i_2, i_3, and i_4 from Eqs. (16-58), (16-60), (16-62), and (16-64) into Eq. (16-79) gives the following for the tip angle ckf:

$$\angle ckf = 36° \qquad (16\text{-}80)$$

From the analysis and earlier discussion related to $i_4 = \gamma$ in Eq. (16-64), it follows that each of the other four tip angles in the skewed star is also given by Eq. (16-80), that is, 36°. So, the skewed star formed when the entry angle γ is different from that, for symmetry still has all its tip angles equal to those of the standard mathematical star [5, 2].

The intersecting lines representing the non-symmetric light paths are very sensitive to departure of angle γ from 54°, as can be seen from examples given in Figs. 16-12 through 16-14. In Fig. 16-12, the entry point was chosen at $0.425 l_2$ from tip P_1 on face A, and the angle γ was taken as 53.5°. Eqs. (16-71) through (16-77) were used to calculate the points of the second reflections in the faces, and the results are drawn to scale. The results drawn to scale for γ = 53.75° and an entry point at $0.9l_2$ from tip P_1 are shown in Fig. 16-13. For a third example, Fig. 16-14 shows the skewed star obtained by non-symmetric, intersecting light paths when the light enters face A at distance $0.95l_2$ from tip P_1, with angle of entry γ = 53.5°.

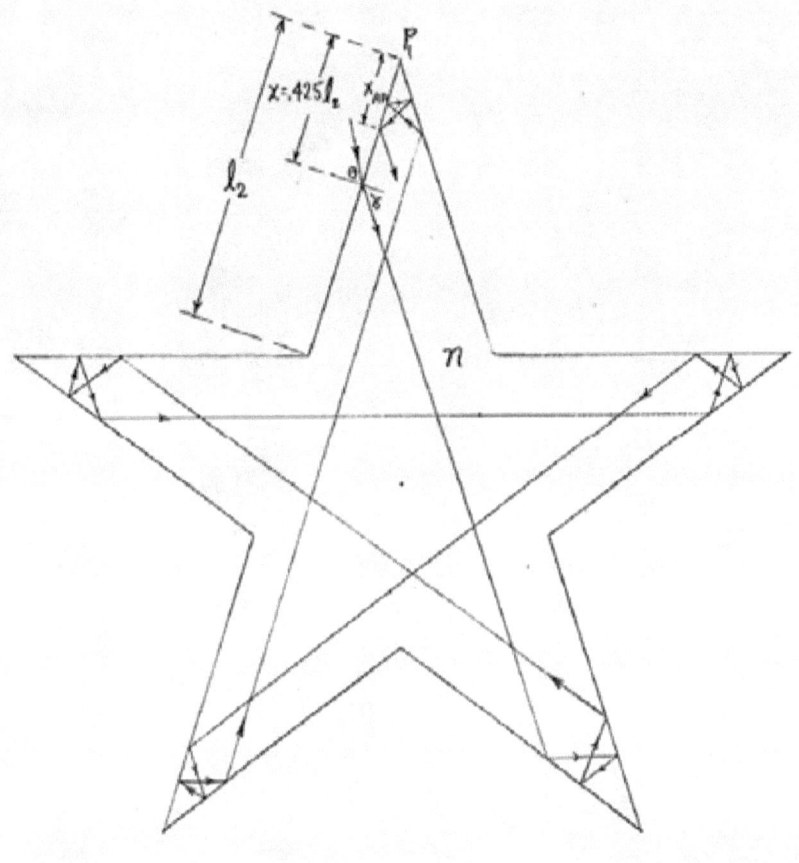

Fig. 16-12. Example of a non-symmetric star formed by the intersecting light paths when light enters a [5, 2] solid star at refraction angle $\gamma = 53.5°$, instead of $54°$ required for symmetry, at distance $0.425\ l_2$ from tip P_1.

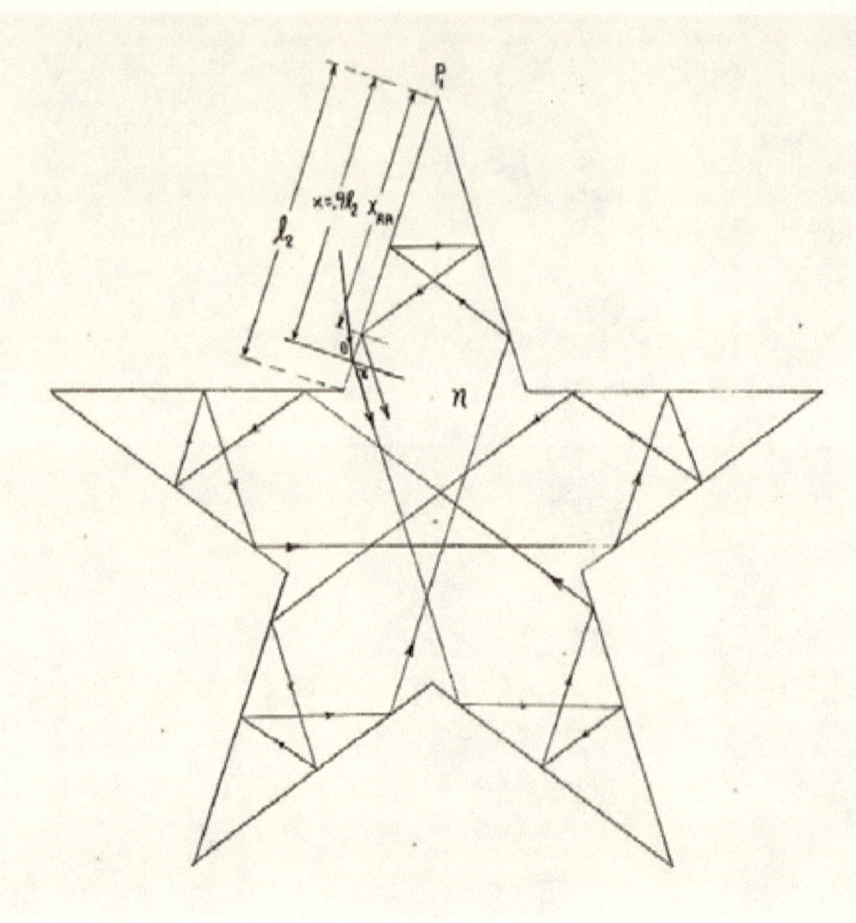

Fig. 16-13. Light enters [5, 2] solid star medium at refraction angle $\gamma = 53.75°$, at distance $0.9 l_2$ from tip P_1, and the slightly non-symmetric intersecting light paths give rise to the skewed star in the central region. Comparison with Fig. 16-12 shows that the skewness depends not only on γ but also on point of entry, x.

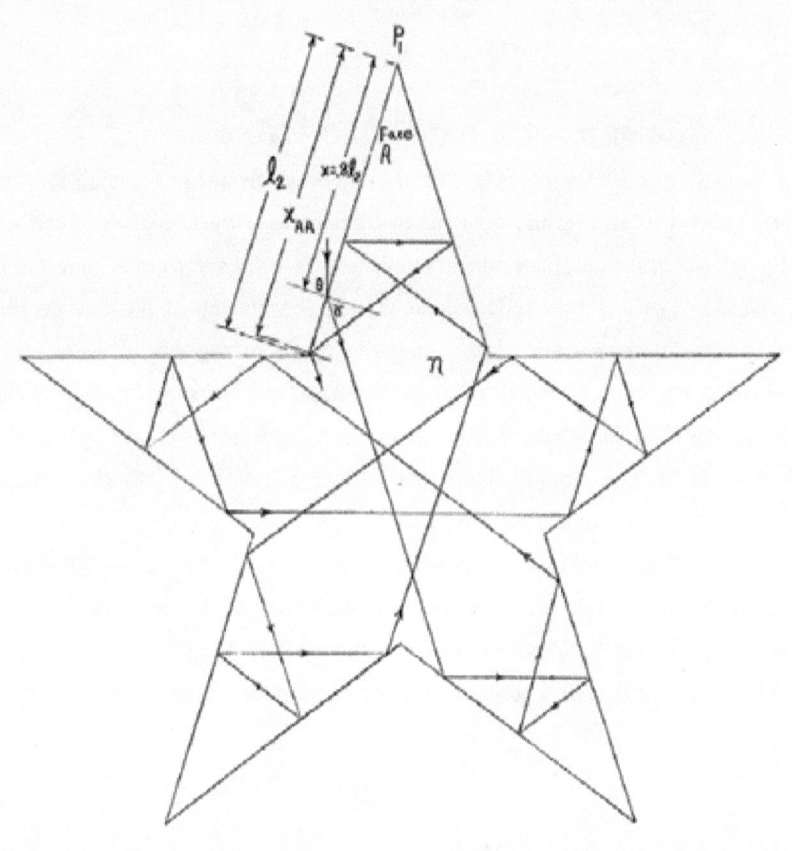

Fig. 16-14. A non-symmetric central star results from the intersecting light paths when light is incident at distance $0.8l_2$ from tip P_1 at angle θ such that the entering refraction angle $\gamma = 54.5°$, or 1/2° greater than that required for symmetry. Here, $\gamma > 54°$ and therefore, after one complete traversal, the light arrives on Face A at distance x_{AA}, exceeding the original point of entry at x. This is in contrast to the case in Figs. 16-12 and 16-13 in which $\gamma < 54°$.

CHAPTER 17
SWINGING SOLID STARS

17-1. Oscillatory motion of solid stars with flat, parallel faces

Suppose that a solid five-point star of the type considered in Chapter 16, with its two-star figure faces parallel and separated by distance t, is suspended about a horizontal axis through one of the tips, perpendicular to the planes of the star faces as shown in Fig. 17-1. The axis is such that the solid star can rotate freely about it. In the absence of any motion, the equilibrium position of the solid star body is with its geometric center O lying on the vertical line through the axis of suspension because it is assumed that the material from which the solid star is made is homogeneous, of the same density throughout. So, if the solid star is displaced from its equilibrium position and released, with what frequency will it oscillate to and fro about the axis of suspension?

To answer the latter question, it is instructive first to consider the so-called simple pendulum consisting of a small or point mass m suspended by a thin wire or string of length L as shown in Fig. 17-2a. When the mass is displaced from its equilibrium position and released, it will oscillate with a period T given by the well-known formula:

$$T = 2\pi \sqrt{\frac{L}{g}}, \tag{17-1}$$

where g is the acceleration due to gravity. It should be noted that the magnitude of the mass is assumed sufficiently large that the mass of the supporting wire or string is negligible in

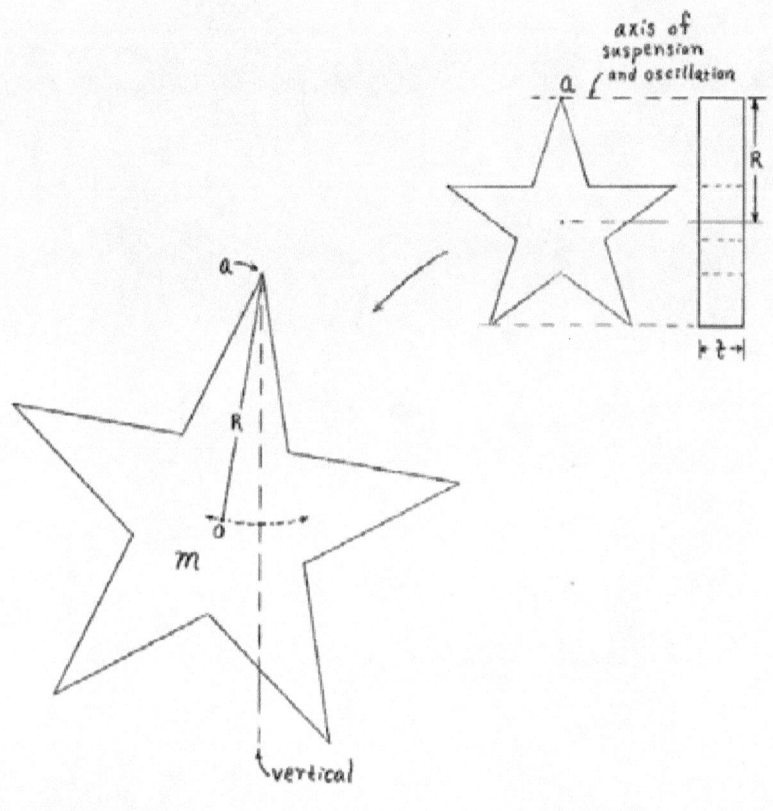

Fig. 17-1. Solid star [5, 2] of radius R, thickness t, and mass m suspended about axis of rotation through a tip at a. The equilibrium position is when the star is oriented with its mass center O lying on the vertical through point a.

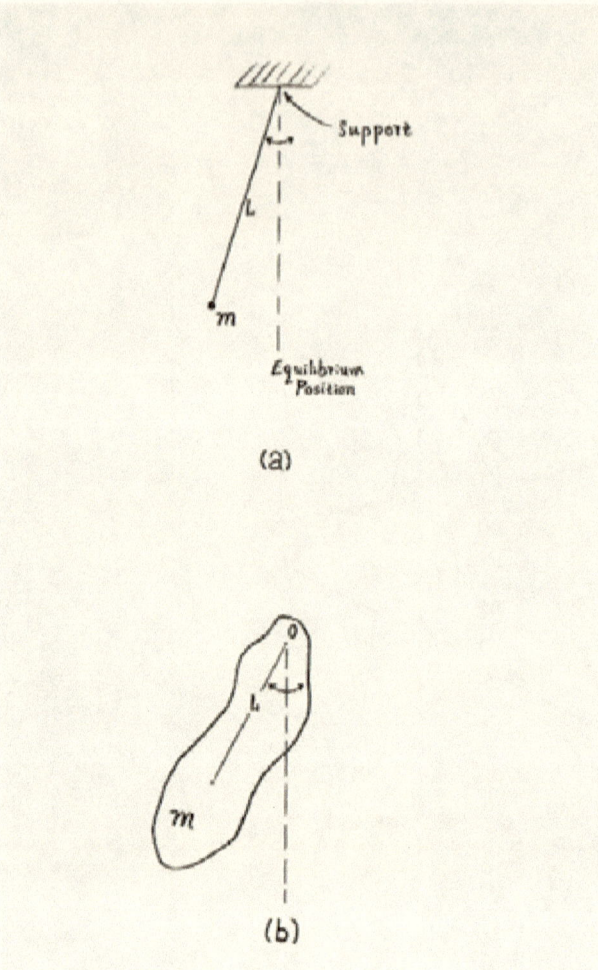

Fig. 17-2. (a) Simple pendulum consisting of "point" mass m suspended by a thin, low-mass, medium-like wire or string and free to rotate about support. (b) "Physical" pendulum consisting of a distributed mass m oscillating about O at distance L from the center of mass.

comparison and furthermore that the wire or string remains taut throughout the motion. Under these conditions, the familiar expression in Eq. (17-1) is very accurate for maximum angular displacements that do not exceed approximately 10° relative to the equilibrium vertical position. The time T given by Eq. (17-1) is the time required for movement of m from one maximum angular position through the center to the opposite maximum position and back through center to the first maximum angular position.

When the small pointlike mass in Fig. 17-2a is replaced by a larger extended mass oscillating about a horizontal axis passing through its periphery, or through its interior, then the configuration is often referred to as a physical pendulum, as shown schematically in Fig. 17-2b. Let L be the distance from the axis of rotation O to the center of mass of this body, and let I_O be the moment of inertia of the body about the axis through O. Then the time T taken for one complete oscillation about the axis is:

$$T = 2\pi\sqrt{\frac{I_O}{mgL}}, \qquad (17\text{-}2)$$

where m is the mass and, again, g is the acceleration due to gravity. As in the case of the simple pendulum, the maximum angular displacement of the physical pendulum must be relatively small to assure a high degree of accuracy in the value of T calculated from Eq. (17-2).

The solid star certainly represents a distributed mass, and therefore Eq. (17-2) must be applied in order to determine the period with which the star suspended as in Fig. 17-1 will oscillate. We note that the homogenous star has its center of mass at its geometric center, and therefore the distance L in Eq. (17-2) is simply the radius R of the star because the axis of oscillation is through the tip, at distance R from the center. The quantity m in Eq. (17-2) is the mass of the solid star. To find I_a, the moment of inertia of the star about the axis through its tip, we refer to Fig. 17-3 in which an x-y coordinate system is oriented with its origin at the tip of the star and the y-axis along the radius. The thickness of the solid star is t and therefore the differential volume of an element of differential area $dydx$ located at point (x, y) is $dv = tdxdy$. If ρ is the density of the star material, then this volume element has differential mass $dm = \rho tdxdy$, and therefore its differential moment of inertia about the axis perpendicular to the plane of the star through the tip at a is:

$$dI_a = (x^2 + y^2)\rho tdxdy, \qquad (17\text{-}3)$$

where $x^2 + y^2$ is the square of the distance from the mass element to the axis through a. The total moment of inertia of the solid star about the axis through a is found by integrating Eq. (17-3) over the limits of x and y corresponding to the boundaries of the star.

$$I_a = \iint (x^2 + y^2)\rho tdxdy \qquad (17\text{-}4)$$

To carry out the double integration in Eq. (17-4), we note that the star figure is symmetric left-to-right about the y-axis in Fig. 17-3 and so the integration can be done for those portions in the first and fourth quadrants, and then the final result will just be twice the value. To do the integrations over the first and fourth quadrants, it is convenient to divide the region into four parts, each

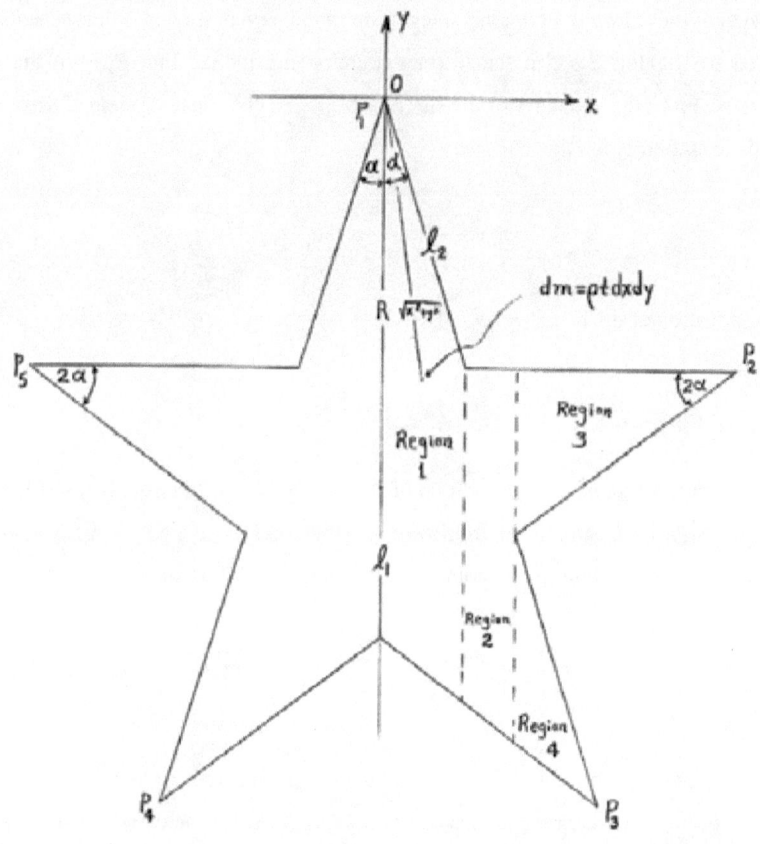

Fig. 17-3. Coordinates used in calculating the moment of inertia of the solid star of uniform density ρ, radius R, and thickness t, about an axis perpendicular to its plane parallel faces passing through its tip P_1 located at the origin of the (x, y) coordinate system.

bounded by vertical lines parallel to the y-axis, and so the final result for half the star figure is the sum of these four integrations. Integrating first over y in Region 1, it is seen that y is bounded by the line P_3P_5 in the lower extremity and by the line P_1P_3 in the upper extremetry. From the geometry of the star relative to the coordinate system chosen in Fig. 17-3, the equation of the line P_3P_5 is:

$$y = -R - l_1 - x \tan 2\alpha, \qquad (17\text{-}5)$$

and the equation of the line P_1P_3 is:

$$y = -x \cot \alpha, \qquad (17\text{-}6)$$

where α is the half-angle, 18°, at each tip of the star, and $l_1 = a_1 R$ in Eq. (4-6) of Chapter 4. The limits on x for Region 1 are from zero to $l_2 \sin\alpha$, with $l_2 = a_2 R$ given in Eq. (4-6), and therefore, the contribution to the moment of inertia in Eq. (17-4), over Region 1 is:

$$I_1 = \rho t \int_0^{a_2 R \sin\alpha} dx \int_{-R-l_1-x\tan 2\alpha}^{-x\cot\alpha} (x^2 + y^2)\, dy, \qquad (17\text{-}7)$$

where the product ρt in Eq. (17-4) is brought outside the integrals because the density and thickness of the solid star are assumed constant, independent of the variables of integration x and y. Carrying out the integration first over y and then over x in Eq. (17-7), the following result for Region 1 is ultimately obtained.

$$\begin{aligned}I_1 = \rho t R^4 \Bigg[&\frac{1}{4} a_2^4 \sin^4\alpha \left(\tan 2\alpha - \cot\alpha - \frac{1}{3}\cot^3\alpha + \frac{1}{3}\tan^3 2\alpha \right) \\ &+ \frac{1}{3} a_2^3 \sin^3\alpha (1 + a_1)(1 + \tan^2 2\alpha) \\ &+ \frac{1}{2} a_2^2 \sin^2\alpha (1 + a_1)^2 \tan 2\alpha \\ &+ \frac{1}{3} a_2 \sin\alpha (1 + a_1)^3 \Bigg]\end{aligned} \qquad (17\text{-}8)$$

For Region 2, the lower boundary on y is given by the expression in Eq. (17-5), and the upper boundary on y is the line P_2P_5 parallel to the x-axis and expressed by $y = -l_2\cos\alpha$. The lower limit on x is the same as the upper limit for Region 1, $x_1 = a_2R\sin\alpha$, and the upper limit on x for Region 2 is $x_2 = l_2\sin\alpha + l_2 - l_2\cos2\alpha$. Therefore, the contribution to the moment of inertia about O from Region 2 is obtained by integrating Eq. (17-7) with these limits on y and x.

$$I_2 = \rho t \int_{a_2R\sin\alpha}^{a_2R(1+\sin\alpha-\cos2\alpha)} dx \int_{-R-a_1R-x\tan2\alpha}^{-a_2R\cos\alpha} (x^2+y^2)\,dy$$

$$= \rho t R^4 \left[\frac{a_2^4}{4}\left(\tan2\alpha + \frac{1}{3}\tan^3 2\alpha\right)\left\{(1+\sin\alpha-\cos2\alpha)^4 - \sin^4\alpha\right\}\right.$$

$$+ \frac{a_2^3}{3}(1+a_1-a_2\cos\alpha+(1+a_1)\tan^2 2\alpha)\left\{(1+\sin\alpha-\cos2\alpha)^3 - \sin^3\alpha\right\}$$

$$+ \frac{a_2^2}{2}(1+a_1)^2 \tan2\alpha\left\{(1+\sin\alpha-\cos2\alpha)^2 - \sin^2\alpha\right\}$$

$$\left. + \frac{a_2}{3}((1+a_1)^3 - a_2^3\cos^3\alpha)\{1+\sin\alpha-\cos2\alpha-\sin\alpha\}\right]$$

(17-9)

In Region 3, the lower limit on y is the equation of the line P_2P_4, which is:

$$y = -a_1R - R + x\tan2\alpha, \qquad (17\text{-}10)$$

and the upper limit on y is the same as the upper y limit of Region 2, i.e., $y = -l_2\cos\alpha$. The lower x limit in Region 3 is the same as the upper limit of Region 2, and the Region 3 upper x limit is $x = l_2(1 + \sin\alpha)$. So, from Eq. (17-4), the moment of inertia contribution from Region 3 is the following:

$$I_3 = \rho t \int_{a_2R(1+\sin\alpha-\cos 2\alpha)}^{a_2R(1+\sin\alpha)} dx \int_{-R(1+a_1)+x\tan 2\alpha}^{-a_2R\cos\alpha} (x^2+y^2)dy$$

$$= \rho t R^4 \left[-\frac{a_2^4}{4}\left(\tan 2\alpha + \frac{1}{3}\tan^3 2\alpha\right)\left((1+\sin\alpha)^4 - (1+\sin\alpha-\cos 2\alpha)^4\right) \right.$$

$$+ \frac{a_2^3}{3}\left(1+a_1 - a_2\cos\alpha + (1+a_1)\tan^2 2\alpha\right)\left((1+\sin\alpha)^3 - (1+\sin\alpha-\cos 2\alpha)^3\right)$$

$$- \frac{a_2^2}{2}(1+a_1)^2 \tan 2\alpha \left((1+\sin\alpha)^2 - (1+\sin\alpha-\cos 2\alpha)^2\right)$$

$$\left. + \frac{a_2}{3}\left((1+a_1)^3 - a_2^3 \cos^3\alpha\right)\cos 2\alpha \right] \qquad (17-11)$$

Finally, for Region 4 the lower limit of y is the equation of line P_3P_5 in Eq. (17-5), and the upper y-limit is line P_1P_3; the equation of which is given in Eq. (17-6). The limits on x are from $l_2(1 + \sin\alpha - \cos 2\alpha)$ to $l_2\sin 3\alpha$. So, the contribution to the moment of inertia about the axis through O from Region 4 is found by integrating Eq. (17-4) with these limits on x and y.

$$I_4 = \rho t \int_{a_2R(1+\sin\alpha-\cos 2\alpha)}^{a_2R\sin 3\alpha} dx \int_{-R(1+a_1)-x\tan 2\alpha}^{-x\cot\alpha} (x^2+y^2)dy$$

$$= \rho t R^4 \left[\frac{a_2^4}{4}\left(\tan 2\alpha - \cot\alpha + \frac{1}{3}\tan^3 2\alpha - \frac{1}{3}\cot^3\alpha\right)\left(\sin^4 3\alpha - (1+\sin\alpha-\cos 2\alpha)^4\right) \right.$$

$$+ \frac{a_2^3}{3}\left((1+a_1) + \tan^2 2\alpha(1+a_1)\right)\left(\sin^3 3\alpha - (1+\sin\alpha-\cos 2\alpha)^3\right)$$

$$+ \frac{a_2^2}{2}(1+a_1^2)\tan 2\alpha \left(\sin^2 3\alpha - (1+\sin\alpha-\cos 2\alpha)^2\right)$$

$$\left. + \frac{a_2}{3}(1+a_1)^3(\sin 3\alpha - 1 - \sin\alpha + \cos 2\alpha) \right] \qquad (17-1$$

As explained earlier, the total moment of inertia I_a of the solid star about the axis perpendicular to its plane through a in Fig. 17-1 is twice the sum of $I_1 + I_2 + I_3 + I_4$, and therefore, substituting α = 18° and using the values of a_1 and a_2 from Eq. (4-6) of Chapter 4 the moment of inertia determined from Eqs. (17-8), (17-9), (17-11), and (17-12) is to the nearest six decimal places:

$$I_a = 2\sum_{j=1}^{4} I_j$$

$$= \rho t R^4 (1.394777). \qquad (17\text{-}13)$$

From Eq. (12-12) of Chapter 12, the mass m_s of the solid star is:

$$m_s = 1.12257 \rho t R^2. \qquad (17\text{-}14)$$

As pointed out earlier, the distance L of the center of mass of the solid star from the axis through a in Fig. 17-1 is simply the radius of the star. Therefore, substituting $L = R$ and the values for I_a and m from Eqs. (17-13) – (17-14) into Eq. (17-2), we find that the period of oscillation of the solid star about the axis through a in Fig. 17-1 is:

$$T = 2\pi \sqrt{\frac{1.394777 \rho t R^4}{1.12257 \rho t R^2 g R}}$$

$$= 1.114668 \left(2\pi \sqrt{\frac{R}{g}} \right) \qquad (17\text{-}15)$$

Notice that the density ρ and thickness t of the solid star cancel in the latter. The period of the oscillating motion is approximately 11.47% greater than that of a simple pendulum of length L equal to the star radius R, as can be seen by comparing Eq. (17-15) with Eq. (17-1).

Eq. (17-15) was used to calculate the period of motion of a solid star of the type in Fig. 17-1 as a function of the star radius, and the results are displayed in the graph of Fig. 17-4. Recall that both the density ρ and the thickness t of the solid star cancelled in the analysis leading to Eq. (17-15), and therefore the results of Fig. 17-4 apply whether the star is made of glass, aluminum, lead, gold, etc., or whether the star is 1 mm or 1cm thick just as long as the material is uniformly dense and the thickness is uniformed. Because T depends on R to the ½ power in Eq. (17-15) it follows, for example, quadrupling the radius of the star only doubles its period of motion. In comparing Eq. (17-15) with Eq. (17-1), it can be seen that the period of the simple pendulum of length R is just $(1.114668)^{-1} \cong 0.897$ times the period of the solid star of radius R.

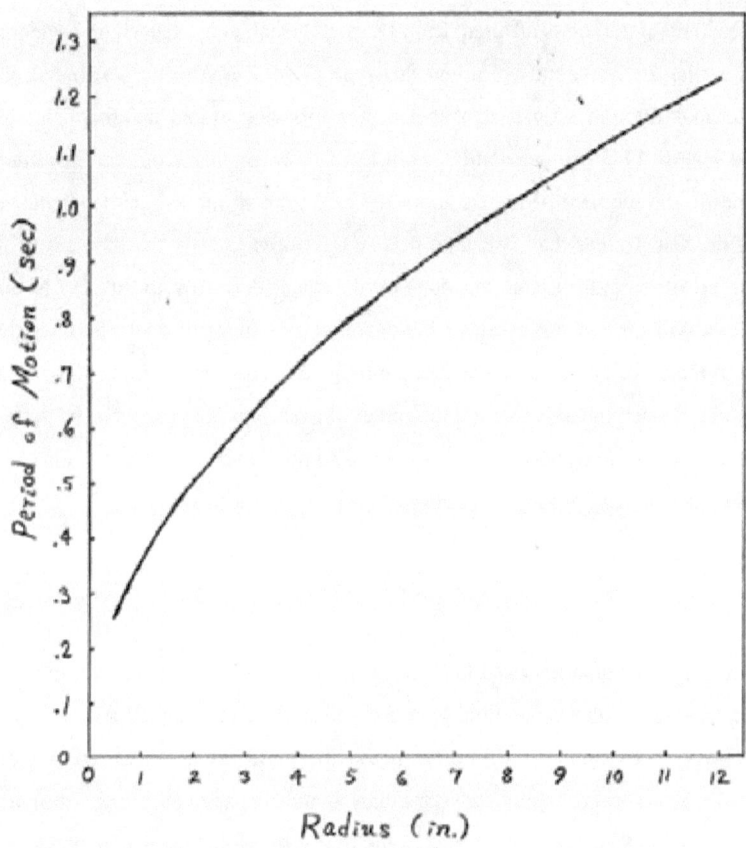

Fig. 17-4. Period of star pendulum about axis through one of its tips, versus radius of star, calculated from Eq. (17-15). The results apply to any [5, 2] star of uniform thickness and density.

17-2. Oscillations of solid stars with variable tip angle

Next, we consider how the period of the oscillating motion is influenced when the angle at each tip of the star is different from 18°. Let the half angle at each tip be denoted by φ, as in earlier analysis, and we allow this type of solid star to be suspended about a horizontal axis through a tip such that it is free to swing to and fro about this axis as indicated in Fig. 17-5. To calculate T from Eq. (17-2) for this geometry, we must first determine I_O, the moment of inertia about the axis through the tip, perpendicular to the plane of the star. Rather than calculate in a straightforward way, the moment of inertia about the axis through the tip, as was done for the star with $\varphi \equiv 18°$ in Eqs. (17-5) through (17-13), we will instead make use of the "parallel axis theorem," which states that the moment of inertia of a body about any axis through it is equal to the moment of inertia of the body about a parallel axis through the center of mass plus the product of its mass times the square of the distance between the two axes. Applied to the solid star in Fig. 17-5 the mathematical statement of this theorem is:

$$I_O(\varphi) = I(\varphi) + m(\varphi) R^2, \qquad (17\text{-}16)$$

where the particular notation used indicates that these quantities depend on the angle φ. Earlier in Chapter 12, these quantities were derived, and the results for $I(\varphi)$ and m(φ) were given in Eqs. (12-18) and (12-20). Referring to Chapter 12, we note that $c(\varphi)$ and $L(\varphi)$ in Eq. (12-14) each is proportional to the star radius R, and $c(\varphi)$ and $L(\varphi)$ appear in such a way in Eq. (12-18) that R^4 is common to each of the five terms within the square brackets. As a result, R^4 can be factored and $I(\varphi)$ can be written as:

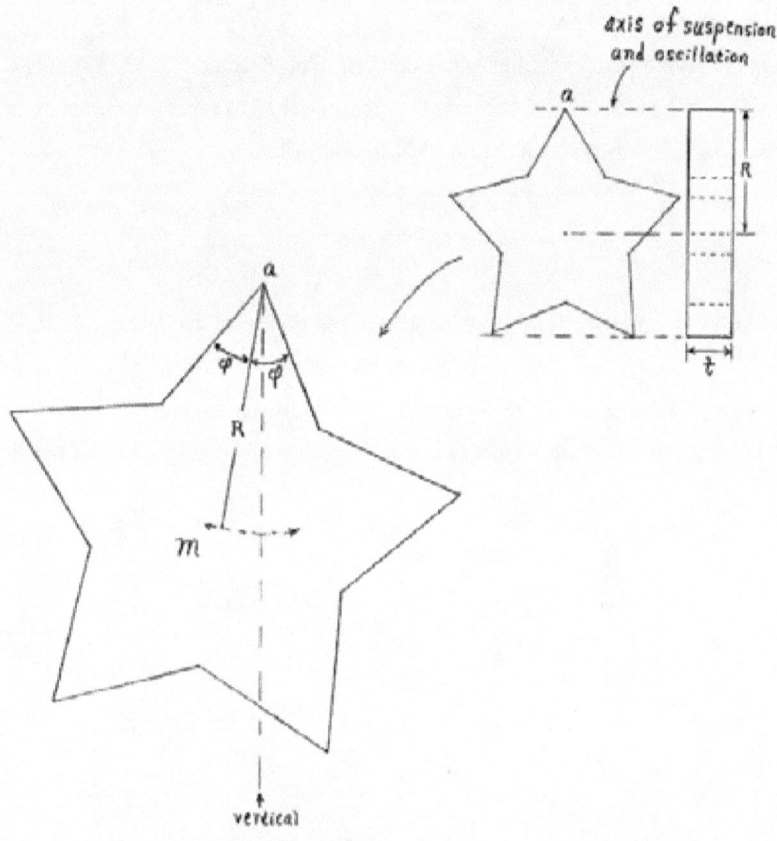

Fig. 17-5. Solid star with tip angle φ, radius R, thickness t, and mass m suspended about axis of rotation through a tip a. The equilibrium position is when the mass center lies on the vertical through point a.

$$I(\varphi) = 10\, \rho t R^4\, I'(\varphi), \qquad (17\text{-}17)$$

where $I'(\varphi)$ is the quantity within square brackets, with R factored out. In a similar manner, we can write the expression for the mass $m(\varphi)$ in Eq. (12-20) slightly different by factoring R^2 from the volume expression of Eq. (12-19) and writing:

$$m(\varphi) = 5\, \rho t R^2\, v'(\varphi), \qquad (17\text{-}18)$$

where $v'(\varphi)$ is simply Eq. (12-19) with R^2 factored from it so that R^2 appears explicitly in Eq. (17-18). So, the period of the oscillatory motion of the solid star in Fig. 17-5, about the axis through the tip, can be expressed as follows by combining Eqs. (17-16) through (17-18) with Eq. (17-2), remembering that the distance L is the distance from the mass center of the solid star to the axis, i.e., $L = R$.

$$T = 2\pi \sqrt{\frac{10\rho t R^4 I'(\varphi) + 5\rho t R^2 v'(\varphi) R^2}{5\rho t R^2 v'(\varphi) g R}} \qquad (17\text{-}19)$$

Factoring the common quantity $5\rho t R^3$ under the radical, the latter can be cast into the following form:

$$T = 2\pi \sqrt{\frac{R}{g}} \sqrt{\frac{2I'(\varphi) + v'(\varphi)}{v'(\varphi)}} \qquad (17\text{-}20)$$

So, when the solid star in Fig. 17-5 is displaced from its equilibrium position and released, it will oscillate to and fro about the axis through a with the period of motion, or time taken for one complete oscillation, given by Eq. (17-20). Note that the quantity $2\pi\sqrt{R/g}$ multiplying the radical containing $I'(\varphi)$ and $v'(\varphi)$ in Eq. (17-20) is the period with which a simple pendulum of length R will oscillate, as can be seen from Eq. (17-1).

The period with which the solid star of Fig. 17-5 will oscillate when displaced slightly from equilibrium and released, as a function of its tip angle φ, can be calculated from Eq. (17-20), making use of Eqs. (12-14) and (12-18) – (12-20) of Chapter 12 to evaluate $I'(\varphi)$ and $v'(\varphi)$. The results, expressed as the factor multiplying $2\pi\sqrt{R/g}$ in Eq. (17-20), are given in the graph of Fig. 17-6. At φ = 18°, corresponding to the mathematical star [5, 2], the factor, as read from the graph, is approximately 1.1147, and this is in agreement with the numerical factor given earlier in Eq. (17-15) for the star with φ = 18°. When φ = 54°, the factor has its maximum value of 1.1768, but this is the limiting value of φ for the solid star and it actually corresponds to a solid pentagon oscillating about an axis through one of its vertices.

When φ = 0° in Fig. 17-6, the value of the factor from Eq. (17-20) is approximately 1.08 as read from the graph. The physical implications of φ = 0° related to the solid star geometry are that the volume, and therefore the mass are zero and likewise the moment of inertia is zero. Still, the factor involving $I'(\varphi)$ and $v'(\varphi)$ in Eq. (17-20) leads to a finite, nonzero value for φ = 0°. That this should be true can be shown as follows. Using the parallel axis theorem stated in Eq. (17-16), we again substitute into Eq. (17-2) for the period and write it in the form:

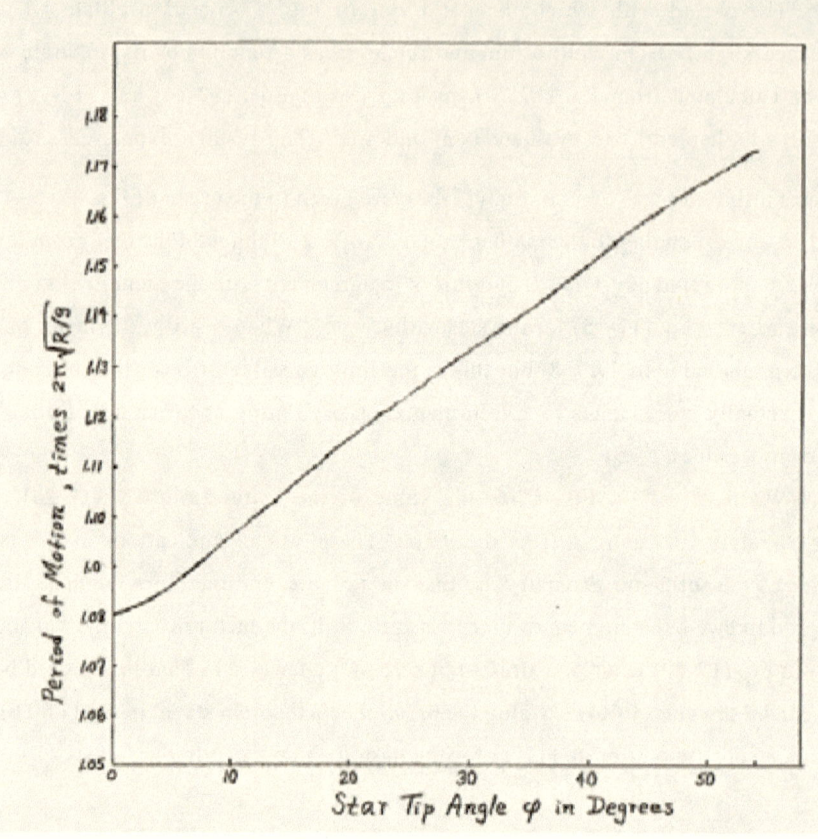

Fig. 17-6. Factor multiplying $2\pi\sqrt{R/g}$ in Eq. (17-20) for calculation of period of motion of five-point star versus its variable tip angle φ. The solid star is of radius R with uniform density ρ and uniform thickness t.

$$T = 2\pi \sqrt{\frac{I(\varphi) + m(\varphi)R^2}{m(\varphi)gR}}$$

$$= 2\pi \sqrt{\left(\frac{I(\varphi)}{m(\varphi)} + \frac{m(\varphi)}{m(\varphi)}R^2\right)\frac{1}{gR}}. \qquad (17\text{-}21)$$

Now, from Eq. (12-19) and (12-20) of Chapter 12, we find:

$$\frac{m(\varphi)}{m(\varphi)} = \frac{\left(\sin\varphi \sin\frac{\pi}{5}\right)/\sin\left(\varphi + \frac{\pi}{5}\right)}{\left(\sin\varphi \sin\frac{\pi}{5}\right)/\sin\left(\varphi + \frac{\pi}{5}\right)} \qquad (17\text{-}22)$$

and clearly, when φ = 0°, the latter is indeterminate because it is zero divided by zero. Using L'Hospital's rule, the limit can be found:

$$\mathrm{Lim}_{\varphi \to 0}\left(\frac{m(\varphi)}{m(\varphi)}\right) = \mathrm{Lim}_{\varphi \to 0}\left[\frac{\frac{d}{d\varphi}m(\varphi)}{\frac{d}{d\varphi}m(\varphi)}\right] = \mathrm{Lim}_{\varphi \to 0}\left[\frac{\frac{\cos\varphi \sin(\varphi+\frac{\pi}{5}) - \sin\varphi \cos(\varphi+\pi/5)}{\sin^2(\varphi+\pi/5)}}{\frac{\cos\varphi \sin(\varphi+\frac{\pi}{5}) - \sin\varphi \cos(\varphi+\pi/5)}{\sin^2(\varphi+\pi/5)}}\right]$$

$$= \frac{\frac{\sin\pi/5 - 0}{\sin^2\pi/5}}{\frac{\sin\pi/5 - 0}{\sin^2\pi/5}} = 1. \qquad (17\text{-}23)$$

The limit of $I(\varphi)/m(\varphi)$ as φ approaches zero was shown earlier in Eq. (12-24) of Chapter 12 to be:

$$\mathrm{Lim}_{\varphi \to 0}\left(\frac{I(\varphi)}{m(\varphi)}\right) = \frac{R^2}{6}. \qquad (17\text{-}24)$$

Using the limits shown in Eqs. (17-23) and (17-24), the limit of T in Eq. (17-21) can now be found:

$$\lim_{\varphi \to 0} T = 2\pi \sqrt{\left(\frac{R^2}{6} + R^2\right)\frac{1}{gR}}$$

$$= (1.08012345)\, 2\pi \sqrt{\frac{R}{g}} \qquad (17\text{-}25)$$

So, although the solid star has no mass and no moment of inertia when $\varphi = 0°$, nevertheless, the mathematical limit of the period of its motion is the nonzero value in Eq. (17-25), and certainly the calculated value of T for nonzero φ, as φ becomes smaller and smaller, approaches this limiting value as seen from Fig. 17-6.

Actual values of the period of motion of the solid star, as a function of its radius R, were calculated from Eq. (17-20) for each of several angles φ, and the results are provided in Fig. 17-7. It is to be remembered that these periods of motion are independent of the density of the medium from which the solid star is constructed and independent of the star thickness as long as the density and thickness are uniformed.

17-3 Period of oscillation versus distance between axis and solid star center

Placement of the axis of rotation through the tip of the solid star in Fig. 17-1 represents an extreme position because it is the maximum distance from the center that lies within the star. How is the period of the motion influenced when the axis is located at some other distance, z, from the center, still lying on the radius, as indicated in Fig. 17-8? To answer this, we make use of the parallel axis theorem which states that the moment of inertia about the axis through a at distance z from the center is $I_c + mz^2$, and therefore the period of oscillating motion can be expressed as follows using Eq. (17-2):

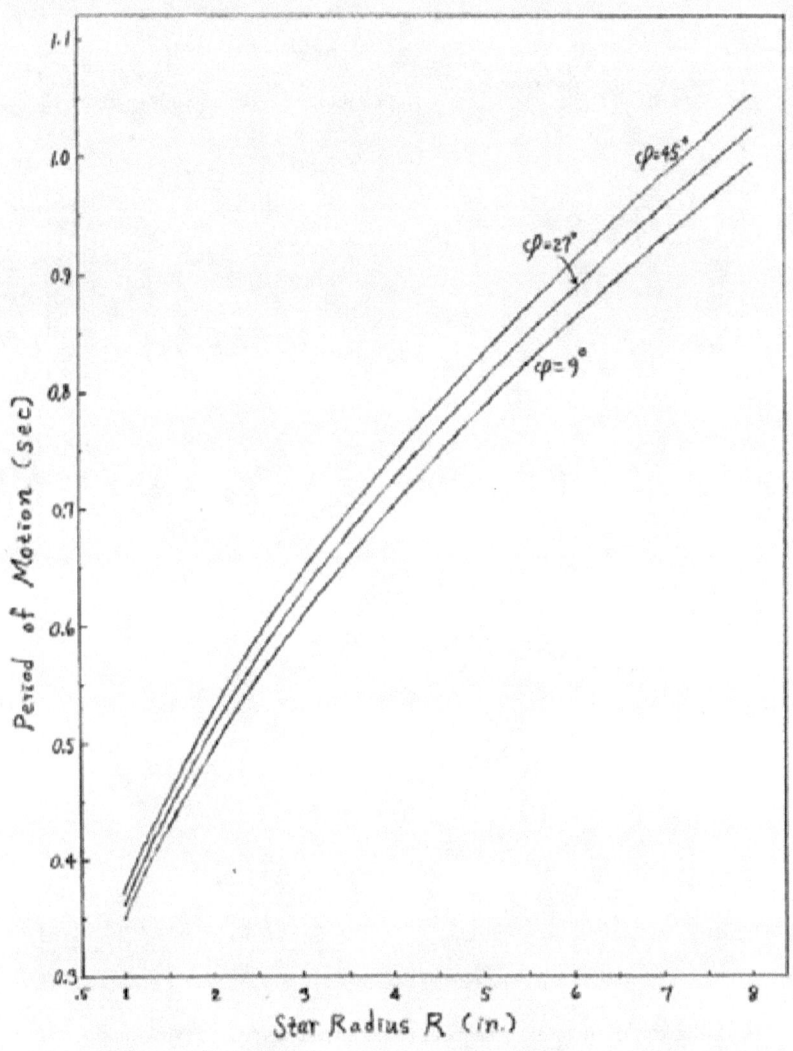

Fig. 17-7. Period of star motion in Fig. 17-5, versus star radius, for each of three different tip angles φ.

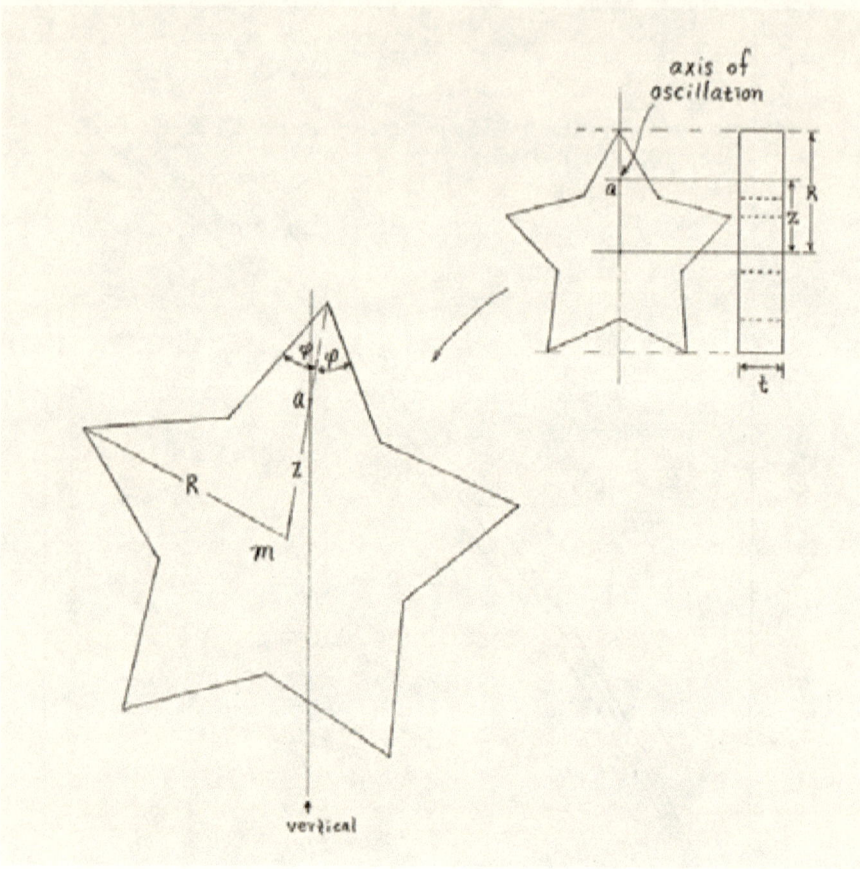

Fig. 17-8. Solid star of tip angle φ suspended on an axis at point a lying on the star radius, at distance z from the center. The equilibrium position is when the mass center lies on the vertical through point a.

$$T = 2\pi\sqrt{\frac{I_c + mz^2}{mgz}} \qquad (17\text{-}26)$$

We note that when the distance z is small, the term mz^2 is small in comparison with I_c, while the term containing z in the denominator causes the value of T to be relatively large in Eq. (17-26). As z increases from small values, the magnitude of T decreases, but for relatively large values of z, the term mz^2 in the numerator increases faster than the factor mz in the denominator so that T again becomes large. Intuitively, a distance z between the center of the star and the axis of oscillation must exist for which the period of motion T is a minimum. At this particular value of z, assuming it exists, the first derivative of T with respect to z must be zero. Now, from Eq. (17-26) the first derivative is:

$$\frac{dT}{dz} = \pi\sqrt{\frac{mgz}{I_c + mz^2}}\left(\frac{mgz(2zm) - (I_c + mz^2)mg}{(mgz)^2}\right), \qquad (17\text{-}27)$$

and the latter will vanish if the distance z is:

$$z = \sqrt{\frac{I_c}{m}}. \qquad (17\text{-}28)$$

For example, for the five-point mathematical star [5, 2], substituting for I_C and m from Eqs. (12-11) and (12-12) into Eq. (17-28) gives the following for z, to the nearest four decimal places. (Note that Eq. (12-11) is the moment of inertia through the center of mass and therefore equal to I_c in Eq. (17-28).)

$$z = 0.4924\, R \qquad (17\text{-}29)$$

Substituting for I_C and m into Eq. (17-26), we can express T in the form:

$$T = 2\pi\sqrt{\frac{a_I R^4 + a_m R^2 z^2}{a_m R^2 gz}}, \qquad (17\text{-}30)$$

where $a_1 = 0.2722$ and $a_m = 1.1226$ are the numerical factors in the expression for I_o and m in Eqs. (12-11) and (12-12), respectively. The period of oscillatory motion was calculated from Eq. (17-30) as a function of the distance z between the star center, and the axis of oscillation, for each of three different star radii, and the results are given in Fig. 17-9. Note that for each radius, the distance z at which the period T is a minimum agrees closely with that calculated from Eq. (17-29).

For the more general case of the solid five-point star with half angle φ at the tip, suspended on an axis perpendicular to its plane at distance z from its center, Eqs. (12-14), (12-18) and (12-19) can be combined with Eq. (17-26) to yield the following equation for the period of the oscillatory notion.

$$T = 2\pi \sqrt{\frac{2R^4 I'(\varphi) + R^2 v'(\varphi) z^2}{R^2 v'(\varphi) g z}} \qquad (17\text{-}31)$$

In the latter, the functions $I'(\varphi)$ and $v'(\varphi)$ are the functions defined earlier in reference to Eqs. (17-17) and (17-18). For given values of star radius R and tip half-angle, the period T exhibits a

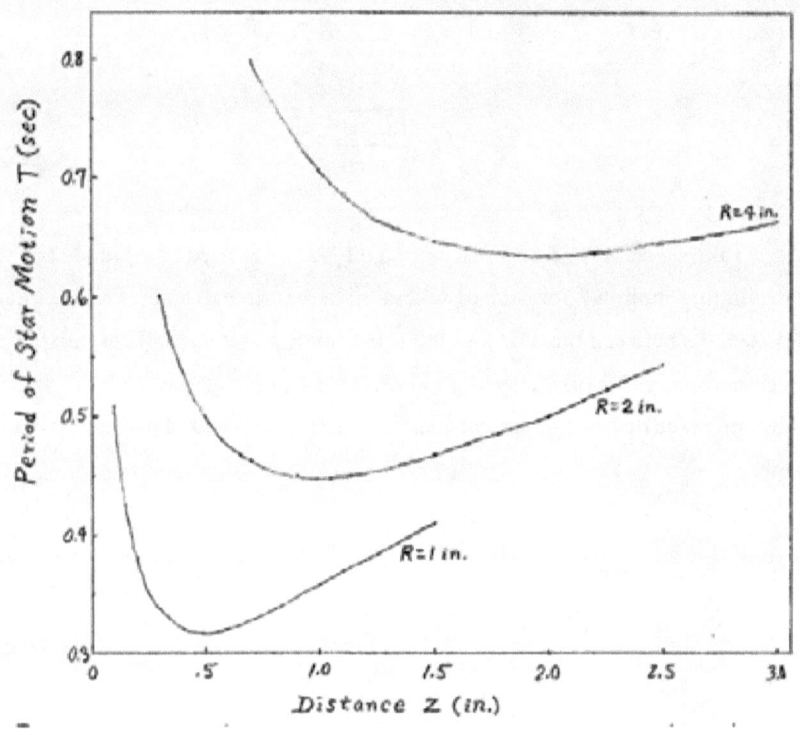

Fig. 17-9. Period of motion T calculated from Eq. (17-30) for the star in Fig. 17-8, with φ = 18°, as a function of distance z between axis and center of star, for each of three different values of the star radius R.

minimum for the distance z between the axis and the star center that causes the first derivative $dT/d\varphi$ to vanish, which according to Eq. (17-31) is:

$$z = \sqrt{\frac{2 I'(\varphi)}{v'(\varphi)}} R \, . \qquad (17\text{-}32)$$

Taking a value of R to be 10 cm, Eq. (17-31) was used to calculate the period of oscillatory motion T for each of several different tip half-angles φ, as a function of distance z between the axis and the star center, and the results are displayed in the graph of Fig. 17-10. Using Eq. (17-32), the calculated value of z at which the minimum value of T occurs for each angle φ agrees well with those appearing in the graph.

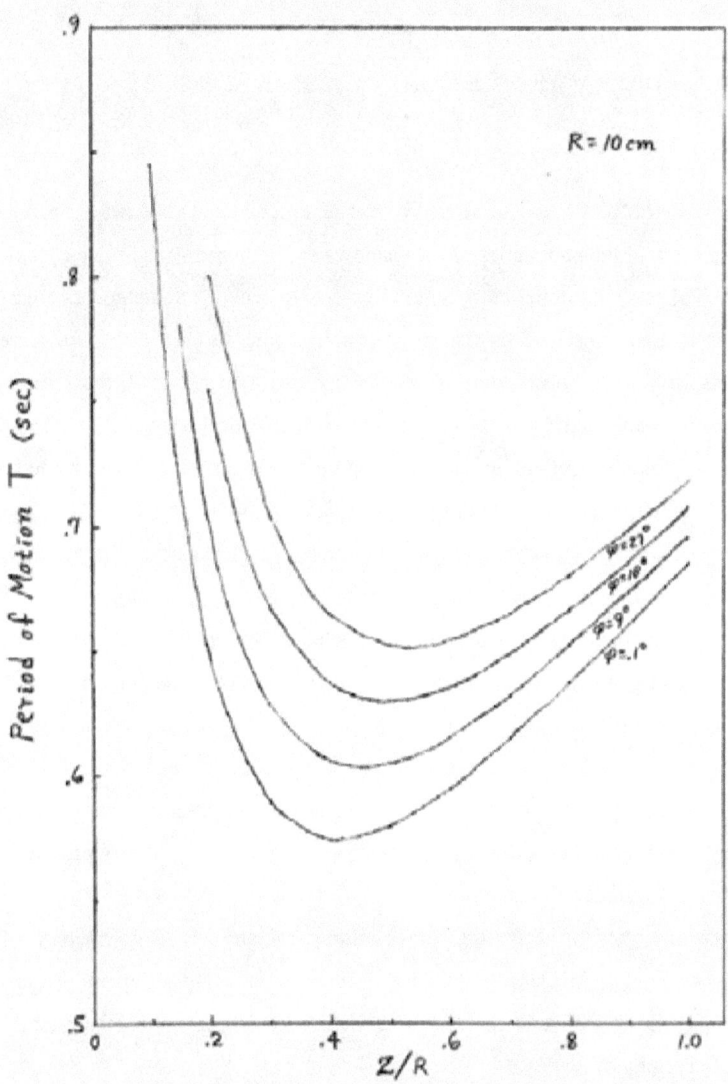

Fig. 17-10. Period of motion T of star in Fig. 17-8 calculated from Eq. (17-31) as a function of distance Z between axis and star mass center, for each of four different tip angles φ. The calculations are for a star radius R = 10cm.

CHAPTER 18

DIFFRACTION OF LIGHT BY A STAR APERTURE

18-1. Introduction

When light is partially obstructed by opaque structure and shadows are produced, we normally think of the boundaries of the shadows as geometric straight lines. Consider, for example, light passing from left to right in Fig. 18-1a in a direction perpendicular to an opaque obstruction represented by the vertical straight line in the figure. If a screen is placed to the right of the obstruction to receive the unobstructed light, then the region above point a is illuminated, while the region below a is dark or shadowed. For purposes of illustration, we can represent the light intensity on the screen, above and below point a, by the profile as shown on the far right in Fig. 18-1a. Of course, we know from experience that the boundary between the illuminated region and the region of shadow on the screen is not mathematically distinct or "sharp." That is, some of the light appears below point a, where it would not be expected to go if light merely traveled in straight lines as it passed by the obstruction, and this situation is illustrated in Fig. 18-1b. This phenomenon is referred to as "diffraction," and the corresponding profile of light intensity on the screen, above and below point a, is represented schematically on the far right in Fig. 18-1b. The profile exhibits an oscillatory nature because this in fact is what is observed under controlled experimental conditions. We know also from experience that the intensity profile varies with distance of the screen from the obstacle.

Other examples of diffraction are common to our everyday experience. For example, when light is incident on an opaque screen containing an aperture, the light passing through the aperture and observed on a second screen consists for the most part of an illuminated region of

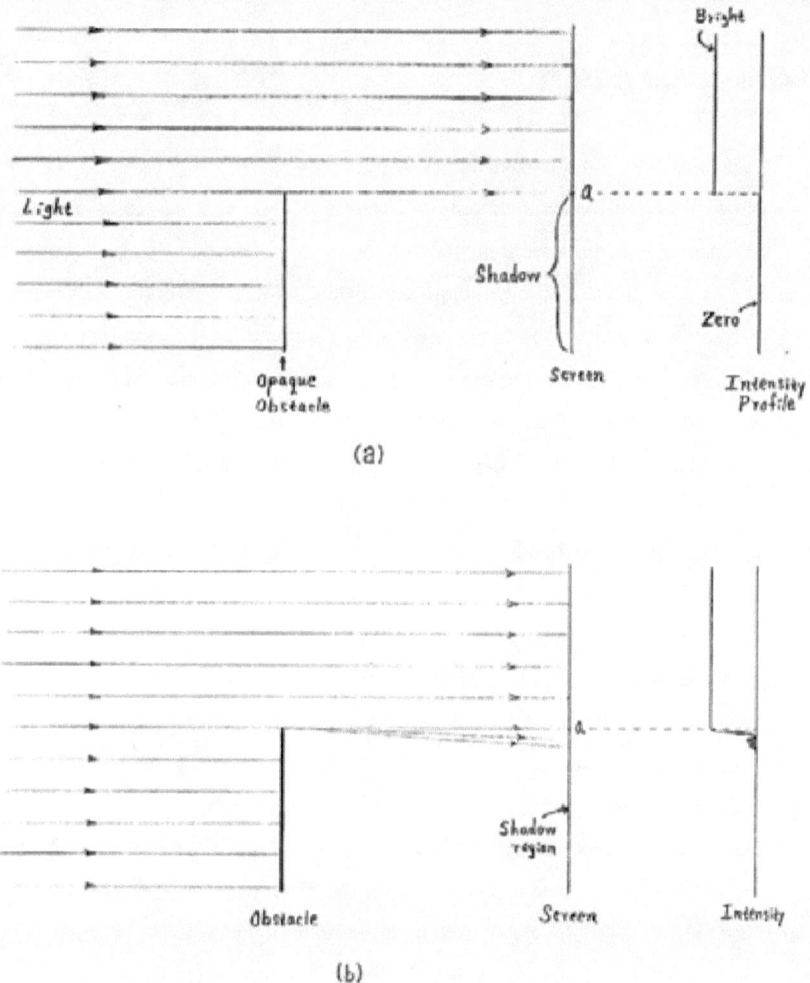

Fig. 18-1. (a) Geometric concept of a shadow based on the assumption that light travels in straight lines past an obstacle, whereas in reality the phenomenon of diffraction illustrated in (b) shows that light "bends" or "spreads" as it passes by the obstacle.

light, having a boundary of the same type as the aperture but the boundary of the light region is fuzzy, and the light intensity profile across the boundary is somewhat like that shown schematically in Fig. 18-1b.

18-2. Diffraction based on the wave theory of light

An explanation for the spreading or bending of light as it passes by obstacles or through aperture in opaque screens began with the work of Christian Huygens nearly three centuries ago, who developed a principle that bears his name. According to Huygens' principle, light consists of waves and at any instant each point on the wave is the source of spherical wavelets that travel at the speed of light, and so at a time later, the new position of the wave is the envelope of all these wavelets. Approximately a century later, Thomas Young and Augustin Fresnel carried the analysis further, and they assumed that each Huygens wavelet consisted of a sinusoidal vibration with a certain light amplitude, and that these amplitudes are added together to give the resultant light amplitude of the propagated wave. As an aid to understanding how diffracted light intensity distributions can be determined based on this theory, consider Fig. 18-2. Light from a source encounters an opaque screen containing an aperture, and the light passing through is observed on a screen at distance H beyond the aperture. Let the screen at H and the screen with aperture be oriented perpendicular to the z axis of an (x, y, z) coordinate system with the origin lying in the plane of the aperture. The location of a point in the plane of the aperture is given by the coordinates (x, y), and the coordinates of a point P in the plane of observation of the screen at distance H will be designated by (x_o, y_o), as shown. Now, based on the diffraction theory referred to above, the light wave amplitude A at a point (x_o, y_o) on the screen is proportional to the double integral over the aperture area, given by:

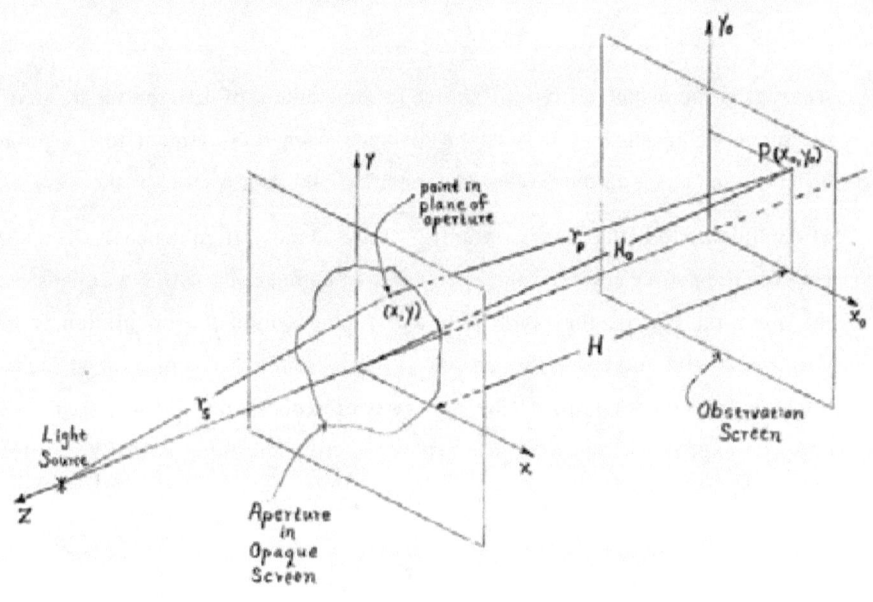

Fig. 18-2. Coordinate system used in describing diffraction of light from a source that passes through an aperture, in reference to Eqs. (18-1) – (18-16) of the text.

$$A \propto \iint e^{ik(r_s + r_p)} dx dy, \qquad (18\text{-}1)$$

where r_s is the distance from the source to the element of differential area $dxdy$ in the plane of aperture, and r_p is the distance from this element to the point of observation (x_o, y_o) on the screen. The quantity k is $2\pi/\lambda$, where λ is the wavelength of the light and i is the imaginary unit $\sqrt{-1}$. As is most often the case, the distance between the source and the aperture is large in comparison with the dimensions of the aperture, that is, the range of x and y over which the integration is to be performed, and therefore the distance r_s is essentially a constant and can be removed from the integrals. Using a property of exponentials, namely, $\exp(a + b) = \exp(a) \cdot \exp(b)$, we can therefore remove r_s from the integration and write Eq. (18-1) as:

$$A \propto e^{ikr_s} \iint e^{ikr_p} dx dy. \qquad (18\text{-}2)$$

Now, the distance r_p in Fig. 18-2 is:

$$r_p = \left[(x_o - x)^2 + (y_o - y)^2 + H^2 \right]^{\frac{1}{2}}, \qquad (18\text{-}3)$$

and the dependence of r_p on x and y makes it impossible to integrate the exponential directly, without resorting to approximate numerical methods. Over the course of time dating back to Fresnel, two approximations for r_p in Eq. (18-3) have proved useful in evaluating the double integral in Eq. (18-2) to determine light wave amplitudes and resultant intensity distributions associated with diffraction phenomena.[5] In one approximation, the range of $x_o - x$ and $y_o - y$ are small compared to H, corresponding to points of observation (x_o, y_o) nearly directly

---

[5] Slater, J.C. and Frank, N.H., <u>Electromagnetism</u>, New York: McGraw-Hill, 1947, ch. 14.

behind the aperture; for this case, referred to as "Fresnel diffraction," the binomial expansion is used to approximate Eq. (18-3) as:

$$r_p \cong H + \frac{1}{2}\frac{(x_o - x)^2 + (y_o - y)^2}{R} + \cdots \qquad (18\text{-}4)$$

The presence of the squared terms in the latter precludes the possibility of direct integration of the exponential but numerical tabulations of the integrals over x and y leading to "Cornu's spiral" have proved useful in diffraction analysis.

In the other approximation, referred to as "Fraunhofer diffraction," the coordinates x_o and y_o of the point of observation in Fig. 18-2 are assumed large compared to the size of the aperture, that is, to the range over which x and y are integrated, and under these conditions, the binomial expansion can be used to approximate r_p in Eq. (18-3) and obtain the following approximation.

$$r_p \cong H_o - \frac{xx_o + yy_o}{H_o} - \cdots \qquad (18\text{-}5)$$

where:

$$H_o = \left(x_o^2 + y_o^2 + H^2\right)^{\frac{1}{2}} \qquad (18\text{-}6)$$

is the distance from the origin in the plane of the aperture to the point of observation (xo, yo) on the screen. Given the form of H_o, it is seen that the quantities x_o/H_o and y_o/H_o in Eq. (18-5) are simply the direction cosines of the point of observation on the screen in Fig. 18-2, and defining l and m, respectively, as the direction cosines in the x and y directions,

$$l = x_o/H_o$$
$$m = y_o/H_o, \qquad (18\text{-}7)$$

allow the expression for r_p in Eq. (18-5) to be expressed as:

$$r_p \simeq H_0 - (lx + my). \qquad (18\text{-}8)$$

Because the distance H is assumed very large compared with x_o and y_o, the quantity H_0 is nearly constant and it can be removed from the integrals by again using the property $\exp(a + b) = \exp(a)\exp(b)$ and substituting from Eq. (18-8) into Eq. (18-2) to arrive at the following for Fraunhofer diffraction.

$$A \propto e^{ik(r_s+H_o)} \iint e^{ik(lx+my)} dx dy. \qquad (18\text{-}9)$$

Now, we know that $\exp(i\theta) = \cos\theta + i\sin\theta$. Further, we are interested in calculating only relative light intensity distributions in Fraunhofer diffraction, and therefore the factor $\exp ik(r_s + H_o)$ will be omitted. Then Eq. (18-9) can be written as:

$$A = \iint \{\cos[k(lx+my)] + i\sin[k(lx+my)]\} dx dy, \qquad (18\text{-}10)$$

where the equality sign is used in place of the proportional sign because the calculations are for relative light wave amplitudes.

Because of the presence of the imaginary unit $i \equiv \sqrt{1}$, we see that the light wave amplitude A on the screen is a complex quantity and it has a real part involving the cosine function, and the imaginary portion involves the sine function. So, from Eq. (18-10), the real part is:

$$A_{Re} = \iint \cos[k(lx+my)] \, dx dy \qquad (18\text{-}11)$$

and the imaginary part is:

$$A_{Im} = i \iint \sin[k(lx+my)] \, dx dy. \qquad (18\text{-}12)$$

In defining A_c and A_s as the double integrals involving the cosine and sine factors, respectively, we can express the complex amplitude A in Eq. (18-10) as:

$$A = A_c + iA_s, \qquad (18\text{-}13)$$

where:

$$A_c = \iint \cos[k(lx + my)]\, dxdy \qquad (18\text{-}14)$$

$$A_s = \iint \sin[k(lx + my)]\, dxdy. \qquad (18\text{-}15)$$

Now, the intensity at point $P(x_o, y_o)$ is the square of the light wave amplitude A, but A is complex and therefore the intensity I_p is equal to A times its complex conjugate, so that from Eq. (18-13), the Fraunhofer diffraction intensity at point $P(x_o, y_o)$ on the screen in Fig. 18-2 is:

$$\begin{aligned} I_p &= A \cdot A^* \\ &= (A_c + iA_s)(A_c - iA_s) \\ &= A_c^2 + A_s^2, \end{aligned} \qquad (18\text{-}16)$$

where the latter follows because the square of the imaginary unit i is simply -1. So, to calculate the Fraunhofer diffraction pattern on the screen in Fig. 18-2 when light passes through the aperture, we evaluate the integrals for the light amplitude A_c and A_s, over the area of the aperture, in Eqs.(18-14) and (18-15), and square them and add to give the intensity in Eq. (18-16) as a function of position (x_o, y_o) on the screen according to the direction cosines $l = x_o/H_o$ and $m = y_o/H_o$ in Eq. (18-7).

Perhaps the most familiar of all Fraunhofer diffraction patterns are those from a rectangular aperture and from a circular aperture as indicated schematically in Fig. 18-3.[6] For a rectangular aperture of length a in the x direction of Fig. 18-3a and width b in the y direction, the Fraunhofer diffraction pattern intensity distribution according to Eqs. (18-14) – (18-16) is:

$$I_p = \left(\frac{\sin \pi la/\lambda}{\pi l/\lambda}\right)^2 \left(\frac{\sin \pi mb/\lambda}{\pi m/\lambda}\right)^2, \qquad (18\text{-}17)$$

where λ is the wavelength of the light. The intensity is a maximum at the center of the pattern on the screen. The distributions along the x_o and y_o directions are indicated schematically, showing that there are minima and relative maxima. The first relative maximum is only a few percent of the intensity at the center, and succeeding relative maxima continually decrease in intensity. In the case of a circular aperture of radius ρ, the intensity of the Fraunhofer diffraction pattern as determined from Eqs. (18-14) – (18-16) is $I_p = (\rho\lambda/l)^2 J_1^2(2\pi\rho l/\lambda)$, where J_1 is the first order Bessel function. The light intensity distribution on the screen, shown schematically in Fig. 18-3b, consists of a central circular bright region surrounded by alternately dark and bright concentric circular rings. The first relative maximum intensity is only 1.75% of the central

---

[6] Born, M. and Wolf, E., Principles of Optics, 5th ed., Oxford: Pergamon Press, 1975, pp. 392-397.

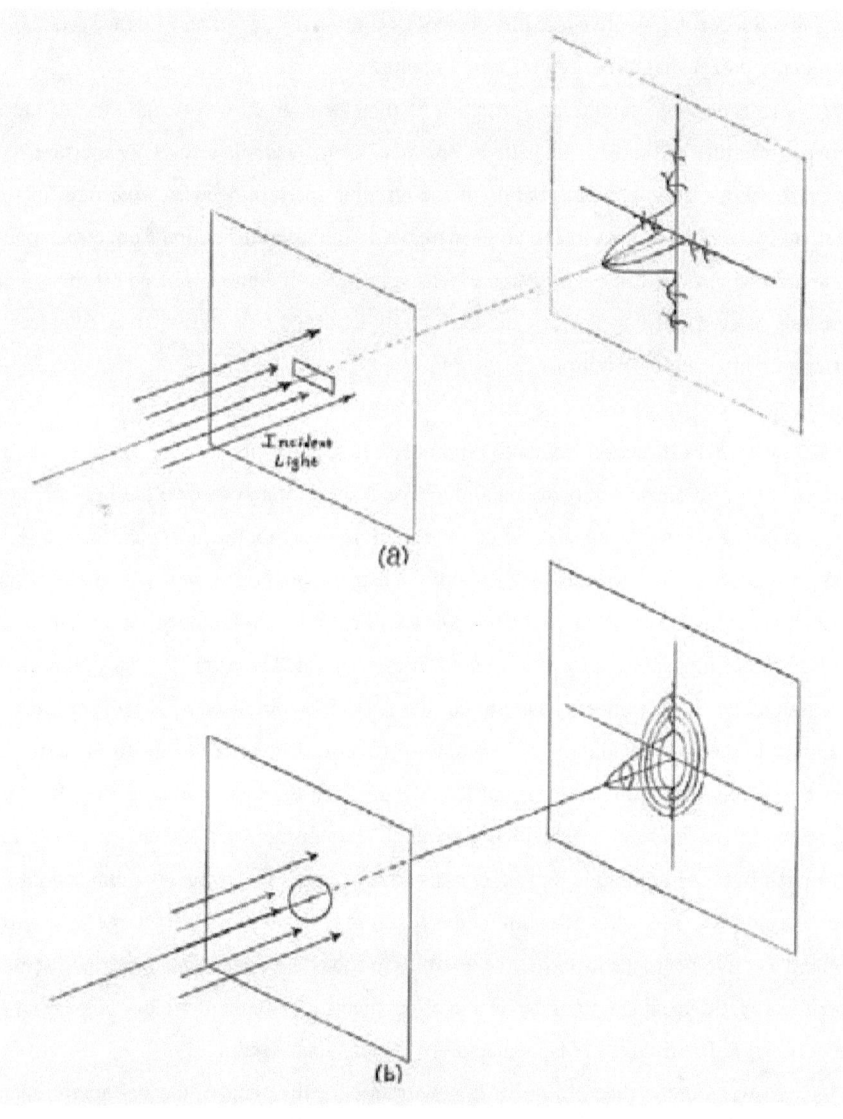

Fig. 18-3. Schematic Fraunhofer diffraction intensity distributions from (a) rectangular aperture and (b) circular aperture.

intensity. Succeeding relative maxima intensities continually decrease, with the second one being only 0.42% that of the central bright region.

An aspect of Fraunhofer diffraction is that for a given wavelength and distance between aperture and screen, the pattern "spreads," or increases in size as the aperture size decreases. For example, as the radius of the circular aperture decreases the radii of the alternately dark and bright circular rings increase. Fraunhofer diffraction from circular and rectangular apertures has been treated extensively in the literature. The comments given here are offered only as insights on the use of Eqs. (18-14) – (18-16) in calculating diffraction intensity distributions.

18-3. Fraunhofer diffraction from a five-point star [5, 2] aperture

If we illuminate a screen containing a star aperture and receive the light passing through it on a screen placed close behind the aperture, then, for the most part, there will be a brightly illuminated region in the shape of the star but the boundaries will be somewhat fuzzy and the light intensity across a boundary will exhibit an oscillatory nature. This is in effect Fresnel diffraction as was discussed briefly earlier. However, for the purposes of discussion here, we are interested in Fraunhofer diffraction produced by a star aperture and therefore to meet the condition of Fraunhofer diffraction, we refer to Fig. 18-4a and note that the screen with the aperture is sufficiently far from the light source so that the light illuminating the aperture is essentially parallel and, further, the screen on which the diffracted light is observed is located at a distance H much larger than the dimensions of the aperture. We note that oftentimes, the requirement that H be very large is met by placing a convergent lens just after the aperture to focus the light on the observing screen and, thereby, the focal length of the lens in effect meets the Fraunhofer requirement that H be very large. The distance H is then actually the lens focal length.

Now, as in the case of Fig. 18-2, we arrange for the plane of the star aperture and the plane of the observing screen at H to be perpendicular to the z-axis of an (x, y, z) coordinate system, and in Fig. 18-4a, the origin of the (x, y, z) system is at the center of the star and the star is oriented with its radius R on the y-axis as indicated. To calculate the Fraunhofer diffracted light distribution on the screen, we must evaluate the double integrals in Eqs. (18-14) and (18-15) over the area of the five-point star, treating the direction cosines l and m as parameters which can be assigned values later to determine diffracted light intensity at a particular point on the screen. To determine the limits on the integrations to be performed over y and x, over the area of the star, we refer to Fig. 18-4b. The area of the star aperture has been divided into eight regions that are bounded along the x-axis by the series of vertical lines parallel to the y-axis as indicated. To calculate the diffraction pattern, the double integrals in Eq. (18-14) must be evaluated over each of the eight regions, and the results added together to give the light amplitude A_c; a similar procedure will be followed to obtain A_s in Eq. (18-15), and then the sum of the squares of A_c and A_s will give the intensity on the screen per Eq. (18-16). So, to begin, we note that for Region 1 in Fig. 18-4b, the integration over y extends from the line P_3P_5 to the P_2P_5 line, and the corresponding limits on x are from $x = -x_4$ to $x = -x_2$, where the values of x_2 and x_4 are indicated in the figures using α to denote the angle 18° in the [5, 2] star aperture. In the (x, y) plane of the aperture, the equation of the line representing the aperture boundary P_3P_5 is:

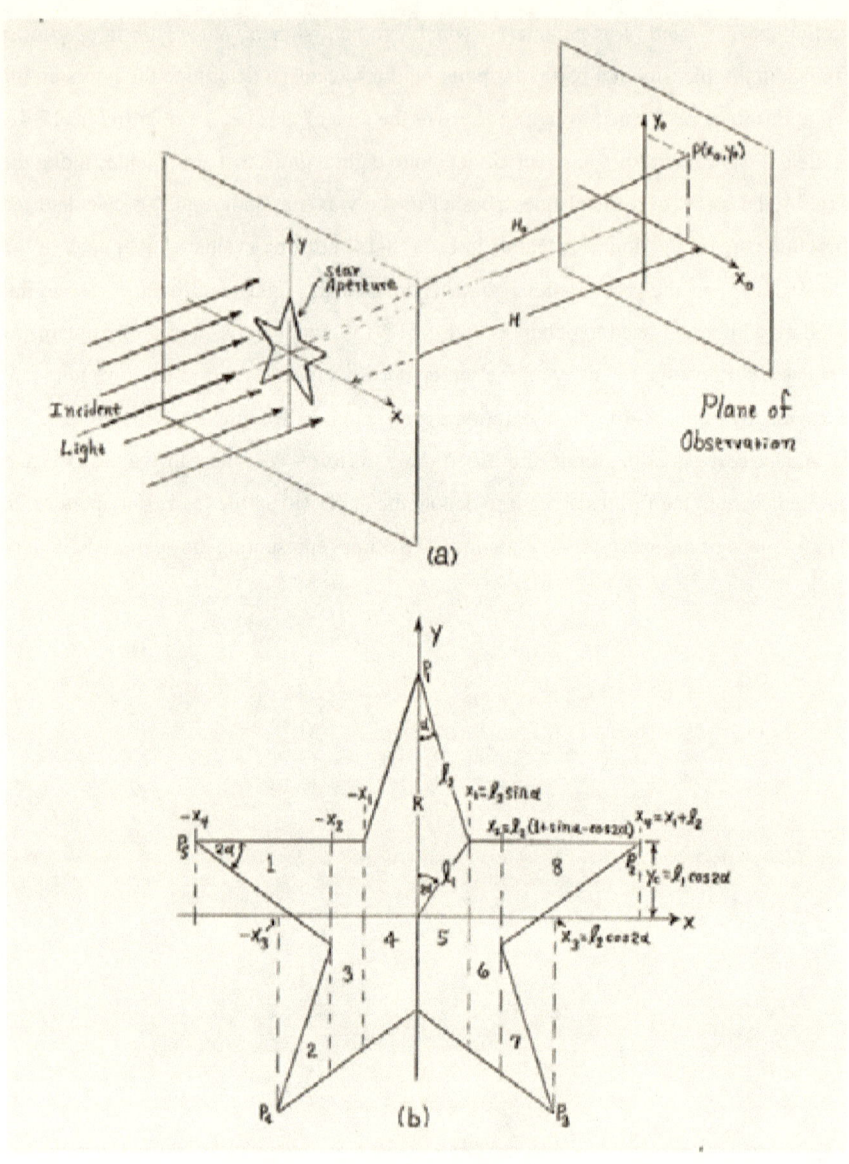

Fig. 18-4. (a) Parallel light incident on a star aperture and (b) geometry of the [5, 2] star used in setting the boundaries and limits of integration in Eqs. (18-14) and (18-15) to arrive at the diffracted light intensity from Eq. (18-16).

418

$$y = -l_1 - x \tan 2\alpha, \qquad (18\text{-}18)$$

and the equation of the aperture boundary line represented by P_2P_5 is:

$$y = l_1 \cos 2\alpha, \qquad (18\text{-}19)$$

Where $l_1 = a_1 R$, as defined in Eq. (4-5) of Chapter 4, along with $l_2 = a_2 R$. So, integrating first over y, then over x, the light wave amplitude A_c from Eq. (18-14) evaluated over Region 1 takes the form:

$$A_{c1} = \int_{x=-x_4}^{x=-x_2} dx \int_{y=-l_1-x\tan 2\alpha}^{y=l_1\cos 2\alpha} \cos[k(lx+my)]\,dx\,dy \qquad (18\text{-}20)$$

The portions of the star aperture boundary line P_2P_4 are represented by the equation:

$$y = -l_1 + x \tan 2\alpha, \qquad (18\text{-}21)$$

and the boundary line P_1P_4 is represented by the equation:

$$y = R + x \cot \alpha. \qquad (18\text{-}22)$$

For Region 2, the limits on x are from $-x_3$ to $-x_2$ and therefore using Eqs. (18-21) and (18-22), the contribution to the light wave amplitude in Eq. (18-14) can be set up for integration as follows:

$$A_{c2} = \int_{x=-x_3}^{x=-x_2} dx \int_{y=-l_1+x\tan 2\alpha}^{y=R+x\cot \alpha} \cos[k(lx+my)]\,dy \qquad (18\text{-}23)$$

Region 3 of the star aperture is bounded in the y-direction by lines P_2P_4 and P_2P_5 and in the x-direction by $-x_2$ and $-x_1$. Therefore, using Eqs. (18-21) and (18-19), the light wave contribution from Region 3 is obtained from Eq. (18-14) as:

$$A_{c3} = \int_{x=-x_2}^{x=-x_1} dx \int_{y=-l_1+x\tan 2\alpha}^{y=l_1\cos 2\alpha} \cos[k(lx+my)]dy. \qquad (18\text{-}24)$$

Region 4 is bounded below in y by line P_2P_4 and above in y by line P_1P_4, with limits on x from $x = -x_1$ to $x = 0$, and therefore using Eqs. (18-21) and (18-22), the light wave amplitude contribution can be expressed from Eq. (18-14) by the following.

$$A_{c4} = \int_{x=-x_1}^{x=0} dx \int_{y=-l_1+x\tan 2\alpha}^{y=R+x\cot\alpha} \cos[k(lx+my)]dy \qquad (18\text{-}25)$$

Regions 5 and 7 are bounded above in the y-direction by line P_1P_3, and the equation representing this line is:

$$y = R - x \cot \alpha. \qquad (18\text{-}26)$$

So, using Eqs. (18-18), (18-19), and (18-21) along with the latter for limits on y and referring to Fig. 18-4b for limits on x, we see that the contributions to diffracted light wave amplitude from the remaining Regions 5-8 can be set up for integration from Eq. (18-14) by the following equations:

$$\left. \begin{aligned} A_{c5} &= \int_{x=0}^{x=x_1} dx \int_{y=-l_1-x\tan 2\alpha}^{y=R-x\cot\alpha} \cos[k(lx+my)]dy \\ A_{c6} &= \int_{x=x_1}^{x=x_2} dx \int_{y=-l_1-x\tan 2\alpha}^{y=l_1\cos 2\alpha} \cos[k(lx+my)]dy \\ A_{c7} &= \int_{x=x_2}^{x=x_3} dx \int_{y=-l_1-x\tan 2\alpha}^{y=R-x\cot\alpha} \cos[k(lx+my)]dy \\ A_{c8} &= \int_{x=x_2}^{x=x_4} dx \int_{y=-l_1+x\tan 2\alpha}^{y=l_1\cos 2\alpha} \cos[k(lx+my)]dy \end{aligned} \right\} \qquad (18\text{-}27)$$

Performing all the integrations in Eqs. (18-20), (18-23), (18-24), (18-25), and (18-27), and adding, and simplifying ultimately lead to the following for the diffracted light wave amplitude A_c at a point $x_o = lH_o$, $y_o = mH_o$ on the observing screen, per Eq. (18-14). Recall that A_c is the real part of the complex light wave amplitude A in Eq. (18-10).

$$\begin{aligned}
A_c &= \frac{1}{mu}[\cos kmR - \cos k(mR + x_1u) + \cos k(mR + x_2u) - \cos k(mR + x_3u)] \\
&+ \frac{1}{mu'}[\cos(mR - x_1u') - \cos kmR + \cos k(mR - x_3u') - \cos k(mR - x_2u')] \\
&+ \frac{1}{mv}[\cos k(x_3v - ml_1) + \cos k(ml_1 + x_2v) - \cos k(ml_1 + x_4v) - \cos km\, l_1] \\
&+ \frac{1}{mv'}[\cos km\, l_1 - \cos k(ml_1 + x_3v') + \cos k(x_4v' - ml_1) - \cos k(x_2v' - ml_1)] \\
&+ \frac{1}{ml}[\cos k(lx_1 + my_c) - \cos k(my_c - lx_1) - \cos k(lx_4 + my_c) + \cos k(my_c - lx_4)]
\end{aligned} \quad (18\text{-}28)$$

In the latter, y_c is defined as $y_c = l_1 \cos 2\alpha$, and the quantities u, u', v, v' are defined in terms of the star tip angle α, and the direction cosines $l = x_o/H_o$ and $m = y_o/H_o$ as follows:

$$\left. \begin{aligned}
u &= l - m \cot\alpha \\
u' &= l + m \cot\alpha \\
v &= l - m \tan 2\alpha \\
v' &= l + m \tan 2\alpha
\end{aligned} \right\} \quad (18\text{-}29)$$

The imaginary part of the complex diffracted light wave amplitude A in Eq. (18-10) is iA_s, where A_s is given by Eq. (18-15). The double integration in Eq. (18-15) must be carried out over the area of the star aperture. Using the limits on y and x referenced above, the integrals in Eq. (18-15) were evaluated for each of the eight regions of the aperture shown in Fig. 18-4b. Adding the individual eight contributions for A_s together and combining terms to simplify leads to the result in Eq. (18-30).

$$A_s = \frac{1}{mu}[\sin kmR - \sin k(mR + x_1u) + \sin k(mR + x_2u) - \sin k(mR + x_3u)]$$

$$+ \frac{1}{mu'}[\sin k(mR - x_1u') - \sin kmR + \sin k(mR - x_3u') - \sin k(mR - x_2u')]$$

$$+ \frac{1}{mv}[\sin km\, l_1 + \sin k(x_3v - ml_1) - \sin k(m\, l_1 + x_2v) + \sin k(m\, l_1 + x_4v)]$$

$$+ \frac{1}{mv'}[\sin k(m\, l_1 + x_3v') - \sin km l_1 + \sin k(x_4v' - ml_1) - \sin k(x_2v' - ml_1)]$$

$$+ \frac{1}{ml}[\sin k(lx_1 + my_c) - \sin k(my_c - lx_1) - \sin k(lx_4 + my_c) + \sin k(my_c - lx_4)] \qquad (18\text{-}30)$$

The diffracted light intensity on the observing screen in Fig. 18-4a is obtained by squaring the light wave amplitudes A_c and A_s in Eqs. (18-28) and (18-30), and adding to get I_p in Eq. (18-16).

18-4. Diffracted light intensity distributions along the x_o and y_o axes

If we let x_o be zero, then the direction cosine $l = x_o/H_o$ *of* observation on the screen in Fig. 18-4b is zero. Then, we can calculate the intensity along the y_o axis by letting the direction cosine $m = y_o/H_o$ *take* on a series of values in Eqs. (18-16) for I_p. At first glance, it appears that setting $l = 0$ in the equations may cause problems because l appears in the denominators of Eqs. (18-28) – (18-30), and some terms combine to give 0/0. However, the use of L'Hospital's rule shows that valid limits exist when $l = 0$. So, the intensity I_p on the y_o axis was calculated as a function of the direction cosine m, and the results are given in the graph of Fig. 18-5. In these calculations, the radius of the star aperture was taken as $R = 0.001$ in., and the wavelength of light as $\lambda = 0.6328$ micrometers (24.913 micro-inches). From Fig. 18-5, it is seen that the first minimum in diffracted light intensity occurs on the screen for a value of direction cosine $m = 0.0235$, and $m = 0.036$ gives a first relative maximum in intensity. The second minimum of intensity occurs for $m = 0.069$, while the second relative intensity maximum is at $m = 0.0815$.

When $l = 0$, corresponding to intensity on the y axis, it can be seen that the factor kmR appears in each term of every cosine and sine function in Eqs. (18-28) – (18-30). Now, k is defined in terms of the light wavelength λ by $k = 2\pi/\lambda$, and therefore under the conditions of

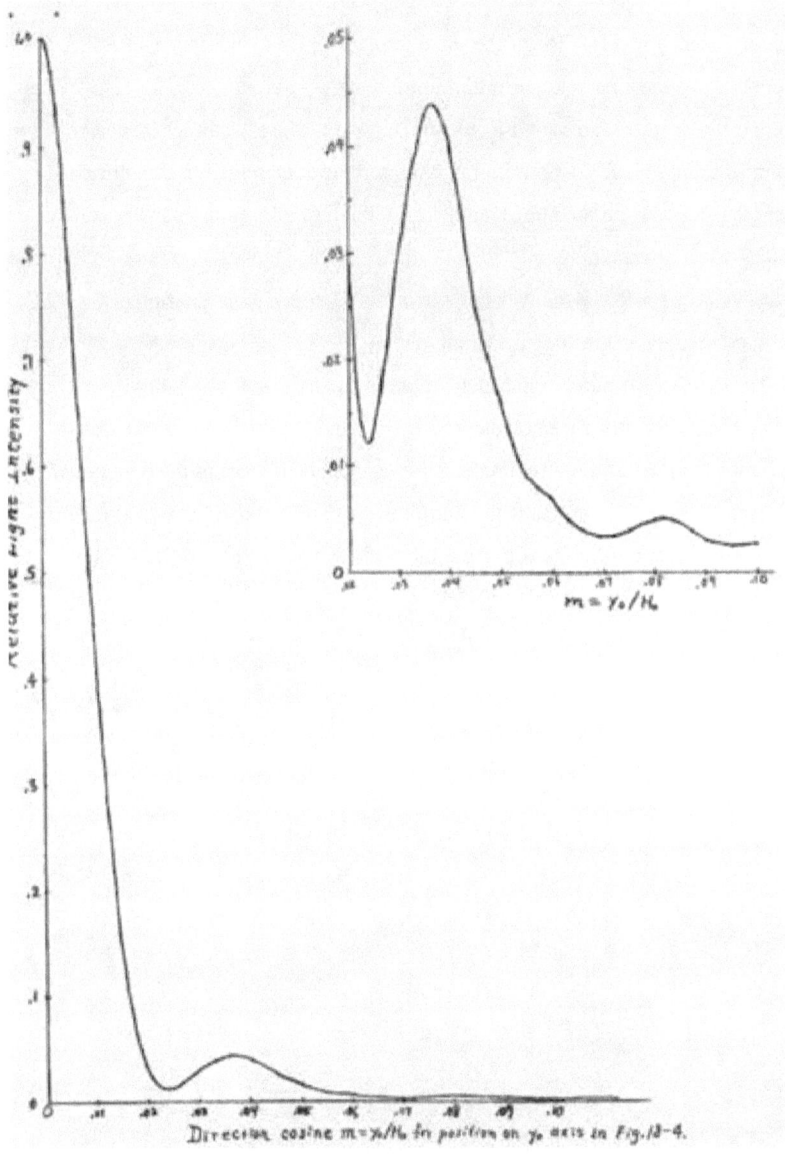

Fig. 18-5. Fraunhofer diffracted light intensity relative to value at center, versus direction cosine of point on y_o axis, for star aperture in Fig. 18-4. The graph above gives detail over the direction cosine range $.02 \leq m \leq .1$.

calculation used for Fig. 18-5, the quantity mR/λ has the value $mR/\lambda = 0.9432$ corresponding to the first relative minimum intensity when $m = 0.0235$. This means, for example, if the aperture radius is a factor of ten greater, then the direction cosine m will be one-tenth as great for the first minimum at the same wavelength. On the other hand, if the wavelength is halved and the radius halved, then the first minimum intensity still occurs for $m = 0.023$. Similar remarks apply for the first relative intensity maximum, for example, when the value of mR/λ is considered for $m = 0.036$ and combinations of m, R, λ are chosen that leave the magnitude invariant.

To find the diffracted light intensity on the x_o axis in Fig. 18-4, we set y_o equal to zero, which equivalently means that $m = 0$. However, setting $m = 0$ in Eqs. (18-28) – (18-30) leads to terms of the form 0/0 because m appears in some of the denominators. Use of L'Hospital's rule, though, leads to valid limits. It is found that, except at the origin, the Fraunhofer diffracted light intensity from the star aperture is zero on the x_o axis.

www.ingramcontent.com/pod-product-compliance
Lightning Source LLC
LaVergne TN
LVHW091656070526
838199LV00050B/2180